THE ORIGINS OF
ANCRENE WISSE

THE ORIGINS OF
ANCRENE WISSE

BY

E. J. DOBSON

OXFORD

AT THE CLARENDON PRESS

1976

Oxford University Press, Ely House, London W. 1

GLASGOW NEW YORK TORONTO MELBOURNE WELLINGTON
CAPE TOWN IBADAN NAIROBI DAR ES SALAAM LUSAKA ADDIS ABABA
DELHI BOMBAY CALCUTTA MADRAS KARACHI DACCA
KUALA LUMPUR SINGAPORE HONG KONG TOKYO

ISBN 0 19 811864 3

© *Oxford University Press 1976*

169368

*Printed in Great Britain
at the University Press, Oxford
by Vivian Ridler
Printer to the University*

IN MEMORIAM

J. R. R. TOLKIEN

PREFACE

I HAVE not been at all sure that an attempt to discover more about the origins of *Ancrene Wisse*—where and when it was written, for whom, and even by whom—was a sensible enterprise, or one of which my friends would approve; and I have therefore been rather secretive about it and have tried to involve them as little as possible. But in the years during which I have been intermittently engaged on it I have inevitably incurred obligations for advice and help, even if those who gave it did not realize the purpose of my inquiries or had to say that nothing was known or discoverable. Dr. David Crook made searches on my behalf in the Public Record Office, and I have had advice on historical matters from Dr. A. B. Emden, Dr. R. W. Hunt, and Dr. D. E. Greenway. Mr. R. E. Latham kindly answered a question about medieval Latin, and Professor I. Ll. Foster one about medieval Welsh. Colleagues in medieval English studies to whom I am indebted include Professor S. T. R. O. d'Ardenne, Mr. John Bromwich, Professor Norman Davis, Dr. A. H. Hudson, Miss E. N. Millett, Professor Geoffrey Shepherd, and Dr. Arne Zettersten. The first draft of the earlier chapters was written in Canberra in 1968 during a term which I spent there as a visiting lecturer at the Australian National University; I owe my thanks to the authorities of the university for making my visit possible, and especially to Professor and Mrs. G. H. Russell, who were then in Canberra, for their great kindness and hospitality to my wife and myself.

E. J. D.

Jesus College, Oxford

CONTENTS

LIST OF FIGURES

I

ANCRENE WISSE AND THE AUGUSTINIANS

Ancrene Wisse is a deliberately anonymous work, which carefully refrains from naming the author and his 'dear sisters' or the places where he and they lived. It is also, in many passages (as for example in the discussion of the Sins), an impersonal work, which might have been written in the same way for any audience; and there can be no doubt that its influence and importance in the later thirteenth and the fourteenth centuries were largely due to this general quality, its easy adaptability, and its relevance to anyone, woman or man, who was interested in the life of religion. But it is by no means always impersonal; the recurrent address to 'my dear sisters' (or 'my dear sister') is no mere trick of style, but shows that the author has constantly in mind the women for whom he is writing, and it would be altogether surprising if he did not sometimes say things that had more meaning for them than they can have for us, who read his work after a lapse of over seven centuries. The most obvious instance of explicitly personal allusion is the well-known passage in the Nero manuscript[1]—undoubtedly original, though truncated or excised in other manuscripts—which says:

You, my dear sisters, are the anchoresses that I know who have the least need of consolation against these trials, except only that of sickness. For I know no anchoress who may have all that she requires with greater ease or with greater honour (*menske*)

[1] Nero MS. (ed. Mabel Day, E.E.T.S. 225, 1952), 85/8 ff.

than you three have, our Lord be thanked for it. For you do not think at all of food or clothing either for yourselves or for your maidens. Each of you has from one friend all that she requires, nor need the maiden seek either bread or food (*suuel*)[1] further than at his hall. God knows, many another knows little of this ease . . . There is much talk of you, what well-bred (*gentile*) women you are, sought after (*iȝirned*) by many for your goodness and for your generosity, and sisters of one father and of one mother, [who] in the flower of your youth renounced all the world's joys and became anchoresses.

These details, obviously, applied only to the women for whom the book was first written (which was why, at a very early stage, the passage was first modified and then omitted from the text), and there must have been not a few people at the time who could have identified the three sisters and their parents, and the patron at whose nearby hall their servants could obtain whatever was needed. Probably much the same people could have put a name to the ascetic who wore both a heavy coat of mail and a hair-shirt, 'so that the sweat therefrom is agony to bear', and yet declared that it did not trouble him, 'and he often asks me to teach him some means by which he could mortify his flesh . . . and weeps to me . . . and says that God forgets him, for He sends him no great sickness';[2] the author here virtually claims to be the spiritual adviser of this *loricatus*, the singularity of whose devotion must have marked him out in the society to which he belonged.

These are references to individuals; others are indicative of social class. All modern scholars have agreed with the late thirteenth-century annotator of the Cleopatra MS. who, in a marginal rubric that he added at the beginning of Part I,

[1] *Suuel* (OE *sufel*) was 'anything, whether flesh, fish, or vegetable, eaten with bread' (Bosworth–Toller, s.v.).

[2] Corpus MS. (ed. J. R. R. Tolkien, E.E.T.S. 249, 1962), f. 103b/8–16 (Morton, p. 382).

referred to 'the devotions of the enclosed ladies' (*de servicio inclusarum dominarum*).[1] There are obvious indications of their rank: they had servants, they were sufficiently well educated to read not only English but French, they were expected to understand and appreciate analogies from warfare and from romance; and beyond all there is the general tone and style of the book that he wrote for them, and its high and cultivated diction. But there are also passages in which his and their social assumptions are made more explicit. Thus in Part VII, dealing with Penance, when he comes to talk of *vilitas et asperitas*, or in his gloss *scheome ant pine*, his example of what he means by 'shame' is significant:

Scheome ich cleopie eauer her beon itald unwurð, ant beggin as an hearlot, ʒef neod is, [his] liueneð, ant beon oðres beodesmon, as ʒe beoð, leoue sustren, ant þolieð ofte danger of swuch oðerhwile þe mahte beon ower þreal.[2]

Shame I call it to be always here accounted of no social rank, and to beg like a wretch, if need is, for one's livelihood, and to be another's pensioner, as you are, dear sisters, and you endure often the arrogance of such a one sometimes as might have been your slave.

And as if to make sure that the meaning of this last phrase was fully understood, a few pages later he writes:

[ʒe ahen] beon bliðe iheortet ʒef ʒe þolieð danger of Sluri þe cokes cneaue, þe wescheð ant wipeð disches i cuchene.[3]

You ought to be happy in heart if you endure the arrogance of Slurry the cook's boy, who washes and wipes dishes in the kitchen.

Even in a book which advocates humility not least of the virtues, it is for him, and he expects it to be for them, a special sign of submission to the will of God, of the self-

---

[1] Cleopatra MS. (ed. E. J. Dobson, E.E.T.S. 267, 1972), f. 9.
[2] Corpus MS., f. 96b/15–18 (Morton, p. 356).
[3] Corpus MS., f. 103a/2–4 (Morton, p. 380).

abnegation demanded by the religious life, that one should put up with insults from one's social inferiors. He does not forget that if they had chosen otherwise they might have had thralls.

Other passages, neither explicitly nor implicitly personal, probably also had a special meaning for the author and his original readers. One minor, but nevertheless significant, instance is revealed by an addition to the basic text in the Cleopatra MS. In Part IV of the Rule,[1] in dealing with remedies against temptations, the author says that not only holy meditations but also other thoughts have sometimes given help against continual temptations—amongst others, 'wonderful and joyful' thoughts, as for example:

ʒef me come ant talde þe þet mon þet te is leouest þurh sum miracle—as þurh steuene of heouene—were icoren to pape.

If someone came and told thee that a man who is very dear to thee by some miracle—such as by a voice from heaven—had been chosen as Pope.

Similarly, he says, 'wonderful and sorrowful' thoughts may help, for example:

as ʒef þu herdest seggen þet mon þet te is leouest were ferliche adrenct, islein, o[ð]er imurðret, þet tine sustren weren in hare hus forbearnde.

as if thou heardest say that a man who is very dear to thee had been suddenly drowned, killed, or murdered, that thy sisters had been burned in their houses.

As the author refers to his 'three dear sisters' as 'the women dearest to me',[2] it is apparent, by reciprocation, that the phrase *mon þet te is leouest*—even if we translate it, not 'the man who is dearest to thee', but 'a man who is very dear to thee'—may well refer to himself; and this presumption is

---

[1] Corpus MS., f. 65b/10 ff. (Morton, p. 242).
[2] Corpus MS., f. 31b/15–16 (Morton, p. 116).

confirmed by the Cleopatra text, which in the second sentence cited above adds, after *adrenct*, the phrase *ase he þet wrat þis boc*.[1] Although peculiar to C,[2] the addition seems characteristic of the marginal annotations which we know the author was in the habit of adding in individual manuscripts and which later copyists embodied in the text— often, as here, with some slight displacement from the position evidently intended. The phrase, though undoubtedly not original (it is lacking even from C's congener, the French text of the Vitellius MS.),[3] seems authentic—at the very least it shows that someone, annotating the exemplar of a manuscript which was itself revised by the author and therefore writing during the author's lifetime, identified the *mon þet te is leouest* and *he þet wrat þis boc*. But in the context, since the 'wonderful and joyful' fate imagined for him is that, by some miracle, he should be elected Pope, it must follow that he is a cleric, not a layman.

This deduction will hardly surprise, for it is inconceivable,

---

[1] Cleopatra MS., f. 107/7. The phrase is clearly misplaced; it should follow *leouest* rather than *adrenct*. The disaster is an imagined one, and there is no probability that 'he who wrote this book' had in fact been 'suddenly drowned'. Hand B of the Cleopatra MS. is, in my view, the author's; it follows that the author was still very much alive when the original Cleopatra scribe was copying the phase *ase he þet wrat þis boc*.

[2] Where it seems convenient, I denote the MSS. by the sigla used in *English and Medieval Studies presented to J. R. R. Tolkien*, ed. Norman Davis and C. L. Wrenn (London, 1962), pp. 128 ff., namely: A for Corpus, C for Cleopatra, F for the French version of the Vitellius MS., G for the Gonville and Caius MS. (usually called the Caius version), L for the Latin version, N for Nero, P for the Pepys version, R for the Royal version, S for the French version of the Trinity College MS., T for Titus, and V for Vernon. For further details, see *English and Medieval Studies*, p. 128, n. 1.

[3] But as C and the English original of F were almost certainly copied simultaneously and directly from a single exemplar, the presence of the phrase in C and its absence from F must be explained by the hypothesis that the addition was present in the exemplar as a marginal note, which the C scribe embodied in his text, the other scribe ignored.

in the conditions of the early thirteenth century, that such a book as *Ancrene Wisse* should have been written by anyone but a highly trained cleric. But there has been no agreement about what sort of a cleric he was. It has been thought that 'he may well have been a secular clerk, a domestic chaplain, or a parish priest'.[1] But to suppose that he was a secular priest, unattached to any order, is against the evidence of the text. There is in the Nero MS., but in that MS. only, an added passage[2] which begins:

Vre leawede breþren siggeð þus hore Vres. Vor Vhtsong ine werkedawes heihte and twenti paternosteres, ine helidawes forti . . .

Our lay brothers say their Hours in this way. For Matins on ferias twenty-eight paternosters, on feast-days forty . . .

and which ends:

3if ei of ou wule don þus, heo voleweð her, ase in oþre obser-uaunces, muchel of vre ordre; and wel ich hit reade.

If any of you is willing to do thus, she follows in this, as in other observances, much of our Order; and well do I advise it.

It is not easy to decide on the status of this passage. That it is an addition is shown by its absence from the chief of the other manuscripts running: Corpus, Cleopatra, and the French Vitellius text. For various reasons, four (TSLR) of the manuscripts of the 'Nero–Titus group' are not running at this point. The failure of the passage to occur in the Pepys version might be due to deliberate omission, since it could be argued that the Pepys redactor would be unlikely to retain a

[1] Geoffrey Shepherd, *Ancrene Wisse: Parts Six and Seven* (London and Edinburgh, 1959), p. xxix, with references to G. Sitwell's introduction to Miss Salu's translation, p. xxi; to C. H. Talbot, *Neophilologus*, xl (1956), 50; and to D. S. Brewer, *Notes and Queries* (N.S.), iii (1956), 232–5.
[2] Nero MS., 10/25–11/5 (Morton, p. 24).

passage referring to the practices in the thirteenth century of the lay brothers of an unnamed religious order. But the passage is also lacking in the Vernon MS., which ordinarily goes closely with Nero; and though it might be possible to explain this by the assumption that the V scribe rejected it because he discovered that it was absent from the revised Corpus-type text which he is known to have consulted,[1] the more obvious explanation would be that the addition was not present in the common ancestor of N and V.[2] But the Nero scribe, or some close predecessor, can be shown to have included in his text certain passages which were not in the antecedent manuscript from which V also descended, but which were found as additions in other manuscripts; and this also could have been an authorized addition made in the margin of some lost manuscript and thence adopted into the Nero text. The addition was certainly not composed by the Nero scribe himself. Throughout his work he was liable to frequent omissions, which he often corrected by interlinear or marginal additions in paler ink, plainly made after further reference to his exemplar. In the passage in question, there are three such corrections of omissions, and there ought possibly to have been a fourth;[3] it must follow that the Nero scribe was copying, and correcting his copy, from a lost exemplar which intervened between the Nero MS. itself and the common ancestor which

[1] Cf. V's omission (as in Corpus) of the entire two paragraphs which include the reference, cited above from N, to the personal circumstances of the three anchoresses. See also my lecture, 'The Date and Composition of Ancrene Wisse', in *Proceedings of the British Academy*, lii (1966), 203–4.

[2] Here and elsewhere I assume the stemma published in *English and Medieval Studies presented to J. R. R. Tolkien*, p. 137. A revised and simplified version is printed below (p. 287).

[3] For the corrected omissions, see the words in caret brackets in Miss Day's edition, 10/26–9, and her footnotes. For the possible uncorrected omission of *pater noster* in l. 33, see p. 73, n. 4, below.

it shares with the Vernon MS., and that the addition was already present in this lost 'proto-Nero'.[1] The phrasing of the passage is entirely characteristic of the author's method in Part I of describing and prescribing the devotions to be practised; if it was not written by the author himself, it was by someone who had completely adopted his mannerisms and who belonged to the same tradition, and it occurs in an early manuscript which preserves the content, though by no means the wording, of the text intended for the original community. Moreover it anticipates, in matter and form, an undoubtedly original passage at a slightly later point in the book[2] which begins:

þe ne con oþer uhtsong oðer ne mei hit seggen, segge for uhtsong þritti Pater nostres, ant Aue Maria efter euch Pater noster . . .

Whoever knows no other Matins or cannot say them, let her say thirty Paternosters, and Ave Maria after each Paternoster . . .

though there are differences in the prescriptions for the various offices. The probability is that the passage in Nero was an addition by the author himself, though doubtless it was an ill-considered one of which he may have thought better (since it is not included in the definitive Corpus revision) because it overlapped too much with the advice that he had already given in the original passage. But if it is

[1] Or else that he was directly copying, and correcting his copy, from the manuscript in which the addition had originally been made; but in either case the addition cannot have been composed by himself. As it is certain that his direct exemplar was not the common ancestor that N shares with V, i.e. that there was a 'proto-Nero' from which he was copying, the likelihood is that the addition was already present in his exemplar, and that he was no more responsible for introducing it into the text than he was for drafting it.

[2] Corpus MS., f. 12a/2–14; Cleopatra MS., f. 19/8–20; Vitellius French version (ed. J. A. Herbert, E.E.T.S. 219, 1944), 32/31–33/17; Nero MS., 20/14–26; Titus MS. (ed. Frances M. Mack, E.E.T.S. 252, 1963), 2/8–21 (Morton, p. 46).

the author's, or even if it is by someone who shared his tradition, it follows that he was a member of an order,[1] and that his order was one which admitted lay brothers.[2]

Fortunately this conclusion is supported by two other passages, better evidenced. One, at the beginning of Part VIII, reads in the Corpus text:[3]

. . . for þi ne schule ȝe beon bute as ure breðren beoð ihuslet, inwið tweolf moneð fiftene siðen.

. . . therefore you shall not take communion except as our brothers do, fifteen times within twelve months.

A's text is here supported both by T, which has *bute as ure breðre beon*, and by N, which has *bute ase ure leawude breþren beoð*. On the other hand the Vitellius French translation, the Latin translation, and the Pepys version all omit the phrase *as ure breðren beoð*. The other manuscripts are either not running (so GSR) or have accidental lacunae which include this sentence (so CV). The agreements run counter to the normal affiliations of the manuscripts; LP disagree with T, which belongs to the same sub-group (the difference between T and P, which often go closely together, is especially striking). It is most unfortunate that a leaf has been lost at this very point in C (whose text resumes a few lines later

[1] It should be observed, however, that in the Nero passage the word *ordre* is not used to mean 'a body or society of persons living . . . under the same religious . . . regulations and discipline' (*OED*, s.v. *order* sb., 7), but rather the regulations or discipline under which the society lives; *muchel of vre ordre* might more appropriately be expanded, in translation, to 'much of the practices of our order'. This is the sense of the word in the title *Liber Ordinis*, the book of the regulations (or rule) of the abbey of St. Victor. But the point can hardly be stressed, since *ordo* is found in this sense ('monastic rule' or 'observation of such a rule') in other sources, e.g. Eadmer, who was a Benedictine and somewhat earlier.

[2] For further discussion of this and the other two passages cited see Chapter II, below.

[3] Corpus MS., f. 111a/23–5; cf. Nero MS., 188/2–4, and Titus MS., 153/14–16 (Morton, p. 412).

in the same passage), for its evidence would almost certainly have been decisive of whether the phrase was an addition. But it seems probable that it was original, for the word-order of the sentence really depends on it; one cannot simply omit it, thus:

for þi ne schule ȝe beon *bute* ihuslet inwið tweolf moneð fiftene siðen,

for *bute* is then nonsensical, nor can one further omit *bute*, since it goes with the negative particle *ne*; one must recast the sentence completely, as the redactor of P found,[1] and read

for þi ne schule ȝe beon ihuslet bute fiftene siðen inwið tweolf moneð.

But if this had been the original form of the sentence, the obvious way to add the phrase *as ure breðren beoð* would have been at the end, not by a complete rearrangement of the word-order; and it would be extremely improbable that NT would share such a rearrangement with A. One must conclude, then, that the two translators and the redactor of P have independently excluded the phrase; and even if it had been an addition, it would have to be regarded as an 'authorized' addition, since it is impossible to conceive of an unauthorized addition which A would share with NT. The adjective *leawude* 'lay' in N's text is of course an addition, almost certainly due to the scribe himself or his immediate predecessor;[2] but an author who in such a context speaks of

---

[1] P's text is: *Now to men and wymmen þat ben bischett hij ne schullen ben yhouseled bot fiftene siþes in þe ȝere* (ed. Påhlsson, *The Recluse* (Lund, 1911), p. 199).

[2] It must also misinterpret the sense intended, for lay brothers took communion much less often; the usual prescription in this period was four times a year, for Augustinians as for Dominicans (see Peter Browe, S.J., *Die häufige Kommunion im Mittelalter* (Münster, Westphalia, 1938), p. 86, who refers to injunctions of Archbishop Odo of Rouen in 1257

'our brothers' is obviously a member of an order, describing its customs.

The second such passage is unobtrusive and occurs only in Corpus;[1] it is therefore absent from Morton's text, and for that reason has not hitherto been discussed in this connection. It is certainly one of the Corpus additions, but this in no way limits its significance; for there are the strongest reasons for believing that the Corpus text is a definitive revision by the original author himself.[2] Early in Part I, after giving instructions for the devotions appropriate to 'the anniversaries of your dearest friends', the author, in the original text, had advised that Commendation should be said either in the morning or at night 'after the suffrages of Matins', with the further comment that it was better still to do this every night except that of Sunday. The additional sentence of the Corpus text comes in at this point, and reads:

In a-mel dei we seggeð ba *Placebo* ant *Dirige* efter þe mete graces, i twi-mel dei efter Non; ant ȝe alswa mote don.

On a one-meal day we say both *Placebo* and *Dirige* after the graces for food, on a two-meal day after Nones; and you may do the same.[3]

and to the observances of Barnwell Priory, Northants.). The 'brothers' meant by *Ancrene Wisse* must be 'those who are not priests', *illi qui non sunt presbyteri*—a recurrent phrase in thirteenth-century documents relating to the taking of communion in Augustinian houses (Browe, p. 85, nn. 125 and 127); but brothers who were non-priests (*Nichtpriester*) were not the same as lay brothers, for there were six recognized clerical orders below the priesthood.

[1] Corpus MS., f. 6b/7–9. The sentence is not present in CFNVP, the other MSS. running at this point (Morton, p. 22); GTSL are not running.   [2] Cf. *Proc. Brit. Acad.*, lii. 194–203.

[3] Miss Salu's translation of this sentence (*The Ancrene Riwle, translated . . . by M. B. Salu* (London, 1955), p. 9) is very free, and in one respect distorts the intended meaning; for she renders *efter þe mete graces* as 'after the Grace before and after meat'. But this is an interpretation of the plural *graces* which neither medieval usage nor the intention of the text warrants; no one could be expected to say the Office of the

On its face, this can only be a description of the prescribed and regular practice of an organized religious community which took meals in common, and it presupposes a knowledge on the part of the readers of who 'we' are. But it has further implications, for its distinction of the practice on a fast-day ('one-meal day') and on an ordinary day ('two-meal day') rests on a routine which is evidently identical with that laid down, in a slightly earlier passage,[1] for the anchoresses themselves. This was that, on a fast-day, the single meal was to be taken after the service of Nones, whereas on an ordinary day the first and main meal was to be taken about midday and was to be followed, in summer, by a sleep and then by Nones. Hence on a fast-day the order of events was (i) Nones, (ii) the single meal, (iii) the Graces after Meat, (iv) the Office of the Dead (*Placebo* and *Dirige*); but on an ordinary day the order was (i) the main meal, (ii) the Graces (not mentioned, but to be assumed), (iii) in summer, a sleep, (iv) Nones, (v) the Office of the Dead. The added sentence necessarily assumes the arrangement of the meal-times prescribed for the anchoresses, and implies that 'we' follow the same routine. But it is a monastic arrangement, derived ultimately from the Benedictine Rule;[2] and though it does not follow

Dead between Grace before Meat and the serving of the food, and then to say the Office again after Grace after Meat. The Graces (in the plural) follow the meal, and are in turn followed by the Office of the Dead. 'Grace before Meat' was normally called *Benedictio cibi*.

[1] Corpus MS., f. 6a/10–14 (Morton, p. 20). The passage prescribes the time of saying Nones in relation to the single or main meal; which is somewhat topsy-turvy, since it is rather a question of the timing of the meal in relation to Nones.

[2] Cf. *The Rule of Saint Benedict*, ed. and trans. by Abbot Justin McCann (London, 1952), c. xli (pp. 98–9). In Lent the single meal was to be taken in the evening, i.e. after Vespers, though Vespers was to be so timed that the meal might be eaten in daylight; otherwise on fast-days the one meal was always to be 'at the ninth hour' (*ad nonam*), and on other days dinner was to be 'at the sixth hour' and supper 'in the evening'.

that the author was a monk, since other orders adopted the originally monastic practice, it does follow that he was a member of an ordered community living under a rule.

It is in fact generally agreed that he cannot have been a monk. No monk could have been so indifferent as he was to the question whether the anchoresses should wear black or white, or have written so scornfully of the *unweote* ('fools') who ask of what order the anchoresses are, the *unwise* who *weneð þet ordre sitte i þe curtel* and ask them *hweðer hwite oðer blake*, and to whom the anchoresses are to reply that they are both white and black *ant of sein James ordre*.[1] It is unlikely, even at so early a date, that a monk would have been so well-disposed to the friars as the author shows himself to be in the two additions in the Corpus version which mention them.[2] The advice *Worltliche leueð lut, religiuse ȝet leas*[3] ('Trust seculars little, religious still less') is evidently wry and self-critical, since any cleric, whether a secular priest or a member of an order, must necessarily come into one or the other category, but it is hard to believe that it could have been written by a professed monk, a 'religious' *par excellence*. There is perhaps no explicit evidence in the text that the author was not a monk, but it would be very surprising if he had been; as Professor Shepherd observes, 'his book owes scarcely anything to the Benedictine Rule'[4] and 'in his liturgical recommendations he is decidedly eclectic',[5] and Mr. Brewer has drawn attention to several

[1] Corpus MS., ff. 2b/28–3a/2, 3b/7–15 (Morton, pp. 8, 10).
[2] Corpus MS., ff. 16b/13–17a/2, 112b/11–12.
[3] Corpus MS., f. 16b/10 (Morton, p. 66).
[4] This is to be qualified to the extent that his and their way of life was deeply influenced by monastic practice and hence ultimately by the Benedictine Rule. But Shepherd is not thinking of this.
[5] Shepherd, *Ancrene Wisse*, p. xxix.

noteworthy differences between monastic practice and the prescriptions of *Ancrene Wisse*.[1]

It has been claimed that the author was a friar, and in particular a Dominican,[2] but the argument has never convinced scholars. The very terms in which he refers to the friars, in the two additions to the Corpus text, show that though he admired and was friendly to them, he was not one himself. In the first of the two passages, after the warning (part of the original text) to 'trust seculars little and religious still less', and the advice not to desire too greatly their acquaintance, the Corpus text adds:

Vre freres prechurs ant ure freres meonurs beoð of swuch ordre þet al folc mahte wundrin ȝef ei of ham wende 'ehe towart te wude-lehe'. For þi, ed euch time þet eani of ham þurh chearite kimeð ow to learen ant to frourin i Godd, . . .[3]

[1] See further below, pp. 28–32.

[2] Notably by the Dominican, V. McNabb, in *MLR*, xi (1916), 1–8; xv (1920), 406–9; and *Archivum Fratrum Praedicatorum*, iv (1934), 49–74. The last of these adds little to the others but is the fullest statement of the case and deigns to give a little more evidence for its assertions. Some of McNabb's arguments, which deserve more respect than they have always been given, though they led him to an impossible conclusion, are considered in more detail below. He spoilt his case by the amateurishness of his presentation, his dogmatism and his failure to cite properly his evidence, his obvious *parti pris*, lack of historical sense, and (it must be added) evident ignorance of Middle English. But he picked on some most important points which others had ignored. Like Professor Shepherd, I find the restatement of the claim by Clare Kirchberger in *Dominican Studies*, vii (1954), 215–38, entirely unconvincing.

[3] Corpus MS., ff. 16b/13–17a/2; also added in the Vitellius French version, 56/11–57/5. The latter part of the passage implies the possibility of regular visits by members of both orders of friars. According to D. Knowles and R. N. Hadcock, *Medieval Religious Houses: England and Wales* (London, New York, and Toronto, 1953), pp. 183–94, Dominican houses were founded at Oxford in 1221, at Bristol before 1230, at Shrewsbury before 1232, at Chester before 1236, at Gloucester before 1241, at Brecon before 1269, and at Worcester in 1347. Franciscan houses were founded at Oxford in 1224, at Worcester about 1227, at Hereford before 1228, at Gloucester and Bristol before 1230, at Chester between

Our Friars Preachers and our Friars Minor are of such a discipline
that all people might be amazed if any of them turned 'an eye
toward the forest-clearing' [i.e. strayed into forbidden pastures].
Therefore, on each occasion that any of them through goodness
of heart comes to instruct you and to comfort you in God, . . .

If he had himself been a friar, he would surely have written
'any of us' rather than 'any of them'. And if he had been a
friar, he must at this date have been either a Dominican or
a Franciscan; and however friendly he may have been to
members of the other order, he could hardly have written
with such complete impartiality of *vre freres prechurs ant
ure freres meonurs*.[1] He seems clearly to be a friendly outsider,
or perhaps rather a member of an order which claimed some
special relationship with the friars ('*our* Friars Preachers
and *our* Friars Minor', phrases in which the word 'friars'
(*freres*) is still used with a strong sense of its literal meaning
of 'brothers'), but he can hardly have been himself either a
Friar Preacher or a Friar Minor.

In any case, simple calculations of chronology rule out the
possibility that a friar could have been the author of *Ancrene
Wisse*. The composition of the work is to be dated 1215–21 or
perhaps a little later,[2] and the Corpus MS. can hardly have

1238 and 1240, at Bridgnorth in 1244, and at Shrewsbury in 1245–6.
It seems that the Dominicans who visited the anchoresses (assuming for
the present that the latter lived somewhere in northern Herefordshire or
southern Shropshire) would have come probably from Shrewsbury, the
Franciscans from either Worcester or more likely Hereford; and that the
earliest possible date for the visits (even assuming that the Dominican
house at Shrewsbury had been founded some years before the first
record of it in 1232) would be about 1228, though 1230 or even 1232
would be a more comfortable date. The date of this reference to the
friars is of course the date of the 'Corpus revision', though the Corpus
MS. itself may be a little later.

[1] Cf. the later, briefer reference in Corpus f. 112b/11–12 (not in F),
which is again to *freres preachurs ant meonurs*, without any distinction.

[2] See *Proc. Brit. Acad.*, lii. 181 ff. The evidence to be cited below,
showing resemblances between *Ancrene Wisse* and the 1220 constitutions

been written much later than 1230;[1] and it is evident that even when the author began to write, his association with the anchoresses was of long standing.[2] But the Dominicans did not come to England until 1221, the Franciscans not until 1224; there is not enough time. And even if we were to grant that the datings were too early by some ten years, that the book was written in the early 1230s and the Corpus MS. about 1240, so as to allow the bare minimum of time that would be necessary for Dominican or Franciscan authorship, it would still be inconceivable that any house of friars would have been able, by 1230 or by 1240, to develop the standardized literary form of West Midland English in which *Ancrene Wisse* and the *Katherine*-group are written, or to train scribes in the regular and consistent use of its somewhat archaic orthography which is displayed by the Corpus MS. and by MS. Bodley 34. Making every allowance for the precocity of the early friars, none of their West Midland houses could have developed such a literary and linguistic tradition within a generation of their first arrival in England.

If then the author was a member of an order, but was neither a monk nor a friar, what remains? The answer to which opinion has been steadily moving is that he was an Augustinian canon.[3] Indeed, the only thing on which Miss

of St. Sixtus, the 1228 and 1238–40 versions of the Dominican *Constitutions*, and the 1236–8 revision of the statutes of Prémontré, strengthens the impression that *Ancrene Wisse* belongs after 1215.

[1] Cf. ibid., pp. 192–3, and the note there. Such a dating, mainly on palaeographic and linguistic grounds, does not of course exclude the possibility that the MS. may be a few years later; cf. p. 14, n. 3, above. The Cleopatra MS. is almost certainly a year or two earlier than the Corpus MS., but in its case there is even less evidence for an absolute dating; if one says that it is '*c.* 1228', it is only because Corpus is dated '*c.* 1230'.

[2] *Ant ȝe, mine leoue sustren, habbeð moni dei icrauet on me efter riwle* (Corpus MS., f. 1a/11–12, restored in spelling; Morton, p. 2).

[3] Cf. D. S. Brewer, *N. & Q.* (N.S.), iii (1956), 232–5; G. Shepherd, *Ancrene Wisse*, p. xxix; G. V. Smithers in Bennett and Smithers, *Early*

Hope Emily Allen and Fr. McNabb were agreed was that the work was Augustinian;[1] the difference between them was that she wished to date it impossibly early, at a time when neither St. Francis nor St. Dominic had founded his order, and that he wished to date it rather too late in order to claim it for one of the offshoots of the Augustinians, namely the Dominicans.

One of McNabb's arguments has received less attention than it deserves, perhaps because he stated it at once too cursorily and too dogmatically, and that is his assertion that *Ancrene Wisse* shows throughout the influence of the Augustinian Rule.[2] There is an evident disproportion in the comparison, for the Augustinian Rule is very brief and for the most part general, *Ancrene Wisse* is long and often detailed. Yet it is undeniable that the author of the later work knew and was influenced by the earlier. The first section of the Augustinian Rule (the so-called *Regula Secunda*)[3] begins:

Ante omnia, fratres carissimi, diligatur deus, deinde proximus, quia ista sunt praecepta principaliter nobis data. Qualiter autem nos oportet orare vel psallere describimus . . .[4]

It proceeds summarily to prescribe the devotions of the brothers, and then equally summarily to deal with their work,

Middle English Verse and Prose (Oxford, 1966; 2nd edn. 1968), pp. 402–3; Basil Cottle in *JEGPh*, lxvii (1968), 143–4.

[1] See her article 'The Origin of the *Ancren Riwle*', *PMLA*, xxxiii (1918), 474–546, and McNabb's rejoinder, 'Further light on the "Ancren Riwle" ', *MLR*, xv (1920), 405–9.

[2] *MLR*, xi. 1–2.

[3] The *Regula Prima* is known not to be Augustinian. On the textual history of the Augustinian Rule, see J. C. Dickinson, *The Origins of the Austin Canons* (London, 1950), Appendix I (pp. 255–72).

[4] Citations from the Augustinian Rule are given in the text published by D. de Bruyne in *Revue bénédictine*, xlii. 318–26, with some typographical changes. Dickinson reprints this on his pp. 273–9, but with a few misprints.

discipline, and other duties. *Ancrene Wisse* is in some sense an elaboration of the same general pattern. In its Preface, among other topics, it stresses the primacy of the Inner Rule, which deals with purity of heart; and when in Part VII it comes to the discussion of Love, its author writes:

For þi, mine leoue sustren, ouer alle þing beoð bisie to habben schir heorte. Hwet is schir heorte? Ich hit habbe iseid ear: þet is, þet ȝe na þing ne wilnin ne ne luuien bute Godd ane, ant te ilke þinges for Godd þe helpeð ow toward him . . .[1]

which is an extended paraphrase of the opening sentence of the *Regula Secunda*, though at this point love of one's neighbour has been replaced by love of those things which help one towards God.[2] But immediately after the Preface, in its Part I, *Ancrene Wisse* prescribes the anchoresses' devotions, as does the beginning of the *Regula Secunda*. The resemblance, however, does not extend to detail; the devotions laid down in the *Regula Secunda* had become so archaic, and its regulations for fasting and for manual labour had proved so oppressive in different times and climes than those for which the Rule was originally designed, that in the early twelfth century Gelasius II, in a papal bull, had given permission for its outworn provisions to be disregarded. Moreover, though Part I of *Ancrene Wisse* covers, in much fuller detail, the ground of the first third of the *Regula Secunda*, and Part VIII that of the rest, these two parts of the Outer Rule are separated, in the English book, by the whole length of the Inner Rule, enclosed within the Outer

[1] Corpus MS., f. 104b/6–9 (Morton, p. 386). See also Shepherd's note on this passage (*Ancrene Wisse*, p. 53, note to p. 20, l. 2); he calls it 'a definition in the Augustinian style'.

[2] But before this sentence the author had referred to *luue . . . to Godd ant to alle men in him ant for him* and to the necessity of doing everything that one does *oðer for luue ane of Godd, oðer for oþres god ant for his biheue* (Corpus MS., f. 104a/14, 28). Love of one's fellow men has not been omitted.

Rule by a deliberate structural device, a piece of formal symbolism.

The second section of the Augustinian Rule, the *Regula Tertia*,[1] begins:

Primum propter quod in uno estis congregati, ut unanimes habitetis in domo, et sit vobis anima una et cor unum in deo, et non dicatis aliquid proprium, sed sint vobis omnia communia...

To this sentence there is explicit reference in the prologue to the twelfth-century Institutes or Statutes of Prémontré,[2] which begins:

Quoniam ex praecepto Regulae jubemur habere[3] cor unum et animam unam in Domino, justum est ut qui sub una regula et

---

[1] The *Regula Tertia* was adapted from St. Augustine's *Letter 211*, written, perhaps *c.* 423, 'for a community of nuns, founded by the saint, whose community life had been undermined by dissensions' (Dickinson, *Origins*, p. 257).

[2] Edmond Martène, *De Antiquis Ecclesiae Ritibus* (rev. edn., 1788), iii. 323. The text printed by Martène (whose first edition was published in 1700–2) under the title 'Primaria Instituta Canonicorum Praemonstratensium, ex ms. bibliothecae S. Victoris', was in fact, according to Lefèvre, the second codification of the statutes of Prémontré, made probably about 1174, though a date after 1190 has been suggested (see Pl. F. Lefèvre, *Les Statuts de Prémontré . . . au XIIIe siècle* (Louvain, 1946), pp. x–xiv). The first codification, made between 1131 and 1134 (Lefèvre, p. viii), was that published by Raphael van Waefelghem, *Les Premiers Statuts de Prémontré* (Analectes de l'ordre de Prémontré, ix; Louvain, 1913), from Munich MS. Clm. 17. 174, of the end of the twelfth or the beginning of the thirteenth century; it does not include the prologue. Lefèvre himself prints a version of the statutes made in 1236–8; its text of the prologue differs only in minor details from Martène's. The same is true of the prologue of the Dominican *Constitutions* both in the earliest surviving recension of 1228 and in the revision made by Raymond of Penafort in 1238–40, both of which are edited by Heinrich Denifle in *Archiv für Literatur- und Kirchengeschichte des Mittelalters*, i (1885), 165–227 (1228 recension; prologue on p. 194) and v (1889), 530–64 (1238–40 recension; prologue on p. 533).

[3] The word *habere* is not in Martène's text, and though it is perhaps unnecessary I have supplied it from the texts given by Lefèvre and Denifle.

unius professionis vote vivimus, uniformes in observantiis canonicae religionis inveniamur, *quatinus unitatem quae interius servanda est in cordibus* foveat et *repraesentet uniformitas exterior* servata in moribus.

Similarly the author of *Ancrene Wisse*, in his Preface,[1] writes:

þer as monie beoð igederet togederes, þer for anrednesse me schal makie strengðe of annesse of claðes ant of oþerhwet of uttre þinges, *þet te annesse wiðuten bitacni þe annesse* of a luue ant of a wil *þet ha alle habbeð imeane wiðinnen*. Wið hare habit, þet is an, þet euch haueð swuch as oþer, ant alswa of oðerhwet, ha ȝeiȝeð þet ha habbeð alle togederes a luue ant a wil euch alswuch as oþer—loke þet ha ne lihen. þus hit is i cuuent.

The phrases that I have italicized are clear proof that *Ancrene Wisse* is here directly dependent on the Premonstratensian institutes of *c.* 1174. But beyond that, all three passages stress that community of worldly goods, or uniformity in religious observances or in clothing and other external matters, is a means towards and a symbol of a single mind and heart— *anima una et cor unum* or *a luue ant a wil*. After this, the *Regula Tertia* goes on to deal at some length with the variations in treatment and diet which may be made necessary by the illness or incapacity of individual members of the community, just as *Ancrene Wisse*, in its Preface, provides that the regulations of the Outer Rule may be varied, as necessity requires and with the advice of the confessor,

efter euchanes manere ant efter hire euene. For sum is strong, sum unstrong . . . sum is clergesse, sum nawt . . . sum is ald ant eðelich . . . sum is ȝung ant luuelich.[2]

Later, after instructing the brothers that in all their actions they should behave in a way befitting their sanctity, the *Regula Tertia* proceeds:

[1] Corpus MS., f. 3b/19–27 (Morton, p. 12).
[2] Corpus MS., f. 2a/9–14 (Morton, p. 6).

Oculi vestri, etsi iaciuntur in aliquam feminarum, figantur in nullam. Neque enim, quando proceditis, feminas videre prohibemini, sed adpetere aut ab ipsis adpeti velle criminosum est. Nec solo tactu et effectu, sed affectu et aspectu quoque adpetitur et adpetit concupiscentia feminarum. Nec dicatis vos animos habere pudicos, si habeatis oculos inpudicos, quia inpudicus oculus inpudici cordis est nuntius.

This passage is directly quoted in Part II of *Ancrene Wisse*, in the section dealing with sight, where—doubtless unwittingly—it is turned back into its original form as an injunction addressed to women:

Inpudicus oculus inpudici cordis est nuncius: Augustinus. þet te muð ne mei for scheome, þe liht ehe spekeð hit, ant is as erndeberere of þe lihte heorte. Ah nu is sum wummon þe nalde for nan þing wilni fulðe to mon, ant tah ne rohte ha neauer þah he þohte toward hire ant were of hire itemptet; ant nu deð sein Austin ba twa þeos in a weie, wilnin ant habbe wil forte beon iwilnet, *non solum appetere sed et appeti uelle criminosum*, 'cuueiti mon oðer habbe wil forte beon icuueitet of monne, ba is heaued sunne'.[1]

In the penultimate paragraph of the *Regula Tertia*, dealing with the obedience due to the superior (*praepositus*) of a religious house, Augustine says:

Et quamvis utrumque sit necessarium, tamen plus a vobis amari adpetat quam timeri, semper cogitans deo se pro vobis redditurum esse rationem.

Ancrene Wisse adapts this to the relationship that should exist between the anchoresses and their servants:

ȝef þet ha sungið þurh ower ȝemeles, ȝe schule beo bicleopet þrof biuore þe hehe deme . . . Ba is riht þet ha ow dreden ant luuien,

---

[1] Edited text, based on Cleopatra MS., ff. 24ᵛ/21–25/12 (Nero 26/5–14; Morton, p. 60), and the other MSS. running; lacuna in Corpus.

ant tah þet ter beo eauer mare of luue þen of drede; þenne schal hit wel fearen.[1]

Finally, the *Regula Tertia* concludes:

Ut autem vos in hoc libello tamquam in speculo possitis inspicere ne per oblivionem aliquid neglegatis, semel in septimana vobis legatur, et ubi vos inveneritis ea quae scripta sunt facientes, agite gratias domino bonorum omnium largitori; ubi autem sibi quicumque vestrum videt aliquid deesse, doleat de praeterito, caveat de futuro, orans ut et debitum dimittatur et in temptationem non inducatur.

This is closely followed, as McNabb pointed out, at the end of *Ancrene Wisse*, with the substitution of a daily for a weekly reading (probably because *Ancrene Wisse* is so much longer and more detailed, and would require many sessions to read through):

Of þis boc redeð hwen ȝe beoð eise euche dei, leasse oðer mare. Ich hopie þet hit schal beon ow, ȝef ȝe hit redeð ofte, swiðe biheue, þurh Godes muchele grace . . . Ȝef ȝe findeð þet ȝe doð alswa as ȝe redeð, þonckið Godd ȝeorne; ȝef ȝe doð nawt, biddeð Godes are, ant beoð umben þeronuuen þet ȝe hit bet halden efter ower mihte.[2]

It is sufficiently clear, from these parallels, that the author of *Ancrene Wisse* knew the Rule of St. Augustine well in both its parts, and drew from it not only general ideas (of which some further examples will be given below), but also

---

[1] Corpus MS., f. 116b/20–6 (Morton, p. 428). The debt of *Ancrene Wisse* to the Augustinian Rule at this point was observed by the late thirteenth-century 'corrector' (scribe D) of the Cleopatra MS., who was himself probably an Augustinian and was almost certainly working on the manuscript after it had been given to the Augustinian abbey (refounded as a house for women) of Canonsleigh in Devon; on f. 198 he adds against the phrase *þet þer beo mare eauer of luue þen of drede* the marginal note 'Augustinus in regula: Et quamuis utrumque sit necessarium: tamen a uobis plus amari appetat quam timeri.'

[2] Corpus MS., f. 117a/26–117b/7 (Morton, p. 430).

on one occasion a direct quotation (or rather two citations from a single passage), on others close paraphrases. But he had also read other Augustinian works which elaborated or commented on the passage from which he directly quotes. One of these was the *De claustro animae*[1] of Hugh of Fouilloy (Hugo de Folieto, a regular canon, and prior in 1153 of an abbey near Corbie),[2] a work sometimes ascribed to Hugh of St. Victor. In chapter iv of Book I, after citing (explicitly from Augustine's 'Regula clericorum') the sentence *Impudicus oculus . . . nuntius*, the author quotes the scriptural verse *Oculi prima tela sunt adulterae*, and proceeds:

Solent homines tribus generibus armorum uti ad defensionem, telis videlicet, hasta, et gladio. Longe positi vulnerantur telis; in illos qui cuspide tangi nequeunt, vibratur hasta; cum pugnatur cominus, officium suum gladius implet. Similibus armis utitur impudicitia ad expugnandum hominem exteriorem . . . *Et inmisit uxor domini sui oculos suos in Joseph* [Gen. xxxix]. Haec sunt impudicitiae tela, quibus vulnerantur multi, licet longe positi. His telis oculorum pudicitiam opposuit . . . Haec est vibratio hastae, blandientis adulterae sermo . . . Hic est gladius, quo configitur cominus, mollis scilicet adulterae tactus.[3]

Similarly in *Ancrene Wisse*, after the passage directly citing the *Regula Tertia*, the author proceeds immediately to quote *Oculi tela prima sunt adultere* and to develop the image of the three sorts of weapons, the arrows of the eyes, the spear of the wounding word, and the sword of touch which gives the death-blow;[4] but he has skilfully abstracted the allegory, and

[1] Migne, *Pat. Lat.*, clxxvi, cols. 1017 ff.

[2] J. de Ghellinck, *L'Essor de la littérature latine au XIIᵉ siècle* (Brussels, Bruges, and Paris, 2nd edn., 1955), p. 204.

[3] Migne, cols. 1026–7.

[4] Cleopatra MS., f. 25/12–25ᵛ/20, Nero MS. 26/14–27/6 (Morton, pp. 60, 62); lacuna in Corpus. It may be added that *De claustro animae*, Book III, c. i, cites the example of Dina, with Gregory's commentary on the passage, which is also used in *Ancrene Wisse* (Corpus MS., f. 14a/16 ff.; Morton, pp. 54, 56).

at once concentrated and elaborated it, from the Latin writer's more discursive and pedantic treatment, in which the symbolism is illustrated by and indeed made subordinate to an account of the stages of Potiphar's wife's attack on Joseph. But *Ancrene Wisse*, after independently extending the allegory to remark on the folly of sticking one's head out of the embrasure of a castle wall while crossbow-bolts are flying about, then turns to yet another source, the commentary on the Augustinian Rule usually attributed to Hugh of St. Victor[1] and its exposition of the passage beginning *Oculi vestri*, which runs as follows:[2]

Sanctus David quia oculos in feminam jecit et fixit, illicito appetitu devictus adulterium et homicidium perpetravit. Si ergo tantus vir per incuriam oculorum cecidit, nos qui longe ab ejus sanctitate distamus, tam mortale praecipitum summopere timere debemus. Teneamus ergo sententiam beati Job qua dicitur: *Pepigi foedus cum oculis meis ut non cogitarem de virgine* [Job xxvi]. Quia enim sensit sanctus vir quod per exteriorem visum interior animus corrumpitur, fecit pactum cum oculis suis ne incaute aspicerent quod illicite concupisceret . . . Nisi enim sanctus David feminam fixe inspexisset, in tantam carnis tentationem minime incidisset. Hinc per prophetam dicitur: *Ascendit mors per fenestras nostras* [Jer. ix]. Mors animae est concupiscentia, domus interior mens nostra est, fenestrae hujus domus sunt quinque corporis sensus. Mors ergo per fenestram ascendit atque domos ingreditur, quando concupiscentiae vitium per sensus prorumpit ad interiora mentis.

Ancrene Wisse had already instanced David's sin with Bathsheba before its citations from the *Regula Tertia*, with an extended contrast between *se hali king as he wes ant Godes*

---

[1] Migne, *Pat. Lat.*, clxxvi, cols. 881 ff. It has been suggested that the commentary is more probably the work of Lietbert of St. Ruf, to whom it is attributed in a number of manuscripts; see C. Dereine, *Revue bénédictine*, lix (1949), 166–7, and *ODCC*, p. 663.

[2] Migne, cols. 898–9.

prophete . . . Godes ahne deorling . . . king ant prophete icuret of alle on the one hand, and *a feble mon*, a *surquide sire*, a *sunful mon* on the other, which is parallel to Hugh's contrast between *tantus vir* and *nos qui longe ab eius sanctitate distamus*; Bathsheba is said to have caused David to commit three deadly sins, *spusbruche*, *treisun*, and *monslaht*, where Hugh, more logically, is content with two, *adulterium* and *homicidium*.[1] After his quotations from the *Regula Tertia*, the English writer goes on[2] to cite a variation on Hugh's quotation from Jeremiah, namely St. Bernard's *Sicut mors per peccatum in orbem, ita per has fenestras intrat in mentem*, but then reverts to the example of David:

Al hali writ is ful of warninge of ehe. Dauid: *Auerte oculos meos ne uideant uanitatem.* 'Lauerd,' seið Dauid, 'went awei min ehnen from the worldes dweole ant hire fantasme.' Iob: *Pepigi fedus cum oculis meis ut nec cogitarem de uirgine.* 'Ich habbe ifestnet foreward,' seið Iob, 'mid min ehnen, þet ich ne misþenche.' Hu deale! Hwet seið he? þencheð me mid ehe? Godd hit wat he seið wel, for efter þe ehe kimeð þe þoht ant þerefter þe dede.[3]

It cannot be accident that Hugh, in a commentary on a passage of the *Regula Tertia*, and *Ancrene Wisse*, in the context of direct quotations from the same passage, have three elements in common: (i) the reference to David and the sins which the sight of Bathsheba caused him to commit, and the contrast between his sanctity and ordinary human frailty; (ii) the citation of Job, with an explanation of his meaning (that the mind is corrupted by, or that thought follows, what the eye sees); (iii) a quotation (in the one case from Jeremiah, in the other from St. Bernard, who is following Jeremiah) which

---

[1] For the *Ancrene Wisse* passage, see Corpus MS., f. 14b/4–22 (Morton, p. 56). The lacuna in Corpus begins just after this point.

[2] Cleopatra MS., ff. 25ᵛ/20–26/1; Nero MS., 27/7–10 (Morton, p. 62).

[3] Edited text based on Cleopatra f. 26/8–17 (Nero 27/17–25; Morton, p. 62), and the other MSS. running; lacuna in Corpus.

says that death ascends or enters by windows, which are equated with the eyes. Such a combination of shared elements cannot possibly be coincidental; the later author must have read the earlier.

This being so, one may cite two other resemblances between Hugh's commentary on the Augustinian Rule and *Ancrene Wisse* which in themselves are not clear enough to bear the weight of proof. The first is at the very beginning of both works. Hugh starts with an etymological definition of *regula*:

Haec praecepta quae subscripta sunt ideo *regula* appellantur, quia videlicet in eis nobis recte vivendi norma exprimitur. Regula autem dicitur, eo quod recte regat, vel quod recte doceat.[1]

Ancrene Wisse begins not so much with a definition as with an extended running illustration of the etymological connections of *regula* (including, significantly, the sort of 'rule' which teaches about a subject):

'Recti diligunt te': in Canticis, sponsa ad sponsum. Est rectum gram[m]aticum, rectum geometricum, rectum theologicum; et sunt differencie totidem regularum. De recto theologico sermo nobis est. Cuius regule due sunt: vna circa cordis directionem, altera uersatur circa exteriorum rectificationem.[2]

The second example comes from Hugh's commentary a little before the passage in which he elaborates on wandering eyes that light on women, at a point,[3] in the same chapter, where he is stressing the importance of unity. He writes:

Sanctorum quoque societas terribilis ut castrorum acies ordinata describitur. Castrorum namque acies cum ad bellum se praeparat, prius se conjungere atque ordinare festinat, ne ab hostibus interrumpi aut penetrari valeat. Sic nimirum nostra spiritualis acies quae bene conjuncta et ordinata simul stare, simul ambulare

---

[1] Migne, col. 881. [2] Corpus MS., f. 1a/1–9 (Morton, p. 2).
[3] Migne, cols. 897–8.

praecipitur, contra diabolum quotidie munitur ad bellum, ut videlicet ex sua conjunctione terreat antiquum hostem, qui in servis Dei nihil tam timet quam concordiae unitatem.

This is also a favourite theme of the author of *Ancrene Wisse*, who, like Hugh, emphasizes the importance of unity as a weapon against the Devil, and the latter's strivings to breach it; he has various similitudes to illustrate it, but one is essentially the same as Hugh's:

Nute ӡe, þer men fehteð i þes stronge ferdes, þe ilke þe haldeð ham feaste togederes ne muhe beo descumfit o neauer nane wise. Alswa hit is in gastelich feht aӡeines þe deouel. Al his entente is forte tweamen heorten, forte bineomen luue þet halt men togederes. For hwen luue alið, þenne beoð ha isundret, ant te deouel deð him bitweonen ananriht ant sleað on euche halue.[1]

It is improbable that the author of *Ancrene Wisse* had Hugh's commentary on the Rule of St. Augustine open before him as he wrote, but he must have read it at some time; and a man who knows well the Augustinian Rule, has studied an Augustinian commentary on it, and can in addition turn to yet another Augustinian work in which a passage from the Rule is cited and extended, is likely himself to be an Augustinian.

The best recent discussion of the Augustinian elements in *Ancrene Wisse* is Mr. D. S. Brewer's,[2] which from now on I mostly follow, though with some rearrangement of the order of his arguments and with some elaboration and modification. Mr. Brewer accepts (though with reserves, as is necessary) Fr. McNabb's liturgical arguments for an Augustinian origin of the Rule; but whereas McNabb had taken the Augustinian influence as indicative of Dominican authorship,

---

[1] Corpus MS., f. 68a/7–14 (Morton, pp. 250, 252)
[2] *N. & Q.* (N.S.), iii (1956), 232–5.

Brewer, mindful of the complications of dating that this would involve, remarks that to suppose that the author was an Austin canon would avoid the difficulty—and, he might have added, would be a more direct interpretation of some of the evidence. He points out that the canons were 'notable for the moderation, learning, and eclecticism which characterize' *Ancrene Wisse*,[1] and that its emphasis on the value of reading is consistent with Augustinian and opposed to monastic practice;[2] and Mr. Cottle has added that 'no order did so much for vernacular composition of the creative sort'.[3]

But Brewer has other arguments much more particular. One is that the instruction in the Outer Rule (Part VIII):[4]

Nest flesch ne schal nan werien linnene clað bute hit beo of hearde ant of greate heorden,

Next to the body none shall wear linen cloth unless it be of hard and of coarse 'hards',

involves the concession that the anchoresses might wear linen, albeit of the roughest; he says that this concession 'may seem slight, but as Hall remarked, it was most unusual', and he goes on to quote J. C. Dickinson's remark that

Few of the differences between monks and regular canons attracted more attention from early controversialists than the fact that the first wore garments of wool, the second of linen.[5]

---

[1] Brewer, p. 233. On the Augustinians' practice of reading and study and on their learning see Dickinson, *Origins*, pp. 186–92.

[2] Cf. Corpus MS., f. 78a/12–21 (Morton, p. 286), which includes the advice *Ofte, leoue sustren, ȝe schulen uri leasse forte reden mare. Redunge is god bone* ('Often, dear sisters, you ought to say Hours less in order to read more. Reading is a good form of prayer'), and f. 11a/22–7 (Morton, p. 44), which enjoins, among other occupations to prevent idleness, *redunge of englisc oðer of frensch.*

[3] *JEGPh*, lxvii. 142.

[4] Corpus MS., f. 113a/26–7 (Morton, p. 418).

[5] Dickinson, *Origins*, p. 184.

But the point is really more particular than this, for Brewer has paid too little attention to the fact that the sentence in *Ancrene Wisse* is a qualified *prohibition* of wearing linen 'next to the body'; and exactly this prohibition, unqualified, is found in the Dominican *Constitutions* of 1228, which say that our brothers 'lineis non utantur ad carnem'.[1] Probably both *Ancrene Wisse* and the Dominican *Constitutions*, in this detail, reflect some early thirteenth-century Augustinian rule, and it is more likely that the Dominican regulation has dropped the qualifying phrase than that *Ancrene Wisse* has added it.[2] Again, the Outer Rule prescribes that the

[1] ed. Denifle, *ALKG*, i. 204, in the chapter (Dist. I, c. 19) 'De Vestibus'. Denifle's footnote records that the MS. adds, after *carnem*, 'nec etiam infirmi, et linteamina omnino removeantur de infirmatoriis nostris', but that these words were first added at the General Chapter of 1236. They are designed to exclude a concession allowed by the Prémontré statutes, and were embodied in the recension of 1238–40.

[2] Though I have found the phrasal resemblance only in the Dominican constitutions, the general implication of the sentence in *Ancrene Wisse* (that linen might be worn otherwise than next to the body, and even next to the body if it was coarse) is in agreement with the *Liber Ordinis* of St. Victor, which, in chapter xx ('De Vestiario', Martène, iii. 261–2), allows for the use of both linen and woollen clothing (and also of furs, providing they are lambskin and not the furs of wild animals—a usual provision). The tunics were to be of white woollen cloth (but office-holders might also have a linen tunic), the copes of black cloth (unspecified); and the considerable list of garments allowed to each canon included two vests or shirts (*interulae, id est camisiae*) and two pairs of pants (*femoralia*), which may well have been of linen though there is nothing to say so. But there is a special warning about linen garments, that they are not to be too fine or expensive (*In lineis quoque vestimentis hoc cavendum statuimus, ne nimis subtilia sint aut pretiosa*; p. 261).

The statutes of Prémontré, both in the recension of *c.* 1174 (Martène, iii. 335) and in that of 1236–8 (Lefèvre, pp. 56–8) are more stringent. They begin their chapter 'De Vestitu' by remarking that those who live in the courts of kings wear soft clothing, but rough and humble clothing is fitting for clerks who have renounced the world. 'For that reason we have resolved not to use linen garments except pants' (*Eapropter proposuimus lineis non uti nisi femoralibus*), and even their woollen garments were not to be too fine or too splendid, or to have the nap shorn, so that the injunction of the Rule might be fulfilled, *Non sit notabilis habitus*

anchoresses should wash themselves wherever is necessary as often as they wish, and observes trenchantly that 'filth was never pleasing to God';[1] and Brewer remarks that 'it was the Augustinians alone among the Orders, as Fr. McNabb noted, who valued cleanliness, accounting dirtiness, in the words of one of them, "a sign of negligence, not a sign of goodness" '.[2] He further argues that the emphasis on wearing warm and sensible clothing, in bed and out,[3] 'is in accord with Augustinian precept and opposed to monastic theory',[4] and that the author's indifference to the question whether they should wear white or black follows 'the Augustinian custom of leaving the regulation of dress to individual houses'. Brewer here refers to Dickinson, *Origins*, p. 185, who in turn cites J. W. Clark, *Customs*, p. 199; the latter states explicitly that there was certainly no uniformity in the colour of the dress of the Austin canons. Nevertheless there were 'black canons' (the ordinary regular canons, so called from the colour of their copes) and 'white canons' (those of Prémontré); and Miss Beryl Smalley says that 'the black cloak which he wore over his white habit distinguished the canon regular from the black and the white monks'.[5]

vester, etc. Linen copes were forbidden (*Lineas cappas habere non licebit*). Even in bed, a linen night-shirt (*linea camisia*) was allowed only to the gravely ill, as a matter of necessity (recension of 1131–4, van Waefelghem, p. 43; of *c.* 1174, Martène, iii. 327; of 1236–8, Lefèvre, p. 22). Despite the exception made for pants, this is more austere than the St. Victor regulations, and is an instance where *Ancrene Wisse* goes with St. Victor against Prémontré.

It may be added that *Ancrene Wisse* is here applying to women a regulation written for men. The first recension (1131–4) of the Prémontré statutes prescribed specially for the clothing of the sisters; see pp. 90–1, below.

[1] Corpus MS., f. 115a/12–14 (Morton, p. 424).
[2] Cf. Dickinson, *Origins*, p. 195.
[3] Corpus MS., f. 113a/22–113b/18 (Morton, pp. 418, 420).
[4] Cf. Dickinson, p. 195.
[5] *The Study of the Bible in the Middle Ages*, p. 83.

This was in particular the dress of the Victorines.[1] Those Augustinians, therefore, whose dress combined both black and white might have special reason to mock at men who ask whether the anchoresses are 'of the black *or* of the white'.[2] When the author says that religion consists in keeping oneself pure and unblemished from the world,

nawt in þe wide hod, ne i þe blake cape, ne i þe hwite rochet, ne i þe greie cuuel,[3]

not in the wide hood, nor in the black cope, nor in the white rochet, nor in the grey cowl,

he is evidently thinking of the dress of the Augustinians, and perhaps only of theirs, for it was the canons (except those

---

[1] *Liber Ordinis*, ed. Martène, iii. 261–2; cf. Fourier Bonnard, *Histoire de l'abbaye royale . . . de St-Victor de Paris*, i (Paris, 1904), 58. It is curious that in Gervase of Canterbury's list of the religious houses of England, in his *Mappa Mundi*, Wigmore Abbey, a Victorine house, is given as an abbey of *canonici nigri* when entered correctly under Hereford-shire, but as a priory of *canonici albi* when wrongly repeated under Shropshire (ed. Stubbs, Rolls Series 1879–80, ii. 435–6); this may suggest some confusion between Victorines and Premonstratensians.

[2] But in the light of evidence to be cited elsewhere, the question may have had a more definite point, whether the anchoresses belonged to the 'black' Augustinians or the 'white' Augustinians. By the time of *Ancrene Wisse*, the Premonstratensians were insisting that their sisters, as well as their brothers, should wear white; see below, p. 112. The questioners are perhaps to be taken as assuming that the anchoresses belong to the Augustinian order, and as asking to which branch of it they adhere. As the ordinary Augustinian clothing combined both black and white, there may even have been an element of private joke in the author's advice to the anchoresses that they should answer that they were both black *and* white—though his stated reason for this (Corpus MS., f. 3b/ 5–15; Morton, p. 10) is the example of the early anchorites, who were both black and white, *nawt tah onont claðes, ah as Godes spuse singeð bi hire seoluen*, Nigra sum set formosa, *'Ich am blac ant tah hwit'*, ha seið.

[3] Corpus MS., f. 3b/18–19 (Morton, p. 12). The text varies in some other MSS. running (Cleopatra, Nero, and the Trinity version), but A's text is exactly confirmed by the Latin version, was probably that of the Vitellius French version (which now has lacunae due to fire-damage), and is also that of Vernon except that V omits *hwite* before *rochet*.

of Prémontré) who wore the hood large enough to cover the head and shoulders, the black cope (*cappa*), and the white rochet of linen,[1] and their lay-brothers who wore a hooded tunic—which might well be called a cowl—of 'country grey';[2] but it may be that 'grey cowl' refers to the dress of the Cistercians, who were often called 'grey monks' in early times, and that the author has more orders than one in mind.

During his discussion, in the Preface, of those who ask to what order the anchoresses belong, the author says that they are to reply that they are 'of St. James's order', and if surprise is caused by this answer they are to counter by asking where in Holy Writ is religion more clearly described than in St. James's canonical epistle, in the words 'Religio munda et immaculata apud Deum et Patrem hoc est, visitare pupillas et viduas in necessitate sua, et immaculatum se custodire ab hoc seculo';[3] and it is later, in expounding this text, that he says that religion consists in keeping oneself pure and unblemished, and not in outward dress. Brewer appositely draws attention to a passage in Dickinson[4] in which he says that the custumal of the Augustinian house of St. Quentin of Beauvais (which was 'enormously influential'),[5] in its prologue, stresses that 'true religion consists not in what is done, but why it is done; not in shaven heads, but in purified hearts; not in white vesture, but in chaste bodies and clean minds'. Dickinson goes on to refer to Arno of

---

[1] Cf. Dickinson, *Origins*, p. 185, and Bonnard, *Histoire*, i. 58.

[2] Cf. *Liber Ordinis*, ed. Martène, iii. 262: 'Tunicae autem et cappae laicorum fratrum, id est conversorum, de grisio rusticano', and p. 262, 'caputium tunicae' (again referring to the clothes of the lay brothers). Grey *cappae* were also prescribed for lay brothers at Prémontré (statutes of 1236–8, ed. Lefèvre, p. 58). But in the context of *Ancrene Wisse* it is perhaps more likely that professed religious are referred to than lay brothers.

[3] Corpus MS., f. 3a/2–10 (Morton, pp. 8, 10).

[4] Dickinson, *Origins*, pp. 175–6.

[5] Ibid., p. 165.

Reichersberg (*d.* 1175), who in his *Scutum canonicorum* (written before 1153, in defence of the canons against the monks) observed that 'God's house has many mansions, and in St. James's words true religion was "to visit the fatherless and widows in their affliction, and to keep himself unspotted from the world", in which, as with other religious practices and pious exercises, all were brethren working alongside the monks *cuiuscunque coloris utantur vestibus*'.[1] Here in Arno is the same association of the citation of St. James and a discussion of vesture, with an eye to the monks; and there cannot be any doubt that *Ancrene Wisse* in this respect is following a well-established Augustinian tradition. The germ of the idea is already in the Augustinian Rule itself, in the sentence 'Non sit notabilis habitus vester, nec affectetis vestibus placere sed moribus'.

Brewer considers that *Ancrene Wisse*'s relaxations in the rule of silence after blood-letting and *hwen ow þuncheð heauie*[2] are 'in accordance with the practice of the uncongregated regular canons',[3] as distinct from what Dickinson calls 'the austere, independent congregations of the order'; but here he pushes the argument too far, for by the early thirteenth century it had become a general practice to permit rest and recreatory conversation after blood-letting.[4] It is to be observed also that in *Ancrene Wisse* conversation with the servants and mutual entertainment by *þeawfule talen* are conceded only for times of bodily weakness or of

---

[1] Migne, *Pat. Lat.*, cxciv, col. 1496. Brewer adds a reference to col. 1502, where Arno, referring to the dress of the canons (wool and fur according to necessity, and linen for the honour and the 'mystery' of the Order), says that in it the brightness (*candor*) of the robes of Aaron and the white tunic (*collobium*) of the apostle James are mingled (assuming that *pertimescitur* is an error for *partim miscentur*—the text printed seems very unreliable).

[2] Corpus MS., f. 115a/2–12 (Morton, pp. 422, 424).

[3] *N. & Q.*, p. 233, referring to Dickinson, *Origins*, pp. 183–4.

[4] Cf. *Proc. Brit. Acad.*, lii. 188.

oppression or grief, and then chiefly as a means to a more
rapid recovery ('it is a great folly to lose for one day ten or
twelve'); and that this is fully in accord with normal Augustinian teaching, from which even a member of the stricter
independent congregations would not dissent. In fact three
separate matters are involved here, which we must turn aside
to examine more closely: the rules for the frequency of
minutio or blood-letting, for relaxations of normal discipline
after it, and for silence.

In the *Liber Ordinis* or book of the regulations of St.
Victor,[1] there is a section 'De minutis'[2] which begins by

---

[1] Martène, iii. 253–91, prints the *Liber Ordinis* under the title 'Antiquæ
Consuetudines canonicorum regularium S. Victoris Parisiensis, ad usum
monasterii S. Evurtii accommodatæ' (i.e. the monastery of St. Euverte,
Orleans, dedicated to Evurtius, a fourth-century bishop of Orleans).
According to his preface (p. 251), this was preserved in a very old manu-
script, written five hundred years before (i.e. about 1200, since he was
writing about 1700), belonging to the library of the abbey of St. Germain,
Auxerre; but though the Bibliothèque Municipale of Auxerre now pos-
sesses a number of manuscripts from St. Germain, including at least one
(MS. 244) with a connection with St. Euverte, Orleans, it does not possess
Martène's copy of the *Liber Ordinis* (*Catalogue général des manuscrits:
Départements*, vol. vi, Auxerre etc.). Martène says that he collated his
text 'diligently' with a Victorine codex, but his footnotes recording the
results are in fact sparse; presumably he found few significant variations.
  The earliest MS. still extant seems to be Paris MS. Bibliothèque Ste
Geneviève 1637, dated to s. xii fin. or s. xiii init. (*Catalogue général des
manuscrits: Paris, Bibliothèque Ste Geneviève*, vol. ii (1896)). MS. Bib.
Ste Gen. 1636 is dated to s. xiii. A partial collation of these two with
Martène's text has not revealed significant differences. They both come
from the monastery of Ste Geneviève, which was subjected to St. Victor
in the mid twelfth century. From St. Victor itself come MSS. Bib. Nat.
lat. 14673 and 15059, dated to s. xiii (Léopold Delisle, *Inventaire des
manuscrits de l'abbaye de St.-Victor conservés à la Bibliothèque impériale*
(1869)); I have not seen these.
  In Martène's text the sections of the *Liber Ordinis* are numbered as
chapters, except for two before and one after chapter lxxii ('De mandato
. . .'), which include two sections that concern us, 'De ordine tonsurae'
and 'De minutis'. But any suggestion that these unnumbered sections
may be later insertions into the text seems unjustified; in the two Ste

Notes 1 and 2 continued on next page

prescribing five general *minutiones* a year, at stated times. As this prescription is already found in the earliest extant manuscript, it must have become part of the regulations by the end of the twelfth century and may be older still. At Prémontré, according to the statutes of *c.* 1174 printed by Martène,[1] *minutio* was at the discretion of the abbot or prior of the house; but the recension of 1236–8, though it retains this statement as an introductory sentence, later contradicts it by prescribing five *minutiones* a year,[2] as in the *Liber Ordinis*. But the Dominican *Constitutions* both of 1228[3] and of 1238–40[4] prescribe four *minutiones* a year, again at stated times; this agrees with *Ancrene Wisse*, which (without

Geneviève MSS. all the sections are unnumbered, and those that Martène leaves unnumbered occur at the same points, and in the same order and with the same text, in the two MSS. His (or his source's) failure to number them must have been due to some oversight.

The composition of the *Liber Ordinis* is ascribed to Abbot Guilduin, who died in 1155 (cf. Bonnard, *Histoire*, i. 48). It does not follow that everything in the extant texts dates from his time; they may embody revisions made up till the late twelfth century. But Martène's text, being essentially that of MS. Ste Gen. 1637, must represent the *Liber Ordinis* as it had become by about 1200, whatever one may think of his own rather vague dating of his lost St. Germain MS.

[2] Martène, iii. 285.

[1] Ibid., p. 328.

[2] Lefèvre, pp. 36–7. But only the total is the same; the five occasions specified are different, as is the form of the prescription.

[3] ed. Denifle, *ALKG*, i. 200. There is an evident connection, though it can hardly be a direct one, between the prescriptions of the *Liber Ordinis* and of the *Constitutions*. Both explicitly prohibit *minutiones* in excess of the specified number, both begin by prescribing the month of September (without closer definition) as the time for the first *minutio*, and both have 'after Easter' as one of the later occasions. The *Constitutions* prescribe 'post Natale' for the second, 'post Pascha' for the third, and 'circa festum Johannis baptiste' (24 June) for the fourth, i.e. they are to be roughly at three-monthly intervals, except for the variable feast of Easter. The *Liber Ordinis* gives for the second 'ante adventum Domini', for the third 'ante Septuagesimam', for the fourth 'post Pascha', and for the fifth 'post Pentecosten'. This looks like an elaboration of the simpler scheme of the *Constitutions*.

[4] ed. Denifle, *ALKG*, v. 540. The text is essentially unchanged.

prescribing times) advises blood-letting four times a year 'or if need is oftener',[1] and may represent more truly an earlier Augustinian tradition than the surviving texts of the *Liber Ordinis* and the 1236–8 version of the Prémontré statutes.

At St. Victor those who had been bled were specially treated for three days, as in *Ancrene Wisse*, and did not fully return to normal duties until Matins at the beginning of the fourth day;[2] this contrasts with the two days of special treatment which, according to Knowles, were usual in Benedictine houses at this time.[3] During this period, the patients at St. Victor were to lie quiet in their beds during times of silence in the monastery, but when speech was permitted in the convent those in the infirmary might converse together 'modeste et religiose', though they must immediately resume silence at the end of the hour of conversation in the convent. However, the abbot should appoint some one person who, in addition to exercising supervision over them, would be able 'in horis silentii, ipsis tacentibus, coram eis ad instructionem et consolationem pariter lectionem recitare'. These readings 'equally for instruction and consolation' are a close parallel to the 'virtuous stories' with which the anchoresses are to 'entertain themselves', though in *Ancrene Wisse* there has been adaptation to the conditions of a smaller and less formally organized community. At Prémontré also, according to the statutes of *c.* 1174, the

[1] Corpus MS., f. 115a/1–2 (Morton, p. 422). But if anyone can do without it, 'I can well permit it'; this, perhaps coincidentally, is the equivalent of the discretion allowed to abbot or prior by the Prémontré statutes.

[2] Bonnard, *Histoire*, i. 79, gives details of the very ample special diet provided at St. Victor in the early fourteenth century during the three days of the *minutio*; by this date the 'austerity' had been tempered a good deal for the bled brothers.

[3] David Knowles, *The Monastic Order in England* (Cambridge, 2nd edn., 1963), pp. 455–6.

patients were specially treated for three days and returned
to normal duties on the fourth; until then they had two meals
a day even on fast-days, 'cum alicujus beneficii superad-
jectione', and at certain times were to go to the dormitory to
rest, each in his own bed, 'cum deputata custodia ad vitan-
dam dormitionem'; presumably the custodian, if he were to
stop them from going to sleep, must have talked or read to
them. According to the 1236–8 statutes, on the second and
third days those who had been bled might be given leave to
converse together 'de honestis' after dinner, 'audita tamen
prius modica lectione de aliqua scriptura facili ad intelli-
gendum, ut de ipsa Scriptura . . . Postmodum, preterquam
infra Horas canonicas, usque ad Vesperas colloquantur.'
This is more generous than the St. Victor rule, obviously
because at St. Victor the rules about silence were themselves
more stringent; after submitting to an easily intelligible
reading of moderate length, the patients at Prémontré are
allowed to talk about decent things, not just during an hour
of conversation, but until Vespers, except in the times of the
Offices.

In *Ancrene Wisse* the instructions concerning silence are
not all given in a single place. The anchoresses, in accordance with the ordinary monastic rule,[1] are to keep silence
from Compline until after 'Pretiosa'.[2] They are always to
maintain silence at mealtimes, as 'other religious' do; if any
of them has a beloved guest, the servants are to entertain
her in the anchoress's stead, though she may undo her window once or twice and make signs of 'glad cheer' towards

[1] Cf. the Rule of St. Benedict, chapter xlii (ed. McCann, p. 100).
A close parallel to the wording of *Ancrene Wisse* is found in the General
Constitutions of the Franciscans in the redaction of 1260: 'Ordinamus
quod silentium a dicto Completorio usque post "Pretiosa" servetur' (ed.
Franz Ehrle, 'Die ältesten Redactionen der Generalconstitutionen des
Frankiskanerordens', *ALKG*, vi (1892), 98–9).
[2] Corpus MS., f. 6a/20–1 (Morton, p. 22).

her guest.[1] This injunction is repeated in an addition to Part VIII in the Corpus MS., where it is stated that silence at meals is to be broken neither for guests nor for blood-letting.[2] Another instruction prescribes days of total silence which are in fact fast-days. They are to keep silence on each Friday of the year unless it is a 'double feast' (and even then they should keep silence on some other day of the week in lieu); on Wednesdays and Fridays in Advent and in Ember Weeks; 'in Lent three days' (*I þe Lenten, þreo dahes*); and for the whole of Passion Week until noon on Easter Eve—though they may make brief remarks, if they wish, to their servants, and listen and reply briefly to 'any good man who has come from afar'.[3] In general they are to talk little, imitating the example of our Lady.

At St. Victor, according to chapter xxxvi of the *Liber Ordinis*, 'Omnibus festis novem lectionum debent fratres tota die[4] tenere silentium, et in primis quatuor diebus Paschae et Pentecostes, licet tunc tantummodo tres fiant lectiones, et in tribus diebus Quadragesimae.'[5] On other days there was provision for an hour of conversation in the cloister, even in Lent—though of course this implies that silence was to be kept for the rest of the day, and there was an elaborate system of signs to enable wishes to be made known without breach of silence. The days specified for complete silence are mostly different from those in *Ancrene Wisse*, and there is indeed a difference of principle; the brothers of St. Victor kept silence on feast-days, the anchoresses did so on fast-

---

[1] Corpus MS., f. 17a/23–17b/1 (Morton, pp. 68, 70).

[2] Corpus MS., f. 117a/20–1.

[3] Corpus MS., f. 17b/3–11 (text imperfect); Nero MS., 30/18–25 (Morton, p. 70).

[4] So Martène, following his St. Germain MS., with which MS. Ste Gen. 1637 agrees. He records that the St. Victor MS. which he collated had *quotidie* for *tota die*, but this is obviously an inferior reading.

[5] Martène, iii. 270.

days and were absolved from the normal rule of silence on Fridays by the incidence of a major feast. But there is one striking resemblance, the elliptical phrases *in tribus diebus Quadragesimae* and *I þe Lenten, þreo dahes*, which leave some doubt whether in Lent there is to be silence on three days of each week (as is probable, especially in the context of *Ancrene Wisse*, and as the translator of the Trinity French version assumed)[1] or simply on three days altogether (which would be the natural translation, of the Latin text in particular). It is difficult not to draw the conclusion that *Ancrene Wisse* is here directly dependent on the *Liber Ordinis*.[2]

The 1236–8 statutes of Prémontré say little about the hours of silence, and (as in *Ancrene Wisse*) there is no separate section dealing with the topic.[3] Silence was to be kept at meals and after Compline, even by the sick. Breach of it was an offence of medium gravity, but necessary remarks made to servants, 'breviter et secreto', by the abbot or the officers of the house in the course of their duties did not count as a breach.[4] There is no evidence that there were days of complete silence, and the lack of provision for an 'hour of conversation' must imply that on ordinary days talking was permitted outside specified times (such as, in the case of those who had been bled and doubtless generally, the times of the Offices). The earlier recensions of the statutes have still less to say. The impression is that Prémontré was content with the ordinary monastic practice, whereas the Victorines specially observed the cult of silence. The

[1] ed. W. H. Trethewey (E.E.T.S. 240, 1958), 182/18.

[2] It almost looks as if there has been an omission of a couple of words in the text of the *Liber Ordinis*, thus *in tribus diebus [uniuscujusque septimanae] Quadragesimae*; if this were so, the direct dependence of *Ancrene Wisse* on the *Liber Ordinis* would be certain. But even MS. Ste Gen. 1637, the earliest extant (of *c.* 1200), has the same text as Martène's; if there was an omission, it must have occurred at a very early stage.

[3] For scattered references to it, see Lefèvre's edition, pp. 22, 29, 31, and 68.

[4] Lefèvre, p. 29.

Dominican *Constitutions* have a separate chapter dealing with silence,[1] but it has no resemblance in form to the rules of *Ancrene Wisse* and of the *Liber Ordinis*; it defines places, not times, where silence is required, though the revision of 1238–40 remembers to add a specific prescription of silence at meals.

It appears, then, that *Ancrene Wisse*, in spite of Mr. Brewer's judgement, does agree with the Augustinian congregations (which at this date include the Dominicans) in its rules for blood-letting and the relaxation of discipline permitted after it, and that it follows (though with a significant difference as well as with an important phrasal agreement) the Victorine practice of complete silence on certain days. In another respect Brewer himself says that the English book 'follows the severer practice of the more austere independent canons of St. Victor, Prémontré, and Arrouaise, who were much influenced by Cistercian practice. This is in the denial of meat, except in sickness.'[2] I have myself argued elsewhere that the severity of the dietary rules in *Ancrene Wisse* is one of the indications that it was written during the period when the reforming legislation of the Lateran Council of 1215 was being published in England, though with the warning that a rigorist might have insisted on these rules at any time.[3] Of the two explanations, Brewer's

[1] So both the recensions, of 1228 (*ALKG*, i. 203–4) and of 1238–40 (*ALKG*, v. 541).

[2] *N. & Q.*, p. 233, with reference to Dickinson, *Origins*, p. 181.

[3] *Proc. Brit. Acad.*, lii. 189–90. A particular instance of the reassertion of traditional rules, about this time, comes from St. Victor itself, of which the dietary practices are described by Bonnard, *Histoire*, i. 77–9, in a long footnote. In the first century of its existence St. Victor, he says, was vegetarian; even fish was one of the dishes conceded only *pro misericordia* to the weak or sick (cf. p. 42, n. 1, below). But by 1200 fish had appeared on the common table on feast days. A further mitigation was introduced by abbot Absalon (1198–1203), who provided on the one hand that the vigils of Whitsun, the Assumption, All Saints', and Christmas should be observed by a fast as absolute as that of Lent, but on the

is certainly the primary one, but they are not inconsistent; a writer whose order observed a strict avoidance of meat might be especially likely to enjoin this practice on his charges at a time when the English bishops were insisting that meat should be eaten only in houses in which it was customary to do so.

Nevertheless there is a qualification to be made. The original text, as preserved unrevised in the Corpus MS., forbids meat and fat altogether to those who are in moderately good health:

3e ne schulen nawt eoten flesch ne seim but for muche secnesse, oðer hwase is ouer-feble.[1]

But at this point in the Vitellius French version there is an addition, found in no other manuscript, which reads:

Solum la riule des chanoignes Seint Augustin, vous ne mangerez char ne seym (si grand maladie nel face, ou grand fieblesce) fors trois iours en la symeyne, nen estee nen yuer: cest a sauer le dymeinge, le mardi, et le jeodi; le jour de Noel poez vous mangier char, quel iour qil auienge fors sul le samadi, si a tiel iour chiet. Solum la riule as freres ou de Seint Benoit, ne deuez vous iames mangier char fors en grand maladie ou quant vous estes trop fieble.[2]

other that food of any sort might be used at the great feasts unless they fell on a Wednesday or a Saturday, and even so fats might be served in such a case on a Saturday. But Jean le Teutonique, his successor as abbot (1203–28), who was active at the Lateran Council of 1215, felt obliged to address a letter on the subject of diet to the foreign priors of the Victorine community, in which he urged on them the strict observance of the fast preceding Christmas, with abstinence even from fats. He permitted the eating of meat only on great feasts, carefully specified, in deference to the relaxations of his predecessors; but apart from that there was to be an absolute prohibition, except for the days of the *minutio*, 'so that, if the rigour and the fervour of the Order are relaxed, it will be attributable only to your negligence'. Unfortunately Bonnard does not give the date of this letter, or a reference to his source.

[1] Corpus MS., f. 111b/14–16 (Morton, p. 412).
[2] ed. Herbert, 304/1–16.

The effect is to offer a choice where both the original text and the Corpus revision had allowed none. It is acknowledged that the stricter rule, though it is that of the *fratres*[1] and of St. Benedict, is not that of the ordinary Augustinian canons, who permit the eating of meat three times a week and on Christmas Day unless it falls on a Saturday.[2] As the addition occurs only in F, its status may be questioned. But there is no sign that F has been adapted in any way for

[1] The word *freres* in the French text probably renders *breðren* in its English original (assuming, as is virtually certain, that the addition, like the surrounding text, is translated from English). It is unlikely to represent Middle English *freres* (as in the two Corpus additions which refer to the Preachers and the Minorites) or to be intended to mean 'friars', for neither the Dominicans nor the Franciscans could be set up as examples of orders whose Rules forbade them ever to eat meat 'except in severe illness or when you are very weak'. The Dominican *Constitutions* of 1228 (ed. Denifle, *ALKG*, i. 199) say that meat is not eaten in their own houses, but 'our brothers are permitted to eat dishes cooked with meat outside the cloister, lest they be troublesome to men (*ne sint hominibus onerosi*)'; similarly the recension of 1238–40 (ed. Denifle, *ALKG*, v. 538–9). The earliest version of the *General Constitutions* of the Franciscans, that of 1260 (ed. Franz Ehrle, *ALKG*, vi (1892), 1–138; text, pp. 87 ff.), says— in words admittedly similar to those used in the Vitellius addition, but probably derived, like them, from the Prémontré statutes—'In locis fratrum fratres carnes non comedant ullo tempore, exceptis debilibus et infirmis' (p. 97); but though the *General Constitutions* are less explicit than the Dominican *Constitutions*, they imply that the brothers, when outside their houses, may eat meat if it is offered, for they lay down, on pain of penalty, that meat meals outside the house are not to be arranged for (*procurentur*) by the brothers themselves (p. 98).

It is therefore much more likely that the 'brothers' referred to in the Vitellius addition are those of the Augustinian congregations, whose members were regularly called *fratres* in their legislation, and which had unqualified rules that the food in their houses was always to be meatless, except that for the weak and sick; so the Prémontré statutes in all three recensions (van Waefelghem, p. 37; Martène, iii. 335; Lefèvre, pp. 20, 33). The *Liber Ordinis* of St. Victor instructs the *refectorius* to serve bread, wine, and vegetables (chapter xiv; Martène, iii. 257), and even for those suffering from some infirmity the leave of the abbot was required before they could be served with fish in the refectory (chapter xli, Note; Martène, iii. 273).

[2] Cf. Dickinson, *Origins*, p. 182.

a community other than the original one; it is a close translation of a good text of the original Rule, which was a near congener of the Cleopatra MS. and was probably made at the same time from the same exemplar.[1] It shares 'authorized' additions of some length with Corpus (and with Vernon), and it also incorporates (at F 3/6–10) a short addition made in the margin of C by 'scribe B', who in my view is the author. The style of the revised passage in F, allowing for the translation into French, is characteristic of the author's manner in giving such instructions; so too is the skill with which the text is adapted, the single original sentence being picked up at the end of the addition without change other than the omission of *ne seim*, which had been made unnecessary by the use of *char ne seym* (representing the English *flesch ne seim*) at the beginning of the added sentence. It is obvious, from collation of the texts and particularly from the visible state of the extant Cleopatra MS., that the author was in the habit of writing additions in individual manuscripts which might or might not be transferred to any other; and it is my judgement that this addition in F is such a revision by the author himself which, as in other cases, was for some reason not incorporated in the definitive revised version of Corpus. Why the author (as I believe) or the translator should have thus modified the strictness of the dietary rule is not my present concern—though it is striking that this is the only alteration of the original text of Part VIII in F, and that it is only in F. It may be merely an instance of his fairness, a belated admission that the ordinary Augustinian practice was less strict; he may have been challenged on the point by some argumentative *clergesse*; or he may have had some special reason connected with the intended recipient, whether of the

[1] See the introduction to my edition of the Cleopatra MS., pp. xxix–xxxvi.

English manuscript on which the translation was based or of the translation itself.[1] He can hardly have meant to permit a general relaxation of the rule that he had originally imposed, for Part VIII was extensively revised in Cleopatra and in Corpus, and yet there the rule was allowed to stand in all its severity. But it is significant for my argument at this point that in an addition to the original text, either in the early and good manuscript from which the Vitellius translation was made or in the translation itself, its author was at pains to comment on the difference between the general practice of Augustinian canons and that of the *fratres* and of St. Benedict prescribed for the anchoresses; for it must show that he, or someone for whom he was writing, was interested in or had raised a question about the Augustinian custom.

We saw above (pp. 14–16) that the author, though he cannot himself have been a friar, was yet friendly to and admired the friars and indeed speaks of '*our* Friars Preachers and *our* Friars Minor'. This attitude would be improbable in a monk, but probable in an Augustinian, since the Augustinians were in the early days well-disposed towards the friars. Indeed the Dominicans were originally called canons;[2] St. Dominic himself was an Augustinian 'black canon' but

[1] See further pp. 307–10, below. The Augustinian Rule (*Regula Tertia*) itself provides that for those *qui venerunt ex moribus delicatioribus ad monasterium* there may be relaxations of the normal austerity in regard to food, clothing, bedding, and bedclothes. The modification of the text in 'proto-F' (or by the translator as he worked) may have been made because this English copy, or the translation based on it, was intended for someone in whose case it was judged inexpedient to insist on the complete renunciation of meat.

Whether the distinction in the French text between *ne mangerez* and *ne deuez . . . mangier* is intended to distinguish between what will be done and what ought to be done is arguable. The latter phrase translates *ne schulen . . . eoten* in the original English text; if the former is rendering something different, it was probably *ne wulleð* (or *nulleð*) *eoten*, since *wullen* in this dialect can be used as a mere sign of futurity.

[2] David Knowles, *The Religious Orders in England*, i. 146.

in his legislation 'made use of the constitutions of the white canons of Prémontré',[1] and the members of his order, as they were first organized in 1216, had the style of canons; though in 1220 they 'abandoned the distinctive dress of canons and the title of abbey for their houses', they never entirely gave up the title of *canonicus*.[2] The Franciscans did not have this close original connection with the Augustinians, yet it would seem natural for an English writer, within a decade or so of their first arrival in the country, to group them with the Dominicans, with whom they had such obvious analogies and associations and whose arrival had so closely preceded their own. Indeed, in the theory of the time they would almost inevitably have been regarded as a special variety of the order of regular canons.[3] For they lived, to a pre-eminent degree, the 'full common life' or 'apostolic life', renouncing personal (and indeed all other) property. Hitherto those who lived this life had been either monks (*monachi*) or canons (*canonici*, *clerici*, or *fratres*); and as the Franciscans, as well as the Dominicans, were plainly not monks, it would be natural to assume that they were yet another of the special independent congregations developed by the Augustinians. Their very name *fratres* would itself aid the identification, since it was one of the appellations of the Augustinians; it would not at once be realized that a

[1] Ibid., i. 148. See further Balme and Lelaidier, *Cartulaire ou histoire diplomatique de Saint Dominique*, ii (1897), 21–30 and 463–4, on Dominic's choice of the statutes of Prémontré as his model.

[2] Ibid., i. 149–50.

[3] The Lateran Council of 1215 decreed that 'no new orders should come into being, but that all in future should choose one of the existing rules' (Knowles, *Religious Orders*, i. 148). It was in accordance with this that St. Dominic had chosen the Augustinian Rule. Such a decree would encourage anyone writing within 15 or 20 years of its passing to regard any new type of religious who was not a monk as an Augustinian; it would be some time before there was explicit recognition that despite the decree two orders of novel type had arisen, and had received papal approval, within five years of the Council.

new class of men living the 'full common life' had developed, and that henceforth there was to be a threefold distinction of monks, regular canons, and friars.[1] It is in this way that I would explain the author's use of the word 'our'—that he looked on the Franciscans, as well as the Dominicans, as a recent offshoot of his own order. But if so, he must have been an Augustinian; no member of a monastic order could have so regarded them.

The evidence cited on pp. 6–14, above, involves the apparent contradiction that the author advises the anchoresses to 'trust seculars little, religious still less', from which one would naturally assume that he was himself a secular, and yet that he speaks of the brothers, or even the lay brothers, of 'our order'. But though the regular canons, and especially those of the independent congregations, followed a life analogous to that of the monks and might seem to us (as indeed they did in the Middle Ages) to be 'religious', they themselves always denied this,[2] and there is no doubt that in legal status they ranked with the secular clergy; they were normally under the supervision of the diocesan bishop.[3] Within the canonical order three divisions were recognized, as we are told by the *Liber de diversis ordinibus* (itself written by a regular canon): 'some as far as possible are completely cut off in life, dress, and habitation from the multitude, others are placed near men, others

[1] It would indeed also require time before *fratres* or the French form *freres* became specialized in sense, to mean specifically 'friars'. The process has evidently already begun, since in the Corpus additions the writer twice uses *freres* and not *breðren* to refer to the Dominicans and Franciscans; but equally his way of using the word shows that it has not yet lost its basic sense of 'brothers'. There is some specialization of application but not yet of meaning.

[2] Dickinson, *Origins*, p. 199.

[3] 'In an age when such technicalities were of significance regular canons were ranked, in theory at least, not with monks, but with the secular clergy' (ibid., p. 201).

dwell among men, whence they are called seculars';[1] but even the first, the members of the contemplative houses of the independent congregations, were in legal theory secular clergy, though members of an order.

Mr. Brewer leaves open the question whether the author was a member of the general Augustinian order of regular canons or of one of the independent congregations; but the normal rule of silence expected to be followed by the anchoresses, the prohibition of meat and fats and the general strictness of their dietary regulations, and the mention of the lay brothers of his order[2] are strongly in favour of the latter. In its origins the Augustinian order had been essentially one of ordained clerics, but later, under the influence of the revived lay element in eleventh- and twelfth-century monasticism, the regular canons also admitted laymen to their houses; and this was especially the case with the independent congregations, 'the orders of canons who retreat far from men', who most closely approximated to monastic houses. There is definite evidence of the presence of lay brothers at Arrouaise, Prémontré, and St. Victor.[3] Similar in tendency is the obvious and pervasive debt of *Ancrene Wisse* to the writings of St. Bernard and his followers, for it was on the contemplative branch of the Augustinian order, the

[1] Migne, *Pat. Lat.*, ccxiii, col. 827.

[2] This assumes that the passage added in the Nero MS., which alone mentions lay brothers, is authentic in the sense that it was written either by the original author (as I believe) or by a member of his community; see above, pp. 6–9.

[3] Dickinson, *Origins*, pp. 203–5. The statutes of Prémontré have provisions dealing with lay brothers even in the first recension of *c.* 1131–4, and they and their duties are frequently mentioned in the *Liber Ordinis* of St. Victor; the latter has a special chapter (xxvi) dealing with the admission of laymen, and in that dealing with communion (ch. l) there are detailed instructions on how the *fratres conversi*, led by their *magister*, are to present themselves at the altar (Martène, iii. 265, 277). Cf. Bonnard, *Histoire*, i. 59–60, 64–5, 67; but his account does not cover all the references to *fratres conversi* in the *Liber Ordinis*.

congregations (including especially that of St. Victor), that St. Bernard and the Cistercians exercised most influence.[1]

In Part VIII especially the author of *Ancrene Wisse* frequently writes that this or the other may be done, or some rule may be varied, with *schriftes leaue* or by *ower meistres read*, and the parallelism of the expressions used can leave little doubt that it is assumed that ordinarily the anchoresses' *meistre* (director) will also be their *schrift* (confessor); they are under the direction of a chaplain. And though in the basic text he never directly says so, and though his injunctions are so phrased as to make it clear that authority belongs to whoever from time to time holds the office of *meistre* or *schrift*, it is difficult to escape the impression that at the time of writing the author himself was their *meistre*. Why else should they have applied to him for a Rule, and why else should he presume to advise, instruct, and even command them? Even in the basic text there is one passage in which it is, as I think, implied that he is their director. This is at the beginning of Part VIII, where he writes:[2]

Biuoren on earst ich seide þet ȝe ne schulden nawiht as i vu bihaten forte halden nan of þe uttre riwlen. þet ilke ich segge ȝetten; ne nane ne write ich ham buten ow ane. Ich segge þis for þi þet oþre ancren ne seggen nawt þet ich, þurh mi meistrie, makie ham neowe riwle. Ne bidde ich nawt þet ha halden ham—ah ȝe ȝet moten changin, hwen se ȝe eauer wulleð, þeose for betere.

Above, at the beginning, I said that you should by no means promise, by way of vow, to keep any of the outer rules. That I still say; nor do I write them for any except only for you. I say this in order that other anchoresses may not say that I, *þurh mi meistrie*, make a new rule for them. I do not at all ask that they keep them— but even you may change, whenever you will, these for better.

[1] Cf. Dickinson, *Origins*, pp. 77–8, 181.
[2] Corpus MS., f. 111a/11–19 (Morton, pp. 410, 412).

The general sense is that he has authority (though in matters of the Outer Rule he does not insist on it) over the anchoresses for whom he is writing, but does not profess to claim it over any others; and this is clear however one translates *þurh mi meistrie*. Miss Salu renders it 'on my own authority', but I do not think it can mean this; she has supplied the word 'own'. The phrase means simply 'by my authority', but if one asks what authority, and if one remembers the etymology of *meistrie*, then it must seem that the full implication is 'by virtue of my position as your *meistre*';[1] this is why he has authority, which he can renounce, over them, but claims none over others. It is he, for the time being, who is their *meistre*, their *schrift*; he is their adviser and director, making rules for their house. This is clearer still in a passage added in the Corpus version[2] in which, reinforcing the advice given in the basic text that each of the anchoresses should recognize well when the Devil speaks in an evil man's tongue, the author proceeds:

ant segge ananrihtes, 'Vre meistre haueð iwriten us, as in heast to halden, þet we tellen him al þet euch of oþer hereð; ant for þi loke þe þet tu na þing ne telle me þet ich ne muhe him tellen, þe mei don þe amendement ant con swaliches don hit þet ich ant tu baðe, ȝef we beoð i þe soð, schule beon unblamet.'

and say immediately, 'Our master has written to us, by way of a command to be observed, that we tell him everything that each hears about another; and therefore be on your guard that you tell me nothing that I cannot tell him, who has the power to put the matter right and knows how to do it in such a way that I and you as well, if we are in the right, shall be without blame.'

---

[1] The Latin version (164/1) has the rendering *per presumptionem*, but even if one overlooks its omission of *mi* it does not seem that *meistrie*, in either OF or ME, normally bore the sense thus attributed to it of 'masterfulness', 'unjustified assumption of authority'.

[2] Corpus MS., 69b/19–24.

Here not only is the writer identified with 'our master', but he is also described as exercising a right—that of being told, in obedience to a command, all that one anchoress hears of another—which can only be that of a confessor.[1] Now one of the duties occasionally, though not regularly, carried out by Augustinian canons was that of acting as chaplains; the Anglo-Norman *Historia Fundationis* of Wigmore Abbey tells a story which shows one of its members acting as chaplain to the founder's son and successor Roger de Mortimer, though he was at that time hostile to the abbey,[2] and Dickinson tells us that 'on the Continent regular canons acted as chaplains to houses of nuns at least as early as the time of Urban II . . . I have found no trace of this practice in twelfth-century England, though it was not uncommon in the thirteenth century.'[3] To be a member of an order, and at the same time spiritual director and adviser of a group of women religious, was something open to an Augustinian.[4]

[1] Once (but only once) the author varies his usual formula 'my dear sisters' by addressing the anchoresses as *deore dehtren* 'dear daughters' (Corpus MS., f. 113a/13; Morton, p. 418), an expression which, admittedly, any priest might use to women in his spiritual charge, but one which is especially appropriate to a confessor, a *schriftfeader*.

[2] Dickinson, *Origins*, p. 236, n. 5, citing Dugdale, *Monasticon*, vi. 348. The AN text is also given, with an English translation, in Thomas Wright, *The History of Ludlow and its Neighbourhood* (Ludlow, 1852), p. 129, and in J. C. Dickinson and P. T. Ricketts, 'The Anglo-Norman Chronicle of Wigmore Abbey', *Transactions of the Woolhope Naturalists' Field Club, Herefordshire*, xxxix (1969), 440. See further pp. 227–9, below.   [3] Dickinson, loc. cit. See also the following note.

[4] Knowles and Hadcock (*Medieval Religious Houses: England and Wales*, pp. 176–7) give a list of priests and brothers of regular orders known to have been attached to nunneries. It includes a number of instances of Augustinian and Premonstratensian canons being attached in this way, two of which date from the twelfth century (contrast Dickinson, cited above): Harrold (Bedfordshire), an Arrouaisian priory (?), of lay brothers rather than canons, attached to a nunnery from 1140–50 until some time before 1181, and Catesby (Northants.), a cell apparently of Canons Abbey, attached to a nunnery from *c.* 1175 until after 1310. Other instances listed belong to the thirteenth century.

Recognition of the Augustinian origin of *Ancrene Wisse* helps to explain the somewhat curious facts of its title. It is commonly known as the *Ancrene Riwle*,[1] a rather more grammatically correct version of Morton's *Ancren Riwle* (which is still also often used, especially by historians). But this is a modern editor's title, a translation into Middle English of *Regula Anachoritarum*, which in its turn seems to have been a librarian's title.[2] In fact no medieval manuscript or version of the 'unrevised' text gives a title, and this can only mean that there was none in their common ancestor β, which, since it obviously gave a very good text, may confidently be identified with the original fair copy delivered to the women for whom the book was written. Evidently the author, at the last moment, held back from giving it a title, but there can be little doubt that the one he had in mind was *Ancrene Riwle*; he repeatedly uses the word *riwle* in the text to refer to what he has written, he subdivides the work into þe uttre riwle and þe inre riwle, and the section of Part VIII which deals with the servants has, in the early Cleopatra MS., the side-heading *Ouwer Meidnes riwle*. Yet the Corpus MS., which alone has a colophon giving a title, calls the work *Ancrene Wisse*, using an otherwise unrecorded noun derived from the stem of the verb *wissin* (OE *wissian*); and as the Corpus revision is authorial, the title finally

---

[1] As in the E.E.T.S. series of editions, with the exception of the Corpus MS., which is given the manuscript title *Ancrene Wisse*. But to distinguish Corpus as *Ancrene Wisse* from the rest as *Ancrene Riwle*, though a common convention, is arbitrary and misleading.

[2] Such titles go back a long way. On f. 3 of the Cleopatra MS. a fourteenth-century hand has written *Regula Inclusarum*; on f. 3ᵛ, in the hand of Robert Talbot (d. 1558), there is *Regula monacharum saxonice*; and on f. 2ᵛ, in the hand of Cotton's librarian, Richard James, *Regula inclusarum veteri Anglicanâ*. The Magdalen College MS. of the Latin version has a colophon which calls the work, in this form attributed to Simon of Ghent, *librum de vita solitaria*, but this colophon is peculiar to the individual copy.

adopted must also be the author's. It is sometimes rendered as 'the anchoresses's guide' and explained by saying that as an anchoress, unlike a nun, was not subject to a formal discipline under a monastic superior, but was required only to vow chastity, stability of place, and obedience to the bishop or his superior, the word *riwle* 'rule' was inappropriate; the author was merely proferring guidance on the conduct of the eremitical life. But this explanation is inconsistent with the repeated use of the word *riwle* within the text, and makes a sharper distinction of sense than was probably intended. In Old English *wissian* is used to render *dictare* and *gubernare*, and Ælfric in his *Grammar* has:

rego ic wissige, of ðam cymð *rex* cyning, ðe rihtlice wissaþ his folce,

and again:

Rex cyning is gecweden *a regendo* . . ., for ðan ðe se cyning sceal mid micelum wisdome his leode wissian.[1]

If then *wissian* meant not merely 'to guide, direct', but also 'to rule', it would seem that the Middle English noun *wisse* may be merely a native equivalent for Latin *regula* or the French-derived *riwle*, and that the title *Ancrene Wisse* was not intended to bear a sense much, if at all, different from *Ancrene Riwle*. But the author must have had some reason for his choice of an otherwise unparalleled noun, especially as he never uses it in his text—nor, as it happens, the verb *wissin* from which it is derived.[2] It is most unlikely that he was influenced by linguistic purism, the preference of a native to a foreign word; that would be uncharacteristic of him, and

[1] Cited in Bosworth–Toller, s.v. *wissian*. The word bears the same sense in ME (see *OED*, s.vv. *wis* v., *wissing*) and can be used of an abbot's government of his monks or of God's government of the world.

[2] See A. Zettersten, *Studies in the Dialect and Vocabulary of the Ancrene Riwle* (Lund, 1965), p. 109, s.v. *iwis*, where the noun *wisse* is entered. But *wissin* and *wissent* occur in the *Katherine*-group.

plainly he had no objection to *riwle* as a word, since he uses it so often. But if he were an Augustinian it would be easy to understand both his initial failure to give the work the formal title *Ancrene Riwle* which he so obviously had in mind and his final *tour de force* in thinking up *Ancrene Wisse* as an alternative. The meaning of so rare a word was probably uncertain even then, and he may have intended the ambiguity.[1] It is noteworthy that though in the twelfth and early thirteenth centuries a series of major sets of regulations—detailed, precise, and extensive—were composed for the leading Augustinian houses, the word *regula* is sedulously avoided in their titles: the *Consuetudines Ordinis* of Beauvais, the *Statuta* of Prémontré, the *Liber Ordinis* of St. Victor, the *Constitutiones* of the Dominicans. The reason was quite simple: to any Augustinian 'the Rule' meant above all else the Rule of St. Augustine, the acceptance of which, however it might be revised, interpreted, or supplemented, was the chief bond between the various branches of the order. It is entirely consistent that the English author should shy away from a formal title involving the word *riwle*, and it would be especially likely if the women for whom he wrote themselves were, or had become, subject to the Augustinian Rule.

There is, then, evidence of various sorts to point to the Augustinian origin of *Ancrene Wisse*. Much of it relates to the order generally, and goes only to show that the author was a canon; but some of it particularly connects him with the independent Augustinian congregations (among which we

---

[1] The word would probably be more likely to convey the basic sense of the verb, 'to make known' and hence 'to point out the way, to guide or direct', than the rarer secondary meaning 'to rule, govern'; but it would be hard to be sure which was meant. I suspect that the author was hunting for an English word that would mean rather more than 'advice' (*read*) and would imply some degree of authoritative direction, but would nevertheless be less strong than command (*heast*), and above all would avoid the word *riwle*.

must reckon, as they themselves did, the Dominicans), and we must now turn to a more detailed consideration of other links between the English work and the regulations and practices of the congregations.[1]

[1] The use of *congregation* to mean (in *OED*'s definition) 'a group of monasteries belonging to some great order, which agree to unite themselves together by closer ties of doctrine and discipline' is anachronistic; in the twelfth and thirteenth centuries the normal word for the Augustinian (and other) congregations was *ordines*, which explains *Ancrene Wisse*'s use of *ure ordre* to refer to what, as we shall see, must in fact have been the Victorine congregation and its usages. But as one has to speak of the Augustinian *order* in general, it is convenient to apply some other word to subordinate organizations within it, and therefore, in this chapter and the next, I have repeatedly followed Dickinson and Brewer in writing of the Augustinian *congregations*.

II

ANCRENE WISSE AND THE
AUGUSTINIAN CONGREGATIONS

In the first chapter we saw that there are passages in *Ancrene Wisse*, one in the basic text and two others in individual manuscripts, in which the author refers explicitly to the members of his 'order', or to its lay-brothers, and their practices; and sound method requires that it should be shown that these practices were, if not specifically Augustinian, at least in use among Augustinians. It was the strength of Fr. McNabb's case that he realized that it ought to be possible to identify the order from the details given in the two passages known to him; his method is not invalidated by the fact that the conclusion which he drew is an impossible one on grounds of date.[1] The difficulty is that information about the detailed practices of religious houses in the late twelfth and thirteenth centuries is fragmentary and often allusive; and though more information may be discoverable in unpublished manuscripts, it is not readily accessible to those whose only concern is to establish the provenance of a literary text. The practices were usually traditional, and the authors of written instructions might assume that they did not need to be very specific about what was already known;

[1] It was not helpful to deny, as R. W. Chambers (*RES* i (1925), 14–15) and Miss Allen did, the authority of the Nero passage, since it does not stand alone in referring to the members of an order and its style appears authentic. The other point taken against McNabb, that it is hard to know what medieval liturgical practice was and how widespread were the customs referred to, was much more cogent; but it is right to try to find out.

moreover there were often variations from house to house, especially among the Augustinians. In view of the imperfections of the evidence, and for a reason that will be obvious from the general argument of the preceding and the following chapter, I confine myself to asking whether the practices described in *Ancrene Wisse* could have been followed in an Augustinian, and particularly in a Victorine or Premonstratensian house; and I intend no judgement, unless specific exceptions are made, that they could not have been followed in others.

There are three passages in question (set out on pp. 8–13, above), and they describe or imply four practices.

(1) The sentence added to Part I in the Corpus MS., about the times when 'we' say the Office of the Dead,[1] implies that on fast-days the single meal was taken, in the author's community, after Nones, but that on an ordinary ('two-meal') day the main meal was taken before Nones (in fact probably about midday, and often separated from Nones by an interval, including in summer a period of sleep). This was the normal monastic routine, laid down in the Benedictine Rule, and as it was also a sensible arrangement it would be expected to apply in all 'regular' houses, whether of monks or of canons; it is therefore not especially significant. The *Consuetudines Ordinis* of St. Quentin, Beauvais, explicitly state that on a fast-day the single meal (*prandium*) is taken after Nones and is followed by certain devotions (see below), after which there is, in summer, a period of sleep until Vespers or a little before;[2] but on days on which two meals are eaten, the main meal is taken after Sext and the evening meal after Vespers.[3] The *Liber Ordinis* of St. Victor does not specify the hours of meals, which it assumes

---

[1] Corpus MS., f. 6b/7–9.
[2] Paris MS. Bibliothèque Mazarine 2005, ff. 98ᵛ–99ᵛ.
[3] Ibid., ff. 100ᵛ–1, 102ᵛ.

to be known, but it contains two passages which imply the ordinary monastic custom. One is in chapter xli, 'De Refectorio', which says:

Quando post prandium in dormitorium vadunt pausatum ad meridianum, tunc egredientes a gratiis . . .;[1]

it follows that there are occasions (in fact ordinary days in summer) when the main meal (*prandium*) will be taken about midday and be followed by a period of sleep. The other is in chapter xxxvi, where provision is made for the brothers to have a period of conversation (the *hora locutionis*, as it is called elsewhere) in the cloister, between Nones and Vespers if it is not a fast-day, but if it is a fast-day, then either between Terce and Sext or between Sext and Nones, depending on the time of Mass.[2] The reason for the distinction is not stated, but the obvious one would be that on a fast-day the single meal took place after Nones, so that the 'hour of conversation' would have to be transferred to some other time.[3] The mealtimes observed at Prémontré are explicitly described in chapters v and vi of Part I of the Statutes;[4] on non-fasting days there were two meals, about midday and in the evening after Vespers, and in the fasting season 'we eat after Nones', except in Lent, when 'we eat after Vespers'.

(2) The same sentence added in the Corpus MS. explicitly says that 'we' say *Placebo* and *Dirige* (respectively the Vespers

[1] Martène, iii. 273.
[2] Ibid., p. 270.
[3] Bonnard, *Histoire*, i. 81, says that on a fast-day the single meal took place 'in the evening', i.e. after Vespers, but he has failed to distinguish the Lenten routine, originally Benedictine, in which this arrangement did apply, from that of a fast-day outside Lent. If he were right, there would be no reason why the 'hour of conversation' should not take place after Nones on fast-days as on ordinary days. The routine at St. Victor must have been the same as that clearly set down in the statutes of Prémontré.
[4] Martène, iii. 336; Lefèvre, pp. 11–14. Cf. pp. 85–6, below.

and Matins constituting the Office or Vigils of the Dead) either after the Graces on a fast-day ('one-meal day') or after Nones on an 'ordinary' ('two-meal') day.[1] In effect the Office of the Dead is always said 'after' Nones, but on a fast-day the single meal (and its accompanying Graces) is interposed between Nones and the Office of the Dead.[2] The *Liber Ordinis* of St. Victor includes a passage which, though it cannot be said to require us to assume this arrangement, is certainly consistent with it. It comes in chapter xli, 'De Refectorio', in prescribing the ceremonial to be followed at the end of the meal. After *Agimus tibi gratias*, *omnipotens Deus* has been finished, the company are to begin the psalms and go in procession to the choir, where the psalmody is to be completed. Then,

dum sacerdos pronunciare debebit *Et ne nos*, eriget se et stans contra altare finiet gratias; et si Nona vel Vigiliae Defunctorum statim postquam egrediantur dici debuerint, dicantur. Quibus finitis, cum processione ibunt ad lavatorium . . .[3]

This shows that there are some occasions when it is appropriate to go straight on to the Office of the Dead after the Graces have been completed in the choir, and that these are alternative to other occasions when it is appropriate to go on to Nones (though the sequel, referred to above,

---

[1] The added sentence immediately follows an original passage (Corpus MS., f. 6a/22–6b/7; Morton, p. 22) in which the anchoresses had been given instructions for the saying of *Placebo*, the Vespers of the Dead, after their ordinary Evensong, and of *Dirige*, the Matins of the Dead, either before Compline or after their ordinary Matins (as well as that of Commendation either 'in the morning' or 'at night after the suffrages of Matins'). These are the regular times; to say *Placebo* and *Dirige* also after the Graces or after Nones, as recommended in the added sentence, is a supplementary devotion, as is clear in the context, and is therefore significant because it is not standard practice; it is suggested as something that 'you' may do in imitation of what 'we' do.

[2] See p. 12, above, for the two alternative sequences.

[3] Martène, iii. 273.

shows that commonly there will be an interval before Nones, which may include a period of sleep). The practice described in *Ancrene Wisse* would explain the more allusive prescription of the *Liber Ordinis*; certainly the latter proves that there were occasions (presumably on fast-days, when Nones would already have been said before the meal) when the Office of the Dead was said immediately after the Graces. What it does not show (nor exclude) is that on non-fasting days the Office of the Dead was said after Nones. That the Office had an important place in the observances of St. Victor is evident from the fact that a separate and longish chapter (lxix) of the *Liber Ordinis* is devoted to instructions on how the brothers shall conduct themselves at the Vespers and Matins of the Dead on the different occasions of the ecclesiastical year.[1] And it may be significant that this chapter immediately precedes those dealing with Vespers and Compline, for the order suggests that at St. Victor the Office of the Dead preceded the ordinary Vespers.[2]

There is much more explicit evidence in chapter lxv of the *Liber Ordinarius* of Prémontré,[3] which provides that the Vigils of the Dead are to be performed 'in conventu' (i.e. as a

[1] Martène, iii. 283.

[2] Cf. also chapter lix of the *Liber Ordinis*, where, in a list of church services, the Vigils of the Dead are mentioned immediately after the Graces: 'quotiens conventus in ecclesia est, terminato eo quod canitur, quidquid illud fuerit, sive Hora regularis sive de S. Maria, sive Missa matutinalis sive major, sive post Gratias, sive post Vigilias Defunctorum . . .' (Martène, iii. 279).

[3] *L'Ordinaire de Prémontré d'après des manuscrits du XIIe et du XIIIe siècle*, ed. Pl. F. Lefèvre (Louvain, 1941), pp. 112–13. The text is based primarily on Munich MS. Clm. 17. 174, of the end of the twelfth or the beginning of the thirteenth century, which, Lefèvre considers, represents the liturgical tradition of Prémontré in the last quarter of the twelfth century; it is later than the Council of Westminster of 1175 but does not include the feast-days of St. Thomas of Canterbury and St. Bernard of Clairvaux, canonized in 1173 and 1174, and is unaffected by the reforms of Innocent III, 1198–1216 (pp. x–xii).

conventual exercise, not privately) at all seasons, except on Sundays, on 'double' and major feasts and the eves of feasts of nine lessons, on the vigils of Christmas, Epiphany, Easter, and Pentecost, and during the whole of the weeks of Christmas, Easter, and Pentecost.[1] From the octave of Easter until the feast of the Exaltation of the Cross (14 September) the Vigils of the Dead

ante canonicas Vesperas continuate dicende sunt, deinceps vero usque ad Quadragesimam post gratias refectionis. In diebus dumtaxat jejunii, Vesperis Mortuorum cantatis, quod reliquium est in Nocturno et Laudibus usque ante Vesperas diei complendum differatur. In Quadragesima quoque, post refectionem Vesperis cantatis, fiat intervallum donec ministri reficiuntur; deinde, signo pulsato, Nocturni et Laudes compleantur.

The main distinction here is between the summer season (in general non-fasting) from Easter[2] to 14 September, and the winter fasting season from then until Easter;[3] but 'days of fasting' as a class are by implication assimilated to the Lenten routine, in which only the Vespers of the Dead are to be said immediately after the meal, the rest of the Office (Nocturns, i.e. Matins, and Lauds) being postponed until before the ordinary Vespers of the day (on fast-days outside Lent) or for an interval while the servants have their meal (in Lent). The principle is that the Office of the Dead is to be said 'before the canonical Vespers' on non-fasting days, but at least its first part, the Vespers of the Dead (*Placebo*), 'after the graces of the meal' (*post gratias refectionis, efter þe mete*

[1] Cf. Lefèvre, p. xxi, summarizing and interpreting the list given in chapter lxv.

[2] The instructions in the *Liber Ordinarius* in fact say 'the octave of Easter', but that is because the Office of the Dead was not to be said in Easter week; the fasting season itself ended at Easter.

[3] Within this period, Lent has a separate place, because then the single meal was taken after Vespers; hence the different instructions for fast-days outside Lent and for Lent itself.

graces) on fast-days. At Beauvais the practice seems to have
been similar, though the exposition in the *Consuetudines
Ordinis*,[1] because of its method of arrangement, is less clear
and indeed incomplete. On a fast-day the single meal is
taken after Nones and at its end, standing in their places,
the brothers say Grace; then, singing Psalm 50, they go to
the church and there 'conclude on behalf of our benefactors'.
Afterwards, if no feast of nine lessons is to follow, they sing
the Vespers of the Dead. Then in summer[2] they go to the
dormitory to sleep, but in winter they sit in silence in the
cloister with their books. Then the prior rings the signal
for the brothers to assemble in the church, and between
successive ringings of the bell, if no feast of nine lessons
follows, the Vigils of the Dead are sung, and afterwards the
canonical Vespers. Presumably, since the Vespers of the
Dead had already been sung, the 'Vigils of the Dead' must
in this passage have the restricted sense of Nocturns and
Lauds, as at Prémontré. But when the writer proceeds to
discuss 'days on which we eat twice' he is so preoccupied
with the issue of diet that he gives no adequate account of
how the daily routine differed and in particular does not

[1] MS. Mazarine 2005, ff. 99^{r-v}, 103^{r-v}.

[2] Summer is defined as 'a resurrectione Christi ad festiuitatem beati
Remigii' (f. 99^{r-v}) and as 'a Pascha usque ad B. Remigii festiuitatem' (f.
103). At the former place there is a qualifying clause 'excepta septimana
quæ inter duo Pascha consistit' (i.e. the week between Easter and its
octave) which, from the way it is introduced, either limits the duration
of the summer season (which can hardly be intended) or applies to the
statement that the brothers go to the dormitory to sleep; compare the
Prémontré instructions (p. 60, n. 2 above).

The postponement of the latter end of the summer season from 14
September (the Exaltation of the Holy Cross) to 10 October (St. Remigius) is a relaxation of the strict rule (though less extreme than the postponement until 1 November, which had become customary by the early
thirteenth century) and an indication that the recorded text of the
Consuetudines belongs to the twelfth century and is certainly earlier than
the Lateran Council of 1215, which set out to enforce the date of 14
September. Cf. *Proc. Brit. Acad.* lii. 189, and the references there given.

mention the Office of the Dead. But he does say that on a two-meal day (*dies geminæ refectionis*) between Easter and the feast of St. Remigius all the brothers, after the end of the midday meal, go to the dormitory to rest, so that they clearly do not sing the Office of the Dead immediately after the meal; and that after the period of rest they congregate in the church to sing Nones 'with the things which follow it' (*cum his quæ ipsam subsequuntur*).[1] This last tantalizing phrase could well cover the Office of the Dead.

The brief sentence added to *Ancrene Wisse* in the Corpus MS. is far less precise than the longer passage in the *Liber Ordinarius* of Prémontré, but as a quick summary, omitting mention of the days on which the Office of the Dead is forbidden, it is accurate in principle, if one allows for its substitution of 'one-meal days' and 'two-meal days' (as in the Beauvais *Consuetudines*) for the fasting and non-fasting seasons. But it differs from the Prémontré regulations in saying that on non-fasting days the Office of the Dead is said 'after Nones', not 'before Vespers'; in this respect the custom of the English author's community might have agreed with that of Beauvais or of St. Victor, but the evidence is insufficient. What is clear is that the three French Augustinian communities had similar practices, comparable to that summarily described in *Ancrene Wisse*.

(3) A passage in Part VIII,[2] certainly original, prescribes that the anchoresses shall take communion on fifteen occasions, carefully specified,[3] during the year; and as we have

[1] MS. Mazarine 2005, f. 103[r–v].

[2] Corpus MS., f. 111a/23–111b/8 (Morton, p. 412).

[3] These are numbered in MSS. AFT but not in CN, and are: (i) 'Midwinter Day' (Christmas Day), 25 December; (ii) 'Twelfth Day' (Epiphany), 6 January; (iii) Candlemas (Purification of the BVM), 2 February; (iv) the Sunday midway between that and Easter, or on Lady Day (Annunciation of the BVM, 25 March) *for þe hehnesse* (because of the importance of the feast), if it falls near the Sunday specified; (v) Easter Day; (vi) the third Sunday after Easter; (vii) 'Holy Thursday' (Ascen-

seen above (pp. 9–10), there can be no reasonable doubt that the parenthetical clause 'as our brothers do' was itself an integral part of the original text. It was partly on this that Fr. McNabb relied in arguing that *Ancrene Wisse* agrees with what was, and still is, the Dominican practice.[1] But according to Browe,[2] the Dominicans had originally gone to communion only seldom, and it was at the General Chapter of 1249 that they adopted the rule that communion should be received at every time of tonsuring,[3] which was in fact on fifteen specified days in the year.[4] The General Chapter of 1266 altered this arrangement in favour of communion every two or three weeks, but there was later a reversion to the rule of 1249. Similarly the Franciscans, after their General Chapter of 1269, were required to communicate as often as they were tonsured, which was then fifteen times a year;

sion Day), the fortieth day after Easter; (viii) Whitsunday (Pentecost), the seventh Sunday after Easter; (ix) 'Midsummer Day' (St. John the Baptist), 24 June; (x) St. Mary Magdalene, 22 July; (xi) Assumption of the BVM, 15 August; (xii) Nativity of the BVM, 8 September; (xiii) Michaelmas, 29 September; (xiv) All Saints', 1 November; (xv) St. Andrew, 30 November.

The fourth of these presents some difficulty, for the latest possible date for Easter is 25 April, and therefore the Sunday midway between 2 February and Easter must at latest fall about 15 March, so that Lady Day (25 March) can never really be 'near' the Sunday specified. The case would be different with Mid-Lent Sunday (the third before Easter), which falls after 20 March in any year in which Easter falls after 10 April, which, on average, is likely to be in three years out of seven. It is possible that the author had Mid-Lent Sunday in mind, but it is certainly not what he says. Probably he just did not work out the calculations.

[1] *MLR*, xi. 3, and *Archivum Fr. Praed.*, iv. 53–4. He not only claimed that the number of times in the year was the same (as is true), but also asserted that the occasions were 'almost identical', 'almost the exact dates'. In fact nine of the fifteen occasions are the same (see below); it depends what one means by 'almost'.

[2] Browe, *Die häufige Kommunion*, p. 82.

[3] Browe refers to *Monumenta O. Fr. Praed. historica*, iii. 44.

[4] According to the *Constitutions* of 1228 and of 1238–40; see further below.

but the General Chapters of 1285 and 1292 increased the number of tonsurings, respectively to twenty a year and to once a fortnight, with a consequent increase in the number of communions, and the chapter of Assisi in 1316 confirmed fortnightly communion.[1]

These are the only two orders for which Browe records the prescription of fifteen communions annually, and it is clear from his evidence that priority in date belongs to the Dominicans. But *Ancrene Wisse* is earlier still, for no one can reasonably suppose that it was written after 1225; its original composition is at least a quarter of a century earlier than the Dominican General Chapter of 1249. It would be legitimate, then, to turn McNabb's proposition on its head, and to say, not that *Ancrene Wisse* must be of Dominican authorship because it follows Dominican practice in regard to the times of communion, but that the Dominican practice must have been derived from whatever earlier order produced *Ancrene Wisse*. The English book, in fact, though apparently unknown to Browe, is an important primary document for the origins of the regulation.

But it is not simply a matter of the total of fifteen. What is really more remarkable is that the number of times of communion should be equated with the number of times of tonsuring, and should be dependent on the latter; for it is by no means an obvious principle. It is understandably not present in the original text of *Ancrene Wisse*, for the simple reason that the book was written for women, who are not tonsured; the author is content to advise that their hair should be cut, or if they wish shaved, four times a year.[2] But in the 'generalized' versions of the Titus and Pepys MSS., adapted (if imperfectly) for a male audience, the text is changed at this point, and the number of haircuts recom-

---

[1] Browe, *Die häufige Kommunion*, p. 81.
[2] Corpus MS., f. 114b/26–8 (Morton, p. 422).

mended is increased to fifteen.[1] The textual readings of the two manuscripts show clearly that they descend from a common ancestor, and in this very passage the identity of the way in which they alter the original text shows that the change must already have been made in the prototype of the 'generalized' version, their common ancestor.[2] Now the Titus MS. is dated to the second quarter of the thirteenth century, probably towards its latter part,[3] and the prototype of the 'generalized' text must of course be somewhat earlier still—one cannot tell how much earlier, but beyond reasonable doubt it must have antedated the Dominican General Chapter of 1249. So in the 'generalized' text one finds implicit the equation which in the Dominican and Franciscan regulations was made explicit—fifteen haircuts or tonsurings a year, and also fifteen communions. Again there is a strong suggestion that the friars had been anticipated in their rule by some other order, whose practice is reflected in the texts of *Ancrene Wisse*.[4]

---

[1] Titus MS., ed. Mack, 156/34–157/1; Pepys MS., ed. Påhlsson, 199/36–200/1.

[2] Of the other versions belonging to the 'Titus-group', Trinity and Royal are not running in Part VIII, and the Latin version (itself made for a community of women) follows the Corpus-type text in Part VIII in the only manuscript (Cotton Vitellius E. vii) which gives it; it therefore reverts to the prescription of four haircuts a year (ed. D'Evelyn, 173/13–17), with the added detail, standard in ecclesiastical legislation on this point, that the hair is to be cut above the ears (l. 16)—though this was originally a prescription intended to apply to men, not women.

[3] See the introduction to Miss Mack's edition, pp. ix–x. As the writing is 'below top line', the manuscript is likely to have been written fairly well into the second quarter of the century; on the other hand its linguistic forms, apart from its obvious Northernisms, seem to me very conservative, and its text, allowing for the 'generalization', is often good.

[4] The argument of this paragraph would not be materially affected if it could be shown that the 'generalized' text of *Ancrene Wisse* was produced in a house of friars, or specifically in the Franciscan friary at Hereford (as is suggested below, pp. 294–9). For it would remain true that the original text had specified fifteen communions, set out in a

We have therefore to consider two apparently distinct matters, not just one: not only the number of communions, but also the number of tonsurings. As already remarked, Browe records no order, other than the Dominicans and Franciscans, that required exactly fifteen communions; but he admits that the evidence is incomplete. Gregory IX in 1235 imposed monthly communion on Benedictine monks and, as far as practicable, on Benedictine nuns also. In Augustinian houses practice was very variable; in Rouen, in the mid thirteenth century, the regular canons of St. Mary Magdalene took communion thirteen times a year, those of St. Lo only three times.[1] In 1339 a bull of Benedict XII imposed monthly communion on 'non-priests' of the Augustinian order.[2] There seems to be no direct evidence on the earlier practice of the Augustinian independent congregations; the *Liber Ordinis* of St. Victor prescribes that the deacon and sub-deacon shall take communion weekly,[3] but does not say how often the ordinary brothers are to do so (though obviously it would be less often), and the same is true of the thirteenth-century version of the *Liber Ordinarius* of Prémontré.[4]

The initial bestowal of the tonsure was a solemn act admitting a man to the clerical estate, and was therefore a form of ordination; its regular renewal was regarded in

numbered list of days, and that the 'generalized' text, wherever produced, had prescribed the same total for the number of haircuts. My argument is not that either text *explicitly* equates the number of days for communions with the number of days for tonsurings in a male community. But even the original text does explicitly say that the anchoresses are to follow the practice of 'our brothers' in taking communion only fifteen times a year, on the specified days.

[1] Browe, *Die häufige Kommunion*, pp. 85–6.

[2] Browe, p. 86, referring to E. Salter, *Chapters of the Augustinian Canons*, p. 262.   [3] Martène, iii. 277.

[4] Michel van Waefelghem, *Liturgie de Prémontré*: *Le* Liber Ordinarius *d'après un manuscrit du XIII*e/*XIV*e *siècle* (Analectes de l'ordre de Prémontré, ix; Louvain, 1913), p. 91 (cited by Browe, p. 47).

religious houses as a matter of importance, to be performed with some ceremony. In consequence it was, comparatively early, subject to regulation,[1] and this may explain why it was sometimes found convenient to define the number of communions by reference to the number of tonsurings. Peter the Venerable (d. 1156) prescribed for the Cluniac branch of the Benedictines thirteen or fourteen[2] *rasurae* in the year, on occasions mostly defined by reference to major feast-days or to specified Sundays. In the Cluniac list,[3] the day for the *rasura* is usually the vigil of a feast or the day before the vigil (or even, in two cases—Easter and Pentecost—a feria some days before the festival); but allowing for this, eleven of the feasts or Sundays mentioned are either identical with, or fall within a few days of, those prescribed as occasions for communion in *Ancrene Wisse*. The two lists are easily distinguishable, but appear to belong to the same general tradition. The Cistercians were tonsured only seven times a year, until, in 1257, the General Chapter permitted twelve *rasurae* annually, prescribed with reference to feast-days or their vigils, or specific Sundays;[4] the Carthusians either six times a year or on the first of each month, according to different sources.[5] The statutes of Prémontré,

[1] See Martène, iv. 236–40 (= *De Antiquis Monachorum Ritibus*, lib. V, cap vii, 'De tonsura et rasura Fratrum').

[2] The seventh occasion in the year, on a day to be fixed between Pentecost and the feast-day of SS. Peter and Paul, was to apply only when the length of time between the two feasts made it necessary.

[3] Martène, iv. 239.

[4] Ibid. Eight of the occasions in this Cistercian list of 1257 (Christmas, Purification of the BVM, Easter, Ascension Day, (the vigil of) St. Mary Magdalene, (the vigils of) the Assumption and the Nativity of the BVM, (the vigil of) All Saints') occur also in the *Ancrene Wisse* list of occasions for communion (or are the vigils of the days specified); of these, the Purification, Ascension Day, and St. Mary Magdalene do not occur in the Cluniac list (which however has St. James, 25 July, in place of St. Mary Magdalene, 22 July).

[5] Martène, iv. 239.

in the second version of *c.* 1174 printed by Martène, do not specify the number of *rasurae* in the chapter 'De rasura et tonsura' (c. xv of the fourth Part, or *Distinctio*),[1] but immediately after the following and concluding chapter there is added a note 'Terminus Rasurae'[2] which lays down eleven numbered occasions for tonsuring during the year, in each case by reference to feast-days or to a division of the interval between them; six of the occasions (including the third, 'halfway between the Purification and Easter'), are the same as those in the *Ancrene Wisse* list of occasions for communion, the rest (four of them in the second half of the year) are different. But in the revision of 1236–8 printed by Lefèvre[3] the number of *rasurae* is increased to sixteen a year, though with the qualification that in cold regions the second (midway between Christmas and the Purification) may be omitted, which would bring the number to fifteen. Eight of the occasions agree with those of the earlier list, but there has been extensive revision between Pentecost and Christmas. The revised list agrees with that in *Ancrene Wisse* (i) in its method of setting out, with the occasions carefully numbered; (ii) in referring to feast-days, not to their vigils or some even earlier day before the feast; (iii) in providing, as the fourth occasion, a day 'midway between the feast of the Purification and Easter';[4] (iv) in eight others of the days specified.

---

[1] Martène, iii. 335.

[2] Ibid.

[3] p. 38.

[4] But the Prémontré statute has the proviso that if the time between the two feasts is (as Lefèvre constitutes the text) *seven* weeks or thereabouts, then there are to be two *rasurae* in the period, and the eighth of the normal list, a day 'midway between Pentecost and the feast of St. John the Baptist', is to be omitted. Lefèvre is here following his base manuscript H, copied at the abbey of Heylissem in Brabant in 1579 by a conservative scribe, which he prefers to T, a Tongerloo MS. copied in the fourteenth century from a thirteenth-century original, because T has been altered to take account of revisions of the statutes made later

But though this list is nearer to that in *Ancrene Wisse*, it is not identical with it. In the Dominican *Constitutions*, in the versions both of 1228 and of 1238–40, the chapter 'De rasura'[1] has obvious links with the Prémontré statutes; its first two sentences, defining the fashion of the tonsure, follow word for word the corresponding Prémontré text, and the manner of setting out the occasions of the *rasurae* is the same as at Prémontré, with reference either to feasts or to days midway between feasts, and with careful numbering of the occasions. There are to be fifteen *rasurae*, against the sixteen (reducible to fifteen) of the 1236–8 Prémontré statutes; nine of the occasions are identical with those in the Prémontré list of 1236–8, and a tenth (the feast of SS. Peter and Paul) agrees with the Prémontré list printed by Martène, against the 1236–8 list, which substitutes (like *Ancrene Wisse*) that of St. John the Baptist (Midsummer Day). Nine of the occasions agree with the list of days for communion in *Ancrene Wisse*; of these, the last two (All Saints' and St. Andrew) agree with *Ancrene Wisse* against both the Prémontré lists. Two of the occasions are peculiar to the Dominican list, though in one case the divergence is

than the codification of 1236–8. But here, where H has *septem septimane*, T has *decem septimane*, which makes better sense; for even if Easter Day falls on its earliest possible date, 22 March, there are 47 (or in a leap year 48) days between 2 February (the Purification) and Easter, which is all but seven weeks, and furthermore if there were two intermediate *rasurae* in a period of seven weeks the intervals between *rasurae* would be only about 16 days, which is inconsistent with a scheme of sixteen *rasurae* to the year (roughly one every 23 days). It is of course possible that T's reading is a deliberate improvement, and that H preserves correctly an illogical original reading; but though it is curious that the calculations of *Ancrene Wisse* go astray at this very point (see p. 62, n. 3 above), one cannot found an argument on a dubious reading which, even if it were original, might demonstrate nothing more than a shared incapacity for simple arithmetic.

[1] ed. Denifle, *ALKG*, i. 205 (1228 recension) and v. 541 (1238–40 recension).

a mere consequence of a difference already noted; this is the eighth, 'between Pentecost and the feast of SS. Peter and Paul', where Prémontré 1236–8 has 'halfway between Pentecost and the feast of St. John the Baptist'. But the fifth occurs only in the Dominican list; this is Maundy Thursday (*Cena Domini*), where both the Prémontré lists and *Ancrene Wisse* have Easter Day.

As far as the occasions specified are concerned, there is therefore no special resemblance between the list of days for tonsuring in the Dominican constitutions and the list of days for communion in *Ancrene Wisse*. There are nine agreements between (i) *Ancrene Wisse* and the Dominican list, (ii) *Ancrene Wisse* and the Prémontré list of 1236–8, and (iii) this Prémontré list and the Dominican list. It would seem best to regard all three as variants on a single formula, especially as the frequent dependence of the Dominican constitutions on the Prémontré statutes is undoubted; and in view of the difference from the Prémontré list printed by Martène (which is presumably to be dated, like the version of the statutes which he gives, about 1174), the resemblance of *Ancrene Wisse* to these lists of 1228, 1236–8, and 1238–40 is a further piece of evidence in favour of its belonging to the thirteenth century, not the late twelfth. The feature that links *Ancrene Wisse* and the Dominican constitutions is of course that they both give the same total, fifteen, against sixteen in the later Prémontré statutes. But this is less distinctive than McNabb thought. The *Liber Ordinis* of St. Victor does not give a list of days for *rasurae*, but instead lays down a general rule;[1] it is that the *rasura* shall take

---

[1] Martène, iii. 284, 'De ordine tonsurae'. Though this is one of the unnumbered sections in Martène, it does not appear to be a later insertion into the *Liber Ordinis*; in MS. Ste Gen. 1637, dated *c.* 1200, in which all the sections are unnumbered, it comes at the same point and with the same text. It must already have been part of the text of the *Liber Ordinis* by the end of the twelfth century.

place every four weeks from All Saints' to Pentecost (i.e. in the winter months), and every three weeks from Pentecost to All Saints'—though regard is to be had to major feast-days falling within a few days before or after these limits.[1] As this means that tonsuring took place, on average, every three and a half weeks throughout the year, the annual total must have been fifteen times,[2] the same as is given for haircuts in the Titus–Pepys redaction of *Ancrene Wisse*, for *rasurae* in the Dominican constitutions, and for communions in the original passage in *Ancrene Wisse*. It is evident that there is a common tradition, from which the sixteen *rasurae* (reducible to fifteen) of the Prémontré statutes of 1236–8 are a

In accordance with the general tendency in the later thirteenth century to increase the frequency of *rasurae*, a General Chapter of St. Victor in July 1277 changed the rule to a scheme which was in principle a fortnightly one, though mostly expressed by reference to the vigils or the morrows of feast-days or their octaves or to Saturdays before specified Sundays (Martène, iii. 293, 'Antiqua Statuta S. Victoris'). This is too late to concern us, but it may be remarked that the list includes (like that in *Ancrene Wisse*) the contiguous feasts of Christmas and Epiphany, Ascension Day and Pentecost—though with more reason, in view of the shorter intervals on which it is based.

[1] Presumably All Saints' Day and Pentecost were to be two of the occasions (as in *Ancrene Wisse* and the Dominican *Constitutions*), since they are the terminal days from which the two parts of the year were reckoned; this deduction is the more likely because All Saints' and Pentecost were not in fact the beginning and end of the winter fasting season.

[2] The precise total in each part of the year would depend on the date of Whitsun. In a year in which it fell on its mean dates of 26–7 May, there would be $29\frac{1}{2}$ weeks in the 'winter' section and $22\frac{1}{2}$ in the 'summer' section; applying the St. Victor rule mechanically, this would mean about $7\frac{1}{2}$ *rasurae* in each. More realistically, if there were *rasurae* on the two terminal dates, there would be either 7 or 6 intermediate *rasurae* in the winter section and 6 or 7 in the summer. In practice it would obviously be most convenient to specify particular days that were to apply every year, perhaps with some possibility of modification (such as is provided in the 1236–8 statutes of Prémontré) in years in which the date of Easter was inconveniently extreme. But the specification of these days might well be left to individual houses, once the general principle had been laid down.

minor aberration, and the three varying thirteenth-century lists of days may be so many partly independent applications of the general principle laid down in the St. Victor *Liber Ordinis*.[1] But the tradition plainly did not originate with the Dominicans; the evidence is that it began among the independent Augustinian congregations, of whom the Dominicans were an offshoot. And the evidence of the texts of *Ancrene Wisse* is that the association of the number and times of communion with the number and times of tonsuring had itself already been made well before the Dominicans adopted this as their rule in 1249.

For the most part the ecclesiastical legislation and the episcopal visitations of the thirteenth and fourteenth centuries were concerned to lay down minimum standards for taking communion, for the laity generally, for the lay brothers and sisters, and for the tonsured brothers and the nuns of the religious orders; the object was to combat the growing tendency towards irregularity and infrequency. But the prescription in *Ancrene Wisse* has the opposite intention; it lays down a maximum.[2] The passage begins by saying that 'one values less the thing that one receives often', therefore they

[1] Nevertheless *Ancrene Wisse* applies the principle imperfectly, for it crowds too much into the 'winter' section of the year; not counting the terminal feasts of All Saints' and Whitsun, there are eight occasions in winter and only five in summer, where the norm should be seven in one, six in the other (see the previous note). Between Christmas and Twelfth Night, and between Ascension Day and Whitsun, the intervals are only of twelve and of ten days respectively, whereas the St. Victor rule specified an interval of four weeks in this part of the year. The difference may be due to the different purpose: tonsuring requires regular intervals (preferably with some regard to the coldness or warmth of the season, as in the rule of the *Liber Ordinis*), communion is concerned with the importance of the festivals as well as with regularity.

[2] Thus it prescribes that, if the sisters by some accident fail to take communion on a day specified, they are to do so on the next Sunday, unless another of the specified days is near, in which case they are to wait until then—in other words, they may omit altogether the day that has been missed.

are to take communion *only* fifteen times a year; and after listing the days it instructs the anchoresses that in preparation for each they are to be 'thoroughly confessed' (*cleanliche ischriuene*), are to submit to 'disciplines', i.e. to penitential punishment (probably flagellation; 'never, however, from anyone but yourselves'), and are to forgo their *pitance* or allowance of food (i.e. to fast completely) for one day. This is in accordance with one line of medieval thought about communion, that it was not to be received lightly or inadvisedly and without due preparation;[1] and though this was not a view confined to any one order or branch of the church, it was current among the Augustinians.[2]

(4) There is, finally, the passage added in the Nero MS. which describes how 'our lay brothers' say their hours;[3] and the problem is of such a nature that the text must be quoted in full.

Vre leawede breþren siggeð þus hore Vres. Vor Vhtsong ine werkedawes heihte and twenti paternosteres, ine helidawes forti; vor Euesonge, viftene; vor eueriche oþer Tide, seouene. Biuoren Uhtsong *Pater noster* and *Credo*, kneolinde to þer eorðe on werkedei and buinde on halidei; and þenne schal siggen hwo se con *Domine, labia mea aperies, Deus in adiutorium meum intende, Gloria patri, Sicut erat, Alleluia,* and ine Leinten *Laus tibi, domine, rex eterne glorie.* Efter þe laste [paternoster],[4] *Kirieleison, Christeleison, Kirieleison, Pater noster,* and efter þe Amen *Per dominum,*

---

[1] Cf. Browe, pp. 145 ff.   [2] Ibid., pp. 148–9.

[3] Nero MS., ed. Day, 10/25–11/5 (Morton, p. 24).

[4] The word *paternoster* is not in the MS. The scribe, in copying this passage, omitted various words, including *paternosteres* in the second line, which he later supplied in paler ink; it seems possible that he has also omitted *paternoster* here, without noticing his error. It is certainly needed for sense, and must be understood if it is not supplied in the text. But the text may be right, for *Efter þe laste* answers to *in fine omnium* in the Dominican *Constitutions* (see below); in the Latin text, however, the arrangement is different, and it is clear that *omnium* refers to the twenty-eight paternosters mentioned immediately before.

Benedicamus domino, Deo gratias. And et alle þe oþre Tiden also biginnen and also enden; bute et Cumplie schal biginnen hwo so con *Conuerte nos, deus salutaris,* and et alle þe oþre Tiden *Deus in adiutorium* wiðvten *Domine, labia mea.* ʒif ei of ou wule don þus, heo voleweð her, ase in oþre obseruaunces, muchel of vre ordre; and wel ich hit reade.

This, like the original passage that, at a later point in Part I,[1] prescribes substitute devotions to be used by any anchoress who could not manage the ordinary Hours, falls into two parts, though the details are different: an opening summary of the essential prayers that are to be (or in fact are) used in lieu of the Hours, followed by further advice about (or a further description of) less simple additions to be used by those who are capable of them. It is this parallelism of construction, allied to the similarity of syntax and style, which I find conclusive evidence of the authenticity of the Nero addition. There is however this important distinction, that the original passage is solely the author's advice to the anchoresses, and may therefore be of his own devising; the

---

[1] Corpus MS., f. 12a/2–14 (Morton, p. 46); for full references, see p. 8, n. 2, above. The prescription of this original passage was that an anchoress who did not know or could not say other Hours was to say instead a group consisting of the paternoster followed by *Ave Maria* and *Gloria patri*—thirty times for Matins, twenty times for Evensong, and fifteen times for all other Hours. At Matins, if she knew them, she was to add the prayers *Deus qui proprium est, Benedicamus domino,* and *Anime fidelium.* The supplementary instructions addressed to one who is more competent are briefer than in the Nero passage (partly because they have been to some degree anticipated by the parenthesis about *Deus qui proprium est* etc. in the main instruction), but are to the same effect: whoever knows how to is to begin by saying at Matins both *Domine, labia mea aperies* and *Deus in adiutorium,* at Compline *Converte nos, deus salutaris,* and at all other Hours *Deus in auditorium.* Anyone who is sick may cut ten paternosters off from Matins and five from each of the other Hours, and if she is more seriously ill she may halve the totals; anyone who is extremely ill is to be fully exempt. In general this demands more from an anchoress who does not know, or is unable to say, the ordinary Hours than the Nero passage says the lay brothers perform.

added passage in Nero professes to be a report of what 'our lay brothers' actually do. It is true that, after its opening summary in the present indicative, the Nero passage, when it comes to what is required of the more competent, shifts to 'shall say . . . and [shall] similarly begin and end'; but though this latter sounds like an instruction, not an account of what is in fact done, the concluding sentences of the addition show that the whole passage has as its object to describe the established usages of 'our order'.[1] The effect of the Nero addition, so interpreted, is that 'our lay brothers' say (i) for Matins, twenty-eight paternosters on ferias and forty on feast-days; (ii) for Evensong (Vespers), fifteen; (iii) for all other Hours, seven. But before beginning the series for Matins they say an introductory *Pater noster* and *Credo*, kneeling to the earth on ferias and bowing on feast-days. Those who know how to then say *Domine, labia mea aperies*, *Deus in adiutorium*, *Gloria patri* and *Sicut erat*, *Alleluia*, and (in Lent) *Laus tibi, domine, rex eterne glorie*. Then, 'after the last [paternoster]', i.e. after the last of the prescribed series for Matins, they say *Kirieleison* etc. and *Pater noster*, and, after the Amen, they add *Per dominum*, *Benedicamus domino*, and *Deo gratias*.[2] At all the other Hours they begin and end similarly, except that (*a*) at Compline, those who know it begin with *Converte nos, deus salutaris* instead of *Domine, labia mea aperies*, and (*b*) at all Hours other than Matins and Compline they begin with *Deus in adiutorium* without *Domine, labia mea*.

Fr. McNabb, followed by Miss Kirchberger, claimed that this 'Office of the Paternosters' was Dominican. But to

[1] The syntactical shift is easy to parallel in the statutes of Prémontré and indeed in the Dominican constitutions, which vary between indicatives describing what 'we' or 'the brothers' do, and hortative subjunctives prescribing what is to be done.

[2] This both compares and contrasts with the ending prescribed for Matins in the original passage; see p. 74, n. 1, above.

substitute 'a short office, which normally consists of a certain number of Paters, Aves, and Glorias'[1] for the standard Breviary offices is a practice by no means confined to the Dominicans; any order which admitted lay brothers or sisters was obliged to provide simpler alternatives to the ordinary Hours, partly because the lay brothers were insufficiently educated to take part in the elaborate services, partly because their duties did not permit them to spend long periods in choir. Thus the earliest recension of the statutes of Prémontré, that of 1131–4, though it has no unified section dealing with the *conversi*, has a number of scattered provisions for them, one of which contains the germ of the whole later development. It reads:

Conversis nostris *Credo in deum*, *Pater noster*, *Miserere mei, deus*, et *Confiteor* et Benedictionem cibi laicis fratribus addiscere licebit. Ceteri vero libelli eis non permittantur.[2]

In the revision of 1236–8 the second sentence becomes 'Nulli vero libelli permittantur eisdem',[3] but whatever the wording, it is clear from the context that the books which are not to be allowed to the *conversi* are the service-books (breviaries, psalters, etc.) requisite for the performance of the normal offices. This being so, any substitutes that the *conversi* used for the Hours must have been made up of the simple prayers that they were allowed to be taught. The second recension, that of *c*. 1174 printed by Martène, omits these provisions for the *conversi*,[4] perhaps because the unique text is from 'a

[1] *Oxford Dictionary of the Christian Church*, ed. F. L. Cross, under 'Lay brother, lay sister' (p. 792). The description fits very well the devotions recommended in the original passage in *Ancrene Wisse*; it is less apt for the Nero addition.

[2] van Waefelghem, p. 48.

[3] Lefèvre, p. 110; see also below.

[4] H. Heijman, 'Untersuchungen über die Prämonstratenser Gewohnheiten', *Analecta Praemonstratensia*, iv (1928), 29, suggests that the sections concerning *conversi* were omitted because it was intended to make

MS. of St. Victor'; the *Liber Ordinis* likewise contains no instructions on how the lay brothers are to conduct their daily lives or their devotions, and Bonnard says that no 'special rules' concerning them are recorded at St. Victor until the sixteenth century.[1] It is possible that St. Victor preferred not to lay down written rules for lay brothers who might be expected to be illiterate, but to rely on traditional oral instructions, which could have the added advantage of flexibility.[2] At Prémontré the regulations for *conversi* reappear in the third recension of the statutes, that of 1236–8, where they are brought together, with important additions as compared with the first recension, in a separate chapter.[3] It is evident, despite Martène's text, that there has been an unbroken development from the version of 1131–4 to that of 1236–8, for the latter takes over its first two sentences from the former with minor changes (including the addition of *Ave Maria* and the Graces to the prayers that may be taught); but then, after a couple of intervening sentences irrelevant to our discussion, it goes on to give a set of rules for the lay brothers' devotions which is not included in the first recension:

Pater noster, Credo in deum, Ave Maria gratia, Confiteor, Miserere

a separate rule for *conversi*, as the Cistercians did about 1174. This does not explain their reappearance in 1236–8.

[1] Bonnard, *Histoire*, i. 58. His cited authority for this statement is a history of Ste Geneviève written about 1760 by a Fr. Cl. du Molinet and preserved in MSS. 609 and 610 (both s. xvii) of the Bibliothèque Ste Geneviève (see *Catalogue général des manuscrits: Paris, Bibliothèque Ste Geneviève*, vol. i). Bonnard refers to the latter of these (formerly MS. in-fol. H. 21²), p. 518.

[2] Thus the *Liber Ordinis*, in setting down the list of clothes for each lay brother, says that they are what he can have *ex consuetudine* (Martène, iii. 262). The clothes are nevertheless listed in detail, because these are the standing orders for the *vestiarius*.

[3] Dist. IV, c. 10, 'De Conversis et de iis que licet eis addiscere, et de orationibus eorumdem'; Lefèvre, p. 110.

mei, deus, et Benedictionem cibi et potus, et Gratias addiscere licebit conversis. Nulli vero libelli permittantur eisdem. . . . In principio quoque Matutinarum dicant *Credo in deum* et *Pater noster*, deinde pro Matutinis viginti quinque *Pater noster*, ad Primam septem, ad Tertiam septem, ad Sextam septem, ad Nonam totidem, ad Vesperas quindecim, ad Completorium septem; post Completorium dicant semel *Pater noster* et *Credo in deum* . . .

This is obviously near to the prescription of the passage added in the Nero MS. of *Ancrene Wisse*, but there are differences. (i) The 1236–8 Prémontré statutes specify twenty-five, not twenty-eight, paternosters for Matins, and omit mention of feast-days. (ii) Both passages agree that *Pater noster* and *Credo* are to be said before the main set for Matins (though Prémontré says nothing about kneeling or bowing), but the Nero passage does not mention that they are also to be said after Compline. (iii) There is no mention in the Prémontré statutes of the additional devotions to be used, before and after the main sets of paternosters, by anyone who knows them; indeed, most of them seem to be excluded by not occurring in the list of things that may be taught to the *conversi*.

The Dominican *Constitutions* of 1228 also have a chapter dealing with the *conversi*,[1] which prescribes their devotions in similar terms.

Eodem tempore surgant fratres nostri conversi quo et canonici, et eodem modo inclinent. Cum surrexerint ad Matutinas, dicant *Pater noster* et *Credo in deum*, quod faciendum est ante Primam et post Completorium. In Matutinis, dicto *Pater noster* et *Credo*

[1] Dist. I, c. 37, 'De Conversis' (*ALKG*, i. 226–7). In the recension of 1238–40 this becomes Dist. I, c. xv (*ALKG*, v. 564), but the text is unchanged except for some rearrangement of the order and other minor details. My text follows Denifle's, but not in typography and punctuation.

in deum, erigant se dicentes *Domine, labia mea aperies* etc., *Deus in adiutorium meum* etc., *Gloria patri* etc. Pro Matutinis in profestis diebus dicant xxviii *Pater noster*, et in fine omnium dicant *Kyrie eleyson, Christe eleyson, Kyrie eleyson, Pater noster*; quo dicto, addant *Per dominum* etc., deinde *Benedicamus domino* etc. In festis ix lectionum xl *Pater noster* dicant. In aliis autem Horis vii *Pater noster* dicant, et in Vesperis xiiii.

Loco 'Preciosa' dicant tria *Pater noster*, pro Benedictione mense *Pater noster* et *Gloria patri* etc. Post mensam pro Gratiis tria *Pater noster, Gloria* etc., vel *Miserere mei, deus* qui sciunt. Et hoc totum cum silentio in ecclesia et ubique.[1]

The resemblance of this regulation to the passage in the Nero MS. is certainly striking, and it is not surprising that McNabb was much impressed by it.[2] There is even the detail of the phrase *qui sciunt*, corresponding to Nero's *hwo se con*, though the contexts are different. The Dominican regulation prescribes, like the Nero passage, twenty-eight paternosters

---

[1] The 1228 text adds a sentence which is dropped in 1238–40: 'Conversis qui nunc habent psalteria tantum duobus annis liceat retinere ab inde, et ipsis aliis psalteria inhibimus'. This shows that in 1228 the Dominicans had only just decided to impose the 'office of the paternosters' on all their *conversi*, for those who had psalters must have been given them so that they could take part in the ordinary offices. The regulation must have been a new one, at least as a compulsory practice applicable to all *conversi*—hence the period of two years' grace.

[2] But it is surprising that in none of his articles did he quote the text of the early Dominican *Constitutions*, for it is the similarity of the various documents in their wording, and not merely in their content, that is so striking. McNabb minimized the significance of the difference between fourteen and fifteen paternosters at Vespers, explaining the latter figure as due to the liking of the author of *Ancrene Wisse* for fives (*Archivum Fr. Praed.*, iv. 51); but in view of the tendency towards fives shown in the Prémontré statutes and in the Gilbertine *Institutions* (see p. 81, n. 1), the point is by no means insignificant if one is seriously trying to trace the history of the practice.

McNabb was careful to acknowledge that the point about the 'Office of the Paternosters' had first been taken by J. B. Dalgairns on p. xii of his introductory essay to Walter Hilton's *The Scale of Perfection* (John Philp, London, 1870): see *MLR*, xi. 1, n., and *Archivum Fr. Praed.*, iv. 51.

for Matins on 'workdays'[1] and forty on feast-days;[2] it mentions bowing on getting up[3] and implies bowing or kneeling while saying *Pater noster* and *Credo* at the beginning of Matins; and it prescribes certain devotions for use before and after the main sets of paternosters at Matins. But there are also differences. The additional devotions are not prescribed, as in the Nero passage, only for those who know them, and the list, though substantially the same, is a little less elaborate; no introductory or concluding devotions are prescribed for the Hours other than Matins (whereas the Nero passage does describe them, with careful distinctions); and the saying of *Pater noster* and *Credo* is prescribed not only for 'before Matins' (as in the Nero passage), but also for 'before Prime' (here the Dominican regulation stands alone) and for 'after Compline' (in agreement with the 1236–8 statutes of Prémontré). The Dominican regulation also goes on, as the Nero passage does not, to prescribe substitutes for 'Preciosa' and the Blessing of the food and the Graces after Meat.[4] But the most significant difference is that

---

[1] By *profestus dies* is meant, not the eve of a festival (so Latham, *Revised Medieval Latin Word-List*), but a week-day lacking the office of any saint, 'dies hebdomadis officio alicujus sancti vacans' (Maigne d'Arnis, *Lexicon Manuale*).

[2] It does not actually say 'for Matins', but the arrangement of the passage in the 1228 recension implies this; moreover it was Matins that was lengthened on a feast-day by having 'nine lessons' instead of the normal three, so that the larger prescription of paternosters on a feast-day is obviously appropriate for Matins. There is greater ambiguity in the 1238–40 recension because of an alteration of the order of the sentences.

[3] Cf. *Ancrene Wisse*, Corpus MS., f. 4b/17–21 (Morton, pp. 14, 16): 'Hwen ȝe earst ariseð . . . biginneð anan *Veni, creator spiritus* . . . buhinde o cneon forðward up o þe bedde'. There is nothing to correspond in the Prémontré statutes or the *Liber Ordinis*, both of which say merely that the brothers, after getting up, are to sit on their beds until everyone is ready to go in procession to the church (statutes, ed. Martène, iii. 325; ed. Lefèvre, pp. 4–5; *Liber Ordinis*, ed. Martène, iii. 281).

[4] The Prémontré statute also continues a little further, without relevance to *Ancrene Wisse*. I have quoted the continuation of the Dominican

for Vespers the Dominican prescription is fourteen pater-nosters, against fifteen not only in the Nero passage but also in the 1236–8 statutes of Prémontré.[1]

Two solutions are possible. (a) If the writer of the Nero addition was a Dominican, he cannot have been the original author of *Ancrene Wisse*; the date of composition of the English work does not allow it. Nevertheless I believe, for reasons given already,[2] that he was the original author; and it is not the case that the Nero passage is simply a translation or paraphrase of the Dominican regulation, for it differs in detail and includes things not present in the latter. (b) The obvious resemblances between all three passages, but also their differences; the close concurrence in date between them, since all are to be dated within at most twenty years;[3]

regulation chiefly because it contains the phrase *qui sciunt*. But it may be added that *Ancrene Wisse*, in Part VIII, provides that the servants, if they do not know the Graces, are to say *Pater noster* and *Ave Maria* before the meal and the same after it with the addition of *Credo* and a special English prayer (Corpus MS., f. 116a/25–116b/3; Morton, pp. 426, 428); this has analogies with, but differs from, the Dominican substitutes for the Graces before and after Meat.

[1] The difference matters precisely because the Dominican number seems more expected; its prescriptions, except only the forty for Matins on feast-days, are in multiples of seven. The Nero passage has multiples of seven for the lesser Hours and for Matins on 'work-days', multiples of five for Vespers and Matins on feast-days; the 1236–8 Prémontré statutes have multiples of five for Matins and Vespers, but seven for the lesser Hours.

In the thirteenth-century Gilbertine *Institutions* (printed by Dugdale, *Monasticon*, vi, Part 2, on pp. *xxix–*xcvii of a special section after p. 946) the offices prescribed are a form of the 'Office of the Paternosters'; they resemble the Nero passage and the Dominican constitutions in the intro-ductory and concluding devotions, but are made up of repetitions of both *Pater noster* and *Gloria patri* (cf. the original passage in *Ancrene Wisse*)— twenty times for Matins and forty on feast-days, fifteen for Vespers *and* for Lauds (an innovation), and ten for the other hours. This is a further development of the Augustinian tradition and carries through consistently a scheme of multiples of five, towards which the Prémontré statutes of 1236–8 tend. [2] See pp. 6–9, above.

[3] It is of course basic to the problem that we do not know the exact

and the known dependence of many of the Dominican regulations on those of Prémontré—all argue that the three documents are variants of a common original of somewhat earlier date. This indeed is probably represented most faithfully by the Nero addition, except for its failure to prescribe *Pater noster* and *Credo* after Compline as well as before Matins (since both the other texts agree against it on this point). The Dominican regulation is close to the Nero addition, but has simplified the instructions somewhat, especially those for introductory and concluding devotions, and has omitted, whether by accident or design, to prescribe these additional devotions for Hours other than Matins; it appears to have innovated by prescribing an introductory *Pater noster* and *Credo* before Prime; and it has certainly changed the number of paternosters in lieu of Vespers from fifteen to fourteen. The Prémontré statutes of 1236–8 have simplified the rules still further, either through aiming at

date at which the Nero addition was written. The Nero MS. itself is dated to the second quarter of the thirteenth century (cf. the introduction to Miss Day's edition, p. ix); six of the thirteen quires are written 'above top line' (all of them by the first scribe, who wrote the text of *Ancrene Wisse*) and seven 'below top line' (including the last quire, which is by the second scribe). This suggests that N is a little earlier than T, which is consistently 'below top line', but N is equally far removed from the archetype and is less faithful to it in textual detail and in linguistic usage (apart from the Northernisms of T). Perhaps N belongs to *c.* 1240. But the Nero scribe did not draft the addition himself; he was certainly copying, and it was probably already embodied in the text in his direct exemplar, which in turn must have derived it from some still earlier manuscript; less probably he himself adopted it from a manuscript other than his normal exemplar (see pp. 7–8 and p. 8, n. 1, above). We can only guess at the date when the passage was added to this lost manuscript. It may have been after the Corpus revision was made *c.* 1230, since the passage is lacking from Corpus; but more probably it was not included in Corpus because it was otiose, in view of the original passage prescribing paternosters etc. in lieu of Hours for those who needed a substitute. The likelihood is that the Nero addition was first written some years before the Prémontré statutes of 1236–8, and perhaps as early as the Dominican *Constitutions* of 1228.

brevity of statement or because of a wish to lighten the burden: they neglect to mention kneeling or bowing during the introductory *Pater noster* and *Credo*; they alter to twenty-five the number of paternosters prescribed for Matins; and they omit, or forget to mention, the distinction between the Matins of 'workdays' and of 'feasts of nine lessons', with the prescription of forty paternosters for the latter.

The Nero passage and the Dominican regulation also agree against the Prémontré statutes of 1236–8 in prescribing, as an addition to the basic sets of paternosters, introductory devotions of a less simple sort (in Nero, only for those who know them; in the Dominican regulation, without this qualification—though the phrase occurs later with a different reference). It is possible that their omission from the Prémontré statutes is a further result of compression or deliberate simplification, but their inclusion would have been contrary to the limitations imposed by the opening sentence, taken over with little change from the statutes of 1131–4. Unless there had been at Prémontré a calculated reversion, after a period of greater complication, towards an original simplicity, it would seem likely that the Nero passage and the Dominican regulation represent a development of the tradition more elaborate than that of Prémontré itself, possibly because lay brothers had proved to be capable of more than the basic Prémontré rule supposed.[1] But whatever the details, it is clear that there is a common tradition, and that it was not Dominican in origin; in this, as in other matters, the Dominicans were following, though with modifications, the earlier usage of Prémontré or of some other allied Augustinian congregation, and the claim that the

---

[1] Cf. p. 79, n. 1, above, which shows that up till 1228 some Dominican lay brothers had been provided with psalters for use in the offices; anyone who could use a psalter would be capable of the additional devotions prescribed by *Ancrene Wisse* and the Dominican regulation.

Nero passage must be of Dominican authorship cannot stand. Indeed, as far as we can judge from the available evidence, all four practices described or implied in the three passages (original or added) in manuscripts of *Ancrene Wisse* which mention what 'we' or 'our brothers' or 'our lay brothers' do are consistent with the customs of the Augustinian independent congregations, and especially (though not only) with those of Prémontré. They agree with, and at least to some extent anticipate, Dominican usage only because it, in its turn, was following Augustinian precedent.

The discussion in Chapter I of Mr. Brewer's arguments, and the examination here of the passages in which the author refers to the practices of his order, have involved frequent comparisons of *Ancrene Wisse* with the regulations of Prémontré, St. Victor, and the Dominicans. But these comparisons have not exhausted the resemblances of *Ancrene Wisse* to the custumals of the Augustinian independent congregations, and in particular to the Prémontré statutes, from which the Dominican *Constitutions* in part derive. The second and third recensions[1] of the statutes (and after them the *Constitutions*) begin with a prologue or introduction, from which *Ancrene Wisse* unmistakably quotes,[2] and are divided into parts called *distinctiones* just as *Ancrene Wisse* is divided, as its author himself explains, into

[1] The account that follows is based on these two recensions, except where the first recension is cited. The recension of 1131–4 is more primitive; though it often agrees in content and even in phrasing with the later versions, it is less organized, and lacks the prologue and the division into *Distinctiones* consisting of numbered chapters. It is also arranged on a different principle, and begins with the regulations concerning the officers of an abbey, starting with abbot and prior; this feature is also found in the *Liber Ordinis* of St. Victor. The second and third recensions often differ in the placing of individual chapters or in the division of material between chapters, but they follow the same general principle of arrangement.   [2] See pp. 19–20, above.

destinctiuns, þet ȝe cleopieð dalen 'which you call parts'.[1]
Long stretches of the statutes have no parallel in *Ancrene Wisse*, being concerned with such things as the organization of an abbey, its officers and their duties, offences against discipline of varying degrees of seriousness, and their punishments. But there is much in common. The statutes, except in their first form, begin by describing the daily round, with special reference to the Breviary offices by which its progression was marked, beginning from the moment when the brothers rise for Matins; they regulate the brothers' devotions and their work, their clothing, their eating and sleeping, their tonsurings and blood-lettings, and their treatment when they are sick; and the 1236–8 recension (and to a minor degree the first) also has chapters near the end dealing with the *conversi*, who are in a sense the servants of a religious house, just as Part VIII of *Ancrene Wisse*, also near the end, has a section which a very early (and perhaps original) marginal rubric describes as *Ouwer Meidnes riwle*.[2]

A particular feature of the statutes is that in describing the daily routine they give considerable prominence to the differences between summer and winter.[3] Even in the first recension the two seasons are carefully defined: the summer routine applies from Easter until the feast of the Holy Cross, and the winter routine from then until Easter. In

[1] Corpus MS., f. 4a/19–20 (Morton, p. 12). In the *Liber Ordinis*, though the chapters are numbered serially throughout in Martène's text, there is no formal division into parts; in this also it agrees with the first recension of the Prémontré statutes.

[2] Cleopatra MS., f. 195; cf. the rubric *La Riule vostre meignee* in F (311/22). It may be added that the three recensions of the Prémontré statutes all tend to deal with miscellanea at the end, including probably recent additions to the statutes, just as in the Corpus version there are various miscellaneous additional notes inserted between the end of the section dealing with the servants and the conclusion (Corpus MS., f. 117a/11–27); but this is perhaps not significant, for it is an obvious way to deal with miscellanea and additions.

[3] van Waefelghem, pp. 31–2; Martène, iii. 326; Lefèvre, pp. 11–13.

summer they eat twice a day, except on the major and minor Rogation Days, the vigil of Pentecost, the Ember Days, the eves of certain Saints' Days, and on Fridays.[1] From St. Cross Day until Easter there is a continuous fast, except on Sundays and major feast-days; on these they eat twice, as in summer, but Nones is said immediately after the main meal, without any intervening period of sleep. Otherwise in this period, and on fast-days throughout the summer, they eat only once, after Nones, except in Lent, when they eat after Vespers. 'Lenten fare' is eaten in the whole of Advent (except on Sundays and feasts of nine lessons)[2] and on the Monday and Tuesday before Ash Wednesday, on the Ember Days of September and December, on the vigils of Ascension Day and Whit Sunday and of certain feast-days.[3] They also fast on all Fridays, unless

[1] Though the first recension includes Fridays, the second and third omit to mention them at this point (thus demonstrating, probably, that the third was based on the second without reference back to the first); the omission is repaired by the second recension in the chapter on Lenten fare (Martène, iii. 335), and by the third in that on food generally, to which the material about Lenten fare is transferred (Lefèvre, p. 20). The first recension in fact says that from Whitsun to St. Cross Day they fast both on Wednesdays and Fridays unless they have had hard work or there is a major feast (van Waefelghem, p. 31); but in the second and third recensions Wednesday is no longer a fast-day. Perhaps it was in removing the reference to Wednesdays that the necessary reference to Fridays was also cut out from the section dealing with the summer routine.

[2] This exception, present in both the earlier recensions, is omitted in that of 1236–8, perhaps by oversight; but cf. *Ancrene Wisse*, cited below, which also forbids *hwit* (milk foods) in Advent, without any exception. The exception is to be expected; its omission, whether accidental or deliberate, would suggest that *Ancrene Wisse* and the 1236–8 recension derive from some lost version, later than that of *c.* 1174 printed by Martène, in which the omission was first made.

[3] van Waefelghem, p. 37; Martène, iii. 335; Lefèvre, p. 20. In the first recension the regulation is ill-drafted (or is spoilt in the Munich MS.), and leaves it unclear whether Lenten fare applies to all the days listed; in the other two recensions there is no doubt.

Christmas Day falls on a Friday; the first and second recensions prescribe Lenten fare for Fridays too,[1] but the third allows eggs and milk foods (*lacticinia*) 'and such like' on Fridays outside Advent and Lent.[2] But the foods[3] served 'in the monasteries of our Order' are always without meat or fat,[4] except for those given to the gravely ill or weak or to hired craftsmen.[5] All this has obvious analogies with *Ancrene Wisse*, both with the passage in Part I defining the relation of Nones to the meals[6] and more especially with the passage in Part VIII which reads:

3e schulen eoten from Easter aþet te Hali Rode Dei—þe leatere, þe is i heruest—euche dei twien, bute þe Fridahes ant Umbridahes ant 3eongdahes ant vigiles. I þeos dahes, ne i þe Aduent, ne schule 3e nawt eoten hwit bute neode hit makie. þe oþer half 3er feasten al, bute Sunnedahes ane, ⟨hwen 3e beoð in heale ant i ful strengðe; ah riwle ne tweast nawt seke ne blodletene⟩. 3e ne schulen nawt eoten flesch ne seim bute for muche secnesse oðer hwase is ouerfeble.[7]

---

[1] The sentence in the first recension, though ill-drafted, leaves no doubt on this point, and the second recension is clear.

[2] Lefèvre, p. 20. *Lacticinia* are the *hwit* of *Ancrene Wisse*.

[3] The word used is *pulmenta* (or *pulmentaria*) which, like Middle English *suuel* (see p. 2, n. 1, above), meant 'anything eaten with bread'.

[4] The word for 'fat' is *sagimen*, the *seim* 'seam' of *Ancrene Wisse*.

[5] van Waefelghem, p. 37; Martène, iii. 335; Lefèvre, p. 20.

[6] Corpus MS., f. 6a/5–14 (Morton, p. 20). Cf. pp. 11–12, above.

[7] Edited text, based on Corpus MS., f. 111b/9–16 (which, however, omits the words after *Fridahes* as far as *þeos dahes*) and the other MSS. running (Morton, p. 412). Note that *Ancrene Wisse* follows the stricter rule of the first and second Prémontré recensions, not the relaxed rule of 1236–8, by prescribing Lenten fare, without *hwit*, for all fast-days in summer, including Fridays; but it does not, like the first recension, name Wednesday as well as Friday as a fast-day. The qualification in caret brackets is an addition to the basic text made only in the Corpus version; in it, the word *tweast*, which occurs only here (but cf. *tuaste* p.t., cited by *OED* s.v. *twist* vb., 8), must mean 'binds' and be 3 sg. pres. indic. of **tweasten* < OE **twæstan*, a variant of *twist* (cf. Zettersten, *Studies in the Dialect and Vocabulary of the Ancrene Riwle*, p. 182). The Corpus addition may be compared with the clause (itself a new one)

This is a competent summary of the same sort of regulations as are expounded at more length in the Prémontré statutes, though it omits certain details (e.g. it does not specify which vigils are fast-days, or mention the two days before Ash Wednesday), and its phrases *muche secnesse* and *ouerfeble* are parallel to such as *graviter infirmi* or *debiles et infirmi* in the statutes.[1] Another verbal parallel is that the statutes have *dies geminae refectionis*[2] to correspond to *twi-mel dei* 'two-meal day' in *Ancrene Wisse*;[3] but I have not noticed *dies unius refectionis* to answer to *a-mel dei* 'one-meal day'.[4] A last resemblance, in dietary regulations, is that the Prémontré statutes forbid any canon or lay-brother to partake of food or drink out of the refectory (i.e. except at the normal times) *sine licentia debita*,[5] just as in *Ancrene Wisse* the ser-

in the 1236–8 recension of the Prémontré statutes which says that those who lie gravely ill in bed are not bound (*non ligantur*) by the rule (*lege*) which lays down that the sick in the infirmary are to be given meat only once a day in the winter and are to keep silence during the times of the Offices and after Compline (ed. Lefèvre, p. 32). But all three recensions have special rules for the sick (van Waefelghem, pp. 46–7; Martène, iii. 328; Lefèvre, pp. 31–2) and for those who have been bled (van Waefelghem, p. 58; Martène, iii. 328; Lefèvre, pp. 36–7).

[1] Cf. van Waefelghem, p. 43; Martène, iii. 327; Lefèvre, pp. 22, 33. The first recension also has *omnino infirmi et debilitati* and a section headed 'De omnino infirmis' (van Waefelghem, pp. 37, 47) which recalls *Ancrene Wisse*'s phrase *ful meoseise*, 'completely unwell' (Corpus MS., f. 12a/14; Morton, p. 46), for which the Cleopatra MS. (f. 19) has *al seke* in the hand of scribe B, whom I take to be the author, correcting an omission by the original scribe. To specify the degrees of sickness is characteristic of all three recensions and of the *Liber Ordinis*.

[2] Martène, iii. 335; Lefèvre, p. 20 (and also p. 37).

[3] See p. 11, above.

[4] But the collocation *in diebus jejunii, ad unam refectionem* . . . does occur (Martène, loc. cit.; cf. Lefèvre, p. 20, with different word-order).

[5] Martène, iii. 328; Lefèvre, p. 30. Cf. also the first recension's prohibition of drinking *extra horam* without permission (van Waefelghem, p. 42). The provisions in the *Liber Ordinis* of St. Victor concerning requests for special food warn the brothers not to ask for things *extra horam* and to take it patiently if, should they nevertheless ask *extra horam*, the request is not granted (Martène, iii. 273).

vants are forbidden to 'munch' anything, whether fruit or anything else, or to drink between meals *bute leaue*, though leave is to be easily given in all matters that are not sin.[1]

Both the Prémontré statutes and the *Liber Ordinis* make it clear that at all times prescribed for sleeping, even at midday in summer, the brothers were to proceed to the dormitory, each to his own bed, and sleep there decorously, just as the anchoresses were to sleep *nohwer bute i bedde*.[2] The brothers of Prémontré were not to presume to lie down except in tunic and shoes and girdle, unless gravely ill, when they might be allowed a linen night-shirt.[3] This instruction is followed and modified in *Ancrene Wisse*, where the author tells the anchoresses that *ȝe schulen in an hetter ant igurd liggen*, 'you are to sleep in a robe, and girdled', but (he adds) loosely enough for the hands to be put under the girdle,[4] and whoever wishes may wear *hosen wiðute vampez* 'drawers without feet';[5] but they are not to wear shoes in bed (*ischeod*

---

[1] Corpus MS., f. 116b/3–5 (Morton, p. 428). But the texts vary; the original form of the sentence (kept in MSS. C and F) had no subject for the verb, leaving 'they' (sc. the servants) to be understood as the subject, whereas MSS. A, N, and T add *ȝe*, thus making the instruction apply to the anchoresses themselves. This cannot be right, since the sentence comes in the section dealing with the servants; but it shows knowledge of the fact that the prohibition, in monastic houses, was not intended to apply only to the servants.

[2] Corpus MS., f. 113b/14–15 (Morton, p. 420).

[3] 'Sine tunice vero, caligis, et cingulo nullus jacere presumat, exceptis pueris et graviter infirmis, quibus per necessitatem linea camisia conceditur' (van Waefelghem, p. 43; so Martène, iii. 327, and Lefèvre, p. 22, with omission of *pueris et* and other slight variations).

[4] i.e. not so tightly that it could amount to a form of mortification of the flesh, as is shown by the way the passage continues; the ability to put the hands under is a test of looseness. The citations from *Ancrene Wisse* are from the Corpus MS., f. 113a/28–113b/14 (Morton, pp. 418, 420).

[5] Hall, *Early Middle English*, ii. 393, followed by Miss Salu, *The Ancrene Riwle*, p. 186, translates 'stockings without feet', which is in accordance with *OED*, s.v. *hose*, where this instance is entered under sense 1β; but sense 2, 'drawers', seems more apposite, though *OED*'s instances begin in the fifteenth century. *OED* may have been influenced

ne slepe 3e nawt). This last, seemingly unnecessary, prohibition of what most people would not think of doing is explained by the Prémontré regulation, and is the proof that
he was writing with the latter in mind. In this he resembles
the *Consuetudines Ordinis* of Beauvais, according to which
the brothers constantly sleep in night-shirts (*camisiis*) and
trousers (*femoralibus*), without mention of girdles, and also
take off their shoes at night *propter vermium importunitatem*,
though otherwise, according to the Rule, they should 'never
and nowhere' go without them nor without them descend
from the dormitory;[1] this contrasts with the permission given
in *Ancrene Wisse* to walk and sit barefoot, and to wear light
shoes, in summer.

It is significant that the author of *Ancrene Wisse*, in these
prescriptions, is adapting for women regulations drawn up
for men, as he also did when he forbade the wearing of
linen, unless it was coarse, next to the body.[2] For the earliest statutes of Prémontré, the recension of 1131–4, had
had a special section on the clothes to be worn by the
sisters of Premonstratensian houses.[3] They were to have
shifts (*camisiae*) of linen or wool, of unfulled cloth so that it
should be less heavy, fur garments of lamb-skin, a black
woollen or linen tunic of thicker cloth, a cloak of lamb-skin
and woollen cloth (which in summer might be separated

by the corrupt Nero text, which suggests that *hosen wiðute vampez* are
an alternative, by day, to going barefoot, as well as night attire.

[1] MS. Mazarine 2005, f. 100ᵛ. The brothers at Beauvais slept on
feather mattresses (*super plumas*) and used bolsters (*puluillis*) and pillows
(*auricularibus*) and also linen bedclothes (*lectisterniis*). But no one was
exempt from sleeping in the dormitory except those who were busy with
some duty or anyone who was afflicted by *nimia debilitate siue senectute
aut infirmitate corporis*.

[2] See p. 29, n. 2, above.

[3] van Waefelghem, p. 65. At this date the sisters were members of
double monasteries; by 1236–8 they had become *sorores cantantes* living
in special nunneries.

from the fleece), a linen alb (a form of white surplice) and above it a black linen veil, a girdle and a sheath with a small knife. All their woollen garments were to be of the same or similar cloth, of their own making (*sui operis*), with the natural colour. For their bed-clothes they were to have a pillow of down 'where supplies permit' (*ubi facultas patitur*), a mattress,[1] and a woollen or linen sheet. But this, with the other regulations dealing with the sisters, disappears from the second recension of *c.* 1174, and though there are rules concerning sisters in the recension of 1236–8 (including one about the colour of their dress) they are quite different; the original regulations drop out and do not return.[2] The author of *Ancrene Wisse* shows no knowledge of them;[3] his

[1] The word in the first recension is printed *wanbitium*, as also *wanbitia* pl. (van Waefelghem, p. 43), but should probably be *wambitium*; the instance on p. 43 shows that it is something soft to lie on, for only *infirmi et pueri* are allowed to have one. In the 1236–8 recension, *wambusios* occurs as a textual variant to *stramina* (Lefèvre, p. 22 n.). These words appear to be variants of medieval Latin *gambesum, wambasium* 'a military tunic, often padded, covering trunk and thighs' (see *OED*, s.v. *gambeson*; cf. also Dutch *wambuis* 'jacket, doublet'); it was padded or quilted because it was worn under the armour to protect the body from the rings. Presumably the word has been transferred to a mattress because it too is padded for comfort.

[2] Heijman, *Anal. Praemon.*, iv (1928), 29, explains their absence from the second recension as a consequence of the decision to admit no more women to Praemonstratensian houses. It is a difficulty that the decree recording this decision is, among others, printed as an appendix to Martène's text of the statutes, as if it were later in date than the revision of the statutes; but even so the provisions about women might have been deleted from existing copies once the decision was taken. One can hardly explain their absence by the fact that Martène's text is based on a manuscript belonging to St. Victor (where rules about women would be irrelevant), for their failure to reappear in the 1236–8 recension must mean that they had been cut out also from the copy or copies kept at Prémontré itself.

[3] The advice in *Ancrene Wisse* that the anchoresses should help to clothe (and to feed) themselves and their servants by their own work (Corpus MS., f. 114b/8–10; Morton, pp. 420, 422), and that they should wear white or black veils over their caps (Corpus MS., f. 113b/19;

own advice concerning clothing is very general, except for a grudging permission to anyone who wishes to wear a *stamin*,[1] a still less enthusiastic reference to breeches of hair-cloth (a sweet and fragrant heart, in his view, is always best), and very explicit warnings against other forms of mortification of the flesh. 'Because men do not see you nor you them', he says, it does not matter whether their clothing is white or black,[2] provided it is simple and warm and well made, and the furs well tawed, and they are to have as many clothes as they need for their backs and their beds. The only really precise recommendation is that instead of wimples they should wear warm caps with white or black veils over them; he felt strongly about wimples.[3] Most of his instructions he must have worked out himself, using his common sense. But the (qualified) prohibition of linen next to the body is shared, as we have seen,[4] with the Dominican *Constitutions* and is likely to be derived from some earlier form of Augustinian legislation, and there is probably a similar link between *Ancrene Wisse* and one of the few rules concerning women that are included in the 1236–8 recension of the Prémontré statutes. This 'strictly forbids' that henceforth any secular girl should by any means be admitted into the houses or cloisters of 'our sisters' as a boarder or lodger

Morton, p. 420), can hardly be taken as evidence that the author knew of the similar (but not identical) provisions in the early Prémontré statutes; these are things that he could easily have thought of independently.

[1] An undergarment made of coarse worsted cloth, little better than a hair shirt and likewise worn by ascetics; see *OED*, s.v.

[2] Cf. the *Consuetudines Ordinis* of Beauvais (MS. Mazarine 2005, f. 104ᵛ): 'Proinde sciendum est quod si in remotis solitudinibus aut siluarum recessibus habitaremus, cujusmodi lanificio, uel infecto seu natiuo, nostra fierent indumenta non magnopere curaremus.'

[3] Corpus MS., f. 113b/18–19 (Morton, p. 420). His objection to wimples is given eloquent and lengthy expression in an addition made at this point in the Cleopatra MS., f. 194 (by scribe B), and embodied with minor revisions in the Corpus MS., ff. 113b/19–114a/13.

[4] See p. 29, above.

(*ad nutriendum vel demorandum*),[1] just as *Ancrene Wisse* says that an anchoress should not degenerate into a school-mistress or turn her house of retreat into a children's school,[2] though it goes on, characteristically, to qualify the prohibition.

This is a restriction designed specifically for women's houses and introduced at a late stage into the statutes; but from the very beginning there had been a considerable list of things that the Premonstratensians had renounced. All three recensions of the statutes have a special chapter about 'the things which we propose not to have'.[3] High in the list are animals and birds 'which are apt rather to provoke curiosity and to be ostentatiously vain than to bring any advantage'. 'We', the brothers of the order, will not act as sureties or make contracts, or keep other men's animals or household goods or crops or money in 'our' granges or houses, 'to our peril, if they were lost'. Similarly the anchoresses are advised, in three consecutive paragraphs, not to keep any animals except only a cat (though the author, mindful of their circumstances, goes on to talk of cows and the trouble they cause, and not—as the statutes do—of stags, bears, chamois, monkeys, peacocks, swans, and so forth),[4] not to engage in trade,[5] and not to keep in their house other men's things, neither their cattle (if *ahte* again bears this sense, as it well may, in view of the Prémontré statute), nor their clothes, nor their documents, and so on, since 'great disadvantages have often come about from such guardianship'.[6]

---

[1] Lefèvre, p. 114.   [2] Corpus MS., f. 114b/20–1 (Morton, p. 422).
[3] van Waefelghem, pp. 45–6; Martène, iii. 335; Lefèvre, pp. 108–9. The three versions vary somewhat; the account given above is a composite one, following especially the second and third recensions.
[4] Corpus MS., ff. 112b/24–113a/8 (Morton, pp. 416, 418).
[5] Corpus MS., f. 113a/8–12 (Morton, p. 418).
[6] Corpus MS., f. 113a/13–18 (Morton, p. 418). *Ahte* certainly means

From almost exactly the date when *AncreneWisse* was written there survives another rule in which the Prémontré statutes were adapted for a community of women: the 'constitutions' of the nunnery of St. Sixtus, a church in Rome which in late 1219 was given by Honorius III to St. Dominic.[1] These constitutions, which their editors hold to have been written by Dominic himself and which they date 'February 1220',[2] are obviously and indeed explicitly Augustinian,[3] and were so described by Gregory IX in 1232.[4] More particularly they are based on the statutes of Prémontré:[5] they begin with a variation on the first sentence of the prologue of the statutes; many of the provisions are verbally identical or else agree with the variant forms of the Prémontré regulations found in the Dominican constitutions of 1228; and (like the latter) they include lists of offences classified according to their gravity—a form of the 'penal code' (of Cluniac origin) which distinguished the Prémontré statutes from most

'cattle' at ff. 112b/26 and 113a/5; in f. 113a/14 it might mean 'possessions' generally in the context of the English text, but is probably still being used in the same sense as in the two closely preceding instances.

[1] ed. Balme and Lelaidier, *Cartulaire ou histoire diplomatique de Saint Dominique*, ii (1897), 425 ff. (no. lxxxviii). For an account of the transference of the church of St. Sixtus from the Gilbertines to St. Dominic, see pp. 405–6.

[2] Ibid., ii. 458–62. The reason for the dating to February is not stated. In 1232 Gregory IX, who as Cardinal Ugolino had been associated with St. Dominic in 1219–20 in founding the nunnery of St. Sixtus, granted the same constitutions to a new German order, the Penitent Sisters of St. Mary Magdalene; and though no copy survives of his bull, it was confirmed and reissued in 1291 by Nicholas IV in a bull of which copies do survive, and from which alone the text of the constitutions is known, since no copy is preserved in the archives of St. Sixtus or of any Dominican house.

[3] Thus it is laid down that the brothers attached to the nunnery 'regulam beati Augustini observant' (Balme and Lelaidier, ii. 453).

[4] His bull, addressed to the Penitent Sisters, rehearses that 'regulam beati Augustini et institutiones ordinis monialium sancti Sixti vobis duximus concedendam' (Balme and Lelaidier, ii. 426, footnote).

[5] Cf. Balme and Lelaidier, ii. 463–4.

other Augustinian custumals, including the *Liber Ordinis* of St. Victor.[1] But there are differences from the Prémontré rules, and in some of these cases the St. Sixtus constitutions have features in common with *Ancrene Wisse*. Thus the prescription for the summer routine is:

A festo resurrectionis dominice usque ad festum sancte crucis in septembri reficiantur bis in die sorores, exceptis sextis feriis, diebus rogationum et vigilia Pentecostes et jejuniis quatuor temporum, vigiliis sanctorum Johannis baptiste, Petri et Pauli, Jacobi, Laurentii, Assumptionis beate Marie ac sancti Bartholomei.[2]

This, like *Ancrene Wisse*, defines which St. Cross Day is meant (that in September, or 'the latter, in harvest-time'), includes Fridays (omitted at this point in the second and third recensions of the Prémontré statutes),[3] but omits the separate mention of *Letania major* found in the statutes. The prescription for winter is:

A festo autem sancti crucis in septembri usque ad Pascha semel reficiantur in die, diebus dominicis exceptis, nisi debiles et infirme vel cum, aliqua ex causa, sit aliter dispensatum.[4]

This again agrees with *Ancrene Wisse* in making an exception only for Sundays and not also for major feast-days, as was done at Prémontré; and its added qualification, not found at this point in the Prémontré statutes, exempting the weak and the sick corresponds to the similar qualification added

---

[1] But not the *Consuetudines Ordinis* of Beauvais, which towards the end (MS. Mazarine 2005, ff. 105–6ᵛ) has a section headed 'De fugitiuis' which is a brief form of the penal code, distinguishing offences of three degrees of gravity. As this section must be later than 1135 (see pp. 102–3, below), it may well be influenced by the Prémontré statutes.

[2] Balme and Lelaidier, ii. 427–8. For the corresponding passage in *Ancrene Wisse* see p. 87, above.

[3] See p. 86, n. 1, above.

[4] Balme and Lelaidier, ii. 428.

to the text of *Ancrene Wisse* in the Corpus revision.[1] The constitutions also agree with *Ancrene Wisse* against the 1236–8 Prémontré statutes (but not the first two recensions) in prescribing Lenten fare for all Fridays as well as for other fasts:

In toto adventu, quadragesima et jejuniis quatuor temporum, vigiliis Ascensionis, Pentecostes, Apostolorum et aliorum sanctorum in quorum vigiliis jejunia sunt indicta, et omnibus sextis feriis, quadragesimali cibo utentur sorores nec tunc que serviunt mixtum sumant.[2]

None of the foregoing prescriptions is modified for women except in wording (*sorores* and *puelle* for *fratres* and *pueri*) and in grammatical gender, though their other variations from the Prémontré statutes show that there is some link with *Ancrene Wisse*. Occasionally, however, there are somewhat more radical adaptations. Thus the St. Sixtus constitutions resemble *Ancrene Wisse* in their treatment of the Prémontré regulation concerning the clothes to be worn in bed, which becomes:

Super stramina et laneis soror jacebit in una veste lanea, et camisia, si voluerit, semper cincta.[3]

Both rules for women prescribe a *hetter* or a *vestis lanea* and girdling, following Prémontré; *Ancrene Wisse* explicitly rejects the Prémontré prescription of shoes, and the constitutions silently drop it; and both add another garment, to be worn either by *hwa se likeð* or *si voluerit*—in the one case *hosen wiðute vampez*, in the other a *camisia*. But in another regulation adapted for women there is a difference: whereas

[1] See p. 87, n. 7, above. The closest parallel in wording to the qualifying clause in Corpus is the provision of the 1236–8 Prémontré statutes cited there; but cf. also the later clause in the St. Sixtus constitutions which runs: 'Porro infirme, valetudinarie vel puelle non debent abstinentia vel jejuniis aggravari' (ii. 432).

[2] Balme and Lelaidier, ii. 429.   [3] Ibid., p. 434.

Ancrene Wisse prescribes that the anchoresses' hair should be trimmed 'or, if you wish, shaven' four times a year, the constitutions prescribe *tonsurae* for the nuns and lay brothers on eight specified occasions in the year.[1] The constitutions provide that if anyone has offended her sister,

tamdiu ante pedes ejus prostrata jaceat, quousque placata ipsam erigat,[2]

which resembles the instruction in *Ancrene Wisse* that if any contention arises between the servants,

þe ancre makie eiðer to makien oþer venie o cneon to þer eorðe, ant eiðer rihte up oðer.[3]

The constitutions also advise the nuns that,

quia otiositas inimica est anime nec non mater et nutrix est vitiorum, nulla in claustro maneat otiosa; sed semper, si poterit, aliquid operis faciat, quia non de facile a temptatione capitur, qui exercitio bono vacat . . .[4]

The opening phrase, *otiositas inimica est animae*, is quoted from the Rule of St. Benedict, c. xlviii, but the rest is an elaboration (supported, after the passage quoted, by scriptural citations) which recalls the instruction in *Ancrene Wisse*:

As Sein Ierome leareð, ne beo ȝe neauer longe ne lihtliche of sum þing allunges idel, for ananrihtes þe feond beot hire his werc þe i Godes werc ne swinkeð, ant tuteleð anan toward hire. For hwil he sið hire bisi, he þencheð þus: 'For nawt ich schulde nu cume neh hire; ne mei ha nawt iȝemen to lustni mi lare.' Of idelnesse awakeneð muchel flesches fondunge. *Iniquitas Sodome saturitas panis et ocium*: þet is, 'Sodomes cwedschipe com of idelnesse ant of ful wombe'. Irn þet lið stille gedereð sone rust; weater þe ne stureð nawt readliche stinkeð,[5]

[1] Ibid.   [2] Ibid.
[3] Corpus MS., f. 116a/6–8 (Morton, p. 426).
[4] Balme and Lelaidier, ii. 449.
[5] Corpus MS., f. 114b/10–20 (Morton, p. 422).

though the English writer's development of the idea is altogether more vivid and lively. Even if the last two parallels are not close in wording, they show some similarity in thought and in the topics chosen for inclusion.

Perhaps the most striking resemblance, however, is in the formulation of the vows required.[1] In the Preface to *Ancrene Wisse* the author writes:

Nan ancre bi mi read ne schal makien professiun, þet is, bihaten ase heast, bute þreo þinges: þet beoð obedience, chastete, ant stude-steaðeluestnesse—þet ha ne schal þet stude neauer mare changin bute for nede ane, as strengðe ant deaðes dred;[2] obedience of hire bischop oðer of his herre.[3]

These, it should be observed, are the maximal, not the minimal, vows, and obedience is defined as being due to 'her bishop or his superior', as is appropriate to anchoresses, or indeed to Augustinians generally who were not members of one of the monastically organized independent congregations. Nevertheless, with allowance for such differences in detail, and for the more striking omission to require the renunciation of property, the sentence is clearly akin to the opening prescription of the St. Sixtus constitutions, which runs:

[1] This was pointed out by McNabb in *Archivum Fr. Praed.*, iv. 60–1.

[2] In the Cleopatra MS., f. 5ᵛ, before *deaðes drednesse* (for Corpus *deaðes dred*), scribe B (i.e. the author) adds the syntactically difficult phrase *as of fur oðer of oþer peril*, apparently to specify the sort of thing that might occasion 'fear of death'. The St. Sixtus constitutions have a clause which provides that 'periculum latronum et ignis' shall absolve from blame and penalty any who, contrary to the normal prohibition, enter the nuns' cloister. But this partial resemblance is probably coincidental; the contexts are different.

[3] Corpus MS., f. 2a/20–5 (Morton, p. 6). The Corpus reading *his herre* is undoubtedly better than Nero's *hire herre*; but it may be significant that the latter is a modification appropriate to women living in a nunnery under a superior.

Quelibet, cum recipitur in sororem, promittat obedientiam, loci stabilitatem et ordinis, vivere sine proprio ac etiam continenter, domum illam in qua professionem fecerit nullatenus egressura, nisi ad conventum alium ejusdem ordinis ex causa necessaria transferetur.[1]

Balme and Lelaidier,[2] believing that nothing corresponding occurred in the statutes of Prémontré, thought that this clause must be an innovation of St. Dominic's; though they granted that the ingredients of the vow—obedience, poverty, chastity, and *stabilitas*[3]—were 'de l'essence de toute vie religieuse', they supposed that it was found opportune specially to formulate the requirements for women who were unfamiliar with the law.[4] But though it is true that no

---

[1] Balme and Lelaidier, ii. 427 (but with *ullatenus* for *nullatenus*).

[2] Ibid., ii. 465.

[3] Balme and Lelaidier seem to regard the vow 'de la stabilité et de la clôture perpetuelle' as something newly added to the basic requirements. But the Rule of St. Benedict (c. lviii) requires that a postulant 'promittat de stabilitate sua et conversatione morum suorum, et obedientiam', and *stabilitas* certainly meant (or comprised) permanence of residence, for a 'pilgrim monk' (*monachus peregrinus*) who desired admittance to a Benedictine house was required 'to bind himself to stability' (*stabilitatem suam firmare*, c. lxi). The actual phrases *stabilitas in loco* and *stabilitas loci* occur, with specific reference to the monastic life, from the time of Louis the Pious (emperor 814–40) onwards (Ducange, s.v. *stabilitas*). The author of *Ancrene Wisse*, in writing his sentence, may well have been influenced, directly or indirectly, by the Benedictine vow (with the substitution of 'chastity' for 'conversatio (*or* conversio) morum'); for he, like it, omits mention of the renunciation of property.

[4] In consequence McNabb, accepting Balme and Lelaidier's view that the formulation was new, but believing (in spite of them) that Cardinal Ugolino was the author, asserted that this was a novel piece of Roman legislation and that *Ancrene Wisse* therefore 'could not be earlier than 1220', since in his view the sentence in *Ancrene Wisse* must have been based on that in the St. Sixtus constitutions (*Archivum Fr. Praed.*, iv. 60–1). But though *Ancrene Wisse* may have been written after 1220, it cannot have been more than a few years later; and it is not easy to see how an English author living in Herefordshire could have become aware in so short a time of the constitutions of a newly founded and as yet undistinguished Roman nunnery.

comparable formula occurs in either the first or the second
recensions of the Prémontré statutes,[1] the revision of 1236–8
includes an almost entirely new chapter on the reception of
brothers, in which are found in close proximity (though not
in a single sentence) the elements of the passages in the St.
Sixtus constitutions and in *Ancrene Wisse*. This version
stipulates that postulants who have finished their novitiate

in Capitulo . . . renunciabunt seculo et proprietati, promittentes
obedientiam, castitatem et vitam communem . . . Postea ad
missam, quam abbas cantabit, faciet novitius professionem hoc
modo: 'Ego, frater N., . . . promitto conversionem morum meorum, emendationem vite et stabilitatem in loco. Promitto etiam
obedientiam perfectam in Christo . . .'.[2]

This is later in date than *Ancrene Wisse* and the constitutions
of St. Sixtus, but it is known that the codification of 1236–8
took account of legislation introduced during the sixty-odd
years that had passed since the recension of *c.* 1174 was made;
and it would seem reasonable to suppose that these formulae
derive from earlier usage. Moreover, even the recension of
c. 1174, as printed by Martène, has appended to it a regulation that

sorores nostrae non egrediantur, nisi forte mittantur de claustro
ad claustrum ejusdem abbatiae ad commorendum,[3]

and this recurs as a clause of the statutes of 1236–8 in the
form

Preterea sorores nostre non egrediantur nec evagentur, nisi

[1] Balme and Lelaidier appear to have known only the second recension
(since neither the first nor the third had been published when they were
writing), though they refer not only to Martène's printed text, but also
to MS. Bibliothèque Nationale latin 14762, which they date to the twelfth
century. I have not seen this manuscript.

[2] Lefèvre, p. 25. The ultimate debt to the Rule of St. Benedict is clear,
but *in loco* is added to define *stabilitas*.

[3] Martène, iii. 335.

forte mittantur de claustro ad claustrum morature ad minus per annum.[1]

By the end of the twelfth century those wishing to become brothers of St. Victor were required to make affirmations which resemble the promises required by the 1236–8 Prémontré statutes.[2] Odo, who was elected abbot of Ste Geneviève after the Victorines were introduced there in 1148, and who died in 1166, wrote in a letter:[3]

In professione igitur nostra quam fecimus, tria, sicut bene nosti, promisimus: castitatem, communionem, obedientiam,

and a twelfth-century manuscript from the priory of St. Nicholas of Regny, in the diocese of Amiens, records that there the formula of profession was:

Ego frater N. . . . stabilitatem corporis mei ecclesiae beati N. promitto . . . et emendationem morum meorum praecipue in castitate, in communione, in obedientia . . .[4]

More conclusively still, the *Consuetudines Ordinis* of Beauvais asserts that the first abbot of St. Quentin, Ivo, who became bishop of Chartres in 1090 and died in 1116,

---

[1] Lefèvre, p. 113.

[2] *Liber Ordinis*, c. xxvii (Martène, iii. 266). Those accepted as novices were required to affirm that they gave themselves to God 'ad serviendum ei in societate et obedientia congregationis hujus, et ad tenendam vitam canonicam secundum regulam B. Augustini, et consuetudines hujus loci'; the abbot required of each of them 'obedientiam Deo et mihi et huic sanctae congregationi, et perseverantiam stabilitatis tuae usque in finem secundum gratiam tibi collatam a Deo et possibilitatem virium tuarum'. When a novice was finally admitted as a brother, he had to make a written profession (c. xxix; Martène, iii. 267–8), but its terms are not given.

[3] Cited by L. Hertling, 'Die Professio der Kleriker und die Entstehung der drei Gelübde', *Zeitschrift für katholische Theologie*, lvi (1932), 171.

[4] Cited by Ch. Dereine, 'Les coutumiers de S.-Quentin de Beauvais et de Springiersbach', *Revue d'histoire ecclésiastique* xliii (1948), 411–42, in n. 5 to p. 436.

Illa tamen quatuor promissa quæ nos in vitæ communis vnitate arctius astringunt et quæ specialiter a nobis in nostra professione primitus exiguntur, id est stabilitatem corporis in ecclesia, obedientiam magistris, vitæ communionem cum fratribus, et præcipue castitatem, districte et immobiliter obseruanda decreuit.[1]

This is essentially the same as, but even more concise than, the formulation of the constitutions of St. Sixtus, and is indeed closer to that of *Ancrene Wisse*; the English author has substituted obedience 'to the bishop or his superior' for obedience 'to the masters' and has dropped 'communal life'—changes appropriate to the situation of anchorites—but he has kept 'chastity' where St. Dominic has 'vivere sine proprio ac etiam continenter'. Though the *Consuetudines Ordinis* survives only in early eighteenth-century copies, one of these (MS. Mazarine 2005, ff. 90–109) is certified, by a note preserved with it (dated 18 November 1713 and signed by a canon of St. Victor) to have been made at the monastery of St. Quentin in Beauvais from a 'very ancient manuscript' (*ex vetustissimo codice MS.*) preserved there.[2] The codification must in fact have been made in the twelfth century, and is certainly earlier than the Lateran Council of

[1] MS. Mazarine 2005, f. 93.
[2] MS. Mazarine 2005, from St. Victor, is a composite of many items copied in the seventeenth and eighteenth centuries, of which the *Consuetudines Ordinis* of St. Quentin, Beauvais, is no. 20. It was originally a separate booklet, with pages numbered from 1 to [39] (last incomplete page unnumbered). The other copy, which I have not seen, is Paris Bibliothèque Ste Geneviève MS. 349, which was used by Dereine (who, though professing to give folio-references, must in fact be giving page-references). This has the *Consuetudines Ordinis* on ff. 1–17ᵛ, followed on ff. 18–31 by *Constitutiones quæ observantur in ecclesia B. M. Magdalenae de Castriduno, ordinis canonicorum regularium divi Augustini*; it is dated by the catalogue 's. xvii–xviii'. Dereine, pp. 433–7, prints the text of the introduction to the Beauvais *Consuetudines* from this manuscript; it appears not to differ significantly from MS. Mazarine 2005, and I suspect that it may be a copy of the latter, with rather more to the page.

1215;[1] it has indeed been dated to the second quarter of the twelfth century,[2] though it must be later than 1136, since it refers to an 'Abbas Radulphus' *bonæ memoriæ* who appears to be abbot Raoul who was elected in 1105 and died in 1136.[3] Even if, therefore, the formulation of the vows was the work of the writer himself and not, as he appears to say, of abbot Ivo, it long antedates both *Ancrene Wisse* and the Constitutions of St. Sixtus. It is very improbable, therefore, that St. Dominic introduced anything new into his regulation, unless in details of wording; he and *Ancrene Wisse* were independently following and modifying twelfth-century Augustinian custumals, and it is indeed possible that they were both influenced by some form of the rule that had already been adapted for women.

The matters discussed above concern, almost exclusively, Part VIII of *Ancrene Wisse*, the practical instructions of the Outer Rule for the life of religion; but there are also apparent similarities between Part I, which concerns the anchoresses' devotions, and both the statutes of Prémontré and the *Liber Ordinis*—with this distinction, that it is in the second and third recensions of the statutes of Prémontré that the regulations concerning devotions are placed, as in *Ancrene Wisse*, at the beginning, whereas the *Liber Ordinis* starts with chapters concerning the officers of the house. In each case the arrangement within the section on devotions

[1] See p. 61, n. 2, above.

[2] Dereine, p. 421, who judges that 'le caractère nettement polémique de l'œuvre l'apparente étroitement avec des ouvrages écrits durant les années 1120–1140'. But see next note.

[3] Dereine, loc. cit., points out that there is a reference (Mazarine MS., f. 104^v) to the prebends owned by the abbey of St. Quentin at the cathedral of St. Pierre, which he says were acquired in 1126; this he takes to be the *terminus post quem*. He also points out the reference to abbot Raoul (Mazarine MS., f. 106), but does not seem to appreciate that its form shows that he was dead.

is to begin with getting up for Matins (*Hwen ȝe earst ariseð
. . .*)[1] and to proceed through the day until its ending (*Hwense
ȝe gað to ower bedd i niht oðer i euen . . .*),[2] but in *Ancrene
Wisse*, in contrast to the other two texts, this is rather a
formal device, for the author in fact has little to say about
the Hours, concerning which the anchoresses have separate
written instructions,[3] and deals almost entirely with private
devotions; he seems to be following a pattern—an obvious
and common one, it is true—which is only partly suitable
for his purposes. Only an expert in medieval liturgical usage
could say whether there are significant detailed resemblances
between the instructions in Part I of *Ancrene Wisse* and
those in the Augustinian ordinals, and distinguish what is
remarkable from what is commonplace. Obviously much is
the ordinary practice of the time and would occur in any
detailed instructions; obviously also much is not, for *Ancrene
Wisse* has impressed those competent to judge by its innovations and modernity. One feature which to a layman seems
distinctive is the author's constant concern with the appropriate posture of the anchoresses during their devotions,
whether and when they should bow or kneel or prostrate
themselves, or sit or stand; and similar directions occur
in the statutes of Prémontré and, perhaps more insistently,
in the *Liber Ordinis* of St. Victor, in the chapters about the
ceremony to be followed in the refectory and at the regular
Hours,[4] where they seem to have impressed Bonnard as
unusual.[5] How significant this is of common origin I am not
able to judge, but I risk drawing attention to one resemblance,
though it is a resemblance with a difference. The Hours

[1] Corpus MS., f. 4b/7 (Morton, p. 14).

[2] Corpus MS., f. 11b/12 (Morton, p. 44).

[3] Corpus MS., f. 6a/2 (Morton, p. 20).

[4] These are chapters xli (*De Refectorio*) and xlii (*De Collatione et
Completorio*) and chapters lxii–lxxi (concerning the Hours, up to Compline); Martène, iii. 273, 280–3.   [5] Bonnard, *Histoire*, i. 71.

recommended to the anchoresses[1] are those of the Little
Office of our Lady, or *Horae Beatae Mariae*, and the
author advises that

ed te an salm ʒe schulen stonden, ʒef ʒe beoð eise, ant ed te oþer
sitten, ant eauer wið *Gloria patri* rungen[2] up ant buhen. Hwa
se mei stonden al on ure Leafdi wurðschipe, stonde o Godes
halue.[3]

[1] Corpus MS., f. 5b/5 ff. (Morton, pp. 18, 20, 22).

[2] The verb *rungen* occurs only in *Ancrene Wisse*, here (Corpus f.
6a/15) and at Corpus f. 79a/12 (Morton, p. 290), in each case followed by
up. Nero (here) and Vernon and Pepys (both times) replace it by forms of
arise; F translates it by *leuer* (16/1) and *drescez vous* (203/28), and S by
seez vus suz (14/24). But the Latin version (109/20)
merely omits *rung up* in translating the equivalent of Corpus f. 79a/12; its
ex(c)erce te ipsam renders the following English phrase *sture þe* (despite
Zettersten, *Studies*, p. 142). The unexplained variants *rueð*, *ruueð*, *runeð*
in *Sawles Warde* (ed. Bennett and Smithers, l. 149) are probably corruptions of *rungeð*; again *up* follows.

As the Corpus infinitive is *rungen* and the imperative sing. is *rung*,
the verb must be either strong (which is improbable, in view of its stem)
or weak class I; in the latter case its *u* must represent OE or ON *y*.
Falk–Torp, *Norwegisch–dänisches etym. Wörterbuch*, s.v. *rangle*, assume
a Gmc. root *ra(n)g*, with gradation-variants, capable of meaning, among
other things, 'to shoot up' (in height), as in ODan. *rangel* 'hoch aufgeschossener Mensch', MLG *range* 'hoch aufgeschossener Junge'. This
root *ra(n)g* they regard as synonymous with Gmc. *ra(n)k*, whence English *rank* adj. (OE *ranc*), which *OED* connects with Danish *rank* and
OIcel. *rakkr* 'erect, upright' and of which it says that 'the root-idea appears
to be that of growing or shooting up'. An OE verb **ryngan* (or ODan.
*rynga), with *i*-mutation of the *u*-grade of the root *rang*, would give the
recorded forms of the Corpus text and the required sense.

The word cannot be a ME formation on the English sb. *rung* (OE
hrung), as posited by Zettersten, loc. cit.; a new ME formation would
belong to class II weak, as this verb plainly does not, and the proposed
etymology does not satisfactorily explain the sense.

[3] Corpus MS., f. 6a/14–16 (Morton, pp. 20, 22). Miss Salu's translation
(p. 9) is unsatisfactory; *rungen up* is 'spring up' rather than the colourless
'stand up', and the last sentence means 'Whoever can stand the whole
time in our Lady's honour, let her stand, in God's name', which has only
a distant resemblance to Miss Salu's rendering.

More detailed instructions for saying our Lady's Matins, with references
to the other Hours, are given before this (Corpus MS., f. 5b/5–6a/1;

This leaves a good deal to discretion; those who can may stand throughout, and it is implied that those who are not well (not *eise*) may sit. But the basic recommendation, to stand for one psalm and sit for the next, is adapted from the rule of the *Liber Ordinis* for the canonical Hours, which the anchoresses themselves do not say; this provides, in chapter lxii, that 'in omnibus Horis regularibus alternatim sedeant fratres', so that in the first psalm half of them sit, and at the beginning of the second 'sedebunt qui prius steterant, et stabunt qui prius sedebant', but 'cum ventum fuerit ad *Gloria*, surgent qui sedebant, et inclinabunt cum aliis, ad *Sicut erat* pariter erigentur'.[1] For the Hours of our Lady, which followed the exacting Hours of the canonical Office, it was the custom at St. Victor to sit for the psalms, as is explained in chapter lxv, 'Qualiter se habeant fratres ad Horas de S. Maria':

Notandum quod horae de Sancta Maria mediocri voce cum cantu dicendae sunt, et in his non inclinatur ad *Gloria patri*. Ad omnes psalmos communiter sedent, cum reinceptione antiphonae surgunt et inclinant donec ad primam lectionem benedictio detur.[2]

In the canonical Hours the brothers who have been sitting *surgent . . . et inclinabunt* at the *Gloria*; in the Hours of our

Morton, pp. 18, 20); they include a direction to bow (or on a feria to prostrate oneself) at a good many points, including *to þe collecte ed eauer euch Tide* (f. 5b/17–18). Similarly the *Liber Ordinis* says that the brothers of St. Victor 'ad *Oremus* inclinant ad chorum, donec suffragia finiantur' (Martène, iii. 282).

[1] Martène, iii. 280. With the last part of this compare the instruction in *Ancrene Wisse* at a slightly earlier point (Corpus MS., f. 5b/12–14; Morton, p. 20): *ant falleð to þe eorðe, ȝef hit is wercdei, wið* Gloria patri (*oðer buheð duneward, ȝef hit* [is] *hali dei*) *aþet* Sicut erat.

[2] Martène, iii. 282. But the text given above is that of MS. Ste Gen. 1637 (supported by MS. Ste Gen. 1636). Martène's differs (i) by reading *et cum cantu*, transposed to follow *sunt*, (ii) by reading *incoeptione* for *reinceptione*.

Lady, in which they all sit together, they *surgunt et inclinant* at the beginning of the antiphon; and the anchoresses, saying their Hours of our Lady as the brothers of St. Victor say the canonical Hours, are always, at *Gloria patri*, to *rungen up ant buhen*. If liturgy is a matter for experts, verbal parallels are for all to observe.[1]

Two other points concerning Part I must be discussed, since they have been raised by Fr. McNabb.[2] The first is also about the Hours of our Lady. Immediately after the sentences just quoted, *Ancrene Wisse* continues:

Ed alle þe seoue Tiden singeð *Pater noster* ant *Aue Maria* ba biuoren ant efter.[3]

This, McNabb asserted, was a practice prescribed by 'no rule but the Dominican'; he claimed that in the thirteenth century the Dominican order was unique in this respect, citing the story of the Blessed Gonsalvo (1187–1259), who was commanded by our Lady 'to enter the order in which her Office began and ended with the *Ave Maria*', which turned out to be the Dominican.[4] This edifying tale of course proves that whoever made it up believed that the practice was confined to the Dominicans; but whether blessed or not, he must have been wrong. For the practice is described in *Ancrene Wisse*, which cannot be a Dominican work, and was obviously therefore not confined to the Dominicans; in this as in other matters their usage must have been derived from the Augustinian congregations from which they sprang, and in which it was a regular practice to say the Hours

[1] McNabb, who to do him justice did not often miss points, claimed that the passage cited from *Ancrene Wisse* gives 'the very rubrics still obtaining in the Dominican liturgy' (*MLR*, xi. 3). But in this instance the documentary evidence is clear that the Victorines had anticipated the Dominicans and that *Ancrene Wisse* derives from the *Liber Ordinis*.

[2] *Archivum Fr. Praed.*, iv. 55–6.

[3] Corpus MS., f. 6a/17–18 (Morton, p. 22).

[4] McNabb cites the Bollandist *Acta Sanctorum*, Jan. 10.

of our Lady after the canonical Hours.[1] The fact that in the immediately preceding sentences *Ancrene Wisse* has directly translated a phrase of the *Liber Ordinis* of St. Victor is a clear indication of the direction in which to look.

McNabb also pointed out that another practice recommended in *Ancrene Wisse*, the inclusion, in private devotions in honour of the Five Joys, of five 'psalms' (the first being the *Magnificat*) whose initial letters make up the name *Maria*,[2] was used by Jordan of Saxony, who succeeded St. Dominic as Master General of the Dominican order in 1221 and who died in 1239.[3] But Jordan is even less likely to have taught the custom to the author of *Ancrene Wisse* than to have learnt it from him; they were contemporaries, and Jordan may have been the younger. It was always probable that they had both learnt the practice from some other source, and this has been confirmed by C. H. Talbot,[4] who cites as evidence a miracle-story related in the *Speculum Historiale* (completed about 1250) by the Dominican Vincent of Beauvais. It concerns Benedictines, an unnamed archbishop of Canterbury, and a bishop of Arras who had formerly been abbot of Cîteaux; the latter is identifiable as Peter, consecrated bishop of Arras in November 1184, who died on

---

[1] The first recension (1131–4) of the statutes of Prémontré devotes a special section to the Hours of St. Mary (van Waefelghem, pp. 66–7), which shows the importance that they had even at this early date, and there are frequent references to them in the *Liber Ordinarius* of Prémontré (ed. van Waefelghem; see the Index, s. *Horae S. Mariae*, p. 402). The *Liber Ordinis* of St. Victor also has a special chapter about them (c. lxv), and there are other references which show that they were regularly said after the canonical hours except on certain days (cf. Martène, iii. 274 and 279, in chapters xliii and lvii).

[2] Corpus MS., ff. 9a/27–10b/22, especially 10b/16–17 (Morton, pp. 38, 40, 42); Salu, p. 17 n.

[3] McNabb cites Gerard de Frachet, *Vitae Patrum*, ed. Reichart (Louvain, 1896), p. 118.

[4] 'Some Notes on the Dating of the *Ancrene Riwle*', *Neophilologus*, xl (1956), 42–3.

19 December 1203, so that the event recounted belongs to the years between those dates. The story, Talbot rightly argues, shows that the *Maria* devotion was known earlier than McNabb thought, and was evidently used in the Latin kingdom of Jerusalem, in southern Italy, and in Northern France before it was brought to England.

In all these matters of semi-liturgical and private devotions, as in the questions of monastic routine that we considered above, *Ancrene Wisse*, though a vernacular work, is an independent authority of primary importance, as Dom Gerard Sitwell recognized;[1] its prescriptions, and the early usages and regulations of the Dominicans, are concurrent testimony to the practices of the Augustinian congregations in the first two decades of the thirteenth century.

The evidence considered in this chapter makes it certain that the author of *Ancrene Wisse* had a good knowledge of some form of the statutes of Prémontré, probably a lost version intermediate between the second (*c.* 1174) and the third (1236–8) of those that survive, since when they differ he agrees exclusively with neither.[2] Though he is independent and original and adds a great deal of his own, the statutes strongly influenced the topics with which he dealt in the Outer Rule, especially in Part VIII, and often determined in detail what he said (even when he disagreed with them) and how he said it, and also to some extent affected the formal arrangement of his work. But it does not follow that he was himself a Premonstratensian. The statutes of Prémontré were widely influential in others of the independent Augustinian congregations, as the Dominican

[1] See his Introduction and Appendix to Salu's translation.
[2] See p. 86, n. 2, and p. 87, n. 7, above, for agreements of *Ancrene Wisse* (or in the latter case the Corpus revision) with the 1236–8 recension against that of *c.* 1174.

Constitutions clearly testify;[1] and it is important to recall
that Martène's text of the second recension was taken from a
manuscript of St. Victor which he dated about 1200,[2] a
sufficient proof that the Prémontré statutes circulated and
were studied in Victorine houses. Moreover, *Ancrene Wisse*
has agreements with the Dominican *Constitutions*—on
underclothing, *minutio*, communion and *rasurae*, and the
'Office of the Paternosters'[3]—which are not shared, or not
so closely shared, by any of the recensions of the Prémontré
statutes and may be evidence of a development of the
common tradition in which Prémontré itself did not take
part.[4] The parallels with St. Dominic's constitutions of St.
Sixtus not only confirm this impression, but may also suggest
the previous existence of some form of Premonstratensian
rule adapted for women. There are other resemblances to the
Liber Ordinis of St. Victor—in the rules for clothing, the
entertainment of those who had been bled, silence on certain
days (though the days are different), the general principle
governing the number of *rasurae* or communions in the
year, and the conduct of devotions;[5] and if these are for the
most part not very particular, there are two striking phrasal
agreements—in the rules for silence[6] and in the directions

---

[1] See also Heijman, *Anal. Praemon.*, iv. 226–41, in the section 'Prémontré, St. Viktor, und Arrouaise'. He holds that the statutes of Prémontré and the *Liber Ordinis* derive independently from their Cistercian
source.

[2] Martène, iii. 251 ('ex codice Victorino ab annis circiter quingentis
conscripto') and iii. 321 ('ex ms. bibliothecae S. Victoris'). MS. Bib. Nat.
lat. 14762, to which Balme and Lelaidier refer for the text of the statutes
and which they date to the twelfth century (*Cartulaire*, ii. 427, n. 2),
would also seem, from its serial number, to belong to the St. Victor
collection.

[3] See p. 29 and n. 1; p. 35; pp. 62–6 and 68–72; and pp. 78–84, above.

[4] But the rule about four, not five, *minutiones* a year may be an earlier
form of the regulation than that in the 1236–8 Prémontré statutes and in
the *Liber Ordinis*, not a divergence.

[5] See p. 29, n. 2; pp. 34–6; pp. 38–9; pp. 70–2; and pp. 104–7, above.

[6] See pp. 38–9, above.

for saying the Hours[1]—which seem to be clear evidence of the dependence of *Ancrene Wisse* on the *Liber Ordinis*. There are signs also of the influence, direct or indirect, of the *Consuetudines Ordinis* of Beauvais. Obviously the author, when called on to compile a rule for his 'dear sisters', did not rely on a single source but made a careful study of various custumals of his order.

There are in fact good reasons why the author of *Ancrene Wisse* cannot have been a Premonstratensian.[2] Appended to Martène's text of the second recension of the statutes are a number of additional regulations, one of which is the resolution of an undated General Chapter that 'henceforth we shall receive no sister' and that anyone who transgresses this statute shall be deprived of his abbacy 'without mercy'. As this is not embodied in the main statutes, one might think that it was later than their revision; but the absence of regulations concerning women from the second recension has been explained as a consequence of the ban on their admission.[3] Certainly the decree cannot be much later than the date of the recension (*c.* 1174), since a bull of Innocent III, of 11 May 1198, addressed to the Premonstratensians, recounts that 'some time ago' (*olim*) they had decided in General Chapter, and had since very often (*sepius*) repeated, under threat of severe penalty, that henceforth no woman should be received as a sister or lay-sister, especially because they had suffered from time to time grave inconveniences from the practice.[4] The prohibition is repeated

[1] See pp. 105–7, above.

[2] I refer here to reasons that appear from the texts. There is a conclusive reason of another sort, that the nearest Premonstratensian house to the area in which *Ancrene Wisse* was written (see Chapter III, below) was Halesowen in North Worcestershire, over 40 miles from the Welsh border, which is far too remote.

[3] See p. 91, n. 2, above.

[4] 'Olim in communi capitulo statuistis, et postmodum sub interminatione gravis pene sepius innovastis, ut nullam de cetero teneamini in

in the statutes of 1236–8, with the qualification 'nisi in locis illis qui sunt ab antiquo recipiendis cantantibus sororibus in perpetuum deputata',[1] i.e. in separate and long-established nunneries. A Premonstratensian, in the face of this reiterated ban, would be most unlikely to assist in the foundation of a new community of women religious in the late twelfth or early thirteenth century, and to go so far as to write a Rule for them. Again, though the first recension of the Prémontré statutes had prescribed a mixture of black and white clothing for the sisters,[2] that of 1236–8 lays down that

vestimenta quoque sororum nostrarum sint alba, nisi in remotis partibus, in quibus ex antiqua consuetudine alium habitum habuerunt, de quibus sustinetur, donec aliter processu temporis, prout melius fuerit, ordinetur.[3]

Though this looks like a new regulation (since it provides that in 'remote regions, in which, by ancient custom, the sisters have had another habit', the change may be put off until, in the course of time, better arrangements may be made), it probably is not; for the 1220 constitutions of St. Sixtus, here as elsewhere evidently following the regulations of Prémontré, already provide that:

vestes autem sint albe quibus utemini et non sint nimis subtiles vel etiam delicate, ne sit notabilis vester habitus . . .[4]

A member of an order which was insisting that its sisters should, like its brothers, wear white henceforth, is unlikely to have expressed, in a book first written about the same time as the St. Sixtus constitutions, the indifference whether the anchoresses' clothes should be black or white that the author of *Ancrene Wisse* displays so prominently in his Preface and

sororem recipere vel conversam, presertim cum ex hoc aliquando incommoda fueritis multa perpessi' (Lefèvre, *Statuts*, p. 114 n., citing J. Le Paige, *Bibliotheca Praemonstratensis Ordinis* (1633), pp. 644–5).

[1] Lefèvre, p. 114. [2] See pp. 90–1, above.
[3] Lefèvre, p. 113. [4] Balme and Lelaidier, ii. 433.

repeats in Part VIII.[1] And the clothes which, again in the Preface, he takes as characteristic of a male religious[2] are not those of the 'white' Premonstratensians, but of the Victorines and the other regular canons—and perhaps also, in his last phrase, those of the Cistercians—presumably because these were the habits to be seen in the area in which he was writing.

To determine what this area was we must turn to a different sort of evidence and another line of inquiry; but we may do so in the belief not merely that the author was an Augustinian, but also that he belonged to one of the independent congregations, to an 'order' strongly influenced by or interested in the statutes of Prémontré but not itself Premonstratensian. This leaves various possibilities open, but one, suggested by his knowledge of the *Liber Ordinis*, must obviously be that he was a member of the congregation of St. Victor.

[1] He might almost be reacting against a contemporary tendency towards greater uniformity and exclusiveness. It is to be remembered that Part VIII was heavily revised both in the Cleopatra MS. (by scribe B, i.e. the author) and in the Corpus version, yet the remark that it does not matter whether the anchoress's clothing is white or black is left untouched.   [2] See pp. 30–2, above.

III

ANCRENE WISSE AND
WIGMORE ABBEY

No investigation of the origins of *Ancrene Wisse* can omit to consider the evidence of its language, or more precisely of that of the Corpus MS., the importance of which was demonstrated by Professor Tolkien in a fundamental study.[1] The outlines of his argument are well known. The Corpus MS. of *Ancrene Wisse* and MS. Bodley 34 of the *Katherine*-group, though written by different scribes, are indistinguishable in dialect; both are in a single form of literary Middle English, with a consistent phonological and grammatical structure and a highly individual but well-observed traditional orthography. The two scribes must have been trained in the same school. But though both manuscripts are copies, not autographs, the most meticulous inspection has failed to reveal internal inconsistencies in the language of the texts, other than in minor details, which are mostly to be explained by the attempt to maintain a traditional spelling which was no longer fully in accord with a changing pronunciation; there is no sign of the dialectal admixture which is so familiar a feature of Middle English documents when a scribe who spoke (or had been trained to write) one dialect copied a text originally written in another. Unless, therefore, we are willing to postulate faultless and consistent translation from one dialect to another not only in the major and obvious features which might well be dealt with by a 'rule-book' in a

[1] J. R. R. Tolkien, '*Ancrene Wisse* and *Hali Meiðhad*', *Essays and tudies*, xiv (1929), 104–26.

well-conducted and self-conscious scriptorium,[1] but also in all the lesser details which are significant to a trained modern philologist but would be apt to escape the attention of a scribe whose duty was merely to produce, in reasonable time, a readable copy of his text, we must conclude, from the uniformity of the language of these two manuscripts, that the author (or much more probably the authors) of the works wrote the same dialect as the two scribes.[2] This was certainly a West Midland dialect, as its main features show; more particularly it was almost directly descended from the Mercian dialect of the Old English gloss to the Vespasian Psalter (which itself has not been precisely located) and there are resemblances to the language of the Worcester version of the Old English Chronicle. The Middle English dialect of the two manuscripts, which Tolkien called 'the AB language',[3] has affinities with the Worcestershire dialect of Laʒamon and with the language of the Westerly lyric. It was evidently a dialect of the Welsh Marches, for its vocabulary includes three distinctive words of Welsh origin: *cader* 'cradle' in *Ancrene Wisse* and *Hali Meiðhad*;[4] *genow* 'mouth' in *Ste Margarete*;[5] and *keis* 'satellites,

---

[1] There is clear evidence that some scribes set out to change regularly certain obvious features of texts which they were copying, and that they even achieved a fair measure of success (cf. Anne Hudson, 'Tradition and Innovation in some Middle English Manuscripts', *RES* (N.S.), xvii (1966), 359–72); but the case under consideration here goes far beyond this.

[2] If 'scribe B' of the Cleopatra MS. was not the author (though I believe he was), then we must add a third scribe, for he also wrote the same dialect, though his use of it has variations in detail; in particular his use of *ea* as a symbol for a long vowel was more restricted.

[3] From the sigla conventionally used for the two manuscripts in which the dialect is found, Corpus Christi College Cambridge 402 (A) and Bodley 34 (B).

[4] *A.W.*, Corpus MS., f. 102b/3 (Morton, p. 378); *H.M.*, ed. A. F. Colborn, ll. 537 and 553 (cf. note on p. 119).

[5] ed. Mack, 22/1; for the etymology, see S. T. R. O. d'Ardenne, *Ste Iuliene*, p. 179.

henchmen' in *Sawles Warde*.[1] The vocabulary also includes a considerable Scandinavian element, but this is not inconsistent with a location in the West Midlands, where Cnut settled a large proportion of his disbanded army.[2] In some respects the forms taken by these words adopted from Norse are distinctively western, not northern or eastern; they have had a phonological history different from that of the same words in the dialects of the Danelaw, and appear in forms which a philologist, knowing their etymologies, can explain, but which no Middle English scribe could have invented if he had been 'translating' into West Midland spellings a text originally written in the east or the north.

The location of the dialect is made more precise by the history of the two manuscripts. Before 1300 the Corpus MS. was given to Wigmore Abbey by John Purcell at the instance of Walter de Ludlow senior, then precentor of Wigmore, who was one of the principal canons in 1299 and was elected abbot in 1302 but refused office. The Purcells were a South Shropshire family.[3] MS. Bodley 34 has on its margins a

---

[1] Joy Russell Smith, '*Keis* in *Sawles Warde*', *Medium Ævum*, xxii (1953), 104–10. Welsh influence may also perhaps be involved in the case of the noun *leohe*, which in *Ste Katerine* (ed. Einenkel), l. 1827, means 'den, lair' and in *Ancrene Wisse* (Corpus MS.), f. 99b/18, means 'bedding' (*stratu* Latin version, *gisir* Trinity French version), so that *hearde leohe* is practically synonymous with the modern naval 'hard lying'. The word has been explained as a blend of OE *hleo(w)* neut. 'shelter, refuge, etc.' and ON *lega* fem. 'lying, place of rest', also 'lair' (cf. Falk–Torp, s.v. *leie*); so by Shepherd, p. 43, and Zettersten, p. 256. This is formally and semantically satisfactory; but it is worth noting that medieval Welsh had a noun *llech* fem. 'covert' (cf. mod. Welsh *llechfa* 'covert, lair'), related to the verb *llechu* 'lurk, shelter, hide' and the nouns *llawch* 'protection' and *lloches* 'shelter, refuge, lair'.

[2] See the introduction to A. Mawer and F. M. Stenton, *The Place-Names of Worcestershire* (E.P.N.S. iv, 1927), pp. xxiii–xxiv, and Stenton, *Anglo-Saxon England* (Oxford, 1943), pp. 407–8. See further pp. 118–21, below.

[3] See N. R. Ker's introduction to J. R. R. Tolkien's edition of the Corpus MS. (E.E.T.S. 249, 1962), pp. xvii–xviii. A John Purcell held

number of scribblings, perhaps pen-trials made in a lawyer's office, of the mid sixteenth century (probably between 1547 and 1562) which record the names of various persons, some of them identifiable as members of known Herefordshire families of the period.[1] In view of the seats of the families, it is probable that the manuscript was then in central or eastern Herefordshire, perhaps in Hereford itself;[2] it is likely to have come from a religious house in the county at the dissolution of the monasteries. As it can hardly be accident that two manuscripts written in a pure West Midland dialect and each containing distinctive words from Welsh have connections with Herefordshire, it is now generally accepted that the 'AB language' is a literary form of Middle English developed either in northern Herefordshire or southern Shropshire.[3] A location in southern Herefordshire

lands at Norbury, near Bishop's Castle, and at Diddlebury, near Ludlow, and occurs in records between 1272, when he was an infant, and 1306 (as was pointed out by Miss V. Bonnell).

[1] See Ker's introduction to the facsimile of MS. Bodley 34 (E.E.T.S. 247, 1960), pp. xiii–xiv. It was Miss H. E. Allen ('The Localization of MS. Bodley 34', *MLR*, xxviii (1933), 485–7) who first pointed out that the scribblings in the manuscript which connect it with Herefordshire were to be dated to the sixteenth century, and not to the fourteenth or fifteenth, as had previously been believed; but Mr. Ker's study is much more detailed and exact.

[2] To the seats of the families identified by Ker (p. xiv) there is to be added Much Cowarne, where William Ewyne (or Gwyne) lived. Much Cowarne is 5½ miles SW. of Bromyard, and Tedstone Delamere is 3½ miles NE. of Bromyard, which itself is 13 miles NE. by N. of Hereford; Castle Frome is 10 miles NE. of Hereford; Ledbury is 13 miles É. of Hereford, and Eastnor is 1½ miles SE. of Ledbury. It seems certain that the scribblings were made by someone living in the Hereford–Ledbury–Bromyard triangle.

[3] One other distinctive feature of the vocabulary supports such a localization: the word *dingle* used in *Sawles Warde* in the phrase *deopre þen eni sea-dingle* (ed. Bennett and Smithers, *Early Middle English Verse and Prose*, no. xix, ll. 333–4). *Dingle* does not recur in literary use until Drayton in 1630, though it is fairly widespread in dialectal use (Wright, *EDD*, records it for Northern dialects, the West Midlands—Worcestershire, Herefordshire, and Gloucestershire—and Suffolk), and in West

would on linguistic grounds be less probable; and the districts of Archenfield and Ewias, which together comprise most of the county south of Hereford and west of the Wye, had still been predominantly Welsh in population and culture at the time of the Domesday survey.[1]

The linguistic argument is reinforced by an analysis of the names of the men who are recorded in Domesday Book as having held lands in Herefordshire and Shropshire before the Conquest, *tempore Regis Edwardi*, i.e. in 1066. The majority have English names, as one would expect, though in Herefordshire there were already some Normans (one of whom had quite extensive holdings), which may help to explain the surprisingly large proportion of French words in *Ancrene Wisse*, and two or three Welshmen even in 'English' districts; at the time of the Domesday survey itself Grifin son of 'Mariadoc rex' held valuable lands which had been granted to his father by William fitz Osbern, earl of Hereford, in four different hundreds.[2] But the largest non-English element, before the Conquest, consisted of landowners with Danish names. In the two counties there occur 45 distinct names of certain or probable Danish origin, belonging perhaps to an even greater number of men.[3] Thirteen of

Midland place-names, in which it is found from the thirteenth century (cf. A. H. Smith, *English Place-Name Elements*, i. 133); one of the areas in which it occurs is northern Herefordshire and southern Shropshire. The Ordnance Survey's 1:25,000 map shows eight named 'dingles' within a radius of 7 miles from Wigmore (from W. through N. to ENE.).

[1] See C. W. Atkin's chapter (c. ii) on Herefordshire in *The Domesday Geography of Midland England*, ed. C. H. Darby and I. B. Terrett (Cambridge, 1954), *passim* (and especially pp. 109–10).

[2] This 'Grifin' was Gruffydd, son of Maredudd ab Owain ab Edwin, king of Deheubarth, who had been an exile in England after his father's death in 1072, living on the Herefordshire manors which William fitz Osbern, earl of Hereford, had granted to his father (J. E. Lloyd, *A History of Wales*, ii. 376, 398). He was killed in 1091 after being recalled to Wales by an offer of his father's crown.

[3] I exclude from the count (i) Earl Harold Godwinson, who held

these names occur in both counties, seven only in Herefordshire, 25 only in Shropshire; and their bearers held lands at 43 different named places in (modern) Herefordshire, at 70 in (modern) Shropshire.[1] Most of these places are identifiable, and when they are plotted on a map (see p. 120) it is clear that they extend from the extreme south-east of Herefordshire to the north-east of Shropshire. But most of them lie to the east of a line drawn through Hereford and Shrewsbury; there are only a couple of places (one now unidentifiable) in north-west Shropshire, and none in southern Herefordshire west of the Wye. In Herefordshire there are a fair number in the sector contained between lines drawn north and west through Hereford; similarly in Shropshire in the sector contained by lines drawn south and west through Shrewsbury. This means that it is only north of Hereford and south of Shrewsbury that Danish landholdings are found towards the western sides of the counties; and in

extensive lands in Herefordshire; (ii) one or two names which could be either OE or ON, e.g. Oslac, which may be either OE *Oslac* or ON *Áslakr*; (iii) the forms *Hunni* and *Huni*, which, despite their resemblance to ON *Húni*, von Feilitzen takes to be variants of the OE name **Hun(n)ing* —probably rightly, as they occur beside the forms *Huning*, *Huninc*, *Hunnic*, and *Hunnit(h)*, which are evidently all variants of the name of a single major landowner.

Some of the Scandinavian names persisted in use into the thirteenth century, when they occur, e.g., in documents preserved in the archives of Hereford Cathedral.

[1] For details, see Appendix I (pp. 369–79). I omit from the Shropshire total the twenty-two named manors in an extensive area north and south of the site of Montgomery Castle (most of them now in Montgomeryshire) over which Azor (a Dane), Oslac (perhaps a Dane), and Sewar held hunting rights. They were all waste in 1066. See Domesday Book, f. 254.

I include in the Herefordshire total places which are now in Herefordshire but at the time of the Domesday Survey were in Shropshire, and I exclude Old Radnor, now in Radnorshire. In the Shropshire total I include Quatt, at the time of the survey in Stoneleigh Hundred, Warwickshire, and exclude Tyrley, now in Staffordshire. But all the last three are marked on the map on p. 120.

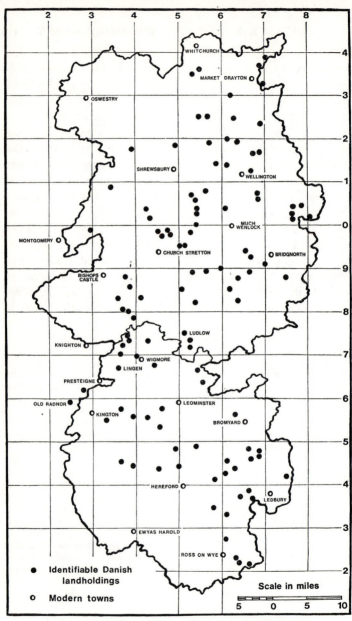

HEREFORDSHIRE AND SHROPSHIRE
Danish Landholdings in 1066

particular it is only in south-west Shropshire and the extreme north-west of modern Herefordshire that any concentration of Danish landholdings is found in the near vicinity of the Welsh border. It is apparent that the local dialects might be markedly influenced by Scandinavian vocabulary almost anywhere in Herefordshire or Shropshire except in the south-west of the former and the north-west of the latter; but on the evidence of the landholdings the area in which one might most reasonably expect to find a strong Scandinavian influence combined with a much slighter but significant Welsh influence would be north-west of Hereford and south-west of Shrewsbury, and more particularly in the extreme north-west of Herefordshire and in south-western Shropshire, on either side of the modern boundary between the two counties.

Tolkien's general argument has implications not only for the localization of the dialect. The texts are written in a consistent literary language with a traditional, though in some ways idiosyncratic, system of spelling; and this spelling-system is a self-conscious one, often directed, even in minor details, to deliberate ends.[1] 'Scribe B', in his corrections to the Cleopatra MS. (itself probably copied from an exemplar in the 'AB language', but by a scribe whose own dialect was somewhat different and who used different spelling-conventions), often shows a careful regard for niceties of spelling. The men who wrote and copied this language did not do so unthinkingly, but had been well trained in its use. We know of at least three such men living between (roughly) 1215 and 1230:[2] the author of *Ancrene Wisse* and the scribes

---

[1] e.g., the distinctions between *godd* 'God' and *god* 'good', and between *oþer* adj. 'other, second' and *oðer* conj. 'or'.

[2] *Ancrene Wisse* is to be dated probably between 1215 and 1222 and was revised about 1228; the Corpus MS. was written probably about 1230, almost certainly copied from the author's holograph, as revised; MS. Bodley 34 is dated by N. R. Ker, in his introduction to the

of the Corpus and Bodleian MSS.[1] But if one widens the chronological range a little, and brings in the authors (perhaps three, and almost certainly more than one) of the *Katherine*-group, and the scribes of the lost intermediate manuscripts in the 'AB language' which must be assumed in the stemmas of the several works of the *Katherine*-group and of *Ancrene Wisse*, one must reckon with at least half a dozen men, and probably more, who were capable of authorship or of acting as scribes in the forty-odd years between about 1190 and 1230. We must therefore assume a centre of literary culture of some size, since not all the members of a religious community would be fit to be trained and used as scribes or be capable of authorship, and also of some age, since it would require time to realize the need for a common literary form of the vernacular, to evolve it, and to train the scribes. Judging merely from the language in which the works are written, we must posit a centre of scholarship (for so formalized and controlled a language can have been developed only by scholarly men) neither small nor newly founded; and if we add consideration of the content of the works, we must assume also that this centre had a good library, probably including English books that preserved at least part of the Old English literary tradition, and that, despite its location in the Welsh Marches, it was in touch with the main literary and cultural movements of the later twelfth and early thirteenth centuries.

A question which bears on the more precise localization of the centre in which the 'AB language' was used is the

facsimile (E.E.T.S. 247, p. x), 'probably in the first quarter of the thirteenth century' (but see further p. 124, below), and the works which it contains, doubtless written at various times, may be dated to the end of the twelfth or the beginning of the thirteenth century (see pp. 163–6, below).

[1] To these one should indeed add the corrector of *Ste Margarete* in MS. Bodley 34, who, though he writes little, uses AB forms.

date at which its orthographical system was evolved. In theory it might have been developed at one centre and transferred to another, but this seems improbable, for it is in some respects (notably in its use of *h*) very unusual and open to criticism, and even scribes who spoke closely related dialects, such as the main scribe of the Cleopatra MS., refused to follow it in these details. It can have evolved only within a restricted geographical area, and would be transferable only within that area; and it is not likely to have been transferred at all except to a centre that was dependent on, and near neighbour to, the one at which it was chiefly practised. To date its evolution is not easy. But its central feature, from the phonologist's point of view, is that it was clearly designed for a language in which there were three short vowel-phonemes expressed by the symbols *e*, *ea*, and *a*; of these, *ea* represented a sound derived from both OE *ǽ* and OE *ĕa*, which in this dialect were kept separate from OE *ĕ* on the one hand and OE *ă* on the other. As *ea* was also used, by the Corpus and Bodleian scribes, for OF *ę* (made short in English) in e.g. *leattres*, *deattes* 'debts', etc., it is probable (unless there has been sound-substitution) that in their speech the short *ea*-phoneme was realized as open /ɛ/,[1] and certain that, when the system was evolved, the short *e*-phoneme was still close /e/.[2] But though the *e/ea* distinction in short vowels is mostly preserved,[3] the

---

[1] Though originally it would have been /æ/, which in closely related dialects (e.g. that of the main scribe of the Cleopatra MS. of *Ancrene Wisse* and of the scribes of the Royal MS. of the *Katherine*-group) later became /a/, identical with OE *ă*. In the 'AB language' itself, raising to /ɛ/ is an assumption which is required (apart from the use of *ea* in words containing OF *ę*) to explain the tendency to identify *e* and *ea*, not *ea* and *a*.

[2] Because otherwise OF *ę*, made short in English, would have been identified with the reflex of OE *ĕ*, as it normally was in ME.

[3] Scribe B of the Cleopatra MS. also observes the distinction, though his usage differs in detail; he seems to represent a somewhat older stage of the development than the Corpus and Bodleian scribes. See the

Corpus and Bodleian scribes sometimes interchange the spellings, using *ea* where by etymology *e* should occur, or *vice versa*, and they do so often enough to show—it is generally agreed—that in their speech the sounds represented by the two symbols had become identical. This happens, however, only in a small minority of instances; for the most part they retain an orthographical distinction between two sounds that had formerly been different but were so no longer. But in the conditions of Middle English, with its spelling-system subject to constant modifications between about 1150 and 1350 because of the pressure of Old French, it is inconceivable that a spelling-distinction peculiar to an isolated West Midland dialect, and receiving no support from general Middle English orthographical practice, should have maintained itself for more than a generation after it had ceased to correspond to living pronunciation, however well-trained the scribes using it were. MS. C.C.C.C. 402 is to be dated *c.* 1230, and certainly was not written before 1224; MS. Bodley 34 is dated, on palaeographical grounds, to the first quarter of the thirteenth century, and on linguistic grounds cannot be separated by more than a few years from the Corpus MS.; it is unlikely to be earlier than 1220.[1] But the spelling-system was not newly developed when the scribes were working, since it expresses an *e/ea* distinction which had evidently ceased to correspond to their pronunciation; it is likely therefore to antedate 1200. On the other hand it is most unlikely to have been

introduction to my edition of the Cleopatra MS. (E.E.T.S. 267, 1972), pp. cxxxi–iii.

[1] Cf. Miss Mack, *Ste Margarete*, p. xx, who says: 'No clear distinction in date can be made between the two MSS. [i.e. Bodley and Royal] either on linguistic or palæographical grounds, and they are usually assigned to *c.* 1230.' This is not strictly true of the Bodleian MS., which on palaeographical grounds has been dated either *c.* 1210 (so Hall and Miss d'Ardenne), or as by Ker.

developed before 1150, and is probably to be dated after 1170. It cannot have developed too early, since we have to allow for a general reorganization of the late Old English system; for a good deal of Old French influence, including the complete displacement of *y* by *u* as the symbol for the short and long vowel-phonemes /y/ and /y:/; for the phonetic identification of OE *ĕa* with OE *ǽ* and the further development of the resulting /æ/ (in free position to /ɛ/, in special circumstances to /a/); and for the complete rejection of the letter *æ* from the system and its replacement by the digraph *ea*. On the other hand it cannot have developed too late, even when one takes into account the probable phonetic conservatism of the dialect: the system allows for a three-fold distinction of short /e/, /ɛ/ < /æ/, and /a/ which is otherwise unknown in Middle English, and which depends on the preservation of close /e/ for OE *ĕ*, though this sound normally became open /ɛ/ during the twelfth century and was certainly /ɛ/ before lengthening in open syllables occurred (during the first half of the thirteenth century); it keeps *a* as the spelling for OE *ā*, and in the word *matin* 'to check-mate' it must identify OF or medieval Latin *a* with OE *ā*, which implies that the latter had not been significantly rounded at the time that the word was adopted into the dialect; its idiosyncratic use of *h* to represent, *inter alia*, the voiced back palatal spirant [ɣ] is based on and extends late OE scribal practice and contrasts sharply with normal thirteenth-century (even early thirteenth-century) usage; and it commonly preserves the OE use of 'silent' *e* between (front) *c*, *sc*, and *g* and a following back vowel, even though these ambiguous OE consonant-letters had in fact been replaced by the unambiguous ME symbols *ch*, *sch*, and ʒ— another remarkable orthographic conservatism, but one also found in the Cleopatra MS. It seems impossible that the spelling-system, as displayed in the Corpus and Bodleian

MSS., could have been worked out before 1150 or after 1200,[1] and the likeliest date for its evolution is the last quarter of the twelfth century.

What is required, then, is a religious centre of some size and culture which had evolved a literary form of the vernacular and a distinctive and self-conscious orthography by 1200 at the latest. It could hardly be a religious house newly founded in 1200; on the other hand, as the spelling-system is unlikely to have been worked out before 1150 and is probably to be dated at least twenty-five years later, it is not necessary to posit a house founded much before 1150. But in fact the choice is limited; in the area in which the 'AB language' must be located religious houses were not numerous, as anyone can see who consults the Ordnance Survey's map of *Monastic Britain*, South Sheet, and discovers how few sites are marked between Hereford to the south and Shrewsbury to the north. Even the small number of sites marked exaggerates the number of houses, for some are markings of successive sites of a single house; those at Shobdon and Aymestrey are earlier locations of Wigmore Abbey, and that at Snead is an earlier location of Chirbury Priory. Others are markings of houses that did not exist at the time when *Ancrene Wisse* was written; thus at Ludlow there are shown houses of Austin and Carmelite friars, but neither of these orders had yet appeared in England and both houses were founded later than 1250. The map is to

---

[1] This is not to say that all the detailed spellings of the two manuscripts were worked out before 1200; I am discussing the evolution of the system, not its application by the two scribes. Thus the lowering of /e/ and /e:/ before *r* to /ɛ/ and /ɛ:/, shown by the scribes' use of *ear* for OE (Mercian) *ĕr*, is almost certainly a more recent feature than the spelling-system itself; scribe B of the Cleopatra MS. does not show it. On the other hand it must be earlier than the tendency towards a general identification of /e/ and /ɛ/, of which the Corpus and Bodleian scribes give less frequent evidence.

be read in conjunction with D. Knowles and R. Neville Hadcock, *Medieval Religious Houses: England and Wales* (London, 1953); it is indeed based on Mr. Hadcock's researches.

We have already seen in Chapter I that it is unlikely that the author of *Ancrene Wisse* was a monk, and this conclusion is reinforced by a consideration of the monastic houses between Hereford and Shrewsbury.[1] Of the Benedictine houses, the priory of Leominster, between Hereford and Ludlow, was a cell of Reading Abbey, and though well endowed was of no great size or importance (in 1283 it had only nine monks);[2] its supposed connection with the well-known MS. Harley 2253, a great collection of Middle English lyrics and other vernacular works, has now been disproved.[3] Livers Ocle, north-east of Hereford, was an alien cell for one or two monks, dependent on Lyre;[4] Monkland, south-west of Leominster, was an alien cell for two or three monks, dependent on Conches;[5] Titley, west of Leominster and near the Welsh border, was another alien cell, dependent on Tiron, and 'appears to have been very small';[6] and Kinsham, a little to the north-east of Titley, also seems to have been an alien priory, about which, apparently, nothing else is known.[7] Bromfield, north-west of Ludlow, was even smaller than Leominster (in 1535 it had just over one-sixth of Leominster's income); from 1155 it was a priory dependent on Gloucester.[8] Clifford, west-north-west of Hereford on the Welsh border, was in

[1] For those of Hereford and Shrewsbury themselves, see pp. 134–5, below.
[2] Knowles, *The Religious Orders in England*, i. 99–100; Knowles and Hadcock, *Medieval Religious Houses*, p. 69.
[3] See N. R. Ker's introduction to the facsimile of MS. Harley 2253 (E.E.T.S. 255, 1966), pp. xxii–iii.
[4] Knowles and Hadcock, p. 86.   [5] Ibid., p. 87.
[6] Ibid., p. 102.   [7] Ibid., p. 86.
[8] Ibid., p. 61.

the twelfth and thirteenth centuries a Cluniac house, a priory dependent on Lewes; it had a prior and eight monks in 1279, and in 1535 was even poorer than Bromfield.[1] Morville, south-east of Shrewsbury near Bridgnorth, and therefore remote from the Welsh border, was from about 1138 a priory dependent on Gloucester, with 'a prior and two monks at most'.[2] Somewhat nearer Shrewsbury, but still remote from the border, was the Cluniac house of Much Wenlock, an alien priory, dependent on La Charité, refounded in 1080–1 and of some size and wealth (there were forty-four monks in 1262, thirty-five in 1279);[3] west of Much Wenlock and dependent on it was Church Preen, a 'very small cell for two monks and two lay brothers'.[4] The Cistercian house at Buildwas, south-east of Shrewsbury, seems, like the neighbouring house of Much Wenlock, too remote from the Welsh border; it was founded in 1135 as a daughter-house of Savigny but was itself not large (there are reported to have been only six monks in 1377).[5] From it comes one of the surviving manuscripts of Andrew of St. Victor.[6] Just over the Welsh border in Montgomery-shire, west of Shrewsbury, was another Cistercian house, Strata Marcella, at this time a house of Welsh monks; it was not until the beginning of the reign of Edward III that the Welsh were replaced by English monks and the abbey was made subject to Buildwas.[7] Of all these monastic houses,[8]

---

[1] Knowles and Hadcock, p. 99.   [2] Ibid., p. 71.   [3] Ibid., p. 101.
[4] Ibid., p. 96.   [5] Ibid., p. 105.
[6] Smalley, *The Study of the Bible in the Middle Ages*, p. 176. The manu-script (of the late twelfth century) is now MS. Trinity College Cambridge B. 1. 29 (27).   [7] Knowles and Hadcock, p. 116.
[8] In addition to the Benedictine, Cluniac, and Cistercian houses, there was a wealthy house of the Knights Hospitallers at Dinmore, north of Hereford, granted to them towards the close of the reign of Henry II (Knowles and Hadcock, p. 242), with a dependent house at Sutton (ibid., p. 249); but obviously the Hospitallers do not come into considera-tion here.

only Much Wenlock seems to have been of the size, age, and importance to have produced the literary language of *Ancrene Wisse* and its group; but it is disqualified on other grounds.

In the area between Hereford and Shrewsbury there were four houses of regular Augustinian canons.[1] Wormsley, 7 miles north-west of Hereford, was a Victorine priory founded *c.* 1216, a smallish house which had eight canons in 1379 and had a net income in 1535 of £83;[2] it was too small, and in particular far too recent a foundation, to have produced *Ancrene Wisse*. Near the Welsh border, less than 3 miles north-east of Montgomery, was Chirbury, a small priory which had been founded about 1190 at Snead and which moved to Chirbury about 1195. It had a net income in 1535 of £66 and is reported to have consisted of a prior and five or six canons, presumably at about the time of its suppression in 1536;[3] it may well have been larger in the thirteenth century, but it was too small and above all too recently founded a house to have developed the 'AB language', since the whole of the *Ancrene Wisse* group must have been written within forty years after, and the spelling-system must have been evolved by the time of, the foundation

---

[1] There were also secular colleges at Bromyard (Knowles and Hadcock, p. 327), Condover (p. 328), Holdgate (p. 331), apparently Ludlow (p. 336), Pontesbury (p. 339), and Wroxeter (p. 345). In the first half of the twelfth century the village church of Wigmore was collegiate (p. 344). All of these were small establishments of less than half a dozen priests. The only large secular college was that of Hereford Cathedral itself (see below, p. 134). In any case we have seen that the author of *Ancrene Wisse* speaks of 'our order' and that he must have been a member of one of the independent congregations; he cannot have been a member of a secular college. But the secular colleges of Hereford and (in the early twelfth century) of Wigmore might well have contributed to the traditions (including the literary and linguistic traditions) of Wigmore Abbey, since it also was Augustinian.

[2] Knowles and Hadcock, p. 160. Rosalind Hill, *Ecclesiastical Letterbooks*, p. 286, puts the date of foundation of Wormsley 'in or before 1222'.

[3] Knowles and Hadcock, pp. 134, 153.

of Snead–Chirbury. Ratlinghope, 4 miles north-west of Church Stretton, was a small cell with never more than three canons, including the prior; it was founded before 1209 and was dependent on Wigmore.[1]

There remains only Wigmore Abbey itself. It was founded before 1148 by Oliver de Merlimond, the steward of Hugh de Mortimer baron of Wigmore, at Shobdon, a village south of Wigmore, after Oliver had built a stone church there about 1140; and the original convent consisted of two canons sent from St. Victor at Paris who, when they became homesick, were replaced by three others of English birth. The site proved unsuitable, and the house was moved to Eye near Aymestrey and then to Wigmore village; and finally, when life in Wigmore proved insupportable, the canons asked for and received permission to look for another site and chose one at or near *Beodune*, just over a mile north of Wigmore village and castle.[2] Here the first stone of the new church was laid in 1172 and the church was dedicated in 1179; but the site would appear to have been decided on before the recall of Abbot Andrew to Wigmore, which was 'between the springs of the years 1161 and 1163, or very soon after',[3] and at least temporary living-quarters for the canons must have been built before the church was begun. The abbey is said to have been intended for an abbot, prior, and seven-

---

[1] Knowles and Hadcock, p. 151.

[2] Dugdale, *Monasticon*, vi. 344, treats *Beodune* as an intermediate site of the house, before a return to Shobdon and the final choice, but this is due to a careless reading of the Anglo-Norman *History of the Foundation of Wigmore Abbey*. The latter clearly states that a canon named Walter Agaymeth 'saw the place where the abbey is now situated and marked the spot' (*vist la place ou l'abbeye est ore assise, et nota le lyu*) while sitting among the reapers in 'the field of *Beodune*' (ed. Wright, p. 118; ed. Dugdale, vi. 346). Professor G. V. Smithers, in Bennett and Smithers, *Early Middle English Verse and Prose*, p. 403, takes *Beodune* as the final site.

[3] Smalley, pp. 114–15.

teen canons; in 1299 bishop Richard Swinfield imposed on the abbot a committee of seven, including the prior and an ex-abbot, which would seem to imply a total community of at least twenty (since even so one in three would be serving on the committee).[1] At its dissolution in 1538 the house was surrendered by the abbot *in commendam*, the prior and sub-prior, and eight other canons. Its net income in 1535 was £261.[2] Its first abbot was the distinguished Biblical scholar Andrew of St. Victor, whose two tenures of office (which were interrupted by an estrangement from his canons and a return to St. Victor) are to be dated from about 1147 to *c.* 1155 and from *c.* 1162 until his death at Wigmore in 1175.[3] As one of the English daughter-houses (the earliest, though not the largest), Wigmore kept in touch with St. Victor; in the early thirteenth century, probably between 1216 and 1222, the communities of Wigmore, St. Augustine's Bristol, and Keynsham (Somerset) wrote twice to the

[1] *Registrum Ricardi de Swinfeld*, ed. W. W. Capes (Canterbury and York Society, 1909), pp. 363–4; Knowles, *Religious Orders*, i. 100.

[2] This compares with the following figures given by Knowles and Hadcock for houses hitherto mentioned: Strata Marcella £64, Chirbury £66, Wormsley £83, Buildwas £110, Much Wenlock £401, Leominster £448. Of houses still to be mentioned, the Benedictine priory at Hereford had £121, Haughmond Priory (Augustinian) £259, Shrewsbury Abbey £532, St. Werburgh's Abbey, Chester £1,003 (and the nunnery, St. Mary's Priory, Chester, £66).

[3] For accounts of Wigmore Abbey see Knowles and Hadcock, p. 159; Beryl Smalley in *Recherches de théologie ancienne et médiévale*, x (1938), 358–73, and *The Study of the Bible*, pp. 112–19; and Bennett and Smithers, pp. 402–3. The Anglo-Norman *History of the Foundation* (preserved in what is now University Library, Chicago, MS. 224, ff. 1–5) is printed in Dugdale, *Monasticon*, vi. 344–8; by T. Wright, *A History of Ludlow and its Neighbourhood* (Ludlow, 1852), pp. 102–32, with a good modern English translation; and (curiously without reference to Wright) by J. C. Dickinson and P. T. Ricketts, 'The Anglo-Norman Chronicle of Wigmore Abbey', *Transactions of the Woolhope Naturalists' Field Club, Herefordshire*, xxxix (1969), 413–46 (text with facing translation, pp. 420 ff.). Dickinson and Ricketts give an account of the establishment of the abbey (pp. 415–18), but it adds nothing new.

abbot of St. Victor, first begging him not to cut them off, for non-attendance, from relations with the Victorine order and sending R., sub-prior of Wigmore, to represent them at the general chapter; and then again to thank the abbot and the general chapter for receiving the English houses back into relations with St. Victor and for their kindness to the sub-prior of Wigmore.[1] Though it was neither very large nor very wealthy, Wigmore Abbey was large enough to have been able to develop its own literary form of English and to assemble a group of trained scribes, and its interest in vernacular composition is evidenced by the fact that the history of its own foundation is, somewhat remarkably, written in Anglo-Norman. The Abbey had been in existence for about three-quarters of a century, and had been settled in its final home for at least forty-five years, when *Ancrene Wisse* was written, and therefore would have had ample time to develop its own tradition; it was firmly established by the probable date of evolution of the spelling-system of the 'AB language'; and its connections with St. Victor would ensure that its tradition was a scholarly one, in close touch with the university of Paris. Yet it was situated only 4 miles east of the Welsh border, patronized and protected by, and in the territory of, an important marcher lordship, in the very district of north-western Herefordshire in which, as we have seen,[2] the social conditions were eminently such as to explain the admixture of extraneous linguistic elements which the 'AB language' displays. Of the Augustinian houses in the area, only Wigmore can possibly have been the centre which developed and used this distinctive literary form of English;[3] and none of the

---

[1] Rosalind Hill, *Ecclesiastical Letter-books of the Thirteenth Century* (privately printed; no place or date), pp. 59–66, 285–7.

[2] See pp. 119–20, above.

[3] On the Augustinian abbey of Haughmond, some four miles north-east of Shrewsbury, see pp. 134–5 and 171–2, below.

monastic houses—even if it were likely, as it is not, that *Ancrene Wisse* was written by a monk—is as suitable.

The main reason for believing that *Ancrene Wisse* and its group were written in Wigmore Abbey is simply this process of exclusion: in the dialectal area to which the works must belong there is only the one religious house that will fit, and this house belongs to the right order. But Wigmore Abbey also suits other subsidiary indications that have not yet been discussed. For instance, its situation serves to explain the passage, in an addition in the Corpus version, in which the author praises the enlarged community of anchoresses for the way in which each is 'turned towards'[1] the other

in an manere of liflade, as þah ȝe weren an cuuent of Lundene ant of Oxnefort, of Schreobsburi oðer of Chester, þear as alle beoð an wið an imeane manere ant wiðuten singularite, þet is, anful frommardschipe . . .[2]

---

[1] This is in reference to the author's interpretation, just before the point where the additional passage is introduced, of Samson's foxes, with their tails tied together and their heads turned away from each other, as a symbol of discord and lack of mutual love. By contrast, when people are united by love they are *euch wiðward oþer*, 'each turned towards the other'.

[2] Corpus MS., f. 69a/19–21. The punctuation of this passage in Bennett and Smithers, p. 231, is mistaken; see p. 267, n. 2, below.

Shepherd, pp. xxiii–xxxiv, and Smithers, in Bennett and Smithers, p. 409, both take this passage as meaning that at the places named there were separate communities of anchoresses belonging (in Shepherd's words) to a 'congregation of recluses' which 'is now quite forgotten'. It seems to me plain that the passage means nothing of the sort. At the beginning of the addition, the author remarks that they are the anchoresses of England—twenty now or more—among whom there is most peace, and none is 'turned away' from the other, as report is; therefore they progress well and prosper because they are united in one manner of life, 'as if you were a religious community of London, etc.' There is no reason at all to suppose that, in the clause of hypothetical comparison introduced by *as þah*, he is comparing them to other communities of anchoresses; the word *cuuent* has its ordinary medieval meaning of 'religious house', whether monastery or nunnery. In a passage in the

The choice of London and Oxford is for reasons that are obvious enough—the one the capital, the other a university town, and both centres where already there were important religious houses (*cuuents*). But as the writer moves to the west, it is perhaps a little surprising that he omits Worcester and Gloucester, and certainly surprising that he omits Hereford. Part of the reason, and possibly the main reason, is that in Hereford there was no 'regular' religious house as important or as wealthy as those in Shrewsbury and Chester. The most important establishment in Hereford was the cathedral, a numerous and well-endowed college of secular clergy.[1] The Benedictine priory, successor during the first half of the twelfth century of two pre-Conquest colleges of prebendaries, was a dependency of Gloucester Abbey; it was neither an independent nor an important house.[2] There were, *c.* 1230, 4 hospitals in the town;[3] the Franciscan friary had been founded by 1228,[4] but the Dominican (a large house of over thirty friars) is not recorded before 1246.[5] In Shrewsbury there was a Benedictine abbey, founded by 1090 and colonized by monks from Séez, which was not large (it seems at times to have fallen below the normal 'full convent') but was well endowed, with a net income in 1535 of £532.[6] By 1230 there were 3 hospitals[7] and 3 or 4 secular colleges;[8] the Dominican friary was founded before 1232,[9] but the Franciscan not until 1245–6.[10] Less than 5 miles

preface that is part of the original text (Corpus MS., f. 3b/27; Morton, p. 12), *cuuent* is used to refer to an organized conventual house, in explicit contrast to those living alone as hermits or anchorites. As the anchoresses' community has so grown in numbers that it exceeds the thirteen that was considered to make up a 'full convent', it has become comparable to an ordinary religious house.

[1] Knowles and Hadcock, p. 331.
[2] Its net income in 1535 is given as £121; ibid., p. 68.
[3] Ibid., pp. 276–7.   [4] Ibid., p. 225.   [5] Ibid., p. 185.
[6] Ibid., p. 77.   [7] Ibid., p. 306.   [8] Ibid., p. 341.
[9] Ibid., p. 187.   [10] Ibid., p. 193.

to the north-east was the Augustinian abbey of Haughmond, founded between 1130 and 1138, which from the extent of its buildings 'would appear to have been intended for some twenty-four canons', though there were only thirteen in 1377, eleven in 1381, and thirteen at the dissolution. Its endowments were similar in value to those of Wigmore, being assessed at £259 in 1535.[1] At Chester was the wealthiest and most distinguished Benedictine house in the three towns, St. Werburgh's Abbey, refounded in 1093 with monks from Bec-Hellouin in Normandy; in 1381 there were twenty monks, and the net income in 1535 is assessed as £1,003.[2] Chester also, alone among the three towns, had a house of Benedictine nuns, St. Mary's Priory (founded about 1140), which had thirteen nuns in 1381, fourteen at its dissolution in 1540; its net income in 1535 is given as £66.[3] There were perhaps 2 hospitals, though neither was certainly in existence by 1230,[4] and a college of secular clergy of more than average size and wealth;[5] the Dominican friary was founded before 1236,[6] the Franciscan between 1238 and 1240.[7] But if the author of *Ancrene Wisse* was concentrating his attention, as he probably was, on well-established monastic houses (*cuuents*), then undoubtedly Chester, with its wealthy monastery and its nunnery, and Shrewsbury, with its independent and adequately endowed Benedictine abbey and its nearby Augustinian abbey, would rank ahead of Hereford, which had only a Benedictine priory, markedly poorer than the Benedictine abbeys in Shrewsbury and Chester.

What is clear is that the author of the passage is thinking as a member of the Anglo-Norman feudal society of the Welsh Marches, confronting the revived power of North Wales. No one else, picking important religious centres for

[1] Ibid., p. 159.
[2] Ibid., p. 62.
[3] Ibid., p. 211.
[4] Ibid., p. 263.
[5] Ibid., p. 327.
[6] Ibid., p. 184.
[7] Ibid., p. 190.

purposes of comparison, would have chosen Shrewsbury and Chester to set beside London and Oxford.[1] Chester was the administrative centre and military base of the northern Marches, Shrewsbury of the central Marches; and similarly Hereford was the centre for the 'southern' or 'western' Marches. The position of the Wigmore district, between Shropshire and Herefordshire, was somewhat ambiguous. At the time of the Domesday survey the extreme north-west of modern Herefordshire (though not Wigmore village itself) was included in Shropshire. But Wigmore Castle was built by William fitz Osbern, earl of Hereford; and nearer to the date of *Ancrene Wisse* the sheriff of Herefordshire dealt with affairs in the Wigmore area,[2] even though his effective power in the barony of Wigmore and in the other marcher lordships along the west of the county was limited.[3] Hereford was 7 miles nearer to Wigmore than

[1] Fr. V. McNabb, pursuing his hypothesis of Dominican authorship, claimed (*MLR*, xi (1916), 4; *Arch. Fr. Praed*, iv (1934), 59) that these four towns were listed because they were 'the first to receive Dominican communities'—London and Oxford (according to him) in 1221, Shrewsbury in 1230, and Chester in 1235. The explanation would be credible only if the Dominican authorship of *Ancrene Wisse* were proved, and would have the consequence that the added passage in the Corpus MS. would have to be dated after 1235. In any case these were not the first four Dominican houses; see the table in Knowles and Hadcock, pp. 213–14, from which it appears that the earliest houses were those in Oxford (1221), London Holborn (before 1224), Norwich (1226), York (1227), Bristol (before 1230), Shrewsbury and Exeter (both before 1232), Northampton (before 1233), Winchester (before 1235), and Chester (before 1236).

[2] Thus when Ralph of Lingen, whose home manor of Lingen lay in the area of north-western Herefordshire that had originally formed part of Shropshire, incurred a debt to the crown for a lawsuit brought before the assizes of Dorset and Somerset, the job of collecting the money was in 1181 transferred to the sheriff of Herefordshire, who, though he failed to obtain the money, duly recorded Ralph's reason for not paying and ultimately his death; see below, pp. 205–7.

[3] 'Geographically the shire included the lordships of Wigmore and Lugharness in the north-west . . . But the power of the sheriff [of Here-

was Shrewsbury, and was more accessible down the valley of the Lugg; it is easy to see why not only Wigmore, but its dependent manors, should come to be within the jurisdiction of Hereford, not of Shrewsbury. This itself may explain why the author, in the passage under consideration, should omit Hereford. If one wishes to emphasize the importance of a group of people by comparing them to established institutions in other places, one does not usually make the comparison with the nearest town, which they are likely to know best—especially if its only relevant institution (in this case, its only monastic house) is not in fact very important; it is more impressive to choose towns at a greater distance, less familiar but often heard of as important centres, where the features being compared (the monastic houses) are truly more important and more numerous, but may also seem even more important than they really are because they are less well known. Even a moderate distance may lend some enchantment. The omission of Hereford probably means that it was the nearest town, the 'local' centre, too familiar to be used in such a comparison; but the trend of the writer's thought suggests strongly that he lived to the north of Hereford—for if he had lived to the south, he would surely have thought of Gloucester and Bristol rather than of Shrewsbury and Chester.

The church of Wigmore Abbey was dedicated to St. James, and *Ancrene Wisse*, in its preface, gives considerable prominence to the teachings of St. James.[1] The coincidence would be more significant if Arno of Reichersberg, in the previous century, had not used the same citation from St. James in much the same way.[2] It might be a sufficient

fordshire] extended over none of these districts' (*VCH Herefordshire*, pp. 360–1).

[1] Both facts are pointed out by Brewer in his article in *N. & Q.* (N.S.), iii. 232–5, though he does not explicitly connect them.

[2] See pp. 32–3, above.

explanation to say that St. James is cited in the preface because to rely on his authority was an Augustinian tradition, and that Wigmore Abbey church was dedicated to him because he was held in reverence by Augustinians; though one may legitimately use this as evidence that the writer was an Augustinian, it does not follow that he was a canon of Wigmore Abbey. But if the anchoresses' director and confessor had been a canon of an abbey whose official title was 'the church of St. James of Wigmore', there would be a special point, an ironic twist, in his somewhat unusual advice that they were to reply, to those who inquired to what order they belonged, that they were 'of the order of St. James'.[1]

It has also been pointed out[2] that before Oliver de Merlimond built his stone church at Shobdon, where the Victorine community was first established, the site had been occupied by a wooden chapel, subject to the church at Aymestrey, which was dedicated to St. Juliana. But if one is to guess why the *Katherine*-group should have included the lives of three women saints, Margaret, Juliana, and Katherine, there is a more obvious possibility, though I do not recall seeing it suggested—that the three sisters for whom *Ancrene Wisse* was primarily written, and for whom (I assume) the related works may also have been intended, were themselves christened Margaret, Juliana, and Katherine, and that the subjects of the lives were chosen in compliment to the recipients. It would not be surprising if three sisters bore these three names, for they were all in common use at the time.[3] If on other grounds we can place *Ancrene Wisse* in the

[1] Corpus MS., f. 3a/2 (Morton, p. 8).

[2] First by Brewer, p. 234, and again by Smithers in Bennett and Smithers, *Early Middle English Verse and Prose*, p. 403.

[3] In 1196–7, at Broughton Hackett, Worcestershire, there was a family of seven girls, the sisters and heirs of one Ralph *armiger*, who were named Margareta, Juliana, Matildis (or Mahalt), Eufemia, Eddusa,

Wigmore district, then it may be significant that the dedication of a twelfth-century chapel should testify to a cult of St. Juliana in the area; for that would perhaps make it more likely that a woman born locally would bear the saint's name, and that in its turn might explain why a life of St. Juliana should be included among the works written for a local group of women religious. But such an argument is entirely speculative. St. Juliana was a well-known saint, and there is nothing remarkable about the choice of her as a subject for a vernacular life; Cynewulf had made the same choice.

That the Corpus MS. was given, towards 1300, to Wigmore Abbey[1] has been seen both as an argument for and an argument against the Wigmore origin of *Ancrene Wisse*. In particular Mr. Brewer asks why Wigmore should have needed a copy if the work had been written there.[2] The question is pertinent, but there might be many answers. The canons may simply have wanted an extra copy; their previous copy may have been damaged or destroyed, or lent and not returned, or lost or stolen, or imprudently sold. Or again Wigmore may previously have had in its library only a copy of the original, unrevised text, and it may have wished to acquire one of the revised version; there is good

Agnes, and Alicia (*Chancellor's Roll 8 Ric. I*, pp. 15, 207; *Pipe Roll 9 Ric. I*, p. 190). It is a pity that Katherine is missing—but perhaps just as well, or someone might have been tempted to see in this over-abundant family (or rather in three of them) the women for whom the *Katherine*-group was written.

[1] According to the *ex libris* inscription on f. 1a of the manuscript; cf. N. R. Ker's introduction to Tolkien's edition, pp. xvii–xviii.

[2] To report more exactly, he asks 'Why had they no copy before?' (p. 233). But this is putting the question in a loaded way; it certainly does not follow that because they accepted this copy they had none before. In modern times even a private person may have two copies of a book; libraries often do, and in the Middle Ages themselves it is easy to find instances of a religious house that possessed more copies than one of a valued work.

textual evidence (notably in the Latin version and the Vernon MS., but also in the Trinity French version and in the Royal version) that the existence of the revised text was known, and that it was consulted by copyists, probably after about 1250, even when they were working primarily from the unrevised text. Though the revised version never really caught up with the unrevised, it is not true that it was unknown or unvalued; and a house that had an interest in the work might well have taken advantage of the chance to acquire an exceptionally good manuscript of the revision, even if it already possessed a copy of the original version. But indeed it is quite possible that the house in which *Ancrene Wisse* was written did not originally possess a fair copy of its own, for the work was not intended for the use of the house that produced it; it was meant for the anchoresses, and any fair copies made in the house of origin may all have been intended to be given away. The *stemma codicum* shows that all the surviving versions based on the original unrevised text go back to a single, unusually correct, manuscript β, which must have been the first fair copy and which must have been given to the anchoresses. The revision is not based on β, but on the author's holograph (since it avoids β's errors); the only extant manuscript of the revised text is Corpus, but there is evidence that the revised copy which exercised influence in the later thirteenth century was neither Corpus nor derived from it, so that it must be assumed that two fair copies were made of the revised text. But both were intended to be given away, Corpus to a single person and the lost copy to the community for which the revision had been undertaken.[1] There may have remained,

---

[1] See pp. 289–92, below, where the revised text and its copies are discussed in more detail and references are given. That Corpus was originally intended for a single person is shown by the form of its scribe's request for prayers (p. 291, below).

in the house that produced the work, only the author's holograph, his 'foul papers', which may have been thrown away after his death and which, even if it survived, would not seem to a medieval librarian to be any substitute for a handsome, well-written fair copy if he had the chance to acquire one.

We are left to guess why Wigmore Abbey should have wanted the Corpus MS. What is significant, and recorded fact, is that even at a time when, in the bishop of Hereford's view,[1] the abbey was in need of reformation, its senior precentor should actively have sought the gift of an unusually fine and accurate copy—far the best that has survived—of a vernacular work; for the inscription in the manuscript explicitly states that the gift was made 'at the instance' (*ad instanciam*) of brother Walter of Ludlow, which can only mean that he had asked for it, and he evidently considered the transaction important enough to wish his part in it to be recorded. At the very least *Ancrene Wisse* must have been a work that was valued in Wigmore; and it looks very much as though brother Walter knew something of the history of this copy, or could recognize a good copy when he saw it. But perhaps he was just lucky; so are we.

In Chapters I and II it was argued that the knowledge shown in *Ancrene Wisse* of the Rule of St. Augustine and of Augustinian custumals was an indication that the author himself belonged to one of the Augustinian congregations. It may seem comparable to found arguments on his reading of other sorts, but in fact a distinction is to be made. A man may read many books, written by members of a variety of orders and institutions, or of none, and yet not belong to the same society as even the writers by whom he is most influenced; it is risky to judge his very nationality by his

[1] Knowles, *Religious Orders*, i. 100.

intellectual debts, but his everyday way of life, and the rules and conventions to which it is subject, may indeed be significant, because they will be determined by the particular society to which he belongs. The author of *Ancrene Wisse* was greatly influenced by the writings of St. Bernard of Clairvaux, yet he was not a Cistercian. It is dangerous to pick out some of his borrowings and to claim special significance for them, unless it can be shown that they are in some way unusual. An argument in favour of the connection of *Ancrene Wisse* and its group with the Victorine house at Wigmore has been based on the knowledge shown in them of the writings of Hugh of St. Victor (1096–1146).[1] We have already seen that the author of *Ancrene Wisse* knew and was influenced by the commentary on the Rule of St. Augustine,[2] and Shepherd, in his notes on Parts VI and VII, has pointed out a number of passages in which the thought of *Ancrene Wisse* has parallels in Hugh's writings.[3] Smithers has claimed[4] that Hugh's influence is apparent in the use of the words 'shadow' and 'painting' in a passage in Part III where the author says that this world's joys and miseries are but shadows and paintings of the joys of heaven and the misery of hell;[5] here, Smithers argues, the words have the technical senses assigned to them in medieval typology, and he cites a passage in Hugh's commentary on Colossians 2 : 17 in which these technical senses are clearly defined. The weakness of the argument is that it is not self-evident, in the *Ancrene Wisse* passage, that the words are being used in any

[1] Smithers in Bennett and Smithers, p. 403.

[2] See pp. 24–7, above.

[3] *Ancrene Wisse: Parts Six and Seven*, pp. 53, 54, 60, 64, 68. The clearest instance is the interpretation of the story of the woman of Sarepta; see Shepherd's text, pp. 26–7 (Corpus MS, f. 108b/12–25; Morton, p. 402), and his commentary, p. 64.

[4] In *Medium Ævum*, xxxiv (1965), 126–8 (summarized in Bennett and Smithers, pp. 404–5).

[5] Corpus MS., f. 65a/25–65b/9 (Morton, p. 242).

but their ordinary meanings—especially as the ordinary meanings are plainly intended in the analogies of the nervous horse that shies at a shadow and of the child who flees from a terrifying picture; the passage can be read with understanding by someone ignorant of medieval typology, and to write it, one would suppose, a man might need to read no more than the two New Testament passages in which *umbra* is similarly used.[1] The strength of the argument is that in *Ancrene Wisse* both *schadewe* and *peintunge* are used as equivalents, contrasted with the thing itself, and that Hugh in his exposition similarly equates *umbra* and *figura*, in contrast to *corpus* and *res* which signify the factual reality. I do not doubt that Smithers is right, but I could wish that the instance had more probative force.

It appears also that the author of *Ancrene Wisse* knew the work of another of the Paris theologians, Richard of St. Victor, a Scot who died in 1173. Shepherd has pointed out that the use of Croesus as an example of the beatitude of wealth in Part VII of *Ancrene Wisse*[2] is an innovation not found in Anselm of Canterbury, the ultimate basis of the passage in question, or in Honorius, who first provided exemplary figures for each of the gifts (of wealth, beauty, and so on), but in Richard's Sermon lxxxviii.[3] There are other places in which the thought of *Ancrene Wisse* has parallels in Richard, but this is the clearest instance. It does not, however, necessarily follow from the author's knowledge of Hugh and Richard of St. Victor that he himself was a Victorine; for the works of both men were widely read and influential, and it is known from surviving manuscripts that Hugh in particular was certainly read in England in many religious

---

[1] Colossians 2: 17, Hebrews 10: 1.

[2] Corpus MS., f. 108a/4–5 (Morton, p. 398).

[3] G. Shepherd, *MLR*, li (1956), 161–7; *Ancrene Wisse: Parts Six and Seven*, pp. 62–3.

houses that were not Victorine. Much more significant, in my view, is the knowledge shown in *Ancrene Wisse* of the commentary on the Rule of St. Augustine attributed to Hugh, since it is for the most part a dull and pedestrian work which would have little interest except for an Augustinian; but even so it is unlikely to have been read only by Victorines.

All who have studied *Ancrene Wisse* are agreed on its author's erudition and on the width of his reading, especially in the religious literature that was relevant to his theme: in the Bible and the commentaries on it, in Augustine, Gregory the Great, Anselm, and above all in Bernard of Clairvaux and other Cistercian authors. Shepherd[1] rightly stresses the importance of the author's reading, and its significance as showing how closely he he was in touch with the intellectual activity of the later twelfth century, of which the most eminent centre was the University of Paris; he was obviously indebted to its biblical scholars and theologians. We must now add the influence on him of Stephen Langton's Paris sermons (the extent of which is still to be determined) and, especially, of the *Moralia super Evangelia* by Alexander of Bath—almost certainly the published form of lectures and homilies delivered in Wells. But he nowhere departs from his normal impersonality to tell us where or under whom he had studied; in this he is characteristic of his time—just as, indeed, it is hard to tell, from a modern scholar's references and citations, which of the writers who have influenced him were his own teachers. But there is one point in *Ancrene Wisse*[2] where the veil of impersonality perhaps drops a little, when he writes, citing Isaiah 2: 10:

Ingredere in petram, abscondere fossa humo. Ga in to þe stan, seið þe prophete, ant hud te in þe [doluen] eorðe, þet is, i þe wunden of ure lauerdes flesch þe wes as idoluen wið þe dulle

---

[1] *Ancrene Wisse: Parts Six and Seven*, pp. xxv–xxix.
[2] Corpus MS., f. 79b/14–22 (Morton, p. 292).

neiles, as he i þe Sawter longe uore seide: *Foderunt manus meas et pedes meos*, þet is, ha duluen me baðe þe vet ant te honden. Ne seide he nawt 'þurleden', for efter þis leattre, as ure meistres seggeð, swa weren þe neiles dulle þet ha *duluen* his flesch ant tobreken þe ban mare þen *þurleden*, to pinin him sarre.

The phrase 'as our masters say' here refers ultimately to the glossators of the Psalms: Anselm of Laon, author of the *Glossa Ordinaria*; Gilbert de la Porrée, author of the *Media Glossatura*; and Peter Lombard, who expanded Anselm's gloss in the *Maior* or *Magna Glossatura* (written between 1135–6 and 1142–3), which displaced all other glosses in the Schools.[1] Specifically it is Peter Lombard who is drawn on; his comment on Psalm 21: 18 (Authorized Version 22: 16) includes the passage

Foderunt clavis gentiles milites *manus meas et pedes meos* (Gl. int.). Et nota quod non ait 'transfixerunt' vel 'vulneraverunt', sed 'foderunt' [Cassiod.], quia sicut terra fossa fructus facit, sic fructum vitæ dedit Christus vulneratus.[2]

Here is the explicit contrast between *foderunt*[3] and *transfixerunt*; the phrase 'non ait "transfixerunt" . . . sed "foderunt"' is almost directly translated in *Ancrene Wisse*, with its 'Ne seide he nawt "þurleden"' and the following contrast between *duluen* and *þurleden*. But Peter's commentary lacks the detail that the nails were blunt (*dulle*), a characteristically graphic addition by the English writer (though he did not necessarily invent it himself). As 'our masters' is a phrase comparable to 'our brothers', which must refer to the brothers of the order to which the author belonged, its use in a passage that is indebted to Peter Lombard may perhaps

---

[1] Smalley, *The Study of the Bible in the Middle Ages*, p. 64.
[2] Migne, *Pat. Lat.*, cxci, col. 234 (punctuation modified).
[3] Taken, as by Cassiodorus (who is referred to) and later writers, in its primary sense 'dug'; though 'pierced' is in fact a well-authenticated secondary sense in Classical Latin.

mean 'the masters of the school in which I studied' and thus be indirectly a claim to have studied in Paris; but I doubt whether it will bear this interpretation. Peter Lombard's *Glossatura* was a standard textbook which would have been used in any school, and 'our masters' may mean nothing more precise than 'the masters of theology whom all scholars follow'. If it means more than this, it might refer to the author's own teachers in some unnamed school, citing Peter Lombard in their lectures and perhaps elaborating him by the addition of the explanation that the nails were blunt. One might perhaps see, in the phrase 'efter þis leattre', the influence of Andrew of St. Victor, the great exponent of the literal interpretation of the scriptures and the first abbot of Wigmore; but this would be to go far beyond the evidence.

In general I do not think that the intellectual and literary debts of *Ancrene Wisse* and the other works of its group can be used as evidence of the order to which their authors belonged. But there is an exception because of the special circumstances of the text of the source. The case concerns, not *Ancrene Wisse* itself, but one of the works of the associated *Katherine*-group. Until recently it has been generally accepted by English scholars that *Sawles Warde* is a translation and adaptation of chapters xiii–xv of Book IV of the *DeAnima* attributed to Hugh of St. Victor, and the supposed fact has been used as an argument for the connection of the *Katherine*-group with Wigmore;[1] but the matter is less simple than we had all supposed. *De Anima* is a collection rather than a work, and is a striking instance of the lack, in the Middle Ages, of any developed sense of individual authorship. It was printed as Hugh's in *Hugonis de S. Victore Opera Omnia* (Rouen, 1648) by the Victorine editors because they had found all the four books of which it consists written

[1] So Smithers in Bennett and Smithers, *Early Middle English Verse and Prose*, p. 403.

under his name 'in an ancient manuscript' (*in vetusto codice*),[1] which must then have belonged to the abbey, since the general title-page claimed that the edition as a whole was based on manuscripts 'preserved in the library of St. Victor'. One such manuscript from St. Victor is Paris Bibliothèque Nationale MS. fonds latin 14507, dated to the fifteenth century,[2] of which the first item (ff. 1–83) is the *De Anima* in four books, with the colophon (f. 1) 'Incipit liber magistri Hugonis de Sancto Victore de anima continens IIII^{or} libros parciales'; but this was certainly not the source of the 1648 edition, as the textual discrepancies show. The edition was evidently based on another manuscript which gave a better text and was presumably earlier (since it does not seem likely that in 1648 a fifteenth-century manuscript would be described as 'vetustus'). The library of St. Victor must have had at least two manuscripts that gave texts of the four-book *De Anima* and ascribed it to Hugh; but this appears to have been a peculiarly Victorine tradition.

The editors of the 1648 edition were themselves uneasy about it, as their prefatory note to the *De Anima* shows. They knew that Books I and III were to be found among works attributed to Bernard of Clairvaux and that Book II was a work attributed (falsely) to St. Augustine;[3] but they

---

[1] *Op. cit.*, ii. 132. It is possible that this attribution to Hugh of St. Victor may originally have been due to association of *De Anima* with a different work, *De claustro anime*, by Hugh of Folieto (Hugues de Fouilloy), who was often confused with Hugh of St. Victor (J. de Ghellinck, *L'Essor de la littérature latine au XIIe siècle*, p. 204).

[2] Léopold Delisle, *Inventaire des manuscrits de . . . St.-Victor* (1869).

[3] All three occur frequently as separate works in manuscripts, the first and third usually attributed to St. Bernard, the second often with the title *De spiritu et anima*, variously attributed. MS. Bib. Nat. lat. 2049 contains all three; MS. Toulouse 191 has the first and third, and also has the pseudo-Augustinian *Manuale* which is the basis of Book IV of *De Anima*. There was evidently some tendency for the component parts of *De Anima* to circulate together.

Migne, *Pat. Lat.*, clxxvii, col. 185 ff., gives mere cross-references **for**

thought that Book IV at least could be ascribed only to Hugh. In this, however, they were wrong. Its chapters i–x and the first half of chapter xi follow (with re-division of the chapters and some variations of text) the preface and chapters i–xxiv of a work often known as the *Manuale*;[1] this occurs as a separate work in many manuscripts, variously ascribed to St. Augustine (or even St. Augustine of Canterbury), St. Anselm, or St. Bernard, but is in fact a conflation, by some unknown author, of passages from the works of these and other writers.[2] After the middle of chapter xi of Book IV of *De Anima* the two diverge; none of the material of chapters xxv–xxxvi of the *Manuale* is used in *De Anima*, and contrariwise chapters xii–xvii of Book IV of *De Anima* have been added by its redactor. But in view of the generally derivative character of his compilation, it is hardly a matter for surprise that even in this section the dialogue which forms chapters xiii–xv should also prove to be found in many manuscripts as an independent work, commonly attributed to St. Anselm, as Hauréau pointed out in 1891;[3] and in 1969

Books I–II of *De Anima* and for all of Book III except its last chapter; it evidently did not trouble him that the texts might have been different. He reprints as Hugh's (from the 1648 edition) only the last chapter of Book III and the whole of Book IV. But he could have given a cross-reference for most of Book IV also; he evidently relied on what the 1648 Victorine editors had said, and did not realize that he had already printed (in *Pat. Lat.*, vol. xl) a version of most of Book IV as St. Augustine's.

[1] Reprinted by Migne, *Pat. Lat.*, xl, col. 951 ff., from the Maurist edition of Augustine's works.

[2] As the Maurist editors pointed out in their introductory 'Admonitio'. See also [J.] B. Hauréau, *Les Œuvres de Hugues de St-Victor* (1886), p. 183, and *Notices et extraits de quelques manuscrits latins de la Bibliothèque nationale*, iii (1891), 177–8. But Hauréau's references to the manuscripts of the Bibliothèque Mazarine are misleading; instead of his 'nos. 868 [*sic*] and 1168' read '858 (formerly 1168)', and for his 'no. 865' read '642 (formerly 865)'.

[3] *Notices et extraits*, ii. 248–9. He observed that if the dialogue was not by St. Anselm, still less was it by Hugh of St. Victor, in spite of its occurrence as 'un chapitre' of a treatise *De Anima* 'où rien n'est de

a critical edition of this dialogue *De Custodia interioris hominis* was published, among other works that come from Anselm's circle, by R. W. Southern and F. S. Schmitt in their *Memorials of St. Anselm*, pp. 354–60. It had, they say, 'an extensive circulation throughout the Middle Ages under the name of St. Anselm', and the ascription to him 'can be traced back to manuscripts of the mid-twelfth century' in both the lines of descent.[1] It was this publication that at last brought the separate existence of the Anselmian dialogue to the attention of Middle English scholars.[2]

Comparison of the texts of the Anselmian dialogue as established by Southern and Schmitt (A), of the version included in the 1648 Victorine edition of *De Anima* (V),[3] and of *Sawles Warde* (*SW*), can leave no doubt that where A and V differ, *SW* goes usually with A. This is perhaps to

lui'. But his criticisms of the text of the 1648 edition of the dialogue are beside the mark; the Victorine editors were giving the text as it occurred in their source, a manuscript of the composite *De Anima*, and were not making a critical edition of the dialogue as a separate work. The faults are not theirs.

[1] Op. cit., pp. 354–5. Their text is based on five manuscripts, two (of the twelfth and fourteenth centuries) representing the English tradition and three (of the twelfth century) the continental. Other manuscripts, both English and continental, are listed by Hauréau, *Notices et extraits*, ii. 248–9, in discussing MS. Bib. Nat. lat. 13576.

[2] Professor R. M. Wilson, in the introduction to his edition of *Sawles Warde*, p. xxx, though he had no knowledge of the Anselmian dialogue, nevertheless pointed out that the fact that this particular extract from *De Anima* had also been translated by Dan Michel in his *Ayenbite of Inwit* 'suggests that it existed as an independent work'; and he deduced from *Sawles Warde*, ll. 312–13 (*for aȝein . . . ihereð*), of which a version occurs in the *Ayenbite*, that the Latin original used by the two independent English translators 'probably differed slightly from the text given by Migne'. This is in fact a sentence which V omits (no. 6 in the list on p. 150, n. 1, below).

[3] I have used the Rouen edition of 1648 itself. Migne's text is a mere reprint (with some spelling changes and, in the dialogue, one error), and Wilson's in his edition of *Sawles Warde* is in turn a reprint of Migne with some further errors (mostly but not only in the Latin spelling).

be expected, since *SW*, like A, is an independent work, not part of a larger compilation as V is. There are eight places where V, as compared with A, has major omissions unlikely to be due to a mere copyist and probably the work of the redactor of the text embodied in *De Anima*; in each of these *SW* avoids the omission and follows A.[1] Minor omissions which might be accidental and due to the scribe of the archetypal Victorine manuscript (or some predecessor) occur at another seven[2] points in V, but again are not found in *SW*.[3] In one case V transfers a clause (with altered wording) to the previous sentence, and in another it alters the order of

---

[1] I refer to A by page and line of Southern and Schmitt's edition, to *SW* by the line-numbering in Bennett and Smithers (though I do not accept their text at all points), and to V, for convenience, by the line-numbering of Wilson's reprint in his edition of *SW*, though for its text I rely on the 1648 edition.

The instances of major omission in V are as follows. (1) A 356/11–13 (*Porro . . . appetitus*), *SW* 48–53, complex sentence omitted at V 20; (2) A 356/30–1 (*eos . . . convincant homines*), *SW* 82 (varied, but note *preouin*), clauses omitted at V 36; (3) A 356/34–5 (*Prudentia. Unde . . . inferno*), *SW* 85–7, question and answer omitted at V 39; (4) A 357/14 (*haec . . . vobis*), *SW* 158–9, simple sentence omitted at V 54; (5) A 358/5–6 (*et audite . . . et ibi*), *SW* 245–7, two principal clauses and introductory words of third omitted at V 75; (6) A 359/12–13 (*Ad earum . . . exaudiat*), *SW* 312–13, complex sentence omitted at V 119–20; (7) A 359/25–6 (*Unde et . . . est*), *SW* 330–1, another complex sentence omitted at V 130–1; (8) A 360/30–2 (*ad quam . . . seculorum*), *SW* 418–21, final prayer, appropriate to end of independent work, omitted at end of what is not the last chapter of *De Anima* (V 169).

[2] In the Rouen edition. There is one more in Migne and hence in Wilson; the fault is of course Migne's.

[3] These are: (1) A 356/20 (*Ego sum timor et memoria Mortis*), *SW* 70–1, V 28 (*Ego sum Timor mortis*; but cf. l. 73, *Timor et Memoria Mortis*); (2) A 356/22–3 (*Ubi est ipse Mors et quando aderit?*), *SW* 73–4 (read *hwenne ha cume*, as T, or better *hweonene ant hwenne ha cume*, conflating BR and T), V 30 (*Ubi est Mors?*); (3) A 358/19, *SW* 274, V 88 (*nominandam dominam Mariam* omitted); (4) A 359/9, *SW* 307, V 116 (*species* omitted); (5) A 359/14, *SW* 314, V 120 (*sed cum* omitted); (6) A 360/2, *SW* 349, V 142 (*absque estimatione* omitted); (7) A 360/12, *SW* 370, V 153 (*de his* omitted after *vobis*; homeoteleuton).

words; *SW* follows the original order of A.[1] At three points there are additions in V to the original text which are not followed by *SW*,[2] and at five or six points there are variations of the wording which also are not (or seem not to be) followed by the English rendering.[3] This evidence is ample to show that *SW* is not directly based on V (or rather on a medieval manuscript giving V's text), but on a version of A. On the other hand there is a smaller number of points where *SW* agrees with V against A, and though some of them are minor variations which might be independent and are not conclusive in themselves, others are significant and therefore serve also to give added weight to the minor agreements. There are, first, seven omissions from A's text shared by V and *SW*, one of them very slight but others of obvious importance.[4] At one point an omission in *SW*

[1] A 356/13–16, *SW* 60–2, V 22–3 (*et ne somnus . . . vigilandum est* transferred to precede *His ita dispositis = As þis is ido þus*); A 359/27 (*naturas et causas et origines*), *SW* 335–6 (*hwet it beo, hwi ant hwerto, ant hwerof hit bigunne*), V 132 (*causas et naturas et origines*).

[2] (1) A 357/16, *SW* 161–2, V 56 (*fideles* added before *prudentes*); (2) A 359/32, *SW* 344, V 138 (complex clause *quoniam bonum . . . in altero* added after *suo*); (3) A 360/3, *SW* 350, V 143 (*secum* added after *aliorum*; but so also in the Paris MS. of A collated by Southern and Schmitt).

[3] (1) A 356/28 *uncos igneos*, V 33 *uncos ferreos* (not translated here in *SW*, but cf. l. 143, *eawles gledreade*); (2) A 357/9 *vermibus consumuntur nec consummantur*, V 49 *vermibus corroduntur* (no direct translation, but cf. *SW* 104–7); (3) A 358/17 *illam gloriosam virginem*, V 87 *gloriosam*, *SW* 273–4 *þe eadi meiden*; (4) A 358/21 *pro hominibus*, V 90 *pro nobis*, *SW* 277–8 *for þeo þet hire seruið* (variation, but based on A?); (5) A 358/29–30 *quod . . . quod*, V 99–100 *qui . . . qui*, *SW* 287 *þet* 'in that, because'; (6) A 360/8–9 *omnes omnipotentes sunt*, V 150 *omnes securi sunt*, *SW* 364 *euchan is almihti*. But the last of these is probably a fault of the particular manuscript of V used by the 1648 editors.

[4] These are: (1) A 358/17–18 *matrem eiusdem dei et domini nostri Iesu Christi*, V 87–8 *matrem eius*, SW 274 *his moder*; (2) A 358/22 *maiestatem et claritatem*, V 91 *claritatem*, *SW* 279 *liht*; (3) A 358/31–2 *quod . . . mutauerunt* (clause of nine words), V 101 omits, *SW* 290 omits; (4) A 358/32 *omnes apostolos*, V 101 *apostolos*, *SW* 290 *þe apostles*; (5) A 359/15–16 *actio quaeve socialis conversatio*, V 122 *actio*, *SW* 316 *blisse*

amounts to a deliberate modification of the allegory to make it more consistent. This is at A 356/8–10, where it is said that the master of the house places Prudence in the outer entrance, 'quae discernat quid sit vitandum, quid appetendum, quid a domo excludendum, quid in domo recipiendum'. Here are four functions, of which the first two, to see what is to be avoided and what desired, are not really those of a doorkeeper. *SW* 43–6, in which the allegory is made more explicit by the use of the word *durewart*, restricts itself to a doorkeeper's functions; Prudence is to watch carefully whom she lets in and out, and to inspect from afar all who approach, to see which deserve to be granted admission or to be shut out. V 17–18 is perhaps intermediate, for it reads 'quae discernat quid sit admittendum, quid vitandum, quid excludendum'; the order is changed from that of A and one of the inappropriate phrases is dropped. But here V and *SW* may independently vary from A. At two points, however, they make identical additions to the text of A, of which one (the completion of a biblical quotation) could be independent, but hardly the other.[1] At four places V and *SW* share variations (one of them very minor) from the wording of A,[2] and at one point they transpose its word-order.[3]

(cf. l. 317, where also *þe imeane blisse* translates *in commune actio*); (6) A 359/24 *dominus Iesus*, V 129 *Dominus*, *SW* 328 *ure Lauerd*; (7) A 360/1–2 *sine comparatione*, V 141 omits, *SW* 348 omits.

[1] A 360/2 *se et alios*. V 141–2 *seipsum et omnes alios secum*, *SW* 348–9 *himseoluen ant . . . alle þe oþre*; A 360/7 '*Beati qui . . . domine*' etc., V 147–8 *Beati qui . . . Domine, in saecula saeculorum laudabunt te*, *SW* 358–60 *Beati qui habitant*, etc.: *Eadi beoð . . . into worlde* (translating full text as in V).

[2] (1) A 357/27 *Adest alius exterius* (v. l. *nuntius*) *prae foribus*, V 66 *Alius nuntius venit*, *SW* 234 *Ich iseo a sonde cumen*; (2) A 359/20 *haec*, V 125 *hoc*, *SW* 320 *þis* (independent misreading of *hec* as *hoc*?); (3) A 360/3 *unusquisque*, V 143 *cor uniuscuiusque*, *SW* 351 (*neauer*) *anes heorte*; (4) A 360/29 *monachus*, V 168 *quisque*, *SW* 406 *mon*.

[3] A 357/2 *ardore intolerabili . . . fetore incomparabili*, V 41–2 *ardore*

The evidence as a whole requires the assumption of the *stemma codicum*:

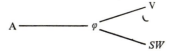

in which φ represents a revised version of the Anselmian text, different from any given by the manuscripts collated by Southern and Schmitt; from it V and *SW* derive the variations from A which they share, though each is an independent further modification (*SW* of course an extreme one, since it is a vernacular rehandling with extensive additions and alterations, not just a version of the Latin text). Now this in itself is a common enough textual situation, but it poses an important question: how did it come about that, in spite of the wide early circulation of manuscripts of the original text (including a good early copy belonging to Hereford Cathedral), the West Midland author of the free and independent English adaptation used, after 1196,[1] the same distinctive version of the Latin as formed the basis of the redaction embodied in the composite *De Anima*? It can hardly be doubted that the latter was compiled in the abbey of St. Victor in Paris, since it appears to survive only in Victorine texts and is ascribed, dutifully but falsely, to Hugh of St. Victor; and the answer to the question would be easy if *Sawles Warde* had been written in Wigmore, where the abbey, as a daughter-house of St. Victor, might well have in its library manuscripts copied from Victorine exemplars. Thus, although the proof that *Sawles Warde* is not directly based on the chapters in *De Anima* appears at first sight to take away an argument for its having originated

incomparabili . . . fetore intolerabili, SW 95–6 **brune uneuenlich** . . . **stench unpolelich**.

[1] On the date of *SW* see pp. 163–4, below.

in an English Victorine house, on analysis it turns out to provide a stronger one; for it is more significant that *Sawles Warde* and the corresponding chapters of *De Anima* should be independently based on an anonymous early variation of a dialogue not of Victorine origin than that *Sawles Warde* should be following, as we formerly supposed, a work attributed to an author so famous and widely studied as Hugh of St. Victor.[1]

The preceding argument assumes, as is generally done by English scholars, that *Ancrene Wisse*, the works of the *Katherine*-group preserved in MS. Bodley 34, and also the prose meditations known as the *Wohunge*-group,[2] were all written in the same cultural centre. It does not seem likely that there will ever be complete agreement on whether or not they were written by a single man. There will probably always be those, like Hall, who will be so impressed by the parallels between the works, in syntax, phrasing, and thought, that they will hold them to be evidence of unity of

---

[1] This is not to say, of course, that Anselm was less famous and influential than Hugh. The point is that the *altered* version of the Anselmian dialogue was anonymous and in itself insignificant; it is just because the version followed was not an important variation, though it was distinctive, that its use both in St. Victor and by the author of *Sawles Warde* becomes highly significant.

[2] i.e. the four pieces (two in variant forms with variant titles) edited by W. Meredith Thompson, *þe Wohunge of Ure Lauerd* (E.E.T.S. 241, 1958). I cannot accept the suggestion, made by Einenkel and supported by Professor Thompson (pp. xxiii–iv), that this group was written by a woman. I do not know how one distinguishes a woman's writing from a man's unless there is some specific reference; allowing for the special stylistic demands of this prose–poetry *genre* and of this type of perfervid devotion, I cannot see any essential difference between the prose meditations and passages of comparable theme in *Ancrene Wisse*. And it seems perverse to me to suppose that 'my dear sister' is a form of address from a man to a woman in *Ancrene Wisse*, but from one woman to another in *þe Wohunge of Ure Lauerd*; of course it could be, but there is no evidence that it is. The hypothesis seems merely fanciful.

authorship, or who will find it hard to believe that there was more than a single man who was capable, in a period which was not rich in distinguished writing in English, of such mastery of vernacular prose. Others will find it more credible, especially in view of the existence of a local form of literary English which was plainly not developed either by or for a single man and which a plurality of scribes had been trained to use, that there was a group of authors, each encouraging and learning from the others and sharing similar ideas and literary techniques, of whom it was the author of *Ancrene Wisse* (probably the last of the series) who, surpassing his teachers, proved the greatest. Many scholars, indeed, find differences between the works which they think are not sufficiently explained by their different *genres* and take to be indicative of diverse authorship. Thus it is often held that the arguments in favour of celibacy and against matrimony in *Hali Meiðhad* are so crude, earthy, and prejudiced that the work could not possibly have been written by the sane and temperate author of *Ancrene Wisse*; so Miss d'Ardenne, who remarks that in *Hali Meiðhad* 'we have left the company of the author of the *Ancren Riwle*, and fallen to a lower and less intelligent level'.[1] I am not so sure that the author of *Hali Meiðhad* was less intelligent, though he was certainly less sensitive; he produced the most original work of the *Katherine*-group and a very remarkable one, arguing his case for all (and more) than it was worth, with forthright vigour, clear sight, and, as Miss d'Ardenne herself says, uncompromising realism. *Ancrene Wisse* itself is neither moderate nor sensible about the relations of men and women.[2] When any question of sex arises, the author reveals a distinct streak of

---

[1] *Ste Iuliene*, p. xlvii.

[2] Cf. Tolkien's remarks on the exaggeration of the difference between the 'humanity' of *Ancrene Wisse* and the 'inhumanity' of the *Katherine*-group, in *Essays and Studies* xiv (1929), p. 116, n. 2.

morbid imagination: about the consequences of hands touching through windows, the methods of seducers, secret strainings and gropings. In any book such as this, addressed to women in religion who, we are told, were generally admired for their goodness, one might expect that in an account of the Seven Deadly Sins the point would be made that Pride is the deadliest of all—and especially, for those devoted to the religious life, Spiritual Pride. But though the author does indeed say that spiritual temptations are more deadly than those of the flesh, he gives, after his description of the Seven Sins (the 'mother-sins' and their offspring) a special warning against one. Spiritual Pride? Not at all; Lechery.

Nu ȝe habbeð ane dale iherd, mine leoue sustren, of þeo þe me cleopeð þe seoue moder-sunnen ant of hare teames . . . Ȝe beoð ful feor from ham, ure Lauerd beo iþoncket. Ah þet fule breað of þis leaste unþeaw, þet is of lecherie, stinkeð se swiðe feor (for þe feond hit saweð ant toblaweð ouer al) þet ich am sumdel ofdred leste hit leape sum chearre into ower heortes nease. Stench stiheð uppart, ant ȝe beoð hehe iclumben þer þe wind is muchel of stronge temptatiuns; vre Lauerd ȝeoue ow strengðe wel to wiðstonden.[1]

It is very strange; either their vocation for the celibate life was slight and uncertain, or he himself was unbalanced in view. But I would agree that *Hali Meiðhad*, with its unashamed and deliberately shocking descriptions of the unpleasantnesses and trials of married life, is different.

The difficulty is to distinguish between writers who shared the same religious beliefs and prejudices, took the same view of life in the world, had been similarly trained, and wrote in a distinctive and remarkably uniform variety of English. Nevertheless it has been argued that underlying the superficial dialectal unity of the *Katherine*-group (as exemplified

[1] Corpus MS., f. 58b/11–23 (Morton, pp. 216–18).

in the Bodleian MS.) and of *Ancrene Wisse* (in the Corpus text) there are certain differences of linguistic usage, both in syntax (especially in word-order)[1] and in the proportions of French-derived vocabulary.[2] The latter are more easily demonstrable. Miss Clark's statistics show that three sub-divisions of the *Katherine*-group can be distinguished. (*a*) *Ste Margarete* has, in its vocabulary, only 2·5 per cent of French-derived words, and *Ste Iuliene* 2·9 per cent. (*b*) *Ste Katerine* has 3·9 per cent, and *Sawles Warde* has 4·2 per cent. (*c*) *Hali Meiðhad* has 6·3 per cent, but still falls well short of the 10·7 per cent found in *Ancrene Wisse*, Parts VI and VII. Differences of literary *genre* and of subject-matter might account for much of the variation, as Miss Clark recognized in her careful discussion, and the difference between groups (*a*) and (*b*) is not very great and need not mean that different authors were involved; it would be possible to assume a single author writing at different times, which would almost certainly mean, in view of the progressive infiltration of French words into English, that group (*a*) was somewhat earlier than group (*b*). But the differences are there, and the separate position of *Hali Meiðhad* within the *Katherine*-group is clear; so too is the difference of *Ancrene Wisse* from the *Katherine*-group as a whole.

The distinctions to be made within the *Katherine*-group on grounds of vocabulary correspond very strikingly with their differences in textual history. MS. Bodley 34 is obviously a 'collected edition' of a number of pieces which were held to constitute a unified group, and it is unlikely that the common factor was no more than that they were all religious

---

[1] R. M. Wilson, 'On the Continuity of English Prose', *Mélanges de linguistique et de philologie Fernard Mossé in memoriam* (Paris, 1959), pp. 486–94.

[2] Cecily Clark, '*Ancrene Wisse* and the *Katherine Group*: a lexical divergence', *Neophilologus* l (1966), 117–23. I have worked out the percentages a little more accurately.

prose works of moderate length. There are compelling reasons for believing that they all originated in the same religious centre, and no one would question that they were all written for women; that is why they are in English. *Hali Meiðhad* is explicitly addressed to women, and the three lives of women saints are obviously so intended; *Ancrene Wisse*, written for the 'dear sisters', refers to 'your English book of St. Margaret'. Only *Sawles Warde* is not specifically written for women, but even in it there is some hint that it was meant for them; the longish reference in the Latin source to the 'glorious multitude of confessors', *viri apostolici et doctores*, and *monachi*, is cut down to a brief sentence about the *confessurs hird*; and that to the 'beauteous and radiant company of blessed virgins' is elaborated and made more prominent. Yet if the several works of MS. Bodley 34 were a recognizable group and were collected in the manuscript for this reason, they had not always circulated as a group, for they have had different textual histories. They may be divided, according to the manuscripts in which they are found and their inter-relationships, into three sub-groups.

(*a*) The lives of *Ste Margarete* and *Ste Iuliene* are found in two manuscripts, Bodley 34 (B) and Royal 17 A. xxvii (R). *Ste Iuliene* differs from *Ste Margarete* and all the other works of the *Katherine*-group in the extent of the divergence between the two texts: that of R has been deliberately (and often clumsily) cut, that of B has been expanded, in part by material derived from *Ste Margarete* and *Ste Katerine*.[1] But in

---

[1] *Ste Iuliene*, ed. S. T. R. O. d'Ardenne, pp. xxxv–xl. But an exception must be made of the passage in *Ste Iuliene* in B, ll. 544–52, which occurs also in R, ll. 427–33. Einenkel in his edition of *Ste Katerine* (*The Life of St. Katherine* (E.E.T.S. o.s. 80, 1884), p. 145) assumed that it was directly based on *Ste Katerine* ll. 1917–44, and Miss d'Ardenne (p. xxxviii) thinks that it shows that *Ste Iuliene* was expanded, during the transmission

other respects there are parallels between the two works. In each there is evidence that the compilers of B had available to them, for collation with the main exemplar, a second copy which resembled but was not identical with R; but it was used in different ways. In *Ste Margarete* the earlier part of the text was corrected, after the ordinary B scribe had finished his work, by a second scribe using an R-type text.[1] In *Ste Iuliene* the readings of the B text and the scribe's own corrections of his work suggest that he 'may have had before him a text more like R, beside the copy mainly followed',[2] which he sporadically conflated with his chief exemplar. Miss Mack assumes, with good reason, that in *Ste Margarete* both B and R were separated by at least one intermediate manuscript from their common ancestor,[3] and the same assumption is made by Miss d'Ardenne for

of its English text, by an addition modelled on the English *Ste Katerine*. But she herself points out (p. xxxix, n. 1) that medieval Latin lives of St. Juliana included an account of this wheel (derived from the Catherine legend), as indeed does the version which she prints from MS. Bodley 285 (see p. 50). The Latin source therefore accounts for the presence of the material in *Ste Iuliene*, and though there are undoubted parallels in wording between the passages in *Ste Iuliene* and *Ste Katerine*, they could have originated in the former. There is no reason to assume that because the material originally belonged to the Catherine legend, the Middle English words used originated in *Ste Katerine*. The parallels prove only that the author of whichever of these Middle English works was the later knew, and was influenced by, the one which was earlier.

[1] *Ste Marherete*, ed. Frances M. Mack (E.E.T.S., o.s. 193, 1934), pp. xiv–xvi. Miss Mack argues that the part of B which was corrected must, in the exemplar, have been written by a different and less careful scribe than the rest, and so have been in greater need of correction; she supports this hypothesis by demonstrating a number of differences of orthography in the corrected portion which presumably derive from the exemplar (since the B text itself was written throughout by a single scribe). The corrections occur up to f. 21 of the manuscript (p. 12, l. 7 of Miss Mack's text).

[2] d'Ardenne, p. xxxviii; cf. n. 2 there, with its cross-references to her notes to the text of B, in which the detailed readings are discussed.

[3] Mack, p. xviii.

Ste Iuliene.[1] It is not easy to judge how correct was the ultimate archetype of B, R, and the lost R-type manuscript.
As there are only two extant texts, the need (real or supposed)
to emend where B and R differ may show no more than that
each has varied from a correct archetype; and even if they
agree, wholly or partly, in what is claimed to be a false
reading, the agreement may be due to the mistaken adoption
by B of an R-type reading.[2] Nevertheless in each case it
seems that the archetype was already corrupt. Miss Mack
finds only a little evidence of corruptions shared by B and
R, and concludes that the archetype, being 'negligible as a
source of common error', 'must have been a first copy of the
author's text'.[3] Miss d'Ardenne, whose examination of her
texts is perhaps more rigorous and who is certainly more
willing to speculate about shared corruptions, finds more
frequent occasion to emend,[4] but none of the assumed errors

---

[1] d'Ardenne, pp. xxxix–xl. But the assumption (pp. xxxviii–ix) of an
ur-text E, of which U (the common ancestor of B and R) was a moderniza-
tion, seems to me extremely doubtful. In general Miss d'Ardenne's
hypotheses about the textual descent of *Ste Iuliene* seem over-elaborate.

[2] Thus in *Ste Iuliene*, B, l. 550, where B and R partly agree and partly
differ, Miss d'Ardenne's reconstructed text (of which I assume the
correctness) rejects one of the points on which the two manuscripts agree
except in spelling (*ouertoke* B, *ouerteoc* R). The simple deduction is that
this error was already present in the archetype; but it could be that B
derived it from an R-type text (i.e. that the B tradition is contaminated by
that of R).

[3] Mack, p. xviii. There is a shared error *meokeliche* for *meaðeliche*
'moderately' at B 34/2 (R 35/2) and an omission of words indicating a
change of speaker at B 38/5 (R 39/4).

[4] See d'Ardenne, p. xl, n. 2, where she says 'the common errors in
B and R are not numerous, and seldom decisive', but her list there is a
little shorter than it should be. Her notes to the text suggest that there are
common errors at B 150 (R 112), probably B 182–3 (R 133), perhaps
B 207 (R 183), B 486 (R 380), probably B 526 (R 412), probably B 568–9
(R 445), B 585 (R 458), B 684 *fiten* (R 536), perhaps B 705 (not in R;
omitted as unintelligible?), B 699 (R 548), B 718 (R 563), B 724 (R 570;
presumed omission of *þe lif*). But I reject *gadien* (B 547, R 429), for it is
inconceivable to me that a form copied five times in extant manuscripts

is of such a nature that it could not be produced by a single process of copying. In both cases, therefore, the archetype seems to have been a direct copy of the autograph, with this difference, that the archetypal text of *Ste Margarete* would appear to have been rather more carefully copied (perhaps by a different scribe) than that of *Ste Iuliene*. But what is clearest is that in both cases the descent was not simple and that the scribe (or the corrector) of B was comparing two variant exemplars, neither of which was accurate and neither of which was fully trusted.

(*b*) The life of *Ste Katerine* and *Sawles Warde* are found not only in B and R, but also in MS. Cotton Titus D. xvii (T).[1] In both cases B and R form a sub-group linked by shared textual errors, and must be derived from a lost manuscript of which T is independent. The archetype of the three manuscripts would appear in each case to have been a relatively good copy of the author's text, probably a direct fair copy. In *Sawles Warde* it had a sprinkling of simple errors; in *Ste Katerine*, which is very nearly twice as long, the errors are proportionately somewhat more frequent, but are still simple.[2]

(*c*) *Hali Meiðhad* occurs in B and T but not in R. The two texts are independent but not widely divergent;[3] B,

(not to mention the antecedent copies which must be assumed in the stemmas of *Ste I.* and *Ste K.* and which must have transmitted *gadien*) was a mere error for **gaden*; these scribes did not hesitate to alter forms of common words which they did not accept as correct. Influence from ON *gadd* (to which *OED* refers *gadien*, s.v. *gad* sb.[1]) will account for the *ð*, OE **gādig* (beside *gād*) for the rest. The sense is 'spikes' rather than 'goads'.

[1] In editions of works of the *Katherine*-group, the siglum C is commonly used for the Cotton MS. But in discussions of the text of *Ancrene Wisse* it is necessary to use T, not C, and it seems to me better to use T regularly.

[2] On the textual tradition of these two works, see Appendix V, below (pp. 421–8).

[3] Perhaps the most troublesome instance is at ll. 324–6 (Bodley text)

which is usually the more faithful, is probably a direct copy of their common ancestor, but T is likely to be separated from it by an intervening manuscript in which the works (other than *Ancrene Wisse*) which T contains were first collected. The archetype itself had a number of errors[1] but they are not complex, so that, once more, it was probably a direct copy of the autograph. *Hali Meiðhad* has the simplest textual history of all the works in the group.

It does not follow, from the fact that the texts of the *Katherine*-group had these different histories, that they were written by different men. It does not even follow, strictly, that they were written and published at different times, but this is the simplest explanation—that *Ste Margarete* and *Ste Iuliene* were written first and therefore had the longest and most complex histories, and that *Hali Meiðhad* was written last and therefore had the simplest. And it is here that there is a striking correlation with Miss Clarke's statistics of the proportions of French-derived vocabulary in the several works; for these statistics, when the conditions of the time are taken into account, again suggest that *Ste Margarete* and *Ste Iuliene* are the earliest works, *Ste Katerine* and *Sawles Warde* somewhat later, and *Hali Meiðhad* the most recent. It is obvious that for none of the pieces did the compiler of the Bodleian collection have available to him the

in the edition by A. F. Colborn (Copenhagen, 1940). Here I assume that the original read:

ʒet of þes þreo had—meiðhad ant widewehad, ant wedlachad þe þridde— þu maht bi þe degrez of hare blisse icnawen hwuch ant bi hu muchel þe an passeð þe oþre.

I would explain the variants of the two texts by assuming that their common ancestor merely corrupted ʒet into ʒef. Then B, retaining the false ʒef, altered *wedlachad þe þridde* to *wedlac is þe þridde* to supply a verb for the *if*-clause; but T simply omitted the false ʒef and as a distinct process altered the word-order to *þe þridde wedlachad*.

[1] Some but not all of these were pointed out by Colborn; others will be in the edition being prepared by Miss E. N. Millett, to whom I am indebted for information about the text.

autograph manuscript; in every case he had to use erroneous copies as his exemplars. This situation is a matter for some surprise, since the dialectal consistency of the texts must mean that all the pieces were originally written in the same literary and religious centre as produced MS. Bodley 34;[1] the easiest explanation would be that not even *Hali Meiðhad* had been recently written, and that enough time had passed for the autographs to have been lost, destroyed, or given away.[2] There is a contrast with the Corpus text of *Ancrene Wisse*, based in all likelihood on the author's original, as revised by himself; on the other hand there is a parallel to all the other manuscripts and versions of *Ancrene Wisse*, which descend from a single manuscript β which already contained errors (though these errors were relatively few). In every case the method of publication seems to have been by a single fair copy, from which all other copies descend directly or indirectly; the exception is the revised text of *Ancrene Wisse*, republished from the revised autograph probably in two copies, of which only the Corpus MS. survives.

It is not easy to date the works of the *Katherine*-group. The Bodleian MS., as we have seen, is on palaeographical grounds assigned to the first quarter of the thirteenth century, but on linguistic grounds cannot be removed by more than a few years from the date of the Corpus MS., which is usually put at *c.* 1230 and must be later than 1224. The Bodleian MS. can therefore hardly be earlier than 1220, and might more safely be dated about 1225. But if none of

---

[1] It must also mean that the copies used as exemplars were written in the 'AB language', or at the least in some closely allied dialect (such as that of R itself) from which consistent retranslation into AB forms was easy. The latter is possible, for B does not always use the expected AB form.

[2] Possibly the authors wrote their drafts in plummet so that, after the fair copy had been made, the parchment could be cleaned and reused.

the works which it contains was newly written, they must all be earlier than 1220 or even 1215 (if the manuscript is dated about 1220). There is, as far as I know, no internal evidence of date in the three saints' lives, which belong to a timeless genre; but there is an indication in each of the other two works. *Sawles Warde* includes a passage[1] which is directly translated from one in the *Visio Monachi de Eynsham*,[2] which claims to be an account of a vision which occurred in 1196; obviously the literary work which describes it may be later still, since even if it is fraudulent (in the sense that no such vision was ever vouchsafed) the author of the alleged record would be especially careful to give a date earlier than that of the publication of his book,[3] and we must allow more time still for the literary account to become available to the author of *Sawles Warde* in Herefordshire. I can see no justification whatever for the suggestion that the lines in *Sawles Warde* are a later addition; though they are, of course, not present in or suggested by the primary source, the Anselmian dialogue, they are so linked both to what precedes and to what follows that it is impossible to conceive how the passage in the English work could have run without them. It follows that *Sawles Warde* is certainly later than 1196 and in all probability later than 1200. The author of *Hali Meiðhad*, who had no single and obvious source, beyond reasonable doubt read at least one passage in the *Moralia super Evangelia* by Alexander of Bath, the influence of which on *Ancrene Wisse* was both extensive and important. The *Moralia*, in Book III chapter 92, contains a

[1] ed. Bennett and Smithers, ll. 131–6 (*hefde a mon . . . arudden him ut þrof*). The parallel was noted by Hall, *Early Middle English*, ii. 512 (note to l. 116), where the Latin is quoted.

[2] ed. P. M. Huber, *Romanische Forschungen*, xvi (1904), 641–733. The passage used in *Sawles Warde* is from p. 663, l. 25 to p. 664, l. 4.

[3] In fact, however, he claims that the event took place in 'the present year' 1196 (p. 646, ll. 7–10), so that he had at least begun to write in 1196.

discussion (duly entered under 'Virginitas' in the index of the Lincoln College MS., so that it would not be difficult to find) which in brief compass expresses a succession of ideas elaborated in *Hali Meiðhad*,[1] and there are certain more precise parallels: both authors quote or paraphrase Isaiah 56 : 4–5, applying it to virgins, and proceed to compare virgins to angels, and to refer to their music in heaven;[2] and the *Moralia*'s phrases 'Earundem preter [lucem] auream est corona aureola'[3] and 'duplex corona' are combined and expanded, in a later passage in *Hali Meiðhad*,[4] in the sentence

Ant alle ha beoð icrunet þe blissið in heouene wið kempene crune; ah þe meidenes habbeð, upo þeo þe is to alle iliche imeane, a gerlondesche schininde schenre þen þe sunne, [*aureola*] ihaten o Latines ledene.

Now the *Moralia* is certainly later than 1189, since it tells a story about *Ricardus rex Anglie*, and indeed, for a variety of reasons, must be later than 1200; and if its author Alexander of Bath is correctly identified with Alexander dean of Wells, it was probably put into its published form between 1205 and the date of the latter's death, which was later than July 1209 but probably before June 1212 (by which time he had been replaced as dean).[5] Once more allowing some time for the work to become known in Herefordshire, *Hali Meiðhad* is in all probability later than 1210.

[1] For the text of the Latin, see Appendix VI (pp. 429–30).

[2] *Hali Meiðhad*, ll. 240–60.

[3] Both manuscripts omit *lucem*, but obviously some feminine noun is required before *auream*. The phrase *lux aurea* occurs in Latin hymns, and the sentence in the *Moralia* reads like a prose version of an accentual verse couplet: *Preter lucem auream | corona aureola*. But I have not identified the source.

[4] ll. 316–19. For *aureola* T has the French form *auriole* and B the gross corruption *an urle*, evidently a misreading of the form retained in T; their common ancestor must have gallicized the Latin word.

[5] See E. J. Dobson, *Moralities on the Gospels* (Oxford, 1975), chapter iv.

This means that we are enabled to assign rough dates to the three stages in the development of the *Katherine*-group which are revealed by their differing textual histories and the proportion of French-derived words in their vocabularies. The latest stage, represented by *Hali Meiðhad* alone, may be put between 1210 and 1220. This work is probably earlier than *Ancrene Wisse* but not necessarily so, since if the two are by different men, as most of us think, the much greater proportion of French words in *Ancrene Wisse* might be an individual feature of its author's vocabulary and not a sign of later date. The second stage, represented by *Sawles Warde* (which is probably later than 1200, though we do not know how much later) and by *Ste Katerine*, might be put between 1200 and 1210, which would be consistent with the fact that MS. Bodley 34 is separated by two inter-vening copies from the autographs of both works. The earliest stage, represented by *Ste Margarete* and *Ste Iuliene*, might be assigned to the last decade of the twelfth century or perhaps to the first years of the thirteenth.[1] It could hardly be earlier than 1190 for the reason adduced by Tolkien, that any greater interval between the date of composition and the date of the Bodleian MS. would have produced more signs than there are of two linguistic strata, the authors' forms and the scribe's. The whole group must have been written at various dates between, at the outside, 1190 and 1220.

Whether or not the *Katherine*-group was written by one man or by several, and whether or not *Ancrene Wisse* was by a different man again (as is most probable), one always comes back to the basic proposition that all these works and the *Wohunge*-group must have originated in a single

[1] Compare Miss Mack's opinion (*Ste Margarete*, pp. xx–xxi) that the opening years of the thirteenth century are a possible date for the composi-tion of *Ste Margarete*.

community. They are all in the same form of language, and are linked by the manuscript tradition.[1] *Ancrene Wisse* refers to 'your English book of St. Margaret'[2] and quotes a verse-paraphrase of a Latin couplet (which, it says, 'was taught you long ago' (*ȝare*), which must confirm that *Ste Margarete* was much earlier); the same verse-paraphrase, incomplete and with some variation of detail, occurs in *Ste Margarete*.[3] There are obvious links of style and thought between *Sawles Warde* and *Ancrene Wisse* (especially Part II), and others between *Ancrene Wisse* and the *Wohunge*-group.[4] *Hali Meiðhad* is indebted to a passage in a work which the author of *Ancrene Wisse* had studied extensively. It is obvious, and not seriously disputed, that the works are the product of a single school of writers. But it does not follow that they were all intended, in the first instance, for the same group of women; one can easily imagine that, if there were several groups of anchoresses in the vicinity of Wigmore, the abbey might have taken more than one of them under its care and that some of the works might have been written for one, some for another. Miss Clark indeed writes, 'The greater "modernity" of *Ancrene Wisse* not only

[1] See the tabular arrangements of the contents of the manuscripts given by Hall, *Early Middle English*, ii. 355, and Shepherd, *Ancrene Wisse*, p. xiv.

[2] Corpus MS., f. 66a/19 (Morton, p. 244).

[3] Corpus MS., f. 65a/16–23 (Morton, pp. 240–2); *Ste Margarete*, ed. Mack, p. 34, ll. 18–21. As the English verses occur elsewhere in Middle English, they were probably not written either by the author of *Ste Margarete* or by the author of *Ancrene Wisse*, and are probably quoted from memory in both works; the textual variations may be due merely to aberrations of memory. But Miss Mack argues (pp. 73–4) that the version in *Ancrene Wisse* may be a revision of that in *Ste Margarete*, and Miss d'Ardenne (*Ste Juliene* pp. xliv–v) holds that the reference in *Ancrene Wisse* to *Ste Margarete*, and its rehandling of the verses, are inconsistent with common authorship. The priority of *Ste Margarete* is in any case not in doubt; nor can it reasonably be doubted that *Ancrene Wisse* is referring to the extant *Ste Margarete*.

[4] Meredith Thompson, *þe Wohunge of Ure Lauerd*, pp. xvi–xx.

in vocabulary but also in syntax may suggest not only a different, perhaps younger, author, but also a different original audience, less traditional-minded, more forward-looking, more cosmopolitan',[1] but this hardly follows from the facts; if one explains the linguistic differences by the assumption of a different author, one does not need and has no warrant to assume a different audience also—and in any case I doubt whether the authors would have varied their language to suit the tastes or capacities of their audiences, and whether the audiences would have so differed in social status as to have varying linguistic capabilities. There is, moreover, the explicit evidence of *Ancrene Wisse* itself that the women for whom it was written possessed *Ste Margarete*. A more cogent reason for assuming that there were more anchorite households than one is the early history of the texts. As we have seen, the *Katherine*-group did not always circulate as a unity; the Royal MS. lacks *Hali Meiðhad*, perhaps because it is a copy of a collection made before *Hali Meiðhad* was written, and the Titus MS. lacks *Ste Margarete* and *Ste Iuliene*, though it has the rest of the *Katherine*-group and also a text of *Ancrene Wisse* and of *Þe Wohunge of ure Lauerd*. In every case the method of publication seems to have been by making a single fair copy from the auto-graph, but from it other copies were made at an early date. The case is clearest with *Ancrene Wisse* itself,[2] where from the first fair copy there were made two further (lost) copies γ and δ; of these, γ was used, a little before the making of the Corpus revision, as the exemplar for two more copies, the surviving Cleopatra MS. and the lost manuscript which was the basis for the French translation of the Vitellius MS., and δ eventually became the ancestor of all other surviving copies and versions except the Corpus MS.

---

[1] '*Ancrene Wisse* and the *Katherine Group*', p. 123.
[2] See the *stemma codicum* printed on p. 287, below.

itself. But there was obviously also an early duplication of copies of all the works of the *Katherine*-group except perhaps *Hali Meiðhad*. The reason can hardly have been to enable each of the three sisters for whom *Ancrene Wisse* was originally begun to have her own personal copy of all the works; if they lived together in a single household, as seems to be implied, they would be able to share a single copy, and to provide each with her own would have been a remarkable extravagance when books were so expensive and so laborious to make. It is much more likely that copies were multiplied because there were more households than one. We read in *Ancrene Wisse* of the sending of messengers from one anchoress to another, which must imply separate anchorite households, though within walking distance of each other;[1] and there is also a disapproving reference to an anchoress who refused to lend another a book.[2] The making of additional copies may have been undertaken to avoid the occasion for such unseemly behaviour. We need not assume that there were as many households as there were copies; a community restricted in numbers might need only a single copy, one increasing in numbers might come to need more. But there is a definite suggestion that there was not merely a single community living in a single place.

It is time to recapitulate the main argument to the point that we have reached. *Ancrene Wisse* was written by a cleric, more specifically a priest, since he acted as confessor to a

---

[1] Corpus MS., ff. 69b/24–70a/1 (Morton, p. 256). The pronouns used show that the messenger (*sondesmon*) envisaged is a woman, presumably one of the servants. Compare also Corpus f. 117a/11–18, in an addition peculiar to Corpus, laying down rules for the anchoresses's conduct when they receive visits from 'your sisters' maidens'. But the following sentence, saying that two nights is long enough for anyone to be entertained, has probably gone on to guests in general.

[2] Corpus MS., f. 67b/2–4 (Morton, p. 248).

group of women religious; and he was a member of an order which admitted lay brothers. It is very unlikely that he was a monk, and for reasons both of chronology and of the way in which, in added passages, he refers to the friars, he cannot have been a friar himself. The Augustinians remain, and there is positive evidence that he was an Augustinian. It is probable that he was a member of one of the independent Augustinian congregations, in view of the existence of lay brothers in his 'order', the strong Cistercian influence, and the detailed parallels with the regulations and practices of Prémontré, Beauvais, St. Victor, and the Dominicans. But the Dominicans must be excluded on grounds of date, and there was no Premonstratensian house in the Welsh marches; on the other hand there is evidence, none of it perhaps conclusive in itself but nevertheless concurrent, to connect *Ancrene Wisse* and its group with St. Victor—verbal parallels with the *Liber Ordinis*, the knowledge of Victorine writings (especially the commentary on the Augustinian Rule), and the independent descent of *Sawles Warde* and the corresponding chapters in the Victorine compilation *De Anima* from a distinctive redaction of the Anselmian dialogue *De Custodia interioris hominis*.

The nature of the language in which *Ancrene Wisse* and the *Katherine*-group are written requires us to look for a religious house of some size and age in the West Midlands, close to the Welsh border and in an area in which there were Scandinavian settlers; but the content of the works also requires the assumption that it was a house in intimate contact with the main centres of contemporary thought, including especially the university of Paris. The area which is most likely on linguistic grounds and in view of the provenance of the two vital manuscripts, Corpus 402 and Bodley 34, is northern Herefordshire or southern Shropshire; and the recorded facts of Danish landholdings in 1066 also point to north-west Herefordshire and south-west Shropshire. But between Hereford and Shrewsbury the only Augustinian house that had the necessary size and age by 1225 or so was Wigmore Abbey, a daughter-house of St. Victor in Paris; indeed, even if houses of all orders in this area (but excluding Hereford and Shrewsbury themselves) are taken into account, Wigmore is still the most suitable. If the area of search is extended to include all English territory within fifteen miles of the Welsh border between the Severn and the Mersey, there are still only six Augustinian houses to be considered. Wormsley, Snead-Chirbury, and Ratlinghope we have already dismissed as too small and too late-founded.[1] The small house at Flanesford, six miles north-east of Monmouth, was not yet in existence when *Ancrene Wisse* was written; it was founded in 1346.[2] There remain only Wigmore and Haughmond, north-east of Shrewsbury. To extend the area to twenty miles from the border would bring in only two more Augustinian houses, both large and important— at the southern extremity Llanthony Priory near Gloucester, which is too far south to fit the linguistic evidence, and at the northern extremity Norton Priory, east of Runcorn, which is too far north (and which, though within twenty miles as the crow flies of the nearest part of Flintshire, is not to be considered as within the Welsh marches).[3] The choice

[1] See pp. 129–30, above.

[2] Knowles and Hadcock, *Medieval Religious Houses*, p. 157.

[3] On Llanthony near Gloucester (known as Llanthony II, to distinguish it from the original Llanthony in the Black Mountains in NW. Monmouthshire) and on Norton see Knowles and Hadcock, pp. 144, 148; both were founded before Wigmore and were larger and richer (allowing for the deliberate understatement of Norton's income by the commissioners of 1535; see p. 148), but neither belonged to one of the independent Augustinian congregations. I omit Llanthony I from consideration because it was in a purely Welsh district; moreover after the foundation of Llanthony II in 1136 it was only of moderate size and importance (thirteen canons remained at Llanthony I in 1136, some twenty-seven went to Llanthony II) and seems progressively to have declined

really lies between Wigmore and Haughmond. But Haughmond is rather too far to the north and in too purely English a district; it was an ordinary Augustinian house, not a member of one of the independent congregations; and it is most unlikely that an author living so near to Shrewsbury would refer to its religious communities in the way that is done in the Corpus addition discussed on pp. 133–7, above. Wigmore, by contrast, fulfils all the conditions—an Augustinian house of the requisite size and length of life, a member of an independent congregation and specifically a daughter-house of St. Victor, situated within the area (north Herefordshire and south Shropshire) to which the linguistic and manuscript evidence directly points, and close to the Welsh border in a district of pre-Conquest Danish land-holdings. There are other subsidiary arguments of more doubtful validity, but the decisive consideration is that there is only this one religious house of the right sort and size and age in the right area. To assign *Ancrene Wisse* and its group to any other house would be to ignore either the evidence of their language[1] or that of their Augustinian origin; to assign them to a priest (or a series of priests) unconnected with any religious house would be to ignore both *Ancrene Wisse*'s evidence that its author was a member of an order and the obvious fact that only an organized community could have produced a number of authors and scribes trained in a single distinctive but somewhat old-fashioned orthography. Only Wigmore Abbey fits.

But this means that we must look in the neighbourhood of Wigmore for the community, or more probably communi-

until in 1481, when Llanthony I had only its prior and four canons, the relative positions were reversed and it became a cell of its daughter-house. Like Lanthony II, it did not belong to one of the independent congregations.

[1] And, it may be added, of the textual transmission, if, as I hold, the Corpus MS. is a direct copy of the revised autograph.

ties, of anchoresses for whom the works were first written; and in view of the probable datings of the various works of the *Katherine*-group and of *Ancrene Wisse* itself we must look for them, not at any time that suits our fancy between the twelfth and the early fourteenth century (the venial but confusing practice of some earlier scholars, guessing before they knew the conditions of time and place that had to be satisfied), but within a closely limited period between 1190 and 1225. This of course was not the end of the anchoresses' history, or perhaps one should say of that of the works written for them, for the revision of *Ancrene Wisse*—partially in the margins of the Cleopatra MS. and definitively in the Corpus MS.—and its first translation into French must be somewhat later; but it was between these dates that the works were written and that the women for whom they were written must have been living near Wigmore in their hermitages.

IV

LIMEBROOK PRIORY

THREE miles to the south-west of Wigmore village, and four miles from Wigmore Abbey, was the small nunnery of Limebrook or Lingbrook, built in an angle of a stream that ran down past the village and castle of Lingen, three-quarters of a mile to the north-west, to join the river Lugg about five furlongs south-east of the priory. Early anti-quaries, asking themselves the question at which the author of *Ancrene Wisse* mocks in his Preface, whether the nuns of Limebrook were 'of the white or of the black', were uncer-tain of the answer; as the 1744 edition of Tanner's *Notitia Monastica* says, 'The *Monasticon* placeth Benedictines; and Speed, ms. Bodl. and Gervase of Cant[erbury] make them White nuns.'[1] They were in fact Augustinian canonesses, as Tanner in this posthumous edition correctly states, citing the evidence of the episcopal register of Charles Booth in 1530, nine years before the dissolution of the nunnery.[2] Much earlier, and therefore more to the point, is the evidence of the register of Thomas de Cantilupe, who in 1279, in a letter to the prioress and nuns of *Lyngebrok*, refers to *ordinem vestrum, a viro vite et literature mirabilis, Augustino . . . institutum*;[3] this is confirmed by two entries in the register

---

[1] T. Tanner, *Notitia Monastica* (1744), p. 176 n. In 1697, however, Tanner himself had described them as Benedictines (*Not. Mon.* (1697), p. 87).

[2] *Registrum Caroli Bothe* [etc.], ed. A. T. Bannister (Canterbury & York Soc. xxviii, 1921), p. 241 (dated 1 September 1530).

[3] *The Register of Thomas de Cantilupe*, transcribed by R. G. Griffiths (Canterbury & York Soc. ii, 1906), p. 200. The date of the letter is lost but it was probably written in March or April 1279.

of his successor, Richard of Swinfield, dated 1287 and 1302, which refer to 'the prioress and convent of the church of St. Thomas the Martyr of *Lingebrok*, of the order of St. Augustine'.[1]

As the church at Limebrook was dedicated to St. Thomas of Canterbury, it must have been founded (unless there had been a rededication) after his death on 29 December 1170 and indeed after his canonization on 21 February 1173. Knowles and Hadcock give the date of foundation as 'about 1189',[2] but investigation shows that we are faced by one of those self-propagating historical legends that grow more definite as they become more remote from their source. For Knowles and Hadcock, as their references show, are only putting into figures the statement of the Royal Commission on Historical Monuments[3] that Limebrook was founded 'in or before' the reign of Richard I, which began in 1189; the Commission in turn is obviously following the nineteenth-century version of the *Monasticon*,[4] which cites the authority of the 1744 edition of Tanner's *Notitia*. With Tanner[5] we at last get a reason for the statement, for a footnote makes it clear that it is a deduction from the mention of Limebrook in Gervase of Canterbury's catalogue of English religious houses in his *Mappa Mundi*. But in this work, as printed by Stubbs from the earliest extant manuscript (MS. C.C.C.C. 438, of which the first part, containing the *Mappa Mundi*, was copied about 1260),[6] there is no

[1] 'Prioresse et conventui ecclesie beati [*or* sancti] Thome martiris, de Lingebroke . . . ordinis sancti Augustini': *Registrum Ricardi de Swinfield*, ed. W. W. Capes (Canterbury & York Soc. vi, 1909), pp. 134 (dated 4 February 1287) and 381 (dated 13 April 1302).

[2] *Medieval Religious Houses*, p. 229.

[3] *Herefordshire*, iii (1939), 136.

[4] Dugdale's *Monasticon*, ed. Caley, Ellis, and Blandinel, iv (1823), 181.   [5] Tanner, *Not. Mon.* (1744), p. 176.

[6] *The Historical Works of Gervase of Canterbury*, ed. W. Stubbs (Rolls Series, 1879–80), vol. ii, p. vii.

Castle ✳ ●Brampton Bryan

✚ Wigmore
Abbey

Adforton ●

Woods

Castle

✳ ●WIGMORE

Deerfold

Modern Road

✚ Chapel
of St.
Leonard

Woods

Lime Brook

Castle
✳ ●

Deerfold

● Lower Lye

LINGEN

Lime

Woods

Limebrook
Priory ✚

Brook

● Upper Lye

Deerfold Bridge

R. Lugg

Aymestrey ●

Shirley
Farm

Kinsham ●

Covenhope●

R. Lugg

Scale in miles

1   0   1   2

● Shobdon

WIGMORE AND LINGEN DISTRICT
After Ordnance Survey 1-inch map, sheet 129

mention of Limebrook among the religious houses of Here-fordshire;[1] and Stubbs himself points out that the work 'was copied at different times with enlarged and improved lists under each head. It is to be found in many MSS. from the fourteenth century downwards.'[2] Obviously Limebrook must have been introduced into the list in one of these later expansions; but the important point is that it is not in the earliest manuscript of about 1260, that in conse-quence there is no reason to suppose that the house was known to Gervase himself, and that Tanner's reason for dating its foundation before the composition of the *Mappa Mundi* (which was about 1200) therefore disappears. Yet ironically the date given, on this false ground, by Knowles and Hadcock is almost exactly right; other evidence shows, as we shall see, that the community from which Limebrook Priory developed must have been founded in or be-fore 1190.

The earliest extant reference to nuns at Limebrook in a contemporary record comes in 1221, when the king's jus-tices at the Worcestershire assizes granted a *deodand*, or charitable gift, of three shillings 'to the nuns of Limebrook' (*monialibus de Lingebrok*); the money was paid to Roger le Poher, who must have undertaken to deliver it.[3] He was a member of a family which held lands in both Worcester-shire and Shropshire; in the latter it held the manor of Romsley of the honour of Richard's Castle,[4] and Roger was therefore a tenant of the estate of Margery de Say (and so,

[1] *The Historical Works of Gervase of Canterbury*, ed. W. Stubbs (Rolls Series, 1879–80), vol. ii, p. 435.

[2] Ibid., p. xlii; cf. also vol. i, pp. xxviii–xxix, on the uncertainty whether even the Corpus MS. preserves the list exactly as Gervase compiled it.

[3] *Rolls of the Justices in Eyre for Lincolnshire 1218–19 and Worcestershire 1221*, ed. D. M. Stenton (Selden Soc., 1934), p. 647 (no. 1524).

[4] R. W. Eyton, *The Antiquities of Shropshire* (1854–60), iii. 197–8. Roger le Poher is recorded from about 1211 to 1231.

at this time, of her third husband, William de Stuteville), from which Limebrook Priory, some twenty or more years later, was to receive its most valuable thirteenth-century possession.[1] It is possible that the nuns of Limebrook were indebted, for their *deodand*, to the influence of Margery or of her husband; and it may be significant that in Easter Term of this same year (1221) William de Stuteville and Margery his wife had brought a custody action against John of Lingen,[2] the son (as we shall see) of the man who is credited by one source with the foundation of Limebrook. If John had come to a settlement with them, he would have had a good chance to commend to their favour the community which his father had established.[3]

The next reference to Limebrook is in 1226, when the king (i.e. the young Henry III, acting presumably through his justiciar, Hubert de Burgh)[4] issued from Shrewsbury a close writ dated 27 August and addressed to Godescall de Maghelines, the bailiff of Montgomery.[5] In this it is recited that the king has granted to Walter of Hukelton 5s. a year in respect of his land at *Aldefelde*, which was in the king's hand and from which named tenants had been accustomed to pay Walter 2s. 8d. a year in rent,[6] and that he has also granted to

---

[1] See below, pp. 185–6.

[2] *Curia Regis Rolls*, x. 96.

[3] William de Stuteville and Margery his wife were concerned in cases heard at the 1221 Worcester assizes; see D. M. Stenton, pp. 491–3, 503, 573–5 (nos. 992, 1016, 1167). But William was not present in person and was represented by attorneys (p. 665, no. 1557); and if Margery appeared in person (it is not clear that she did), it was only to change her attorney (p. 627, no. 1297) in a case brought against her and her husband by her father's widow.

[4] Cf. F. M. Powicke, *The Thirteenth Century* (1953), p. 43, who says that Hubert de Burgh got possession of the castle and honour of Montgomery in 1223.

[5] *Rotuli litterarum clausarum*, ii (1844), 134–5.

[6] Walter de Hukelton or Hokelton took his surname from the manor of Hoccleton (in Chirbury parish in SW. Shropshire, ENE. of Montgomery),

Engeram de Bouleres 16s. a year for the land at *Ristone* and
Acle which had belonged to his brother William de Bouleres
and which also was in the king's hand.[1] The writ then orders
Godescall to pay 5s. and 16s. respectively to Walter and to
Engeram and concludes: 'Also pay to the nuns of Limebrook (*monialibus de Lingebroc*) half a mark of our gift.'[2]
This seems inconsequential, but may not be. In October
1223 the crown had taken over the honour of Montgomery
from the ruler of Southern Powys, and had commenced the
building of the new castle of Montgomery;[3] the land-cases
dealt with in the writ are obviously in consequence of the
take-over, since the places mentioned were dependent on
Montgomery. The king had almost certainly visited Montgomery on his way to Shrewsbury,[4] and the purpose of the
writ is to record his decisions and to authorize payment.

which he held of the honour of Montgomery. He is first heard of in 1224
(Eyton, xi. 159–61) and died in 1250 (*Cal. I.p.m.*, i. 45 (no. 180)). *Aldefelde* has not been identified, but as some of the tenants bore distinctively
Welsh names it must have been in this area, probably in Montgomeryshire itself.

[1] *Ristone* is Rhiston in Shropshire, south of Chirbury and ESE. of
Montgomery, and *Acle* is Ackley in Montgomeryshire, NNE. of Montgomery; both were members of the honour of Montgomery (Eyton,
xi. 72, 153–4). The writ records that Engeram had a 'charter' (*cartam*)
of his brother's in respect of the land, but that the oral testimony (*ut
dicitur*) was that he had not had seisin of it.

[2] In both the last two sentences, *facias habere* is used with the dative,
evidently to mean no more than 'pay'.

[3] J. E. Lloyd, *A History of Wales*, ii. 662. King John had granted
Montgomery in 1216 to Gwenwynwyn, prince of Powys (Lloyd, p. 649);
the English Crown resumed possession in 1223 in its alarm at the power of
Llywelyn ab Iorwerth, prince of Gwynedd.

[4] The king was at Hereford until 21 August, at Leominster on the
22nd, and at Lydbury North, SE. of Bishop's Castle, on the 23rd; he
was at Shrewsbury from the 27th (when the writ to the bailiff of Montgomery was issued) until the 29th, to meet his half-sister Joan and her husband Llywelyn (Lloyd, p. 665 and n. 58). As Lydbury North is off the
direct route from Leominster to Shrewsbury and is no further from
Shrewsbury than it is from Leominster (so that the king, if he had gone

Evidently his attention had somehow been drawn to the nuns of Limebrook during his consideration of the affairs of Montgomery,[1] and certainly it was to the account of the bailiff that he charged his not very princely gift. Though its profit was small, Limebrook had achieved the distinction of royal notice.

After 1226 there is a gap before we again hear of Lime-brook Priory. We know that the church of Clifton-on-Teme was appropriated to it between 1240 and 1268 and that it received at least one benefaction from the lands of Margery de Lacy, who died in 1256,[2] but contemporary records do not survive. A charter of (probably) about 1252, surviving in a fourteenth-century copy, refers to and names a prioress of Limebrook.[3] In 1277 the prioress was defendant in an action concerning lands, discussed below; this is closely followed in date by bishop Thomas de Cantilupe's letter of 1279 to the prioress and nuns of Limebrook (*Lyngebrok*, *Lyngbrok*) about a visitation of their convent.[4] There is, I think, no necessary significance in the fact that the records of 1221 and 1226 speak simply of 'the nuns of Limebrook' (*moniales de Lingebrok*), in contrast to the phrases 'the prioress and nuns' (*priorissa et moniales*) and 'the prioress and convent' (*priorissa et conventus*) found in later records;

straight on, could have reached Shrewsbury on the 24th) it must seem probable that he was diverging to deal with affairs in Montgomery and had spent two or three days doing so.

[1] Both Walter of Hukelton and Engeram de Bouleres were connected with the neighbourhood of Chirbury, which Lloyd (p. 389 and n. 107) says was 'the ecclesiastical centre of a wide region' and 'the mother church of Churchstoke, Forden, Hyssington, Snead, and Montgomery'; in particular, at this time, it was the site of an Augustinian priory (see p. 129, above). One possibility is therefore that the Augustinian canons of Chirbury had found means to commend to the king's favour the Augustinian canonesses of Limebrook. But there may have been a more direct link between Limebrook and the honour of Montgomery; see p. 283, below. [2] See below, pp. 186–90.

[3] See below, pp. 211 ff.   [4] See above, p. 174 and note 3.

even after the fuller formulae were in use, the simpler is still found,[1] and it should not be assumed, from the mere lack of mention of a prioress in 1221 and 1226, that the house had not yet been organized as a priory.

It is important for our understanding of the origins of Limebrook to determine whence, and more significantly when, it acquired the little property that it possessed in the thirteenth century. Apart from the charter of about 1252, of which I defer consideration, the earliest surviving record directly bearing on this issue is the court case of 1277. In Michaelmas Term of that year Agnes de Muscegros and other heirs and kin of Walter de Muscegros[2] sued the prioress, under the terms of the Dictum of Kenilworth, for his lands at places which were probably Winforton, on the Wye, Tretire, and Bodenham.[3] The details of the case are unclear,

[1] It occurs, for example, even in the *Taxatio Ecclesiastica* of 1291 (*Tax. Eccles. P. Nicholai IV* (Record Commission, 1802), pp. 165b, 172b).

[2] At his death (before 2 December 1264) his heirs were his seven surviving aunts and the children of two others (*Cal. I.p.m.*, i. 192–3 (no. 606)). It was essentially the same array of aunts and cousins who thirteen years later sued the prioress. As Agnes heads the list, it may be suspected that her son John of Monmouth was the prime mover in the action.

[3] *Abbreviatio Placitorum* (1811), p. 193. The date given in the heading is Michaelmas Term 6 Edw. I, but this should properly be 5–6 Edw. I (M.T. 1277). The place-names all seem corrupted. (i) *Lingebork* is obviously for *Lingebrok*, Limebrook. (ii) *Wlfreton* agrees with *Wlferton* in the Close Rolls, but there is no Woolverton in Herefordshire, and the return to the inquisition *post mortem*, the originating document, has *Wynfreton*, Winforton. (iii) *Reccir* is plainly a misreading of *Rettir*, the *Retir(e)* of the Close Rolls and the *Ryttyr* of the inquisition; these are the normal medieval forms of a place-name that was corrupted to *Tretire* in the sixteenth century (Bannister, *Place-Names of Herefordshire*, and Ekwall, *ODEPN*, s.n. *Tretire*). Tretire (spelt *Rythir*) had been held by Walter's grandfather of the same name in 1210–12 (*Red Book of the Exchequer*, ii. 497). (iv) *Bordham* must be an error for the *Bodeham* (Bodenham) of the inquisition and the Close Rolls.

partly owing to the devious part played in the affairs of the Muscegros estate by John Lestrange the younger;[1] but in outline Walter de Muscegros had been a Montfortian when he died in late 1264,[2] and after the royalist triumph at Evesham, Lestrange (who had changed sides in time)[3] was given possession of Walter's properties. But in consequence of the Dictum of Kenilworth (October 1267) he came, a year later, to an arrangement with John of Monmouth (the son of Agnes de Muscegros), acting as attorney for the heirs; in return for £140, payable in instalments over

[1] See *Cal. I.p.m.*, i. 192–3 (no. 606); *Close R. 1264–8*, pp. 24–5, 100–1, 110, 489–90; *Cal. Pat. R. 1258–66*, p. 602. After Muscegros's death Lestrange seized his lands by force and had to be ejected by the Montfortian government, yet he had already promised timber from Walter's manor of Monnington in Straddel for building work in the chapel in Hereford Priory in which Walter was buried. He was an executor of the will, yet after Evesham he again took possession of the estate and had to be bought out, and even so kept part of it for himself.

[2] He held lands of the honour of Brecon, i.e. of Humphrey de Bohun the younger, who remained a leader of the Montfortian party until the end and died of wounds received at Evesham; this is probably why Muscegros himself was a Montfortian. The agreement of October 1268 says that his 'transgressions', on account of which the king had given his lands to Lestrange, had been forced (*impositae*) on him. About 10–11 November 1264 Muscegros was one of the wardens of Hereford castle when the town was attacked by a Marcher army under Roger de Mortimer and including Hamo Lestrange among its lesser leaders (*Cal. Inq. Misc. 1219–1307*, pp. 100–1 (no. 291); his death may have been a consequence of this fighting.

[3] On 7 March 1265, despite his recent forcible seizure of the Muscegros lands, the Montfortian government committed Montgomery castle to 'John Lestrange the younger' and ordered him to come to court for urgent discussions, and on 2 April it repeated the order for the delivery of Montgomery to him, allegedly with the compliance of 'Edward the king's son'. But Lestrange had joined his father John and his brother Hamo on the royalist side before Evesham (T. F. Tout, *Collected Papers*, ii. 70). Eyton, *Shropshire*, x. 272–3, who seems to have taken a rather simple-minded view of Marcher manoeuvrings at this time (Tout, ii. 42, n. 2), did not realize this, and assumed that John the younger remained a 'traitor', i.e. a Montfortian. He was probably playing a double game, like Gilbert de Clare.

eighteen months, he surrendered most of their properties.[1]
He gave back, however, only the moiety of Tretire (and of
Lassington in Gloucestershire),[2] and he must have kept the
whole of Winforton, which is not mentioned (either as
Winfreton or as *Wlfreton*) in the agreement; it is also possible,
though not probable, that he had acquired a parcel of Muscegros land at Bodenham.[3] He could, therefore, have given
land at two of these places, and possibly at all three, to
Limebrook Priory either before his death in December
1275 or by his will.[4] The lawsuit against the prioress followed
within two years. I have found no further record of it,[5]
but it may well have been compromised; the search in the
Chancellor's rolls which the court ordered would have dis-
closed that Walter de Muscegros, at the time of his death,
had held the manors of Tretire and Winforton (*Wlfreton*),
but no land at Bodenham, so that the prioress may have been
obliged to surrender any land that she had temporarily held
at the first two places, but not at the third. Certainly there is

[1] *Close R. 1264–8*, pp. 489–90. The memorandum is enrolled after
one dated 28 October 1268, witnessed by Lestrange, and is probably of
the same date. The first payment of £20 was due on St. Martin's Day,
11 November.

[2] This also caused litigation, in Hilary Term 1290 (*Abbrev. Placit.*,
p. 221).

[3] In 1242–3 Walter de Muscegros held a half hide at Bodenham of
the honour of Brecon (*Book of Fees*, ii. 805, 813). But the return of the
inquisition *post mortem* of February 1265, and later records, mention
only two mills at Bodenham, both of which were to be returned under the
agreement of October 1268, and say nothing of lands. Nevertheless the
inclusion of *Bordham*, i.e. Bodenham, in the lawsuit of 1277 seems to
imply that the Muscegros family believed, or wished it to be believed,
that it had been deprived of lands there.

[4] Eyton, x. 277, fixes his death before 28 December 1275, though the
writ of *diem clausit extremum* did not issue until 26 February 1276.

[5] The reason may be the fate of John of Monmouth, who before
3 August 1279 killed a chaplain in Wiltshire and fled, but before 17 May
1281 was hanged for his crime in Wilton (*Cal. Fine R.*, i. 115, 146, 147,
151, 185; *Cal. Inq. Misc. 1219–1307*, p. 363 (no. 1233); *Cal. Close R.
1279–88*, p. 90).

no later record that the priory held lands at Tretire or at Winforton (*Wlfreton*), and in 1292 members of the Muscegros family were in possession of Tretire.[1] At Bodenham, however, the priory had land producing rent valued at £2 in 1291; this may have been, or have included, the half hide that Walter de Muscegros held there in 1242–3 but not at his death in 1264—but it may have come rather from the Lacy honour of Weobley.[2] In any case, even if the land at Bodenham had come from Walter's holding, the priory must have acquired it after 1242–3, and it cannot have formed part of the original endowment.

By the time of the ecclesiastical taxation of Pope Nicholas IV in 1291, Limebrook owned property in a number of places.[3] It seems possible that the prioress, like other tax-payers at other times, did not make an absolutely full statement of her affairs to the papal commissioners,[4] but the

[1] It was held by John Tregoths (Tregoz, Tregos) jointly with his wife Mabilia (otherwise Amabilia, Amabilis), one of Walter de Muscegros's aunts (*Placita de Quo Warranto*, p. 266).

[2] See below, pp. 186–90. The value of the rent (£2), which is little less than the whole value of the priory's manor at Marston and four times the value of its carucate at Eardisland, suggests that it held more than half a hide at Bodenham.

[3] *Tax. Eccles.*, pp. 165b, 172b; cf. Dugdale, *Monasticon*, ed. Caley, Ellis, and Blandinel, iv. 182. The forms of the place-names are not in all respects accurate and have to be compared with those used by the Ministers' Accounts of the Augmentation Office in 33 Henry VIII (1541–2), for which see Dugdale, iv. 184. I normally give the modern forms of the names first.

[4] There is at least one minor omission. On 18 May 1282 a licence was granted for the alienation in mortmain by John 'de Crofta', to the prioress and nuns of *Linggebrok*, of one acre of meadow in *Ayston* (*Cal. Pat. R. 1281–92*, p. 20; misprinted *Dyston* in text, but see the Index). This is identified by the Index as Aston (east of Ross on Wye), but in view of the location it is much more likely to be Ashton (4 miles NNE. of Leominster) or Pipe Aston (4 miles NNE. of Croft) or Aston (2 miles SSE. of Croft); *Ays-* is a common ME variant of *Ash-* and *As-*. Of these places, Ashton is the most likely, for in 1541–2 the Ministers' Accounts of the Augmentation Office listed among the possessions of Limebrook

list undoubtedly includes all the major possessions of the priory. The properties were as follows, arranged in their probable order of acquisition.

(1) At Limebrook (*Lingebrok*) itself, in Herefordshire: two carucates of land valued at 13*s.* 4*d.* a year, and a mill valued at 3*s.* a year: total, 16*s.* 4*d.* a year. This, the domain or 'home' estate, will be discussed in more detail below.

(2) The church at Clifton-on-Teme, Worcestershire, which was the only spirituality which Limebrook possessed in 1291; it was valued at £6. 13*s.* 4*d.* a year and was at that time the priory's largest single source of income.[1]

The manor and church of Clifton were among extensive properties in Doddingtree Hundred, Worcestershire, that were part of the inheritance of Margery de Say, daughter and sole heiress of Hugo de Say, lord of the baronies of Richard's Castle in Herefordshire and Burford in Shropshire.[2] After a childless first marriage, she was married in 1210 to Robert de Mortimer, son of another Robert de Mortimer of Essex, and had by him a son and heir Hugh de Mortimer and another son William. Robert died before July 1219, and by the end of the year, at the king's bidding, she had married her third husband, William de Stuteville.[3]

a property worth 11*s.* in rent at *Morton*, i.e. Moreton 3 miles N. of Leominster, and Ashton is in the same parish, less than a mile ENE. of Moreton. John of Croft was a member of the distinguished family which held (and still lives in) Croft Castle, but which also held other lands (e.g. in 1249 Hugo of Croft had held the eighth part of a knight's fee at Marston, of the honour of Weobley; *Book of Fees*, ii. 1482); Croft Castle is 3½ miles WNW. of Moreton.

[1] In July 1543 Richard Callowhill received a grant of messuages in Clifton, Worcestershire, called 'Hakes Lande', with several fields called 'Cookes Felde', and 'le Personage landes', which formerly belonged to 'Lymbroke Priory' (*Letters and Papers of Henry VIII*, vol. xviii, part 1, no. 981 (47), p. 534); they were evidently the glebe lands of the church.

[2] On Margery de Say's inheritance and her marriages, see *The Complete Peerage*, ix. 258 ff., esp. p. 261.

[3] William promised the king two palfreys and a sum of money in return for the marriage, but he did not pay; on 20 September 1231 the

She appears to have died before the autumn of 1242, and William de Stuteville before 20 May 1259, when Hugh de Mortimer, Margery's heir, was stated to be 40 years old (obviously a round number).[1] The church at Clifton was appropriated to Limebrook Priory at some unrecorded date during the episcopate (1240–68) of Peter de Acquablanca, bishop of Hereford; this was stated when the appropriation was confirmed in 1287 by bishop Richard of Swinfield.[2] As Margery de Say died within two years of the beginning of Peter de Acquablanca's episcopate, and possibly earlier, it is perhaps unlikely that the church was given to Limebrook during her lifetime; she may have bequeathed it by her will, or it may have been given in her memory by her son after her death.[3] What is certain is that it was not given before 1240.

(3) (a) At Marston in Pembridge,[4] Herefordshire: land worth £2. 6s. 8d. a year, and the pleas and perquisites of the manor court, valued at 5s. a year. (b) At Bodenham, Here-

king remitted the debt and ordered that the matter should be closed (*Close R. 1227–31*, p. 560).

[1] *Cal. I.p.m.*, vol. i, no. 439 (p. 120).

[2] *Registrum Ricardi de Swinfield*, p. 134.

[3] The date of Margery's death is deduced from the fact that in autumn 1242 her son Hugh de Mortimer sued his stepfather William de Stuteville for waste of his woods in Worcestershire. The matter was finally settled by William granting Hugh, among other things, the service of Robert of Clifton for Clifton manor (*Complete Peerage*, ix. 261 n.). From this it would seem that the manor of Clifton had been included in that part of Margery's property which William, as her widower (by whom she had also had at least one son), had retained 'by the courtesy of England', and that he was transferring it to Hugh as part of the compensation for his waste of the woodlands. It does not perhaps follow that the church went with the manor; but it may have been after the settlement of this case that the church was appropriated to Limebrook, and if so it was after Margery's death.

[4] The name is given as *Merton* in *Tax. Eccles.*, by error for *Merston*; as *Merston* in *Feudal Aids*, ii. 387 (of date 1316); as *Marston* (*Marson*) *in Bembridge* by the Ministers' Accounts of the Augmentation Office (1541–2).

fordshire: annual rent of £2. (c) At Nun Upton, Hereford-shire: four carucates of land under grass valued at 1s. 8d. per carucate, i.e. a total of 6s. 8d. a year.[1]

These three properties may have come from a single source. Marston was one of the manors of the honour of Weobley, the patrimony of the de Lacy family. In 1242 Marston was held by William Pichard of Milo Pichard, who held of the heirs of Walter de Lacy,[2] and in 1249 William Pichard still held it.[3] But by 1291 the manor and the manorial court belonged to Limebrook Priory, and in 1316 the prioress paid the feudal aid assessed on Marston.[4] At Bodenham there were three manors, two belonging to the honour of Weobley and the third to that of Brecon (which passed to Humphrey de Bohun 'the younger' by his marriage to Eleanor de Braose and in 1242–3 was already in the hands of Humphrey's father, the earl of Hereford); at this date the first two manors were held, by named tenants, of the heirs of Walter de Lacy,[5] and the third was divided between two tenants, one of whom was Walter de Muscegros.[6] The identification of the property at Upton occasions some

---

[1] 'De feno apud Upton', *Tax. Eccles.* The low value set on the land was presumably because it consisted of hayfields and was not arable. The name Nun Upton is due to the connection with Limebrook. The Augmentation Office list describes the 'messuage' at Nun Upton as being in Worcestershire (Dugdale, iv. 184), but this is an error; in 1544, when it was granted to Richard Andrews and George Lisle, it was correctly described as being in Herefordshire, in a parish given as 'Bromehyll *alias* Bremehill', by which Brimfield is meant (*Letters and Papers of Henry VIII*, vol. xix, part 2, no. 166 (41), p. 76).

[2] *Book of Fees*, ii. 803, 816.

[3] Ibid., p. 1480.

[4] *Feudal Aids*, ii. 387.

[5] *Book of Fees*, ii. 805, 817. But in 1249 Bodenham Furches was said to be held by William de Furches of the king in chief (ibid., p. 1482), whereas in 1242 it was held in dower by Isabella de Furches of William de Furches, who held of 'Walter de Lacy of the honour of Weobley'. See, however, p. 188, n. 5, below.

[6] Ibid., pp. 805, 813. See also pp. 181–4, above.

difficulty, for within a radius of less than half a mile there are now three Uptons—Nun Upton in the parish of Brimfield, and Lower Upton and Upton Court in the parish of Little Hereford; and to distinguish these in the early records is not easy.[1] In Leominster Hundred (according to *The Book of Fees*)[2] there was an Upton which in 1242–3 was held by John de Waudebuef of the honour of Brecon; this may be Upton in Little Hereford, for Little Hereford at this time was itself held by another tenant of the earl of Hereford, who himself held of the bishop of Hereford.[3] But in Wolphey Hundred there was an Upton where Thomas of Upton held one and a half hides, in 1242–3, of Roger Pichard,[4] who belonged to a family dependent on the de Lacys,[5] and a fragmentary entry records that in 1249 Thomas of Upton held in Upton of the honour of Weobley;[6] this must be Upton in Brimfield, i.e. the place later known as Nun Upton.[7]

The common feature that connects all three of these

[1] The admirable index to *The Book of Fees* attributes all the entries here cited to 'Upton in Little Hereford', but this seems to me to be mistaken.

[2] ii. 800. John de Waudebuef also held of the earl of Hereford at Gattertop in Hope under Dinmore (ibid., pp. 800, 813).

[3] *Book of Fees*, ii. 810, 813. Leominster 'Hundred' consisted of a number of scattered vills belonging to the manor of Leominster (O. S. Andersen, *The English Hundred Names* (Lund, 1934), i. 162).

[4] *Book of Fees*, ii. 810.

[5] On 25 May 1248 the king acknowledged that Roger Pichard (who evidently had died) held his lands in Herefordshire of John de Verdun (the husband of Margery de Lacy) and not of the king in chief, and ordered that the said John should be given full seisin, without delay, of all Roger's lands which had been seized into the king's hand. (*Close R. 1247–51*, p. 52.)

[6] *Book of Fees*, ii. 1483.

[7] It is, however, difficult to reconcile the one and a half hides held by Thomas of Upton with the four carucates held by Limebrook in 1291, if the carucate and the hide are to be equated. There must have been some rearrangement of the landholdings.

places, Marston, Bodenham, and Nun Upton, is the association with the honour of Weobley and the de Lacy family;[1]
and the case is clearest at Marston, where the whole manor
and the manorial court were given to the priory, but obviously after 1249 when William Pichard still held it. When
Walter de Lacy died in 1241 his heirs were his two granddaughters, Margery and Matilda,[2] who were then minors.
But by 1244 they were both married, Margery to John de
Verdun and Matilda to Peter de Geneve,[3] and on 12 May
of that year an order was issued for the delivery to their
husbands and themselves of the lands of Walter de Lacy.[4]
In the division of the property, the castle of Weobley fell
to Margery and her husband John de Verdun,[5] that of Ludlow
to Matilda and Peter de Geneve, though in each case the

[1] The honour of Brecon and the Bohun family come into the
picture at Bodenham and Upton but not at Marston. The Pichards
come in both at Marston and Upton, but they were tenants of the de
Lacys, not tenants-in-chief, and seem to have had no connection with
Bodenham. On the possibility that the land at Bodenham came from the
Muscegros estate see pp. 181–4, above.

[2] Eyton, v. 240, seems to make Matilda the elder, but the Close Rolls
regularly give precedence to Margery and her husband.

[3] Peter died in 1249, before 17 July (*Close R. 1247–51*, p. 179).
Matilda (or Maud) was remarried, between 22 July and 18 August 1252,
to Geoffrey de Geneville (Joinville), the friend of Edward I (*Close R.
1251–3*, pp. 128, 142). Their daughter Joan de Geneville married in
1306 Roger de Mortimer, the future first earl of March, to whom Geoffrey gave seisin of Matilda de Lacy's properties in Ludlow and in Ireland
in 1308 (Powicke, *The Thirteenth Century*, p. 517, n. 1).

[4] *Close R. 1241–4*, p. 186.

[5] Ibid., p. 210 (of date 15 July 1244). Sir Maurice Powicke (*The
Thirteenth Century*, p. 404 and Index) describes the mid thirteenth-
century Roger de Mortimer as 'lord of Wigmore and Weobley', but this
is a mistake, unusual in so learned a scholar; Weobley passed from Margery
de Lacy to her surviving son Theobald de Verdun, by whom it was held
at his death before 28 August 1309 (*Cal. I.p.m.*, vol. v, no. 187, pp. 95–6).
Theobald's son of the same name married in 1302 Maud, daughter of
Edmund de Mortimer, the son of Roger de Mortimer and Maud de
Braose (*Complete Peerage*, ix. 283).

lands dependent on the castles seem to have been partitioned.[1] Margery died in 1256.[2] Her immediate heir was her elder son Nicholas, who himself died before 5 August 1271, leaving as his heir his brother Theobald, then aged '23 and more';[3] and her husband John died before 17 October 1274.[4] He had married a second wife Eleanor, whose dower occasioned a complex dispute in 1276 with her stepson.[5] Theobald lived until 1309. Though there is no direct evidence, the probability is that Marston and the land at Nun Upton, and possibly that at Bodenham, were given to Limebrook during Margery's lifetime; until Theobald succeeded his father in 1274 no one else would have had a clear right to dispose of them. A suitable opportunity for the endowment may well have arisen some time after Roger Pichard's lands had fallen into the hands of John of Verdun (by right of his wife) in 1248.[6] But what matters for our purpose is that in 1249 William Pichard still held Marston and Thomas of Upton held Upton;[7] the transfer to Limebrook must have been after this date.

(4) At a place listed as *Burton* in the *Taxatio Ecclesiastica*: five acres of land and two acres of meadow, the whole valued at 2s. a year. This land must have been in the parish of Bourton (or Burton), 3 miles south of Much Wenlock in Shropshire. On 17 May 1281 a licence was granted for the alienation in *frank almoin* by Reginald de la Legh to the

[1] The inquisitions *post mortem* on Nicholas de Verdun (*Cal. I.p.m.*, vol. i, no. 767) and his father John de Verdun (*Cal. I.p.m.*, vol. ii, no. 78) both speak of their holding 'the moieties' of Ewyas (Harold), Weobley, and Ludlow.   [2] Eyton, v. 240.

[3] *Cal. I.p.m.*, vol. i, no. 767 (p. 249).

[4] *Cal. I.p.m.*, vol. ii, no. 78 (pp. 58–60).

[5] *Cal. Close R. 1272–9*, pp. 288, 322–3, 342–3.

[6] See p. 188, n. 5, above.

[7] Before 3 June 1260 a Thomas of Upton (not necessarily the man who held Upton in 1249) killed himself *per infortuniam* within the jurisdiction of the sheriff of Worcestershire (*Close R. 1259–61*, p. 53).

prioress and nuns of *Lyngebroke* of 24*s.* (evidently an error for 24*d.*) of rent in *Westbradeleye.*[1] This is the modern Bradeley (or Bradley) in Bourton parish one mile south of Bourton itself, which is named *West-Bradeley* in a record of 1244,[2] doubtless to distinguish it from two other Bradleys in the near vicinity (the modern Bradley Farm one mile northeast of Much Wenlock, and Bradleys Coppice 4 miles east of Much Wenlock); Bradeley in Bourton is the westernmost of the three. Reginald de la Legh was a Shropshire knight, much employed by the crown on inquisitions and judicial inquiries, as an assize judge, and on other duties, between 1275 and 1292, chiefly in Shropshire, Herefordshire, and Staffordshire; and on two occasions (in July 1282 and August 1284) he was rewarded by a royal gift of two bucks from the forest of Cannock.[3] It is not known when he died, for he seems to have been succeeded by a son of the same name (since the name continues to occur until 1337–8) and it is uncertain when one gave place to the other. He belonged to a family that took its surname from its manor of *Leye* (*Lega, Leghe, Lee*), later *Hugh Leghe* (the modern Hughley),

[1] *Cal. Pat. R. 1272–81*, p. 434. If the calendered record reports the original correctly, 24*s.* (for 24*d.*) must be a copying error of the Chancery clerk. So small an area of land would not have been worth 24*s.* a year; the record of the *Taxatio Ecclesiastica*, which gives 2*s.*, must be right. The index to the calendared volume identifies *Westbradeleye* with Bradley West in Somerset, but this is a bad guess; there is no evidence at all to connect either Limebrook or Reginald de la Legh with Somerset.

[2] See E. W. Bowcock, *Shropshire Place Names* (Shrewsbury, 1923), p. 51.

[3] Records relating to him occur in *Cal. Pat. R. 1272–81*, pp. 234 (of date 1277), 412, 466, 470; *Cal. Pat. R. 1281–92*, pp. 65, 76, 92, 212, 254, 281, 286, 342–3; *Cal. Pat. R. 1292–1301*, p. 44 (of date 30 December 1292); *Cal. Close R. 1279–88*, pp. 117 (of date 1281), 162, 173, 274, 323; *Cal. Close R. 1288–96*, p. 120 (perhaps not the same man); *Cal. Inq. Misc.*, i. 401 (no. 1403), 403 (no. 1416), 603 (no. 2257); *Cal. Charter R.*, ii. 424 (of date 4 September 1292). See also Eyton, vi. 302–8 (especially 306–8), who cites records from 1275 until 1289 (and indeed later, but these may refer to his son).

which it held of St. Milburga's Priory, a Cluniac house at Much Wenlock,[1] to which Bourton also belonged. Bourton is 2 miles to the south-east of Hughley, above Wenlock Edge, and at the time of the Domesday survey both had been held by a single tenant, of Anglo-saxon name, from whom the de la Legh family may have descended;[2] evidently it had retained (or regained) interests in the Bourton parish, since Reginald was able to endow Limebrook with rents at Bradeley.

(5) At Eardisland (*Erleslen, Erselen*),[3] Herefordshire: one carucate of land worth 10s. a year, and an annual rent of 2s., a total of 12s. a year. This land came into the possession of Limebrook in 1285, when Maud, the widow of Roger de Mortimer, gave the manor of Eardisland and the advowson of the church at Old Radnor to the abbot and convent of Wigmore and the prioress and nuns of Limebrook;[4] the properties listed as Limebrook's in the *Taxatio Ecclesiastica* of 1291 must be the priory's share of her benefaction. Maud or Matilda, who married Roger de Mortimer before 8 Novem-

[1] Eyton, loc. cit.; Ekwall, *ODEPN*, s.n. *Hughley*.

[2] Eyton, loc. cit., doubted whether the de la Legh family can have descended from the Domesday tenant of Hughley and Bourton, since he could find no record that this family had ever held Bourton as well as Hughley; but the force of his argument is perhaps weakened by Reginald de la Legh's ability to dispose of parcels of land at Bradeley.

[3] The Ministers' Accounts of the Augmentation Office (1541–2) say *Barrow in Eresland*, but there is no place called Barrow in Eardisland now. There is, however, a place called The Barr, and there is a Barrow in the neighbouring parish of Pembridge (A. T. Bannister, *The Place-Names of Herefordshire* (1916), p. 14).

[4] *Inquisitions ad quod damnum*, vol. i (P.R.O. Lists and Indexes xvii, 1904), p. 13. The originals in the P.R.O. (Chancery Inquisitions A.Q.D. (C. 143), File 8, no. 1) show that in the writ (dated 28 May 13 Edward I) addressed to the sheriff of Herefordshire the forms of the place-names are *Erleslane, Radenonere* for Radnor, *Watmor* by error for Wigmore, and *Linbrok*'; in the return to the writ (which states that the inquisition was held on Thursday, 28 June) the forms are *Erleslen, Radenor, Wygemore,* and *Lyngebroke*.

ber 1246,[1] was a great heiress, the eldest daughter (and co-heiress with her sisters, one of them the Eleanor who married Humphrey de Bohun) of William de Braose, who was hanged by Llywelyn ab Iorwerth in 1230 for his adultery with Llywelyn's wife Joan, William's step-grandmother—an event tactfully described by a contemporary official document as 'the misfortune which has befallen him'.[2] Maud and her sisters also shared in the division of the lands of William Marshall, earl of Pembroke, after 1245. She could well afford to give a little to the poor nuns of Limebrook, and she may perhaps have felt that she had something to expiate, for it was to her at Wigmore that the head of Simon de Montfort was sent after his defeat and death at Evesham in 1265.[3] The castle and honour of Radnor[4] and the advowson of the church there[5] were part of her inheritance from her father, and at her death Eardisland and Kingsland were declared to be dependent on the castle of Radnor.[6] Maud's

[1] *Close R. 1242–47*, p. 484.

[2] 'infortuniam quod de eo accidit', *Close R. 1227–31*, p. 368. He was the grandson of the great William de Braose, who died in 1211. The 'misfortune' was not allowed to interfere with the projected marriage of Llywelyn's son and William's daughter; the marriage was business, the hanging hot-blooded vengeance for a private wrong.

[3] Powicke, *The Thirteenth Century*, pp. 202–3.

[4] Cf., for example, *Close R. 1231–4*, p. 375; *Cal. Pat. R. 1281–92*, pp. 69, 317; and the return of the inquisition *ad quod damnum*.

[5] *Cal. Pat. R. 1225–32*, p. 390.

[6] *Cal. I.p.m.*, iii. 19 (no. 41). But in 1242–3 Ralph de Mortimer is recorded as holding Kingsland and Eardisland (including Burton in Eardisland); see *Book of Fees*, ii. 805, 814. In 1249, probably by coincidence, John of Lingen appears to have held Burton in Eardisland of Roger de Mortimer. Nevertheless these were de Braose lands; *The Book of Fees* (ii. 1186, 1187, 1246, 1247) records in 1250 two serjeanties, held by different persons, of summoning 'the lords of Wigmore at Wigmore, of Braose at Kingsland, and of Lacy at Weobley'. Roger de Mortimer held Kingsland and Eardisland in 1249 by virtue of his marriage to Maud de Braose. His father Ralph must have held them in 1242–3 because they had been transferred to his custody in view of the projected marriage of Maud to Roger, just as in July 1238 William de Cantilupe

husband Roger de Mortimer had died in 1282, and may have left a small cash bequest to Limebrook Priory;[1] she herself died in March 1301. Two of her granddaughters, Joan and Elizabeth, the daughters of her heir Edmund de Mortimer, became nuns at Limebrook.[2]

Of the properties held by Limebrook in 1291,[3] all but one were acquired after 1240, and some as late as 1281 and 1285, whereas there are records of 'nuns of Limebrook' as early as 1221 and again in 1226. The chief properties came from the estates of heiresses—of Margery de Say, Margery de Lacy, and Maud de Braose. The only properties not accounted for by gifts made later than 1240 are those listed as being at

'the younger' had been given custody of the lands and person of Eva de Braose, though she was not yet of full age, in anticipation of her marriage to him—ten years before the final division of the de Braose lands between the heiresses.

[1] Roger of Luggovere (presumably 'Lugg-bank', a place on the banks of the river Lugg), one of the executors of the will of Roger de Mortimer (*Cal. Pat. R. 1281–92*, p. 130), acknowledged on 21 November 1289 that he owed the prioress of Limebrook 20 marks (*Cal. Close R. 1288–96*, p. 110).

[2] *Complete Peerage*, ix. 283; cf. *Cal. Pat. R. 1330–4*, pp. 335–6 (of date 12 September 1332), which confirms Joan's right to a pension of 10 marks yearly, granted to her by her dead father Edmund de Mortimer and charged against the receipts from a number of manors in the vicinity of Limebrook, including that of *Lyngebroke* itself (probably an alternative name for *Lyngeyn*, which is not mentioned, since there is no other evidence for a manor of Limebrook). Cf. p. 210, n. 2, below.

[3] Others were acquired later. On 13 April 1302 the church of Stoke Bliss was appropriated to Limebrook (*Reg. R. de Swinfield*, ed. Capes, p. 381); this was evidently by gift of a Mortimer (*Cal. Pat. R. 1307–13*, p. 163 (of date 20 June 1309), which says that the advowson was acquired from Roger de Mortimer; but he did not succeed his father Edmund until 1304. In 1320 John de Aquablanca, dean of Hereford, left by his will 5s. to the nuns of Limebrook to say the office of the dead 'in their churches' for his soul (*Charters and Records of Hereford Cathedral*, ed. W. W. Capes (Cantilupe Society, 1908), p. 188). In 1336 the priory acquired 116s. 6d. in rent at Adforton in Shropshire from Thomas of Baryngton (*Cal. Pat. R. 1334–8*, p. 343). In 1349–50 it acquired the manor of Broxwood Power by the gift of a clerk called Adam Esger (Inq. ad quod

Limebrook itself: the two carucates of land valued in 1291 at 13*s*. 4*d*. a year, and the mill valued at 3*s*. a year. That these were, or included, the original endowment is obvious from the fact that, from the earliest records onwards, the nunnery was situated at Limebrook; but what is of most significance for our inquiry is that the whole of the original endowment cannot have been greater than the small and not at all valuable 'home estate' of 1291.[1]

The antiquary John Leland, in his *Itinerary* (based on his researches during a tour of England between 1534 and 1543), says that 'Mortimers Erles of the Marches were founders of Wygmore, Lynebrook, and Feverlege'.[2] A different tradition is, however, preserved in British Museum MS. Harley 1087, a still later source, which on f. 66 gives what purports to be

damnum, in Dugdale, *Monasticon*, iv. 182; cf. *Calendarium I.p.m.* ii (1808), 167 (no. 33)); on 20 February 1351 the king gave his licence for this alienation in mortmain for a fine of 100*s*. (*Cal. Pat. R. 1350–4*, p. 319). In 1426 this property was described as the fourth part of a knight's fee, to be held of the earldom of March by the prioress of *Lyngebroke* at 25*s*. (*Cal. Close R. 1422–9*, p. 253). On 10 February 1355 the king, 'out of compassion for the great poverty and indigence of the prioress and nuns of Limebrook at the present time' *and* for a fine of 30*s*. which they had agreed to pay, gave his licence for the alienation in mortmain by William de Waldebouf of a messuage and 80 acres of land in 'Draycote', Herefordshire (*Cal. Pat. R. 1354–8*, pp. 168–9; cf. *Calendarium I.p.m.* ii (1808), 189 (no. 5)); this was possibly Drayton by Nun Upton, since it must have been an ancestor of this Waldebouf who held at Upton in 1242–3 (see p. 188, above).

[1] There may of course have been benefactions in cash, for somehow funds must have been found for the buildings at Limebrook, which are dated to the thirteenth century (Royal Commission on Historical Monuments, *Herefordshire*, iii. 136: 'The remains now consist of a single ruined building (41 ft. by 22½ ft.) lying E. and W. . . . It would appear to date from the 13th century . . . [There are] extensive foundation-mounds in the field to the E.').

[2] John Leland, *The Itinerary*, ed. T. Hearne (2nd edn., 1744), v. 11; *The Itinerary in Wales of John Leland*, ed. Lucy Toulmin Smith (1906), p. 48.

a family tree, headed *Genelogia illorum de Lingan*,[1] which is
of such importance for our study that I reproduce it on p. 199.
At its top is the name of *Radulfus de Lingan*, or Ralph of
Lingen (the village north-west of Limebrook on the same
stream), who is described as *dominus de Lingan, primus
fundator prioratus de Lingbroke*, 'lord of Lingen and first
founder of the priory of Limebrook'. This is obviously
based on some entirely different source from Leland's. I
shall now turn to examine the two traditions, beginning
with the later one.

MS. Harley 1087[2] is written in a hand of the later sixteenth
century, and contains material which may in general be
described as antiquarian and genealogical. From f. 5 to
f. 54ᵛ it has a long list of men who had been created peers
since the Conquest;[3] the last three names, on f. 54ᵛ, are
those of Henry Cheney of Tuddington (Toddington), Henry
Compton, and Henry Norris of Rycote, all of whom were
created peers on 8 May 1572. Obviously the rest of the
manuscript was copied after this date. Most of the material
from f. 55 onwards relates to the west of England, especially
to Herefordshire and Shropshire, and comes from a variety
of sources. Item 3 is extracted from the chronicles of 'Tin-
terne in Wallia', item 4 from those of Llanthony Priory by
Gloucester. The material from f. 77 to f. 81 is extracted from

[1] Printed in Dugdale, iv. 182. My transcript has been made from the
manuscript.

[2] Nothing seems to be known about the origin of this manuscript.
Many of the Harleian manuscripts came from the collections of the
Elizabethan antiquary John Stow (1525(?)–1605), but this is not in his
hand. In view of its contents it seems likely to have been compiled by
some West Midland (perhaps Herefordshire) antiquary; and as the
Harley family had its seat at Brompton Bryan, in N. Herefordshire 3½ miles
from Wigmore, it may well be that the manuscript had been acquired
locally by Robert Harley or one of his forebears.

[3] According to the *Catalogue of the Harleian MSS. in the British
Museum*, i (1808), 543, this 'treatise' is 'commonly ascribed to Robert
Cooke Clarencieux, and ought to be read with caution'.

the *Testa de Nevill* or *Book of Fees*. On ff. 74ᵛ–75 is a list of the
bishops of Hereford beginning with bishop Walter who
died (it is said) in 1079 and ending with Thomas Spofford,
who is stated to have been formerly bishop of Rochester;
Spofford was translated from Rochester on 18 November
1421 and resigned his see of Hereford on 4 December 1448.[1]
Evidently this list is copied from one compiled in the second
quarter of the fifteenth century, during Spofford's episcopacy.
On f. 66, the upper part of the page which also gives the
Lingen 'genealogy' is occupied by a summary of the line
of descent and inheritance from Gilbert de Lacy (*fl.* 1150)
to Richard 'now' Duke of York and Earl of March and
Ulster (after whose name is the word *Finis*); this also must
be a copy of a document originally compiled between 1425
(when Richard inherited the earldom of March) and 1460
(when he died). More significant still is an entry on f. 68,
headed *Say* as if it were a genealogy of the de Say family
(in conformity with the interest of the compiler of MS.
Harley 1087), which is in reality of a very different nature.
It reads:

Hugo de Say dominus de Castro Ricardi [fuit][2] filius Hugonis
de Say qui dedit Rogero de Alreton[3] Hildburye.[4]

Hugo de Ferrarijs dedit eidem Rogero eciam Hilburye quam

---

[1] John le Neve, *Fasti Eccl. Angl.*, ii: Hereford Diocese, compiled by
Joyce M. Horn (1962), p. 2.

[2] I supply the word *fuit*, assuming that it stood in the original document.   [3] Alderton, Salop.

[4] *Hilburye* appears to be the modern Hillborough (< OE **Hilde-
burge worþ*) in Temple Grafton, Warwickshire (west of Stratford on
Avon); in 1235–6 *Hilbewrth'* (identified by the Index of *The Book of
Fees* with Hillborough, Warwickshire) belonged to the fief of William de
Stuteville, the third husband of Margery de Say, who received therefrom
a rent of half a mark for half a knight's fee (*Book of Fees*, i. 509, 513, 516).
But Hillborough in Warwickshire seems rather remote from the Alderton
SSW. of Wem from which Roger took his name; the distance between the
places is almost 50 miles.

Hugo de Say prius dedit et quiquidem Rogerus de Alreton dedit abbati et canonicis.

Robertus de mortuo mari dominus de Castro Ricardi filius Roberti de Mortuo mari desponsauit Margaritam filiam et heredem Hugonis de Say et pro Salute anime sue et Margarite vxoris sue confirmauit donacionem predictam Abbati et conuentu de Wigmore.

The original purpose of the note was obviously not genealogical, but to establish the undoubted right of Wigmore Abbey to *Hilburye*, which it must have been given about 1200;[1] and it must have been written at Wigmore, for only there would a man refer, without further specification, to 'the abbot and canons', as this writer does in his second sentence. Evidently, therefore, the sixteenth-century antiquary who compiled MS. Harley 1087 had, among his other materials, at least one document, probably of early date, that had come from Wigmore Abbey.

The genealogy of the Lingen family that he gives on f. 66 is, considered as a genealogy, very defective. Its chief fault is the omission of generations, possibly by copying error on the part of the Harleian scribe himself and almost certainly because of the constant recurrence, in the direct male line, of two Christian names only, Ralph and John—a circumstance that complicates the task of tracing the family through the public records. Two generations, a Ralph and a John, have been omitted in the later thirteenth century: where the list begins with the sequence Ralph–John–John–John, it should really go Ralph–John–John–[Ralph]–[John]–John.[2] The last of these is identifiable with a man who succeeded to the estate in 1304, and he and his son and grandson (both named Ralph, and included in the Harleian list) carry us through to

[1] The confirmation of the gift by Robert de Mortimer was during his marriage to Margery de Say, 1210–19.
[2] See Appendix III (pp. 393 ff.) on the Lingen succession.

1390. But then the list omits two more generations, a John and a Ralph; the latter died in 1452. Finally it gives Sir John Lingen, who was prominent in the public affairs of Herefordshire in the latter part of the fifteenth century and who died in 1507. But his is the last male name on the list; it does not give his son, Sir John Lingen 'the younger',

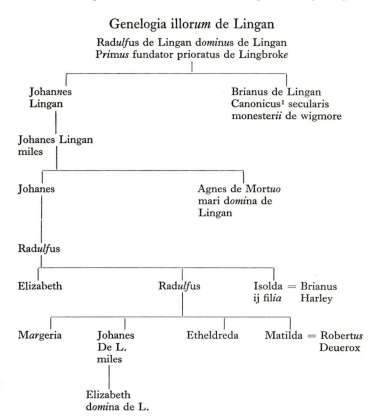

Genelogia illorum de Lingan

Radulfus de Lingan dominus de Lingan
Primus fundator prioratus de Lingbroke

Johannes
Lingan

Brianus de Lingan
Canonicus[1] secularis
monesterii de wigmore

Johanes Lingan
miles

Johanes

Agnes de Mortuo
mari domina de
Lingan

Radulfus

Elizabeth   Radulfus   Isolda = Brianus
                                 ij filia Harley

Margeria   Johanes   Etheldreda   Matilda = Robertus
            De L.   Deuerox
            miles

Elizabeth
domina de L.

[1] Miswritten in manuscript; probably to be read, strictly, as *Conino-nicus*, i.e. *an* miscopied as *oni*, with flourished mark of suspension over *i*.

who died in 1530, nor this Sir John's son and grandson (both named John), of whom the latter died in 1554; nor the last John's only daughter and heiress Jane, who lived until 1610 and was the contemporary of the antiquary who copied the list. If he himself had compiled it, the easiest part of his task would have been to trace the descent in the sixteenth century; yet it is the sixteenth-century Lingens that he altogether omits. Nor can it be said that he omits what was common knowledge, as one might have argued if he had left out only the name of his contemporary, the heiress Jane; he stops with her great-great-grandfather.

The Harleian list has other peculiarities. It shows little interest in the men of the family other than the direct male heirs; the only younger son mentioned is *Brianus de Lingan Canonicus secularis monesterii de wigmore* in the second generation, though examination of the public records reveals no lack of names of other male members of the family, some of them perhaps only distantly related, but others certainly younger brothers or close cousins of the contemporary head of the family and active in Herefordshire and Shropshire.[1] By contrast the list gives the names of a number of women of the family. In the later fourteenth century it names the two sisters of the Ralph who died in or before 1390: an elder sister 'Elizabeth' (to be identified with the Isabel known from other sources, for the two are forms of the same name), and Isolda, who is carefully distinguished as the 'second daughter' and whose marriage to Brian Harley is recorded. In the later fifteenth century it names the three sisters Margery, Etheldreda, and Matilda of the Sir John who died in 1507, and notes that the last-named was married to William Devoreux. Younger brothers do not interest its compiler, but sisters and their marriages do.

[1] See Appendix III.

Two other women are named on the list, both described
as *domina de Lingan*. The first is named as 'Agnes de Mort*uo*
mari', and she is entered as if she were the sister of the early
fourteenth-century John of Lingen who succeeded to the
estate as a minor in 1304 and was knighted in 1306. But a
Lingen daughter could not be *domina de Lingen* unless she
were heiress to the estate, which she would not be if she had
a brother living who had children. Nor could she be called
'de Mort*uo* mari' unless she had married a Mortimer; in that
case she might conceivably be *domina de Lingan* if she had
married the lord of Wigmore himself, since he was the
tenant-in-chief and the overlord of the Lingen family. But no
such marriage occurred; the fourteenth-century Mortimers
of Wigmore, who became the earls of March, did not achieve
their great position in the state, close to the crown itself
('Not we from kings, but kings from us'), by marrying
the daughters of their tenants and retainers. Nor, for that
matter, did they marry their daughters to their tenants.
Agnes must have been the daughter of some cadet branch
of the Mortimers who had been married to Sir John Lingen
and by virtue of her marriage had become 'the lady of Lingen'. The clue is provided by the record that on the death
of his father, the wardship of the young John Lingen, with
the right of arranging his marriage, was given by Edward I
to his yeoman, Walter of Woodham.[1] At Woodham in
Essex there were three manors, Woodham Ferrers, Woodham
Walter, and Woodham Parva, the last also known as Woodham Mortimer because it was held by the descendants of a
Robert de Mortimer (the father of Margery de Say's second
husband) who had held it in 1212, and to whose father

---

[1] *Cal. Pat. R. 1301–7*, p. 245 (30 July 1304, at Stirling). In 1310
Walter of Woodham was chief forester of the king's forest at Windsor,
but he died before 8 October 1311 (*Cal. Close R. 1307–13*, pp. 281, 382,
389, 501).

it had been given by Henry II on his marriage.[1] It seems probable that Walter of Woodham had made use of his right as guardian to marry his ward John Lingen to the daughter of a neighbour, perhaps his own kinswoman, who would have been a distant cousin of the Mortimers of Richard's Castle. Agnes de Mortimer, then, was Sir John Lingen's wife, not, as the Harleian list appears to show, his sister.[2]

The other woman described as *domina de Lingan* comes at the very foot of the list, entered as if she were the daughter of the Sir John who died in 1507. But again a Lingen daughter could be *domina de Lingan* only if the direct male line had failed (as it did in 1554, when Jane Lingen was the heiress); and in 1507 it is known, from the public records, that it did not fail, that Sir John 'the elder' was succeeded by Sir John 'the younger'. Indeed the Welsh antiquary Simwnt Vychan, who was related by marriage to the Lingens, asserts that the elder Sir John had fifteen children,[3] an ample insurance against the failure of the line. The 'Elizabeth' at the foot of the list can have been 'the lady of Lingen' only if she were the wife of a lord of Lingen. But she was not the elder Sir John's daughter-in-law; his son, the younger Sir John, married first, about 1490, Eleanor Myl(e)water, and secondly, in 1522, Elinora, widow of Sir Thomas Cresset.[4] The solution must be that the 'Elizabeth' of the list is here (as in the case of the sister of the Ralph Lingen who died in or before 1390) a more formal substitute for 'Isabel', and that *Elizabeth domina de Lingan* is Isabel Burgh, the wife (not the daughter)

---

[1] *Book of Fees*, i. 121; cf. Ekwall, *ODEPN*, s.n. *Woodham Ferrers*.

[2] It may be noted that his mother was named Matilda (*Cal. Pat. R. 1301–7*, p. 245), and his son Ralph's wife was Margery, daughter of Fulk of Pembridge (see below, p. 398 and n. 2). The Harleian list has undoubtedly put Agnes de Mortimer in the right generation; its error is only in showing her as if she were Sir John's sister.

[3] Burke, *The History of the Commoners of Great Britain and Ireland*, iv (1838), 266.　　　　[4] See below, p. 404.

of Sir John 'the elder', whom he had married about 1460 and who died in January 1522, when she must have been a very old woman.[1] She was buried beside her husband in the chancel of the parish church of Aymestrey, her name being given, in the memorial inscription, in the form Elizabeth; and there they lie to this day.[2] It would seem that the document of which the Harleian list is a copy was unskilful, or at least ambiguous, in showing schematically the relationship of husband and wife; but on each occasion on which the phrase *domina de Lingan* is used its purpose was to designate the wife of a lord of the manor.

The list is, then, no ordinary genealogy. Except for the direct male line (in which there are gaps), it is less interested in the men of the family than in the women. It does not continue the descent to the contemporaries of the Elizabethan antiquary who copied it into the Harleian MS., but stops with a man who died in old age in 1507, his sisters, and his wife who died, also old, in 1522. It does not include his son who died in 1530. It must have been compiled or last revised between 1522 and 1530, some dozen years before the dissolution of the monasteries between 1536 and 1540;[3] and it is

---

[1] Uncalendared I.p.m. in the P.R.O.; cf. *Index of Inquisitions preserved in the P.R.O.*, vol. i: Henry VIII to Philip and Mary (P.R.O. Lists and Indexes xxiii, 1908), p. 145. The returns to the writ make it clear that she is the mother of Sir John 'the younger', who is named as her heir. For further details, see p. 403, below.

[2] See R.C.H.M., *Herefordshire*, iii. 10 (the date 1506 given for Sir John Lingen's death is presumably Old Style), and Duncumb, *History and Antiquities of the County of Hereford* (1812), ii. 184 (who wrongly gives 1522 as the date of Sir John's death, by confusion with that of his wife).

[3] Limebrook itself was dissolved in 1539; Julian(a) Barbour, its last prioress, surrendered the house to the king on 28 December of that year. She must by then have been an old woman, for she had been ordained as a nun of Limebrook on 21 September 1481 (*Registrum T. Myllyng*, ed. A. T. Bannister (Canterbury and York Soc. xxvi, 1920), p. 71) and was already prioress in 1514 (*Registrum Ricardi Mayew*, ed. A. T. Bannister

a list of the dead, not of the living.[1] It begins with a man described as 'first founder' of the priory of Limebrook, though he was not the founder of the family,[2] or even, perhaps, the first Ralph of Lingen to appear in surviving records.[3] It bears, in fact, every sign of being really a list, compiled in a religious house and probably in a nunnery (which can only mean in Limebrook Priory), of dead founder's kin,[4] for

(Canterbury and York Soc. xxvii, 1921), p. 194). Tanner says that there were six nuns at the dissolution, 'but only four, beside the prioress, appear to have had pensions' (Dugdale, *Monasticon*, iv. 182–3; cf. *Letters and Papers of Henry VIII*, vol xiv, part 2, p. 283 (no. 752); vol. xv, p. 554). Their names were Katharine Dodde (who in 1530 had asked for and been given permission to go to a Cistercian nunnery because she desired a stricter discipline (*Registrum Caroli Bothe*, p. 241) but who must have returned), Margaret Tytley and Elizabeth Adams (ordained as nuns of Limebrook on 23 April 1514; *Registrum Ricardi Mayew*, p. 194), and Marie Sturie.

[1] We may, I think, assume that Sir John Lingen's sisters, as well as his wife, had died; they must all have been born by 1453, since his father died in January of that year.

[2] The family is believed to descend from the Turstin who in 1086, at the time of the Domesday survey, held Lingen, Shirley (SE. of Lingen, near the confluence of the Lingen brook with the river Lugg, and one of the continuing properties of the Lingen family), and Huntington in Ashford Carbonel (another Lingen property), all as a tenant of Ralf de Mortimer. On this see Eyton, v. 75. But Eyton did not clearly distinguish the Turstin who held Lingen and Shirley in 1086 from 'Turstin the Fleming', *alias* 'Turstin of Wigmore', who for a time after 1066 held Wigmore Castle before he was supplanted by the first Ralf de Mortimer, though he was aware of the difficulties of the identification. The two Turstins were in fact different men; see J. H. Round in *VCH Herefordshire*, i. 303–4. Turstin was a common Norman name. Round himself seems not to have distinguished the Turstin who was Ralf de Mortimer's tenant at Lingen, Shirley, and Huntington, from other Turstins who were the tenants of other men at other places.

[3] See below, p. 205.

[4] Or possibly of dead benefactors who belonged to the family of the founder (since this would be one way of explaining why some of the Lingen male heirs are omitted from the list). But I think this less likely; the omissions are probably errors occasioned by the recurrent Christian names Ralph and John, not deliberate exclusions. As the compiler of MS. Harley 1087 gives a copy of a document from Wigmore Abbey

whose souls the nuns would be under an obligation to pray. And it had been added to, or more probably recopied,[1] until the third decade of the sixteenth century, within seventeen years at most of the dissolution of the priory.

If this is indeed the origin of the Harleian 'genealogy', special authority attaches to its claim that Ralph of Lingen was the 'first founder' of Limebrook. It gains added credibility from the fact that it fits the chronology, which cannot have been known to any one in the sixteenth century. For the identification of this Ralph of Lingen, despite the omissions of the Harleian list, is not difficult. In the thirteenth century there is no record of a Ralph of Lingen until 1276, which is far too late; from 1194 until 1270 the records know only successive men called John of Lingen. To find Ralph, the reputed 'first founder', we must therefore go back to the twelfth century. Among the muniments of Hereford Cathedral there is a document, dated 'about 1150', recording a grant of land to the chapter of the cathedral which is witnessed by, among others, 'Radulphus de Lingen'.[2] If the document is correctly dated, I doubt whether this is our man; it was probably his father. But it is undoubtedly our Ralph[3] who appears in the Pipe Roll for 23 Henry II,

---

(see p. 197–8, above), it is perhaps possible that the 'genealogy' of the Lingens also came from Wigmore; but this would not account for its evident interest in the women of the family. Even if it came from Wigmore Abbey and not from Limebrook itself, its authority would be undiminished.

[1] That it was recopied, and not merely added to, seems to follow from its omissions and its failure ever to use the early forms *Lingein*, *Lingeyn*, *Lingain*, etc. of the name Lingen (for which it has only the unusual spelling *Lingan*). It is not likely that both these features are to be attributed solely to the scribe of the Harleian copy.

[2] *Charters and Records of Hereford Cathedral*, ed. Capes, p. 15.

[3] As assumed by Eyton, v. 76. It is probably also our Ralph of Lingen who appears in the Pipe Roll of the previous year (1176) as 'Radulphus de Lingieura', where he is mentioned, with Hugo 'de Crofta', Richard

i.e. for the financial year ending at Michaelmas 1177. He had begun an action concerning land[1] and had been debited with a fine:

Radulphus de Lingein debet c. *m.* pro habenda parte sua de feodis .x. militum versus Robertum de Maisi.[2]

Ralph of Lingen owes 100 marks for having his share of 10 knights' fees against Robert de Maisi.

The debt is recorded in the section of the roll headed 'Dorset and Somerset', doubtless because the case had been begun before the assizes there. Ralph did not pay, and for the next three years the entry is unchanged.[3] But in the roll for the year ending at Michaelmas 1181 there is added to the stereotyped record of the debt the note *sed requirendus est in Herefords[ci]re* ('but he is to be sought in Herefordshire'),[4] and in the next year the entry is transferred to the Hereford-shire part of the roll, with the note *qui requirebatur in Dorseta* ('he who was sought in Dorset');[5] the sheriff of Hereford-shire has been given the job of collecting the money. In the financial year 1182–3 the debt is still merely recorded,[6] but in the next year the sheriff adds to the record an explanation why Ralph of Lingen has not paid up: *sed nondum potuit habere rectum*, 'but he has not yet been able to get judgement'.[7]

'de Dilun', and Reginald 'de Haia', as a knight of the shire of Hereford-shire; in view of the company he keeps, *Lingieura* must be an error for *Lingein.* (*Pipe R. 22 Hen. II*, p. 45.)

[1] Entries in later rolls give more details. The land in question appears to have been at Castle Eaton and Milston in Wiltshire and at Poulton in Gloucestershire; see Lady Stenton's Index to the *Chancellor's Roll* for 8 Rich. I (Pipe Roll Soc., vol. xlii). An outline of Ralph's litigation, based on the Pipe Rolls, is given by Eyton, v. 75–6.

[2] *Pipe R. 23 Hen. II*, p. 21.

[3] *Pipe R. 24 Hen. II*, p. 41; *Pipe R. 25 Hen. II*, p. 68; *Pipe R. 26 Hen. II*, p. 107.   [4] *Pipe R. 27 Hen. II*, p. 6.

[5] *Pipe R. 28 Hen. II*, p. 14.   [6] *Pipe R. 29 Hen. II*, p. 110.

[7] *Pipe R. 30 Hen. II*, p. 27.

For three more years the record is unchanged,[1] but then there is a slight variation (*sed nondum habuit rectum vel habere potuit*).[2] And so we come to Michaelmas 1189, twelve years after the case had begun; by this time Ralph must have despaired of his action, and the Exchequer of its fine.

Meanwhile Ralph had been involved in other cases. In the financial year 1182–3 he was fined half a mark at the Shropshire assizes,[3] and in 1184–5 he is recorded as owing a fine of half a mark, imposed at the Herefordshire assizes, for unjust disseisin.[4] In the following year he paid this,[5] but at the Worcestershire assizes was fined another half mark for disseisin.[6] In the year 1186–7, at the Shropshire assizes, he was fined and paid 20s. for novel disseisin, and he also paid the half mark owing from the year before.[7] Finally, in the year ending at Michaelmas 1190, he was fined and paid half a mark *pro wasto*, for the offence of cutting timber contrary to the forest laws;[8] and in this year also we find the last record of his old debt of 100 marks for the case begun in 1176–7:

Radulphus de Lingein debet c. *m.* pro habenda parte sua de feodo x militum uersus Robertum de Maisi. Sed non potuit habere rectum et mortuus est et ideo non debet summoneri.[9]

Ralph had died during the year, at some time after the assizes at which he had been fined *pro wasto* but before Michaelmas, still without getting judgement against Robert de Maisi; and the sheriff thinks that the matter ought to be dropped.

But this was not quite the end of it. Four years later, in

---

[1] *Pipe R. 31 Hen. II*, p. 198; *Pipe R. 32 Hen. II*, p. 31; *Pipe R. 33 Hen. II*, p. 131.

[2] *Pipe R. 34 Hen. II*, p. 211; *Pipe R. 1 Rich. I*, p. 142.

[3] *Pipe R. 29 Hen. II*, p. 3.   [4] *Pipe R. 31 Hen. II*, p. 199.

[5] *Pipe R. 32 Hen. II*, p. 31.   [6] Ibid., p. 41.

[7] *Pipe R. 33 Hen. II*, pp. 64, 218.   [8] *Pipe R. 2 Rich. I*, p. 48.

[9] Ibid., p. 46.

the financial year 1193–4, John of Lingen sued Robert the son of Robert de Maisi, at the Wiltshire assizes, to get his fair share of a fee of 15 knights (an increase of 50 per cent in the size of the fee), and was, like Ralph before him, debited with a fine of 100 marks.[1] There can be no possible doubt that this John of Lingen is Ralph's son and heir, suing the son of his father's adversary. But he must have been equally unsuccessful in his action, for he was equally unwilling to pay the fine; the rolls record the debt for two more years,[2] but then give up, with no indication that it was ever paid,[3] nor is there any evidence that the later Lingens held lands at the places in Gloucestershire and Wiltshire that had been in dispute. John must wisely have dropped the case.

The importance of the litigation is twofold. First, it establishes the period of Ralph of Lingen's *floruit*, from 1177 onwards, and the date of his death, in 1190. Secondly, it establishes the succession, that his heir was John of Lingen. It is unlikely that Ralph was an old man when he died. His son John survived until shortly before 1236, when his successor, also named John, was evidently newly enfeoffed at Lingen, and it may be the elder John who was engaged in litigation in 1235; he was certainly still alive in 1231.[4]

---

[1] *Pipe R. 6 Rich. I*, p. 200.

[2] *Pipe R. 7 Rich. I*, p. 139; *Chancellor's R. 8 Rich. I*, p. 26.

[3] There is no record of the debt in the Pipe Roll of 9 Rich. I, either under Wiltshire (where it had been recorded in the previous three years) or under Herefordshire; and the same is true for the rolls for 10 Rich. I and for the whole reign of John.

[4] See Appendix III, pp. 393–6, below, for details of the careers of these two Johns, with citation of the evidence. There seems to be a clear distinction between the John who from 1194 to 1231 (or 1235) is known almost entirely from his litigation, and the John of 1236 onwards, a much more active, successful, and influential man, highly trusted by the Mortimers (for whom in 1247 he delivered the large sum of £200 to the king's treasury in Winchester) and eventually by the Crown (by which

He had lived for at least forty-one, and probably for forty-five, years after his father's death in 1190; and the second John was granted protection for the duration of a projected Welsh campaign in 1263, witnessed a dated charter of 24 February 1270,[1] and probably lived until about 1275.[2] It is evident that the younger John can hardly have been born before 1200, and may well have been born later; and the elder must have been a young man, probably still unmarried, when his father died in 1190. He must have been of full age when he resumed the litigation with the son of Robert de Maisi in 1193–4, but the delay of three or four years before he did so may mean that he was still a minor in 1190.[3] In any case, as he seems to have lived for another forty-five years, it would be reasonable to guess that he was only about twenty years old in 1190; and this would be consistent with the probability that his heir was not born until 1200 or after.[4]

MS. Harley 1087, then, attributes to a man who died in 1190 the 'first foundation' of a religious house which was certainly in existence, as a contemporary record testifies, in 1221; and it does so though the dates of Ralph of

he was employed, from 1259 to 1262, as one—apparently the first in precedence—of the 'dictators' of the truce with Llywelyn ap Gruffydd, prince of Wales).

[1] Eyton, vii. 30.
[2] See below, pp. 395–6.
[3] But it could equally well be due to the seizure of Wigmore Castle by the Crown in 1191, and the exile for three years of Roger de Mortimer.
[4] The alternative would be to suppose that the younger John was the grandson of the elder, and that the elder John's son had predeceased his father. But even so, if the elder John lived until 1235, he must have been young in 1190. I can see no reason, in the records, for supposing that there were three, not two, Johns from 1190 to 1270. The evidence of the Harleian list is not of much use, since it certainly omits generations; but if we were to suppose three Johns between 1190 and 1270, we should have to assume one more omission in the list. The second John on the list, singled out for the description *miles*, corresponds with the John of Lingen who was so prominent from 1247 to 1263, and who is described as a knight in several records from 1253 onwards.

Lingen's life and death, and of the foundation of Lime-brook, cannot have been known to the antiquary who copied the Lingen 'genealogy' into the manuscript and are unlikely to have been known, with any accuracy, to those who had brought the list up to date between 1522 and 1530 but had retained the ascription to Ralph of the 'first foundation' of the priory. In other respects too the tradition seems credible. Limebrook is only three-quarters of a mile downstream from Lingen, midway between Lingen and Shirley, which was also held by the Lingen family; indeed it is encircled by properties (Lingen itself, Shirley, Kinsham, Covenhope, and Aymestrey) which from an early date belonged to the family. Eyton observes, as tending to confirm 'the legend which attributes the founding of Lymbroke to a Lingen, that at the dissolution the nuns had lands in Shirley, Ames-trey [i.e. Aymestrey], Cowarne Magna, and Lingen;—in all of which places we can trace a previous interest of the Lingens';[1] and there are even indications in the records that the manor of Lingen was sometimes called *Lingebrok*.[2] We have also seen that there is evidence (albeit that of liti-

---

[1] Eyton, v. 76, n. 8. It does not follow, of course, that all these proper-ties were part of the original endowment; they only demonstrate a family interest in the nunnery. Though Eyton speaks of a 'legend', it seems to me, for reasons given above, that the statement in the Harleian MS. must be based on earlier documentary evidence and is not merely a sixteenth-century record of an oral tradition (which is what I presume Eyton to mean by 'legend').

[2] The published calendar of the *Curia Regis Rolls*, x. 96, records that one roll has the name John of *Lingeine*, the other John of *Lingeb'* (for *Lingebrok*). *Cal. Pat. R. 1330–4*, pp. 335–6, lists, among other manors in the neighbourhood, that of *Lynebroke* where Lingen must be meant. The Black Book of Wigmore itself (on which see immediately below) lists *Lynebrok* among the 'manoirs et parcelles' dependent on Wigmore concerning which documents were preserved among the muniments of Wigmore Castle, but does not list Lingen, under any spelling (MS. Harley 1240, f. 4), though it contains various documents witnessed by members of the Lingen family and indeed one undated grant made by a John of Lingen.

gation) to connect John of Lingen, the son of Ralph, with Margery de Say and her third husband William de Stuteville, in the same year as that in which a *deodand* intended for the nuns of Limebrook was paid to one of Margery's tenants,[1] and that this is in fact the earliest occurrence of a reference to the nuns of Limebrook in an extant public record. There is much in the discoverable facts to support the claim of MS. Harley 1087 that Ralph of Lingen was the 'first founder' of Limebrook Priory.[2]

On the other hand there is the tradition recorded by Leland that the Mortimers were the founders of Limebrook; and this appears to be confirmed by a copy of a mid thirteenth-century charter preserved in the Black Book of Wigmore (*Liber Niger de Wigmore*), now British Museum MS. Harley 1240. This manuscript is a companion to British Museum MS. Additional 6041; the two were written between 1375 and 1380 by a single scribe, presumably the archivist at Wigmore Castle.[3] MS. Additional 6041 consists of two parts, originally intended as separate, though complementary, volumes (since they were foliated separately by their scribe), though they survived together and had evidently been bound as one (as they now are). The first part (ff. 1–48 in the modern foliation) is imperfect at the beginning, folios i–viii in the medieval foliation having been lost, and another

---

[1] See pp. 177–8, above.

[2] A further detail of the 'genealogy' of MS. Harley 1087 which tends to confirm its authenticity is its description of Brian of Lingen, in the second generation (i.e. in the early thirteenth century), as *canonicus secularis monesterii de wigmore*. Anyone inventing a description of a canon of Wigmore, at any date after those who had known him were dead, would assume that he was a *canonicus regularis*, for Wigmore was a Victorine house. See further pp. 322–3, below.

[3] The accounts of the two manuscripts given by E. Owen, *Catalogue of MSS. relating to Wales in the British Museum*, ii. 230 (Harley 1240) and iv. 924–5 (Additional 6041), are inaccurate and misleading, especially that of Harley 1240.

leaf (originally f. xvi) has been lost between ff. 8 and 9; this part is a calendared list of muniments concerning the possessions of Edmund de Mortimer, third earl of March. The second part (the modern ff. 49–106) lacks the original folios ix–xvi (between the modern ff. 56 and 57) but is complete at the beginning; the scribe himself heads it 'Remenbrance de les munimentz touchantz leritage dame Phelippe la compaigne Esmon de Mortimer. Counte de la marche & dulnester', and it consists of an alphabetical index to the muniments followed by a calendared list of them. MS. Harley 1240 (*Liber Niger*) corresponds to the first part of MS. Additional 6041,[1] but is perfect at the beginning (though leaves have been lost elsewhere, as is shown by gaps in the scribe's original foliation); its heading reads 'Ici comence le kalender des munimentz touchantz le heritage le tres honourez seignour le Counte de la Marche'. It begins, as MS. Additional 6041 does (though imperfectly), with an alphabetical list of the places ('manoirs et parcelles') concerning which there were documents in the archives; against each is noted the 'title'[2] under which the document was filed and the number endorsed on the document. There follows a calendared list of the documents, arranged under the same main headings (Wigmore, etc.), in the order of the numbers endorsed on them; this order in no way corresponds to their date, or indeed to the location of the places concerned. In MS. Harley 1240 the number of the document is preceded by a cross-reference to the folio of the manuscript on which a copy of the document is given; this is not found in MS. Additional 6041 because in it the documents are merely

[1] Presumably there was originally another manuscript, since lost, to correspond to the second part of MS. Additional 6041.

[2] i.e. the division of the muniments, or box, in which the document was kept; these divisions were according to the honours (e.g. Wigmore) to which the manors or other holdings belonged. The Wigmore division comes first.

calendared and not copied out in full. I should judge that the alphabetical index and the calendared list in MS. Harley 1240 are copied from those in MS. Additional 6041, though with some modifications and elaborations; but the reverse might be possible.[1] As Owen opined, MS. Harley 1240 may have been a fair copy intended for the earl of March, MS. Additional 6041 the archivist's own copy; the former is much larger in format, more elaborate (e.g. in its method of setting out the alphabetical list), and generally more impressive. But the great difference between the two is that MS. Harley 1240 appends to the calendared list complete copies of the Latin texts of the documents, with an Anglo-Norman summary of each (identical except in minor details with that in the calendared lists of Harley 1240 itself and of Additional 6041) written in the margin beside the copy of the document. The two manuscripts are impressive evidence of a well-organized and well-stocked muniment room.[2]

The date of the manuscripts can be fixed within narrow limits. It is obvious, from the form of the headings, that

[1] Owen, iv. 925, thinks that MS. Additional 6041 'may have been derived from the Liber Niger', but the text of Additional 6041, where it differs, seems to me more correct. Moreover the calendared list in Additional 6041 is more detailed in one respect than that in Harley 1240: it adds to the Anglo-Norman summary of each document its date, or the note 'sa(u)nz date'. I think it more likely that the archivist first made a calendar of the documents, preceded by an alphabetical index of places (as in Additional 6041), and then decided to produce a more elaborate book, in which he added to the index and calendar a complete copy of the documents; knowing that the documents were to be copied in full, including their dating clause (if any), he dropped from the calendar of MS. Harley 1240 the notes on the date (or lack of date).

[2] It is surprising that the evidence of the two manuscripts has not been used more for place-name studies. Bannister obviously made no use of them for his *Place-Names of Herefordshire*, and I doubt whether either was used by Ekwall. The documents relate to Ireland and Wales as well as to England. The *Liber Niger* was known to and used by Eyton, though without (so far as I have discovered) any indication of where it was to be found or of what its modern shelf-mark was.

they were made during the lifetimes of Edmund de Mortimer and his wife Philippa. She died at the end of 1380 or early in 1381 (her will was proved on 9 February 1381), he on 27 December 1381.[1] Equally obviously they were made after their marriage in 1369; but in fact they must be later still, for they include a writ of Edward III dated November 1374 (48 Edw. III).[2] The manuscripts must therefore have been written between 1375 and 1380; and this is consistent with the style of the handwriting.

The document that concerns us is an undated[3] charter of which an Anglo-Norman summary is given in both manuscripts and the original Latin text in MS. Harley 1240, f. 40. From internal evidence it can have been issued only by the Roger de Mortimer who was lord of Wigmore from 1246 to 1282, the husband of Maud (Matilda) de Braose. As he mentions in it not only his wife, whom he married in 1246 (before 8 November)[4] when he was about 15 years old, but also his children (in the plural), the charter can hardly have been issued earlier than 1250 and may well be later. Beyond this the dating depends on the list of witnesses—'dominus' Henry de Mortimer, Hugh of Croft, John of Lingen, Ralph de Arraz, Robert Corbet, Brian of Brompton (i.e. Brampton), William de Mortimer, 'and others'. Five of these names— Brian of Brampton,[5] John of Lingen, Hugh of Croft, Ralph

---

[1] *Complete Peerage*, viii. 447–8.

[2] The full copy of this writ is in MS. Harley 1240, ff. 45ᵛ–46.

[3] That it was undated is specifically stated in MS. Additional 6041, f. 6ᵛ, which adds to the summary of the document the note 'sanz date'. Most of the early (thirteenth-century) documents in the register are undated in MS. Harley 1240 and are stated by Additional 6041 to be 'sa(u)nz date'. The scribe has not merely omitted the dating clauses.

[4] *Close R. 1242–7*, p. 484. Roger is said to have been born 'about 1232' (*Complete Peerage*, ix. 276) but may have been a little older; his father Ralph was married in 1230. But Roger must have been under 16 when he married Maud de Braose.

[5] The name Brian of Brampton does not help in dating, as successive heads of this family from 1214 to 1294 bore the same Christian name,

de Arraz (or 'Adraz'), and Henry de Mortimer—are to be found among those of other witnesses of grants[1] made by or to Ralph de Mortimer, Roger's father, who died in 1246; nevertheless three of them survived into the 1270s.[2] Robert Corbet died before 7 January 1270.[3] The William de Mortimer who witnessed the charter is not easy to identify, as the name was recurrent in the family; moreover by this date we have to distinguish the Mortimers of Richard's Castle from those of Wigmore. Hugh de Mortimer of Richard's Castle had a younger brother William,[4] who must have been the man who accompanied Henry III on his expeditions to Gascony and Scotland between July 1253 and September 1255[5] and who is described in July 1266 as the 'bailiff' of Hugh de Mortimer.[6] But there was at the same time a William de Mortimer connected with the Wigmore family. A document in the Black Book records an exchange of the land in Leinthall Starkes held by William de Mortimer for that held in Leinthall Earls by Roger, the eldest son of Richard of Burley; it seems to belong to the lifetime of the Ralph de Mortimer who died in 1246.[7] On 23 September

and it is therefore not possible to tell which of them witnessed any particular charter unless its date has been determined by other means.

[1] MS. Harley 1240 (*Liber Niger*), f. 40ᵛ (nos. xxx and xxxii).

[2] On John of Lingen see pp. 394–6, below; he was undoubtedly living in 1270 but had probably been succeeded by his son Ralph before August 1276. Ralph de Arraz witnessed a grant by Robert Corbet in late 1269 (Eyton, i. 179, citing *Rot. Cart.*, 54 Hen. III, m. 9) and was justice for gaol-delivery at Shrewsbury in 1274, but had probably died before November 1279 (Eyton, iii. 57–8). Henry de Mortimer witnessed the same grant by Robert Corbet in late 1269.

[3] Eyton, i. 179, citing *Rot. Cart.*, 54 Hen. III, m. 9.

[4] *Complete Peerage*, ix. 262.

[5] *Cal. Pat. R. 1247–58*, pp. 235, 286, 330 (the last a grant of free warren to Hugh de Mortimer at the instance of William de Mortimer); *Close R. 1253–4*, pp. 203, 218; *Close R. 1254–6*, pp. 79, 140.

[6] *Cal. Inq. Misc.*, i. 266–7 (no. 875).

[7] MS. Harley 1240, f. 40ᵛ (no. xxxi). It is undated, but the list of witnesses overlaps with that of the following document (no. xxxii),

1255 Roger de Mortimer and William de Mortimer were given a quittance from the common summons before the justices in eyre in Herefordshire.[1] Also in 1255 William de Mortimer was returned by the Claverley Inquest as lord of the manor of Shipley (which was held of the Mortimers of Wigmore and was a dependency of Claverley), and he was named as a defaulter in due attendance at the assizes of January 1256.[2] In February 1262 John de Braose complained that Roger de Mortimer and William de Mortimer with an army of Welsh, outlaws, and suchlike had seized, and still held, the castle of Corfham (Shropshire), in the March of Wales, which he claimed was his.[3] On 22 March 1263 William de Mortimer was granted protection during the Welsh war.[4] Later references to a William de Mortimer may refer to Roger's fourth son, who in August 1264 was given as a hostage for his father[5] and who died before 30 June 1297;[6] but up to 1262–3 we are clearly dealing with an elder kinsman of Roger's who could have witnessed his charters at any date after he had been granted livery of his inheritance on 26 February 1247.[7] The critical witness is Hugh of Croft. The Croft family was another in which the same Christian name tended to recur in successive genera- tions, and in this instance it seems that we have to choose between two Hughs, one of whom, after a long and dis-

which records the grant of an acre of land at Leinthall Starkes by Ralph de Mortimer to Alan le Starker; Hugh of Croft and John of Lingen were among those who witnessed both documents. Other documents in MS. Harley 1240 (nos. xlii and xliiii, f. 42^{r-v}) record grants of land by Richard of Burley, the father of Roger, to William de Mortimer in Leinthall Earls and in Easthope.

---

[1] *Close R. 1254–6*, p. 225.   [2] Eyton, iii. 75, 210.

[3] *Cal. Pat. R. 1258–66*, p. 231.

[4] *Cal. Pat. R. 1258–66*, p. 286. But this might perhaps be William de Mortimer of Richard's Castle.   [5] Ibid., p. 344.

[6] *Cal. I.p.m.*, iii. 269–70 (no. 407).

[7] *Complete Peerage*, ix. 276, citing *Excerpta e Rot. Fin.*, ii. 7; Roger was then still a minor.

tinguished career, was dismissed from his post as escheator
of Herefordshire on 1 July 1255 on account of 'his old age
and feebleness' (after a previous order for his replacement,
on 1 May 1254, had seemingly been ineffective), but may
have lived on until about 1260, and the other of whom held
Croft from 1265 onwards; the two were briefly separated by
a John of Croft, recorded in 1263 in a way that can leave no
reasonable doubt that he was then the head of the family.[1]
Though the younger Hugh cannot absolutely be excluded,
since Robert Corbet did not die until the end of 1269, the
elder is much more likely to be the man who witnessed the
charter, for the whole tenor of its list of witnesses is that it
was issued while Roger de Mortimer was still being advised
by his father's counsellors.

It would seem, from all the evidence, that the charter to
Limebrook transcribed in MS. Harley 1240 is to be dated
between 1250 and 1255, after the young Roger de Mortimer
had had time to beget a plurality of children[2] and before the
old Hugh of Croft had become incapable of public business.
But Roger de Mortimer, like Hugh de Mortimer of Richard's
Castle, was serving in Gascony in 1253–4.[3] The charter
must therefore have been issued either before August 1253,
when the king left for Gascony, or after December 1254,
when he returned; and as Hugh of Croft had already been
adjudged ripe for dismissal by May 1254, it is more likely
to antedate the Gascon expedition. The probability is that
it was issued in or about 1252, though a date of about 1255–6
cannot be excluded.

[1] For details of the family descent, and for references, see Appendix
IV, pp. 413–20.
[2] Roger's second son Edmund, who succeeded him in 1282 owing to the
death in 1274 of his eldest son Ralph, is thought to have been born
'about 1250' (*Complete Peerage*, ix. 283).
[3] *Complete Peerage*, ix. 276–7 (citing *Cal. Pat. R. 1247–58*, p. 232;
Close R. 1253–4, p. 70; and Bémont, *Rôles Gascons*, vol. i, nos. 2719,
etc.).

The copy of the charter in MS. Harley 1240 begins incomplete at the top of f. 40 in the modern foliation (f. xliii in the medieval); the opening line or two must have been at the foot of the verso of the preceding leaf, one of several that have been lost. The surviving text, in translation,[1] begins:

. . . of my [tenants?] have given and granted and by this present charter have confirmed to God and to the church of St. Thomas the Martyr of *Lingebroc* and to the nuns there serving God,[2] in free, pure, and perpetual alms, the whole valley in which was founded the church of the Blessed Mary and of St. Leonard of *Sutelesford*, which [valley] is now[3] called *La Derefaud*, and all the lands and tenements, possessions, rents, easements, and other things below my woods and the way out into the valley of Wigmore, as they are more fully, better, and more openly contained in charters of my grandfather, Roger de Mortimer, of happy memory, which he made for the sisters formerly living in[4] *Le*[5] *Derefaud*; within the boundaries and limits within which the said sisters were in possession and had seisin, and by the same seisin as the aforesaid sisters at all times had possession.

The grantor[6] goes on to impose two conditions. The first is that the nuns shall provide and maintain a chaplain to cele-

---

[1] The original Latin begins: '. . . meorum dedi et concessi et hac presenti carta mea confirmaui deo et ecclesie sancti Thome martiris de Lingebroc et monialibus ibidem deo seruientibus in liberam puram et perpetuam elemosinam totam vallem in qua fundata est ecclesia beate marie et sancti leonardi de Sutelesford que modo vocatur la Derefaud et omnes terras et tenementa possessiones redditus eisiamenta et alia infra nemora mea et exitum in valle de Wygemore sicut plenius melius et liberius continentur in cartis bone memorie Rogeri de Mortuo mari aui mei quas fecit sororibus quondam existentibus apud le Derefaud per fines et metas per quas dicti sorores vsi fuerunt et seisinam habuerunt et per eandem seisinam sicut sorores predicti omni tempore vsitauerunt.'

[2] In the Anglo-Norman summary, this becomes simply *la maison de Lyngebrok*; but this is of course due to the late fourteenth-century archivist.   [3] Or perhaps 'sometimes' (*modo* in the Latin).

[4] Or perhaps 'at' (*apud*).   [5] So MS. here, though elsewhere *La*.

[6] His name, lost at the beginning of the Latin text, is given in the Anglo-Norman summary in the margin of f. 40 as 'mons*ire* Roger de

brate the divine offices in the church of *La Derefaud*, 'for my soul and those of Matilda my wife, my children, my ancestors and parents in perpetuity'. The second is that he and his heirs shall have the right to present two women 'to be made nuns or lay-sisters' (*ad moniales vel sorores faciendas*) as 'we' choose, on the terms that when one or the other dies, other women are to be received in their place 'at our presentation'. He and his heirs will guarantee this gift and grant against all mortals in perpetuity (he did not foresee Henry VIII, who was, very indirectly, his heir). 'We' and the aforesaid nuns have therefore set 'to this document, made in the fashion of a deed of transfer',[1] 'our' seals and that of Wymarc the prioress,[2] in the presence of the witnesses whose names are discussed above, 'and others'.

This is, for the present study, a remarkable and important document which requires careful elucidation. 'My grandfather' is Roger de Mortimer, lord of Wigmore from February 1181, who died on 24 June 1214; he held the barony when Ralph of Lingen died. *La* (*Le*) *Derefaud* (*Dereuaud* in the Anglo-Norman summaries written by the late fourteenth-century archivist) is the modern Deerfold (or Deerfold Forest, according to Bannister).[3] This is now the name

Morteme*r*', and similarly in the calendars of both MS. Harley 1240 and MS. Additional 6041.

[1] 'huic scripto ad modum cirographi confecto alenatiui'. The meaning intended by *cirographum alenatiuum* would here seem to be 'deed of transfer', since the grantor is transferring property originally granted to the 'sisters' to the nunnery; but it might mean simply 'deed of grant', since *alienator* is used to mean 'grantor' (*Revised Medieval Latin Word-List*, citing sources of *c.* 1290 and *c.* 1315). But most charters are deeds of grant, and something special seems to be meant here.

[2] The copy of the charter in MS. Harley 1240 says *tunc Priorisse*, but the *tunc* is an obvious embellishment of the copyist. He does this elsewhere in lists of witnesses, so that 'X seneschal of Wigmore' becomes 'X *then* seneschal of Wigmore'.

[3] *The Place-Names of Herefordshire*, p. 57. But Bannister, misled by the forms *Darweld* (dated 1532, but properly 1534–5), *Darwalde* (dated

of a stretch of high ground running north from the point where the Lime Brook, coming down from Lingen, joins the river Lugg just west of Shirley Farm. Immediately below the confluence the bridge over the Lugg is named Deerfold Bridge, and the name Deerfold is marked at two other points on the modern map;[1] the first, one mile north of the bridge, is on the northern slopes of a steep hill (summit 928 feet, some 530 feet above the river-flats by the bridge), and the second, one mile further north, is across the summit of a somewhat lower hill (about 850 feet), steep-sided to north and west, situated $1\frac{1}{4}$ miles NNE. of Lingen and 2 miles west of Wigmore. The modern road-signs lead to this second point, but the name Deerfold evidently belongs properly to the whole of the two-mile-long ridge which is

---

1539, but properly 1541–2), and *Darvoll* (1603), derives the first element from OE *daru* 'hurt', which is absurd, and the second from OE *weald* 'forest', which is more reasonable. But this leaves the modern form unexplained, and the medieval forms support the modern (as indeed does the second element of the 1603 form, in which -*voll* is a reduction, with the common loss of final -*d*, of -*vold* 'fold'). The name is what it seems to be, a compound of OE *dēor* 'deer' and *fal(o)d* 'fold'. The *dar*- of the sixteenth- and seventeenth-century forms shows shortening in the first element of a compound (OE *dēor* > ME *dĕr*), followed by the change of *ĕr* to *ăr*; cf. the name Darley < OE *dēorlēah*. The *w* of the forms *Darweld*, *Darwalde* is probably best explained as a false substitution, by a scribe, for *u* in his original (cf. *Dereuaud* in the Anglo-Norman summaries); this *u* is of course for Western /v/ < OE *f* at the beginning of the second element. But it is possible, though unlikely, that there may have been two names, *Deerfold* and *Deerwald* (Deer Wood); if there were, the same stretch of country must have been meant.

In the medieval forms of MSS. Harley 1240 and Additional 6041, the occurrence of *u* for original *l* in -*faud*, -*uaud* is an Anglo-Norman not an English phonetic development, reflecting the general OF vocalization of back /l/ to /u/ before a consonant, which had occurred before the middle of the twelfth century (Pope, *From Latin to Modern French* (Manchester, 1934), §§ 385, 387). Cf. the surname *Wauton* for *Walton* (p. 416, below) and the form *Anseume* for *Anselm* in MS. Cleopatra C. vi, f. 147^v.

[1] Ordnance Survey 1:25,000 series, Sheet SO 36 (Presteigne). See the sketch-map on p. 176, above.

bounded on the south-west by the Lime Brook and on the west by a tributary which runs south from near Birtley to meet the main brook just below Lingen. Some five furlongs to the south-east, at the hamlet of Limebrook, a second southward-flowing tributary joins the brook; its narrow wooded valley breaks into the Deerfold cluster of hills. In the charter, however, the name *La Derefaud* is given a more specialized application, to 'the valley in which was founded the church of the Blessed Mary and St. Leonard of *Sutelesford*'; this is also the application of *Darweld*, *Darwalde* in documents (cited below) of 1534–5 and 1541–2. *Sutelesford* is a lost place-name, which was evidently falling into disuse in the thirteenth century, but its location is indicated by the modern Chapel Farm (grid reference 395685), $1\frac{1}{4}$ miles WSW. of Wigmore, which is built on the site of the chapel of St. Leonard.[1] Chapel Farm is on the bank of a stream which flows in a generally southerly direction until, one mile below the farm, it first curves to the south-east, then east to pass south of Lower Lye, and finally, turning again to the south-east, enters the river Lugg one mile north-west of the Aymestrey bridge. A crossing near Chapel Farm, on the road from Lingen to Wigmore, may have been the ford of *Sutelesford*; the valley in which Chapel Farm stands, east of the Deerfold ridge, must be the one referred to in the charter. To the north and east of Chapel Farm is high wooded ground (Burnt Coppice and Barnett Wood), between the farm and Wigmore; viewed from the west, the modern farm is very much 'below' Barnett Wood, which rises steeply on the other side of the stream. These woods are undoubtedly *nemora mea*, though in the Middle Ages they may well have differed in extent.[2] By 'the way out into the valley of

[1] Cf. the Ordnance Survey map cited.
[2] In particular, the woods north of Chapel Farm are now mostly a modern plantation of conifers.

Wigmore' (*exitum in valle de Wygemore*, governed by *infra*)
must be meant the road from Lingen to Wigmore, which
now runs in an ENE. direction north of Chapel Farm, on
higher ground, to cross a ridge of some 750 feet (Tucknell
Bank) half a mile north-east of the farm and then, turning
ESE., runs down the southern rim of the Wigmore valley
to the village of Wigmore itself; a direct continuation of
the line of the road ENE. from the ridge, along a surviving
footpath (according to the Ordnance Survey map), would
have led to the valley directly beneath Wigmore Castle,
built on an eminence to the north. The road crosses the
Chapel Farm stream below Tucknell Bank, and now divides
its wooded upper valley from the cleared lower valley; it
therefore makes good sense to speak of 'the whole valley
below my woods and [below] the way out into the valley of
Wigmore'.[1]

There are, however, points about the charter which are
not entirely clear. The first is what is meant by 'the whole
valley'. It would, I think, be reasonable to suppose that it
means the valley from Chapel Farm southwards to where the
stream, after receiving tributaries from side-valleys to the
west, turns south-east away from the Deerfold ridge; in its
lower course it could hardly be called the Deerfold valley,
nor could it be well said to be 'below my woods'.[2] Then again
some doubt might be possible where exactly the 'sisters' had
lived. The modern evidence is that the name Deerfold applies
to a tract of country or, as Bannister says, to a forest, and

[1] The 'way out' must have followed much the same route in the Middle
Ages as now, since it is aiming for the col between two hills and its line
is therefore dictated by the topography. It is the 'way out' from the
Deerfold forest to the Wigmore valley on the most direct route from
Lingen to Wigmore Castle.

[2] The southern boundary of Wigmore parish crosses the stream 5 furlongs south of Chapel Farm and 2 furlongs north of the point where the
main tributary from the west comes in. This parish-boundary probably
marks the southern limit of the *Sutelesford* valley.

this is of course consistent with its etymological meaning, 'deer-park'.[1] But the draughtsman of the charter plainly applies the name of *Sutelesford* to the valley; and we must therefore accept that in his understanding of the matter the sisters were living, at the time of the original grant, not at some unspecified place in the Deerfold forest, but at *Sutelesford* (or at least in its valley), where a church or chapel had been founded and dedicated to the Virgin and St. Leonard. And finally we must ask in what sense the word *sorores* is used. In the latter part of the charter, in the expression *moniales vel sorores*, it must mean 'lay-sisters', since there is an evident intention to distinguish between alternative forms of membership of the nunnery; but in the earlier part, where the context does not require this special meaning, *sorores* (which is used thrice, without qualification) should be construed more widely. It may still be used in a religious sense, less definite than 'lay-sister', to mean that the women, though not nuns (*moniales*), were members of some form of community vowed to religion. But it may equally well be used in its natural meaning, that the women were sisters by birth; though neither their names nor their

---

[1] The word occurs, in the form *derfald*, in the *Peterborough Chronicle*, s.a. 1123 and 1127 (ed. Clark (Oxford, 2nd edn., 1970), p. 42, l. 5, and p. 50, l. 67), the first referring to the royal deer-park at Woodstock, where the bishop of Lincoln (as befitted an enemy of monks) fell dead from his horse as he rode with the king (Henry I), and the second referring to a diabolic hunt that occurred wherever the diabolic abbot Henry of Poitou, unjustly appointed to Peterborough, chose to go, as was seen 'on þe selue derfald in þa tune on Burch & on ealle þa wudes ða wæron fram þa selua tune to Stanforde'. A deerfold, like a deer-park, must have been enclosed by a fence or ditch, but such enclosures might be very extensive. It is not conceivable that the 'valley of *Sutelesford*' was itself the Mortimers' deer-park, in spite of the name applied to it in the charter; no medieval noble would have granted away his deer-park, least of all to women unconcerned with hunting. It must have been a valley adjoining, and therefore named after, the deerfold itself, which is what the modern map implies.

parentage are stated, the later charter is explicitly merely summarizing the details 'more fully . . . contained' in the earlier.

There can be no reasonable doubt that the elder Roger's grant, like his grandson's, was made for religious motives, but the community to which the 'sisters' belonged (or which they constituted) cannot have been so organized that it could be regarded as a legal entity, a body corporate able to hold lands. For it seems to be explicit, from the recital of the extant charter of *c.* 1252, that the original grant had been not to a body corporate (such as 'the church of the Blessed Mary and of St. Leonard'), but to 'the sisters living in *Le Derefaud*' in their own persons. So long as any of them survived, she would have a clear title under the earlier Roger's charter; but difficulty would arise after the last had died. The prioress and nuns of the church of St. Thomas the Martyr at Limebrook may have been in some way the successors of 'the sisters living in *Le Derefaud*' and may even have come *de facto* to control the property granted to them, but they would have had a dubious legal right to inherit it. The later charter, drawn up, as its draughtsman explains, in the form of a deed of transfer, conveys the title in express words to a body corporate, 'the church of St. Thomas the Martyr at Limebrook and the nuns there serving God', in perpetuity. But as a grant in perpetuity is a much more serious matter than one to sisters who will in due course die, the younger Roger de Mortimer has exacted his price— the maintenance of the original chapel as a chantry where prayers might be offered for his soul and the souls of his family, and the right, for ever, to nominate two women as members of the community.

It does not necessarily follow, from the argument of the preceding paragraph, that the last of the 'sisters' had recently died in 1252 or so; the clerks of Roger's chancery may have been inspired to find a flaw in the prioress of Limebrook's title to property long in her effective control, by their lord's desire to impose conditions for its renewal. But it is by no means impossible that the last of the 'sisters' had recently died, and indeed I think it is probable; for the later charter is explicitly a transfer of property which, when the sisters died, the lords of Wigmore would have been entitled to take back into their own possession. A woman who had been born in 1175 or later might well have been one of the recipients of a grant made (at the outside limits) between 1181 and 1214, and probably after 1200;[1] and in 1250, if she had lived, she would have been 75 or less. The transfer of the title may not have been a legal device to enable a new, young, and energetic lord to tidy up his affairs to his own advantage; it may have been a genuine necessity, occasioned by the recent death of the last of the original grantees.

Between the evidence of the charter of MS. Harley 1240 and that of MS. Harley 1087 (that Ralph of Lingen was the 'first founder' of Limebrook Priory) there is no real inconsistency; we have only to assume two separate acts of endowment. There is not even any evidence that the original recipients of the grants were the same women; indeed the probability is that they were not. Roger de Mortimer's grant,

[1] Even if the original grant had been made in the first year possible, 1181 (which is very unlikely), one would only need to imagine a woman born in 1165 who would have been 16 years old in 1181; for in those days women often entered religion at a very early age, 'in the flower of their youth', as *Ancrene Wisse* itself says. In 1250 such a woman would have been 85; but this of course is by no means impossible. The widow of the elder Roger de Mortimer did not die until 1252 (*Complete Peerage*, ix. 273), though her eldest son Hugh must have been born by about 1190 (he was married before 1210); she must have been about 80 at her death. 'The sisters in the Deerfold' may well have been younger than their benefactor's wife. If the grant had been made about 1210, a woman born as late as 1190 could have been one of the original grantees; and in 1250 she would have been only 60.

though it eventually passed to the prioress and nuns of Limebrook, was originally made to 'sisters living in *Le Derefaud*', two miles from Limebrook across steep wooded hills; Ralph of Lingen is credited with the initial endowment of a religious house whose buildings were at a slightly later date, and probably from the beginning, sited in the south-eastern corner of Lingen parish, surrounded, except to the north-east, by lands traditionally held by the Lingen family. The likelihood is that there were originally two distinct communities, separately endowed. But even if we were to assume, despite the difference of site, that there had never been more than a single community and that the 'sisters living in *Le Derefaud*' were the nucleus from which there developed the priory of Limebrook, it would still be possible that this community had received two early endowments which gave rise to two traditions of its foundation. Ralph of Lingen may have given lands in the valley of the Lime Brook on which the community eventually built its permanent house, Roger de Mortimer the chapel of St. Leonard and the lands about it because that was where the community originally lived; both may have had some claim to be the founder, but priority may have belonged to Ralph of Lingen. Wigmore Abbey itself is a parallel case: it was originally established, as a priory, by Oliver de Merlimond, the steward of Hugh de Mortimer, but the latter subsequently confirmed Oliver's benefactions, added others of his own (including the final site of the abbey), and was thenceforth regarded as the founder.

The hypothesis that Ralph of Lingen's endowment was earlier than Roger de Mortimer's the evidence allows and almost invites, for Roger lived for 24 years after Ralph's death and must have been a much younger man. Though the charter gives no indication of the date of the elder Roger's grant, it is unlikely to have been in the early years of his barony after his succession in 1181. The Anglo-Norman *History of the Foundation of Wigmore Abbey*,[1] written in the early thirteenth century, records that Roger, at the time of his succession,[2] was in the king's custody because of the death

[1] For bibliographical references, see p. 131, n. 3, above. The chronicle ends with its account of the elder Roger de Mortimer's gift of the piece of land known as 'the treasure of Mortimer' to the abbey, i.e. before his death in 1214, and there is no indication that it breaks off incomplete. It was undoubtedly used as a source by the compilers of the Latin chronicle entitled *Fundationis et Fundatorum Historia* (largely an account of the founder's family and its history) in the same manuscript (printed by Dugdale, *Monasticon*, vi. 348–54). The latter was, from internal evidence, written at various dates up to the early fifteenth century, when it ends, but the passages based on the Anglo-Norman chronicle precede one which refers to the later Roger de Mortimer 'qui nunc est' and who is said to have held the barony for 15 years (i.e. this latter passage, taken at face value, was written in 1262). The Anglo-Norman chronicle must therefore be earlier than 1262. On the other hand it includes a sentence referring to the death and burial of the elder Roger's widow Isabella, who died before 29 April 1252 (*Complete Peerage*, ix. 273). But this sentence looks like a later insertion, made perhaps when the Anglo-Norman chronicle was being used for the compilation of the Latin *Historia*. Otherwise the Anglo-Norman chronicle reads like an account written soon after the events which it describes, i.e. probably before 1225.

[2] The chronicler does not explicitly say that it was at the time of his succession that Roger was in the king's custody, but the order of his narrative gives this clear impression; it is so taken by Eyton, iv. 205–6. The chronicler's account is accurate; as Eyton points out, the sheriffs of Herefordshire and Shropshire both accounted for lands, variously described as those of Hugh or of Roger de Mortimer, for a period which was evidently six months up to Michaelmas 1181 (*Pipe R. 27 Hen. II*, pp. 4, 19; *Pipe R. 28 Hen. II*, p. 14), this being presumably the length of time that elapsed between Hugh's death in February and Roger's recovery of his freedom. Cadwallon ap Madog of Maelienydd, a cousin and adherent of the Lord Rhys, had been killed in 1179 by Roger's followers while he was returning under safe-conduct from the king's presence; this accounts for the seriousness with which Henry II regarded the affair. Some of the offenders were put to death and others were forced to seek refuge in the woods, and Roger himself was imprisoned (cf. J. E. Lloyd, *A History of Wales*, ii. 567). The sheriff of Herefordshire received payment at Michaelmas 1179 for sending the prisoners to 'the court at Windsor and at Worcester' (*Pipe R. 25 Hen. II*, p. 39). The essential facts are thus confirmed by the contemporary official records of the Pipe Rolls.

of one Cadwallon, killed by Roger's men, and his lands were in the hands of the king's servants;[1] and when he was freed and recovered control of his lands, he was quick to challenge one of his father's benefactions to the abbey. Thereafter he was hostile to it, resenting his father's alienation of valuable lands, and at one time[2] compelled the abbot and most of the canons to withdraw to Shobdon, though they were soon enabled to return to their main house by the king's intervention. The chronicler explains that Roger was a gay young man, changeable and headstrong and bent on his pleasures, and under the influence of unwise and sycophantic counsellors.[3] This continued until one day (an anniversary as it happened of his father's death, though he did not remember that), as he rode on his pleasures, exclaiming to his companions at the fertility of the abbey's fields and repining that his father's generosity had been at his own expense, he heard the abbey bells ring out and, asking why, was told by his chaplain, one of the canons, that it was because of the services in commemoration of his father; thereupon he was changed in heart and himself became a generous benefactor of the abbey, giving to it the land known from its value as 'the treasure of Mortimer'. The story implies that his 'persecution' (as it is expressly called) of the canons was of some duration, and so does the wording of the chaplain's reply, 'Sir, to-day is so many years since your father, the founder of our house, died';[4] the indefinite expression *tantz des anz*, 'such-and-such a number

---

[1] Dugdale, vi. 347; Wright, p. 124; Dickinson and Ricketts, p. 436.

[2] The chronicler says that it was before Christmas, without specifying the year, but he may mean the Christmas immediately following Roger's release from custody, i.e. Christmas 1181; certainly it was during the reign of Henry II, i.e. before July 1189.

[3] Dugdale, vi. 348; Wright, p. 127; Dickinson and Ricketts, pp. 438, 440.

[4] 'Sire, hieu a tantz des anz morut vostre pere. fundour de nostre mesun' (Dugdale, vi. 348; Wright, p. 129; Dickinson and Ricketts, p. 440).

of years', though obviously the chronicler's substitute for
whatever the chaplain had actually said, would hardly have
been used if the death had been comparatively recent and
the number of years small. Roger's conversion to a more
charitable frame of mind is unlikely to have occurred during
the first ten years after his succession; and a man who was
still actively resentful of his father's transference of ancestral
lands into the dead hand of the church can hardly be supposed to have himself given, during the same period, a size-
able tract of land to the 'sisters' of the Deerfold. Between
1191 and 1194 he could not have done so; for in 1191 he
rose in unsuccessful rebellion in support of Prince John,
his castle of Wigmore was seized on behalf of the crown, and
he himself was exiled for three years. He was again absent
from Wigmore between 1205 and 1207; for on landing at
Dieppe in 1205 he was captured and eventually had to pay
a ransom of 1,000 marks for his liberty. He was back in
England by June 1207.[1] The probability is that his benefactions to Wigmore Abbey and to the Deerfold sisters[2]
were made between 1194 and his death in 1214; it is a matter
of common observation, and indeed implied by the Wigmore
chronicler, that increasing age makes men more willing to
make grants for religious purposes. But if Roger's endowment of the Deerfold sisters was later than 1190, then it
must have been later than Ralph of Lingen's endowment of
Limebrook.

Considerations of topography, already briefly mentioned,
support the hypothesis that there had been two distinct
endowments. The site of Limebrook Priory is within the
territory of the Lingen family, as Chapel Farm and its
valley are within the territory of Wigmore;[3] the two, though

[1] *Complete Peerage*, ix. 272.
[2] And to other religious houses; see *Complete Peerage*, loc. cit.
[3] The valley north of Limebrook, including the modern Upper

near enough to be managed as a single estate, are separated
by the main ridge of the Deerfold hills. In 1291, according
to the *Taxatio Ecclesiastica*, the priory owned two carucates
of land at Limebrook, and there is no mention of the Deerfold
(or *Sutelesford*) valley. But it is very hard to see how there
can have been room for more than a single carucate in the
south-eastern corner of Lingen parish, in the valley of the
Lime Brook and on the slopes to the south-west;[1] and it is
equally difficult to see how there can have been room for
more than a single carucate in the valley around and south
of Chapel Farm.[2] It seems probable that in 1291 two separate
properties were lumped together and treated as one.

This conclusion is supported by sixteenth-century documents relating to Limebrook Priory. The *Valor Ecclesiasticus*
of 1534–5 (26 Henry VIII) gives a very summary account of
its possessions,[3] but distinguishes the 'farm' (*firma*) of

Limebrook Farm, as well as the Chapel Farm valley, is now within the
parish of Wigmore—as indeed is the whole of the Deerfold except its
southernmost extremity west of Upper Lye. But the actual site of the
ruins of Limebrook Priory is just within the boundary of Lingen parish.
At this point the Lime Brook and its northern tributary are, for about
half a mile, the boundary between Lingen and Wigmore parishes.

[1] The land to the NE., on the left bank of the brook, is very steep and
wooded.

[2] The extent of a carucate is doubtful. According to the tractate known
as *Fleta* (which Denholm-Young thinks may have been written in the
Fleet Prison between 1290 and 1292 by the lawyer Matthew de Scaccario;
see Powicke, *The Thirteenth Century*, p. 356, n. 2), a full carucate contained 180 acres if a three-field system was in use (60 in each field, one
being fallow), but 160 if a two-field system was used (80 in each field,
one being fallow). But according to *OED*, 'Commonly only the land
under plough in any one year was reckoned . . . Hence in ancient deeds
the normal carucate is either 120 acres or 80 acres.'

[3] Dugdale, *Monasticon*, iv. 184. The spiritualities (Clifton and Stoke
Bliss) were valued at £4. 6s. 8d., the temporalities at £19. 11s. 0d. (from
which was deducted £1 for the fee of the bailiff John Grene); the latter
comprised the nunnery with the rents etc. assigned to it, valued
at £15. 17s. 8d., the domain lands, valued at £2. 13s. 4d., and the 'farm'
of *Darweld*, valued at £1.

Darweld, valued at £1 *per annum*, from the domain lands, valued at £2. 13s. 4d. The Ministers' Accounts[1] of 1541–2 (33 Henry VIII, Augmentation Office), by contrast, list the properties (both spiritualities and temporalities) under no less than thirty-three distinct headings, with a total value of £32. 10s. 4d.; the last four listed under Herefordshire are the mill at *Lymbroke* (valued at 10s.), the 'farm' of *Dorwalde*[2] (also valued at 10s.), the chapel of St. Leonard at *Dorwalde* (valued at £2), and the site and appurtenances of the priory at *Lymbroke* (valued at £5. 12s. 11d.). It is impossible to reconcile the figures of the *Valor Ecclesiasticus* with those of the Ministers' Accounts,[3] but they have in common that they both distinguish the 'farm'[4] and chapel of Deerfold from the domain lands of the priory, while the grouping of the items in the Ministers' Accounts seems to depend on the recognition that Deerfold and Limebrook were in the same area. There are, finally, the particulars of the domain lands of Limebrook drawn up on 3 February 1553 (7 Edward VI), in preparation for their sale by the Crown.[5] These recite that, in addition to the buildings and other appurtenances of the former priory, there was an estimated total of 84 acres of pasture (though the separate items listed add up only to 61 acres) and of 122 acres of arable (in this case the items listed add up to 123 acres); the value of the whole was

[1] Dugdale, iv. 184.

[2] *Dorwalde* in the *Monasticon* must be a misreading of the form *Darwalde* cited by Bannister (see p. 219, n. 3, above) from '*Aug. Off.*'; but Bannister's date 1539 must be a mistake, just as his dating to 1532 of the form *Darweld*, which is evidently taken from the *Valor Ecclesiasticus*, is also too early. He is two years out in each case.

[3] Except that in each the Deerfold properties are valued at approximately two-fifths of the Limebrook properties (counting 'farm' and chapel together in the one case, mill and site in the other).

[4] The word may perhaps be used in its modern sense, which is recorded from 1522, but is more likely to have its older meaning of 'fixed rent'.

[5] *Dugdale*, iv. 183.

assessed at £5. 16s. 4d. *per annum*, which agrees well enough with the £5. 12s. 11d. of the Ministers' Accounts eleven years before. The whole property, of 84 (or 61) acres of pasture and 122 (or 123) of arable, appears to correspond almost exactly with a single medieval carucate of the three-field type, with its 60 acres of fallow and 120 of arable, especially if the fallow had been added to the common land, as it often was, in reckoning the extent of the pasture. This seems to confirm the hypothesis that at Limebrook itself there was only a single carucate, and that the second carucate of the *Taxatio Ecclesiastica* of 1291 was in the Deerfold valley, which is not separately mentioned.

Quite apart from the evidence of the charter of MS. Harley 1240 (*Liber Niger*), and from any deductions to be drawn from topography and from the sixteenth-century evidence, Ralph of Lingen cannot have had any intention of founding a full-scale nunnery. Even if the original endowment at Limebrook consisted of two carucates, and even if both were his gift, it was utterly inadequate. In 1291, when Limebrook owned temporalities valued at £6. 8s. 8d. a year and a spirituality, the church at Clifton, valued at £6. 13s. 4d. a year, the house was poor; one of the manuscripts of the *Taxatio Ecclesiastica* itself speaks of the *pauperes moniales de Lyngebrok*.[1] The nuns were unable to pay the papal taxes, and were therefore placed under sentences of excommunication; the bishop of Hereford had to intercede with the commissary of the papal nuncio to get them let off, in March 1299, on account of their great poverty (*considerata . . . magna paupertate earundem*).[2] But if they were very poor in 1291, what can they have been before 1240, when, as we have seen, they possessed only their original endowment (or

---

[1] *Tax. Eccles.*, p. 165b n.
[2] *Registrum Ricardi de Swinfield*, ed. Capes, p. 366.

endowments) in the area of Limebrook itself, valued in 1291 at 16s. 4d. a year? This is little more than a halfpenny a day. The wage of an ordinary manual labourer in the late twelfth century was a penny a day;[1] a foot-soldier got twopence or even threepence.[2] In 1222 the *minimum* annual salary of the vicar of an appropriated church was set at five marks a year, i.e. 66s. 8d.;[3] but the original endowment of Limebrook was in 1291—after a century in which agricultural prices had risen—valued at just under a quarter of this sum. Dickinson says that 'by the later years of the twelfth century . . . many founders were small men whose piety might well be greater than their pence',[4] but no one can have supposed that a full nunnery could be founded with an endowment that even a hundred years later produced little more than half the wage of an ordinary labourer, and somewhat less than one quarter of the minimum salary of a paid vicar. In fact, as we have seen, it is virtually certain that of the two carucates listed in 1291 as being at Limebrook, one was really in the Deerfold valley and was the elder Roger de Mortimer's gift to the sisters who had lived there; if we credit to this property half the value of the lands as assessed in 1291 (i.e. 6s. 8d.), the value of Ralph of Lingen's gift is reduced to 9s. 8d. a year (at 1291 values). It is inconceivable that he can have intended, with so exiguous an endowment, to found a nunnery. But he may well have intended to provide a basic assured income for a very small community of two or three women, vowed to a religious life of simple poverty, who for the rest would look for food and clothing to their own work and the charity of their neighbours. And in the social conditions of the time

[1] A. L. Poole, *From Domesday Book to Magna Carta* (Oxford, 2nd edn., 1955), p. 414.

[2] Poole, p. 372; D. M. Stenton, *English Society in the Early Middle Ages* (Harmondsworth, 1951), p. 88.

[3] Poole, p. 227.

[4] *Origins*, p. 151.

he would be most likely to do this if they were kinswomen of his own, perhaps his sisters, who had devoted themselves to the life of religion and for whose maintenance he had an obligation to provide.

Limebrook Priory must be an instance of a religious house that developed where none had been intended. Dickinson, in *The Origins of the Austin Canons*, tells us that many Augustinian houses began as hermitages that developed into larger communities;[1] among other English examples he cites Snead–Chirbury, in south-western Shropshire. All the evidence tends to show that Limebrook originated in this way. There is the pitifully inadequate initial endowment; the fact that the tradition recorded in MS. Harley 1087 describes Ralph of Lingen as the 'first founder', as if in recognition that there had been distinguishable stages in the foundation; the issue of the elder Roger de Mortimer's charters not to a body corporate, but to 'the sisters living in *Le Derefaud*', and the likelihood that these 'sisters' were distinct from whatever community there was at that time at Limebrook; and the gap of thirty-one years between the death of Ralph of Lingen in 1190 and the first extant record of *moniales de Lingebrok* in 1221. But the use, in the records of 1221 and 1226, of the term *moniales* must mean that by then the house at Limebrook was a recognized nunnery, and though it is not until some thirty years later, in the younger Roger de Mortimer's charter, that we find a record referring to a prioress and still later that we learn explicitly that the house was one of Augustinian canonesses, we need hardly doubt that this was already the case in 1221. At some stage in the course of its unrecorded history between 1190 and 1221 the nature of the community at Limebrook must have changed; the few women for whom the original small endowment would have been barely adequate must have attracted

[1] Op. cit., p. 143.

disciples until their number had grown to that required of a 'full convent' and they could be organized as a regular nunnery; and gradually they began to acquire other endowments, including, soon after 1250, those originally granted to the 'sisters' in the Deerfold and now legally transferred to the 'church of St. Thomas the Martir'.

During this same period, after the death of Ralph of Lingen and about the time when the elder Roger de Mortimer was endowing the 'sisters' in the Deerfold, there is contemporary evidence of an anchoress who lived somewhere within the jurisdiction of the sheriff of Herefordshire and of the March of Wales; her name was Margaret. The Pipe Roll for 1202–3 records that the sheriff has paid 15s. 2½d. for a half-year 'to Margaret the recluse' (*Margarete incluse*) in obedience to a royal writ (*per breve R.*).[1] Thereafter he paid annually 30s. 5d., exactly a penny a day, until the year ending at Michaelmas 1212.[2] The Pipe Roll for the next year (15 John) is missing; in that for 16 John there is no mention of any payment to Margaret. She may have died, but another reason for the cessation of her pension is more probable. It had certainly been paid for nine and a half years, from 5 John (a half-year's pension) to 14 John (a full year's pension). It may well have been granted originally for ten years, since such payments were commonly authorized for a fixed term and not indefinitely; and if so, since it started from Lady Day 1203, it would have been due to be discontinued at Lady Day 1213, during the year for which the Pipe Roll is missing. Unfortunately the writ ordering the pension seems not to survive; it would have stated the

[1] *Pipe R. 5 John*, p. 55.
[2] *Pipe R. 6 John*, p. 16; *7 John*, p. 271; *8 John*, p. 65; *9 John*, p. 157; *10 John*, p. 190; *11 John*, p. 60; *12 John*, p. 145; *13 John*, p. 232; *14 John*, p. 158.

conditions on which it was granted, and probably have given some indication of where Margaret lived and at whose instance King John—who was not ungenerous in doling out 'small sums to religious houses, particularly to small nunneries'[1]—had made the grant. We are left to guess from the bare accounting record of the Pipe Roll. Margaret the recluse, like the 'sisters' in the Deerfold and the community at Limebrook, lived within the jurisdiction of the sheriff of Herefordshire. The king's orders for her pension must have been received, and were probably issued, between Michaelmas 1202 (when the new financial year started) and Lady Day 1203, since the pension was paid for a half-year in 1202–3, i.e. from Lady Day 1203; they must therefore have been issued from France, where the king was engaged, from the spring of 1202 until December 1203, on his last unsuccessful campaign in defence of Normandy. Roger de Mortimer, in whose Wigmore barony both the Deerfold 'sisters' and the Limebrook community lived, was with the king in Normandy for part at least of this time; on 1 April 1202 he witnessed a charter of the king's at Montfort-sur-Risle, and he 'appears to have been with John at Bonport in July following'.[2] If Margaret had lived within Roger's domains and been under his patronage, it would be easier to understand how a recluse living in Herefordshire came to be granted a pension by a king on campaign in Normandy. There is no indication whether Margaret lived alone or was a member of a group of recluses, receiving the pension on behalf of them all. It was a standard rate of grant. Nevertheless, though its daily rate was only that of a labourer's wage, it was almost twice as much as the income that Limebrook Priory derived in 1291 from its home estate. Margaret may not have been one of *þeose riche ancres þe*

---

[1] Poole, p. 428.
[2] *Complete Peerage*, ix. 272–3.

tilieð oðer habbeð rentes isette,[1] but so long as her pension lasted she was insured against the extremes of poverty.

[1] Corpus MS., 112a/25–6 (Morton, p. 416); but Corpus here reads *chirch*, probably by mere error, for the *riche* of the other MSS. The author probably had in mind the widows or daughters of the higher nobility, who, if they entered the life of religion, were often very amply provided for, and who might still have to concern themselves with the cultivation of their estates (hence *tilieð*). He can hardly have meant persons with small endowments or small pensions.

V

ANCRENE WISSE AND LIMEBROOK

THE evidence cited in the previous chapter shows that between about 1190 and 1225 there were at least two groups of women religious in the neighbourhood of Wigmore. At Limebrook there was the community founded, with a small endowment, by Ralph of Lingen, who died in 1190; by 1221 its inmates were described as *moniales* and it had almost certainly already been organized as an Augustinian priory. In the Deerfold west of Wigmore there were the sisters to whom Roger de Mortimer had granted the chapel of the Blessed Virgin and of St. Leonard, and the valley in which it was situated, between his succession in 1181 and his death in June 1214, probably in the latter part of this period, after 1200. There was also the anchoress Margaret, who may have been a member of one of these two groups (and if so, more probably of the latter), to whom King John paid a pension for at least nine and a half years, and perhaps for ten, from Lady Day 1203, possibly at the instance of Roger de Mortimer.

The main reasons for believing that *Ancrene Wisse* and the *Katherine*-group were written for one or other of these groups are that the dates fit so well and that the locations are so suitable. We have already seen[1] that the *Katherine*-group must have been written, at the outside, between 1190 and 1220; the narrower limits of 1200 and 1215 would be rather more likely. I have argued elsewhere[2] that *Ancrene*

[1] pp. 163–6, above.
[2] *Proc. Brit. Acad.* lii (1966), 181–208, esp. p. 206.

Wisse is to be dated after 1215, and 'even possibly after . . . 1222'; but it is not in fact likely to have been written after 1222, in view of the number of copies that had been made by the time that the Cleopatra MS. had been completed[1] and the extent of the revisions both in that manuscript and in Corpus, written about 1230 or perhaps a little later—certainly after 1224, when the Franciscans came to England, and probably after 1227, the approximate date of the founding of their house in Hereford. To this a further argument may be added. In the passage from Part I quoted on p. 249, below, the anchoresses are directed to remember

the torments which prisoners suffer and have where they lie heavily fettered with iron—especially [those] of the Christians who are in pagan lands, some in prison, some in as much servitude as an ox is or an ass.

This is undoubtedly influenced by the propaganda in favour of a new crusade to recover the kingdom of Jerusalem and to free Christian captives and slaves;[2] and in particular, though the graphic phrase 'as an ox is or an ass' is evidently the English author's characteristic addition, there is a clear dependence, direct or indirect, on Innocent III's encyclical

---

[1] See the *stemma codicum* on p. 287 (reproduced, in simplified form, from *English and Medieval Studies presented to J. R. R. Tolkien*, ed. Davis and Wrenn, p. 137). There were at least four copies in existence when C was completed: the first fair copy β; γ (probably a direct copy of β); the English manuscript from which F was translated (made at the same time as C from the same exemplar, but finished sooner); and C itself. There were probably several others (δ and its descendants ϵ, ζ, and η); these retained and transmitted the more important of the original passages about the three sisters, though only N preserves it in full. See further below, pp. 286–9.

[2] In 1187, after Saladin's victory at Hattin and the fall of Jaffa, a very large number of Christian prisoners was sold into slavery; see Stephen Runciman, *A History of the Crusades* (Cambridge, 1951–4), ii. 460–1. There was also a steady capture of Christian pilgrims by pirates.

De negotio terrae sanctae,[1] in which the Pope wrote:

Nam et quomodo, secundum praeceptum divinum, diligit proximum suum sicut seipsum, sicut scriptum est, qui scit fratres suos, fide ac nomine Christianos, apud perfidos Saracenos ergastulo diri carceris detineri ac jugo deprimi gravissimae servitutis, et ad liberationem eorum efficacem operam non impendit . . .? An forte nescitis quod apud illos multa millia Christianorum in servitute ac carcere detinentur, qui tormentis innumeris cruciantur?[2]

The encyclical was issued in April 1213,[3] which gives a definite *terminus post quem* for the composition of Part I of *Ancrene Wisse* (though on other grounds it is to be put later still, since it shows the influence of the Fourth Lateran Council of November 1215). But when the Fifth Crusade began, under Innocent's successor Honorius, in late 1217, England took no active part owing to troubles at home. In September 1221 the crusade ended in ignominious failure, with Jerusalem still in the hands of the infidel and the Christian captives unredeemed; indeed, the lot of Christians in Muslim lands was worse than ever.[4] It would argue an extraordinary insensitivity on the part of the English author if he had summarized the Pope's words calling for the liberation of the captives after the news had become known in the West that the crusade which he

---

[1] J. D. Mansi, *Sacrorum Conciliorum Nova et Amplissima Collectio*, xxii (1778), cols. 956–60; Migne, *Pat. Lat.*, ccxvi, cols. 817–22. The letter was addressed to England, among many other countries.

[2] Mansi, col. 957; Migne, col. 818.

[3] The letter is undated but comes fairly early (no. 28) in the register for the sixteenth year of Innocent's pontificate, which began on 22 February 1213. It is assigned to April in *Calendar of Papal Registers relating to Great Britain and Ireland: Papal Letters* i (1893), 38. It should be noted that a reference in the letter (Mansi, col. 959; Migne, col. 820) to the Lateran Council refers to that of 1179 (specifically its Canon 24; Mansi, cols. 230–1), and not to that of 1215, which repeated these provisions in much the same words. [4] Runciman, iii. 169–70.

had planned had utterly failed; and in any case it is probable that the passage was written during or shortly after the period between the Lateran Council and the summer of 1217, when the preaching of the crusade was at its height. Once written it was left unaltered; it was not the author's normal practice to delete, and he was an unsystematic reviser. The extreme range of dates for the original composition of the *Katherine*-group and of *Ancrene Wisse* itself is therefore between 1190 and 1222;[1] which agrees very closely with the dates for the development of Limebrook, for the sisters who lived in the Deerfold, and for the anchoress Margaret.

It is clear, from the internal evidence of *Ancrene Wisse*, that the women for whom it was written lived near the author, who could visit them regularly: he was their director, and apparently their confessor; he knew their circumstances well and they were to tell him of everything that each heard about the other. The evidence of the various texts requires the same assumption, for it was the author's practice to write additions or explanations in the margins of the various early copies; these we can see in the extant Cleopatra MS., and analysis of the text shows that similar additions must have been made in copies now lost.[2] Yet the additions spread to manuscripts other than those in which they were first made, and the author, when he came to make the Corpus revision, was able to collect in it most of the additions originally made in other manuscripts; this implies either that the various early copies were from the start all held in a single centre

[1] Compare Tolkien's opinion in 1929 that 'the events in the textual history of each [i.e. *Ancrene Wisse* and the *Katherine*-group] took place within less than a generation and round about A.D. 1225' (*Essays and Studies*, xiv. 122).

[2] *English and Medieval Studies*, pp. 157–62, and (for the additions and corrections in C) more fully and correctly in my edition of the manuscript (E.E.T.S. 267, 1972), pp. xciii–cxxx.

(which hardly seems likely, since a single small community would not need multiple copies) or that the communities which owned the several copies were near to each other and to the author's own community, so that copies could readily be borrowed for purposes of collation. But if 'the author's own community' was Wigmore Abbey, then the groups of women must have lived within a short radius of Wigmore. Limebrook and the chapel of St. Leonard are only two miles apart; Limebrook is four miles, in a direct line, from Wigmore Abbey, and the chapel of St. Leonard only two miles. Furthermore, the original passage concerning the three sisters, preserved in full only in the Nero MS.,[1] says that the author knows no anchoress who can have all that she requires with greater ease or honour than they can, for they do not have to worry about food or clothing for themselves or their maidens:

Each of you has from one friend all that she requires, nor need the maiden seek either bread or food further than at his hall.

It is plainly implied that they lived very near a well-disposed and generous patron of some rank, since they got their requirements not only with ease but also with honour, and his residence might be described as, or included, a hall. Limebrook Priory is only three-quarters of a mile down the valley of the brook from Lingen castle, the residence until about 1235 of the son of the priory's 'first founder', and three miles in a direct line from Wigmore castle; but the chapel of St. Leonard fits the condition better, for it is only one mile, across a wooded ridge traversed by 'the way out into the valley of Wigmore', from Wigmore castle, the most important and wealthiest centre in the district and the seat, after 1214, of the son of the Roger de Mortimer who had granted the chapel to the sisters living in the Deerfold.

[1] ed. Day, 85/8 ff.; translated on pp. 1–2, above.

The confirmatory charter of Roger's grandson explicitly says that the chapel was dedicated to the Blessed Virgin and St. Leonard, and it was still called the chapel of St. Leonard in the sixteenth century; the secondary dedication seems to have become the one by which it was commonly known. St. Leonard is said to have been of noble birth and appears to have lived in the sixth century; he became a hermit at Noblac near Limoges and later founded a monastery there. His cult spread widely in the twelfth century and became popular in England, and he would obviously have been a suitable patron for well-born anchoresses. He was, according to the *Oxford Dictionary of the Christian Church*, 'the special patron of prisoners and also of peasants and of the sick'.[1] But in the numerous medieval hymns, sequences, and other sacred poems devoted to him, though he is most commonly celebrated as the liberator of captives,[2] and, somewhat less frequently, as the healer of the sick and of those suffering from physical infirmity or defect,[3] there is no mention of peasants; the words used are *pauperes* (or *paupertas*),[4] and also *afflicti*,[5] *desolati*,[6] *languidi* (*languentes*,

[1] p. 800.

[2] Dreves *et al.*, *Analecta Hymnica Medii Aevi*, iii. 124–6 (no. 8), iv. 179–80 (nos. 330, 332), vi. 168–9 (nos. 219, 221), xvii. 138 (no. 50), xviii. 119–21 (no. 44), xxii. 163 (no. 276), xxiii. 225 (no. 395), xxvi. 243–50 (nos. 84–7), xxix. 159 (no. 300), xxxiii. 130 (no. 148), xxxiv. 220 (no. 269), xxxix. 205 (no. 230), xlii. 246 (no. 271), xliv. 189 (no. 209), xlv. 144–7 (no. 57), xlvi. 286 (no. 252), xlix. 365 (no. 773), lii. 238 (no. 261), lv. 251–2 (nos. 222–3).

[3] Dreves *et al.*, iii. 124–6 (no. 8), iv. 180 (no. 332), vi. 168 (no. 219), x. 239 (no. 316), xxii. 164 (no. 278), xxiii. 225 (no. 395), xxvi. 243–4 (no. 84), 252 (no. 87), xxxiii. 130 (no. 148), xxxiv. 220 (no. 269), xxxix. 205 (no. 230), xlii. 246 (no. 271), xlv. 144–7 (no. 57), xlvi. 286 (no. 252), lii. 238 (no. 261), lv. 251 (no. 222).

[4] Dreves *et al.*, iii. 124–6 (no. 8), vi. 168 (no. 219), ix. 210 (no. 280), xvii. 138 (no. 50), xlvi. 286 (no. 252).

[5] Dreves *et al.*, xxvi. 246 (no. 86), 253 (no. 87), xxxiv. 219 (no. 268), xlv. 144–7 (no. 57), xlvi. 286 (no. 252).

[6] Dreves *et al.*, xxvi. 244 (no. 84), xxxiii. 130 (no. 148).

languor),[1] *maesti*,[2] *miseri*,[3] *oppressi*,[4] *tristes*,[5] *turbati*,[6] and the nouns *anxietas*[6] and *cura*.[7] The various ideas are often combined in a single poem. So in a hymn by the late fourteenth-century Carthusian Albert of Prague;[8]

> Nam vinctos, quos visitasti,
> Omnes certe liberasti,
>   Dei cum potentia.
> Vinctum me nunc visitare
> Et dignare[9] liberare
>   Mea a malitia . . .

> Ad hunc locum aegri currunt,
> Surdi, muti, et recurrunt
>   Sani atque omnium
> Dominum pie laudantes,
> Toto corde venerantes
>   Sed et te piissimum.

> Eja lucens lux virtutum,
> Pauperum solamen tutum,
>   Leonharde nobilis . . .

and in verses in British Museum MS. Harley 211, dated to the fifteenth century:[10]

> Salve, pater pietatis,
> Leonharde, desolatis

[1] Dreves *et al.*, xxii. 164 (no. 278), xliv. 189 (no. 209), xlv. 144–7 (no. 57).
[2] Dreves *et al.*, xlvi. 286 (no. 252).
[3] Dreves *et al.*, vi. 169 (no. 221), lv. 252 (no. 223).
[4] Dreves *et al.*, xxxiv. 219–20 (nos. 268–9).
[5] Dreves *et al.*, x. 239 (no. 316), xi. 175 (no. 313).
[6] Dreves *et al.*, xxix. 159 (no. 300).
[7] Dreves *et al.*, vi. 168 (no. 219).
[8] Dreves *et al.*, iii. 124–6 (no. 8, stanzas 2, 8–9).
[9] Imperative singular of *dignari* 'deign'.
[10] Dreves *et al.*, xxxiii. 130 (no. 148).

> Singulis refugium,
> Febro, morbo fatigatis
> Et in partu cruciatis
>   Celere praesidium,
> Vinctis et incarceratis,
> Mente rapta consternatis
>   Singulare gaudium.
> Tu, qui tot iam caritatis
> Servis confers dona gratis,
>   Sis nobis solacium
> Deprecando pro peccatis
> Ut ad sanctae trinitatis
>   Ducamur palatium.

There is frequently, as in these pieces, a prayer to be released from sin or temptation,[1] and the analogy of the chains of captives and the bonds of sin is often made explicit. So in verses in a fifteenth-century manuscript:[2]

> Afflictorum consolator,
> Captivorum liberator,
> Nos peccatis catenatos,
> Cippo labis vinculatos,
> Nos absolvas et non tarde,
> Precamur, sancte Leonharde,

and again in others in a text dated 1507:[3]

> Confessor Leonarde,
> Nos, qui sumus mentis tardae
>   Malis vinctos, evincula;
> Ut multos catenarum
> Sic nos a vinc[u]lis culparum
>   Absolve prece sedula.

---

[1] Dreves *et al.*, iii. 124–6 (no. 8), ix. 210 (no. 280), xvii. 138 (no. 50), xxiii. 225 (no. 395), xxvi. 244 (no. 84), 245–6 (no. 85), 246 (no. 86), 249 (no. 87), xxxiii. 130 (no. 148), xxxiv. 219 (no. 268), xxxix. 205 (no. 230), xlii. 246 (no. 271), xlv. 144–7 (no. 57), xlvi. 286 (no. 252).

[2] Dreves *et al.*, xxvi. 246 (no. 86).

[3] Dreves *et al.*, xxxiv. 219 (no. 268).

I

In France St. Leonard was already celebrated for his inter-cessions in favour of prisoners by the early eleventh century,[1] and in England in the first half of the twelfth William of Malmesbury, with a touch of honest doubt, remarks:[2]

Fertur enim in primis ille sanctus absolvendorum vinculorum potens, ut, videntibus nec mutire audentibus adversariis, pondera sua captivus liber asportet.

His most famous exploit in this field (which William was narrating) was the liberation of the swashbuckling crusader Bohemond Prince of Antioch from a captivity which he perhaps deserved and which was certainly convenient for several of his associates.[3] In August 1100, advancing into border territory with too few men and too little care, Bohe-mond was ambushed by the Turks, defeated and captured, and carried 'loaded with chains' to the fortress of Niksar in Pontus, where he was held imprisoned and in fetters for almost three years. In addition to other more worldly expedients to secure his release, he prayed to St. Leonard for his intercession, vowing that if he were freed he would honour the saint's shrine; and in due course he did so, first sending gifts and then himself going on pilgrimage to Noblac during his visit to France in 1105–6. By the 1130s the story had been widely reported.[4]

[1] A. Poncellet, 'Boémond et S. Léonard', *Analecta Bollandiana*, xxxi (1912), 24–44; see p. 28.

[2] *De gestis regum Anglorum*, iv, § 387 (ed. Stubbs, Rolls Series 1887–9, ii. 454).

[3] For the story, see Poncellet, pp. 24–9, who gives detailed citations of the original sources, and Runciman, *A History of the Crusades*, i. 321–2, ii. 38–9.

[4] Poncellet, p. 29, cites Raould de Caen, *Gesta Tancredi* (1112–18), c. 152; the *Historia Peregrinorum* (after 1131), c. 140; the Anglo-Norman Ordericus Vitalis, *Historia Ecclesiastica*, Book X c. 23 and Book XI c. 12 (which Poncellet dates 1135–6); and William of Malmesbury, *Gesta Regum*, iv, §§ 375, 387 (ed. Stubbs, ii. 438, 454). The account in William must be one of his later additions to the *Gesta Regum*, for it is apparently

There is good reason why a chapel built in the territory and within the gift of Roger de Mortimer should have had a dedication to St. Leonard, for the Mortimers had had experience of captivity. Roger himself, at the time of his succession in February 1181, was in prison by the orders of Henry II and had been in some danger of his life, and he was again a prisoner of war in France in 1205–7.[1] His son and heir Hugh was married to Annora, the daughter of William de Braose, a former favourite of King John's who by 1210 was a declared traitor; in that year the king, invading Ireland in pursuit of William and his helpers, drove him into exile and captured his wife and eldest son, who died of starvation later in the year in Windsor Castle, where they had been imprisoned.[2] Annora herself was imprisoned by the king during the family's troubles, and was indeed still in prison at the time of her father-in-law's death and her husband's succession in July 1214; she was released on 27 October 1214.[3] Her sister Margaret, the wife of William de Lacy, was granted by King John, on 10 October 1216, a piece of land in the forest of Aconbury, south of Hereford, where she was at liberty to found a nunnery for the souls of William her father, Matilda her mother, and William her brother.[4] It is perhaps not fanciful to suppose that the

derived from Ordericus Vitalis (or his source); where Ordericus says that Bohemond sent to the saint's shrine silver foot-shackles, William, embroidering this, says that in his prison he was shackled with silver chains (which is highly improbable) and that it was these which, after his release, he sent to the saint. But certainly the story was known in England by the middle of the twelfth century.

[1] See pp. 227–9, above.
[2] See, for example, Poole, *From Domesday Book to Magna Carta*, p. 315.
[3] F. M. Powicke, 'Loretta, Countess of Leicester' in *Historical Essays in honour of James Tait* (Manchester, 1933), p. 260, n. 2.
[4] Powicke, p. 263.

secondary dedication to St. Leonard of the chapel in the Deerfold may have been added by the Mortimers between 1210 and 1214; certainly it would have had an added significance for them in those years. We shall have further occasion, in this chapter, to mention Annora de Braose; for the present it is enough to notice the fact of her captivity, and that from 1214 until her husband's death in November 1227, the period during which *Ancrene Wisse* was written, she was the lady of Wigmore castle.

Whatever the reason, it is recorded fact that the chapel was dedicated to the Virgin and St. Leonard. Now *Ancrene Wisse* Part I is notable for the prominence which it gives to the cult of the Virgin and the elaboration of the devotions prescribed in her honour; and these are only the private devotions, for the sisters also said the Hours of our Lady. The fact in itself may not be significant in a book written for women; but it has occasioned remark, and in particular Sitwell observes that the English book 'seems to give the earliest known example of the devotion to the Five Joys of Mary set out in an elaborate form'.[1] We have already seen also that *Ancrene Wisse* is distinctive in prescribing that the *Ave Maria* was to be sung before and after all the seven offices of our Lady, and in its inclusion, in the devotions in honour of the Five Joys, of five 'psalms' whose initial letters make up the name *Maria*—these two practices having links, in the thirteenth century, with the Dominicans.[2] The Virgin is not of course the only object of the devotions recommended in Part I, but those in her honour predominate and are especially noteworthy for their modernity. St. Leonard is not mentioned by name in *Ancrene Wisse*, but in Part I, immediately after the paragraphs in which the anchoresses are advised to say as many paternosters as occurs to them in honour of the saints whom they love best and six for their

---

[1] *The Ancrene Riwle*, trans. Salu, p. 196.   [2] pp. 107–9, above.

benefactors, and either four or, better, nine for all the souls of the faithful departed, there follows a special paragraph, distinct from those dealing with the paternosters, in which they are directed that each day or night they are to remember the sick and the afflicted, the poor, prisoners, and those who are strongly tempted:[1]

Bi dei sum time oðer bi niht gederið in ower heorte alle seke ant sarie, þet wa ant pouerte þe poure þolieð, þe pinen þe prisuns þolieð ant habbeð þer ha liggeð wið irn heuie ifeðeret—nomeliche of þe cristene þe beoð in heaðenesse, summe i prisun, summe in ase muche þeowdom as oxe is oðer asse; habbeð reowðe of þeo þe beoð i stronge temptatiuns. Alle hare sares setteð in ower heorte, and sikeð to ure lauerd þet he neome reowðe of ham ant bihalde toward ham wið þe ehe of his are. Ant ȝef ȝe habbeð hwile, seggeð þe salm *Leuaui oculos*; *Pater noster*; verset, *Conuertere domine usquequo*; *Et deprecabilis esto super seruos tuos*; oremus, *Pretende domine famulis et famulabus*.

The prescriptions at the end show that the author was thinking of votive masses (and indeed in his next paragraph he goes on to devotions to be said at mass); for the psalm *Levavi*, the versicles *Convertere* and *Et deprecabilis*, and the collect *Pretende, domine, famulis et famulabus* were all used in appropriate masses.[2] In particular the votive mass for prisoners in the Sarum Missal links the petition that 'thy

---

[1] Corpus MS., f. 8a/7–18 (Morton, p. 32). But the Corpus text is corrupt at the beginning; the text printed above is an edited one based on collation of all the manuscripts. See *English and Medieval Studies*, pp. 160–1, and my edition of the Cleopatra MS., p. cviii.

[2] In one of the medieval manuscripts of the Sarum Missal the psalm *Levavi* and the two versicles are used in the votive mass *Pro iter agentibus* (*The Sarum Missal*, ed. J. Wickham Legg (Oxford, 1916), p. 451, nn. 2, 5). The collect is used in the mass *Pro benefactoribus uel pro salute uiuorum* (ibid., p. 410). In the Lesnes Missal the collect is used in the votive mass *Pro salute Vivorum* (*Missale de Lesnes*, ed. Dom Philip Jebb (Henry Bradshaw Society, xcv, 1964), p. 138); this is an Augustinian missal of the beginning of the thirteenth century.

servant N.' be released from the chains in which he is held by his enemies with one that he be freed from the bonds of sin,[1] just as the hymns, sequences, and other verses in honour of St. Leonard do; and *Ancrene Wisse* similarly proceeds from those in prison and in servitude to those 'in strong temptations'. But the whole collocation of ideas in the passage—the sick and 'sorry', the poor, prisoners and especially prisoners held *in heaðenesse* as Bohemond had been[2]—can leave no reasonable doubt that this is an instruction for women devoted to the cult of St. Leonard; the distinctive feature is the concern for prisoners, but the others are confirmatory.

I conclude, then, that the three sisters at whose request *Ancrene Wisse* was written and for whom it was initially intended were 'the sisters living in the Deerfold' to whom Roger de Mortimer gave the chapel of the Blessed Virgin and of St. Leonard, since this explains two of the cults that have left clear and distinctive marks on the devotions recommended in Part I.[3]

[1] *The Sarum Missal*, ed. Legg, pp. 407–8 (*Missa pro eo qui in uinculis detinetur*). The collect includes the phrases 'deprecamur ut famulum tuum N. a cunctis peccatorum suorum nexibus et ab hiis quibus captus tenetur inimicorum suorum uinculis . . . absoluas'; the Secret speaks of 'omnibus . . . peccatorum sordibus' and 'inimicorum suorum . . . insidiis et uinculis'; and the Postcommunion of 'omnibus . . . periculis et . . . angustiis quas patitur, et uinculis'.

[2] The author was not of course referring to Bohemond, who had been dead for a century, but to Christians held captive and enslaved by the infidel in his own time; see above, p. 239 and n. 2.

[3] The chapel of St. Leonard was built in a clearing in the woods, and its site is still overlooked by woods on the north and east; lower down the same stream the villages of Upper and Lower Lye, as their name implies, were also built in clearings. It may have been in allusion to the site of the chapel that the author quoted the line *Eauer is þe ehe to þe wude-lehe* (Corpus MS., f. 25b/3; Morton, p. 96), though the verses which it suggested to the scribes of the Nero and Cleopatra MSS. would not seem very suitable for the ears of anchoresses; see my edition of the Cleopatra MS., p. 77. But he again half-quotes the line in the Corpus addition referring to the friars (f. 16b/15); it was evidently something that ran in his mind and therefore probably had no special point.

This is the short answer, but it is not the whole answer, for the author had more objects than one in view even from the start and changed his plan as he went on. He often writes for Christians generally, as he himself admits towards the end of Part V;[1]

Mine leoue sustren, þis fifte dale, þe is of schrift, limpeð to alle men iliche. For þi ne wundri ȝe ow nawt þet ich toward ow nomeliche nabbe nawt ispeken i þis dale; habbeð þah to ower bihoue þis lutle leaste ende.

Even when he is writing 'for all mankind alike', however, he usually remembers that his intended readers are women, though the results are sometimes incongruous to the situation of recluses: thus in Part IV he lists, under the sins to which lust gives rise, the taking of measures to prevent conception or to induce abortion,[2] and in Part V, giving examples of how confession should be 'naked' and reveal all the circumstances of the offence, he imagines a woman making confession, largely of sexual offences.[3] But even when he is writing specifically for anchoresses he is not always addressing himself to the particular women who had asked for his book. It is true that at the beginning of Part VIII he explicitly says that he writes 'none of the outer rules except for you alone', and continues:[4]

Ich segge þis for þi þet oþre ancren ne seggen nawt þet ich, þurh mi meistrie, makie ham neowe riwle, ne bidde ich nawt þet ha halden ham.

But despite this disclaimer (which applies especially to Part VIII) it is obvious that from the start he had been aware of the possibility that other anchoresses than his own charges

[1] Corpus MS., f. 93a/2–6 (Morton, p. 342).
[2] Corpus MS., f. 56b/14–18 (Morton, p. 210).
[3] Corpus MS., ff. 86a/22–87a/22 (Morton, pp. 316–20).
[4] Corpus MS., f. 111a/15–18 (Morton, pp. 410–12).

might read his book and had borne it in mind in phrasing his instructions. Clearly he knew all about his original charges, whether they were strong or weak, learned or unlearned, old and plain or young and beautiful, yet in his Preface (which may of course have been written last) he writes that the Outer Rule may be altered in various ways, 'according to each one's manner and her capacity',

for sum is strong, sum unstrong, ant mei ful wel beo cwite ant paie Godd mid leasse; sum is clergesse, sum nawt, and [mot te] mare wurchen ant on oðer wise seggen hire bonen; sum is ald ant eðelich ant is þe leasse dred of, sum is ȝung ant luuelich ant is neod betere warde. For þi schal euch ancre habben þe uttre riwle efter hire schriftes read, ant hwet se he bit ant hat hire in obedience þe cnaweð hire manere ant wat hire strengðe.[1]

The women for whom he had begun to write were literate, had books both in French and English, and could at least recite Latin psalms, prayers, and versicles, but in Part I he provides for the saying of paternosters and aves by anyone who cannot say her Hours.[2] It is to be observed that he has two ways of formulating his directions. Sometimes he addresses *mine leoue sustren* in the plural and uses plural pronouns and verbal forms; but sometimes the address is to *mi leoue suster* and the pronoun used is *þu*. The latter may seem more particular, but is in fact more impersonal; it is the mode of address of an author to an unknown reader and is normally accompanied by more general instructions, whereas passages assuming particular circumstances are addressed to the sisters in the plural. Those in the singular (whether in the second person or the third) commonly assume the 'typical' situation of a single anchoress living alone with her servants. This ambivalence in the author's own

[1] Corpus MS., f. 2a/9–18 (Morton, p. 6).
[2] Corpus MS., f. 12a/3–11 (Morton, p. 46).

attitude often makes it difficult for us to understand clearly his allusions and serves to increase the anonymity of his book (as it may have been intended to do), and there are some specially puzzling transitions. Thus in one of the passages[1] which assumes a particular building and its three windows, and which to begin with uses the plural *ȝe*, there is at the end a general instruction using singular forms:

Ȝef ei haueð deore gest, do hire meidnes as in hire stude to gleadien hire feire; and heo schal habbe leaue forte unsperren hire þurl eanes oðer twien, ant makie sines toward hire of a glead chere.

This, by seeming to imply that each anchoress has her own individual window, is inconsistent with what precedes; he has apparently switched to the hypothetical case of the single anchoress alone in her cell, with her women and the guest in an outer room. Even in the passage in the Nero MS. concerning the three sisters there is a change from plural to singular forms (in the sentence quoted on p. 242, above) which may occasion some doubt whether the sisters lived together with servants in common or separately each with her own servant.

Nevertheless, despite the author's diverse aims, it is unquestioned that he wrote in the first instance for a particular group of women who, as he says at the beginning of his Preface, had for many a day begged him for a Rule, and it is generally and rightly accepted that these were the three sisters to whom reference is twice made: first near the end of Part II, in a brief mention of 'all three of you, my dear sisters, the women dearest to me',[2] and secondly in the Nero passage, early in Part IV at the end of its brief first section on external temptations and immediately before the author launches out on his long discussion of inner temptations and

[1] Corpus MS., f. 17a/18–17b/1 (Morton, pp. 68–70).
[2] Corpus MS., f. 31b/15–16 (Morton, p. 116).

the Seven Deadly Sins.[1] There are also references, in Parts I
and II,[2] to their house or rather to its windows, of which
there were three. The one most often mentioned is the
parlures purl, the window of the 'parlour' in its original
sense of a room in a religious house set aside for conversation with outsiders; but it is implied that the anchoresses
will normally not receive visitors within the parlour but
speak to them through its window, which was the smallest
and was to be well curtained, obviously because it gave on
to the outside world. The second was the *huses purl*, the
window of their main living-room,[3] through which they could
talk to their servants; either it opened into the servants'
quarters or on to an inner courtyard beyond which were the
servants' quarters. It is not stated whether the sisters slept
in this room or had a separate dormitory, but there is no
mention of a dormitory window. The third window was the
chirche purl, through which they could see into the church,
hear mass said, and receive the sacrament;[4] they were never
to converse through it.[5] Presumably the 'high altar', with the
consecrated elements preserved above it, which is mentioned
at the beginning of Part I,[6] is that of the church, not an altar
in their own house. There is a much later reference, in Part
IV,[7] to the fact that 'night and day' there is only a wall

---

[1] The placing is logical; as the author explicitly says at the beginning
of the second of the two paragraphs of the passage, the sisters' comparatively easy circumstances constitute a strong external temptation—the
world's flattery, consisting in plenty of worldly things—which might
quickly deprive them of much of their (spiritual) reward.

[2] Corpus MS., ff. 12b/21-5, 13a/12-13, 15b/18-21, 17a/18-23 (Morton, pp. 50, 64, 68).

[3] Cf. *OED*, *house* sb.[1], sense 1 (*c*), though its instances are much later
in date.

[4] Corpus MS., ff. 8a/19-20, 8b/18, 11b/2-5 (Morton, pp. 32, 34,
44).

[5] Corpus MS., f. 17a/18-21 (Morton, p. 68).

[6] Corpus MS., f. 5a/1-3 (Morton, p. 16).

[7] Corpus MS., f. 72a/5-9 (Morton, p. 262).

between the anchoresses and Christ's body, i.e. the Host preserved in the church, and 'each day he comes forth and shows himself to you . . . in the mass'. The church was served only by a single priest, to whose Hours they were to listen as far as was possible, but they were not to say the versicles or sing with him so that he might hear them doing so;[1] it seems to be implied that when they were at the *chirche purl* they were very near the priest, as would be the case if the 'church' were in fact a small chapel. Obviously, if they had a window that looked into the church and only a wall, night and day, separated them from the Host, their house was built on to the wall of the church; and the same is clearly implied by the passage[2] in Part III which says that recluses who live under the eaves of churches are betokened by the *nihtfuhel i þe euesunges* and that an anchoress is called *ancre* because she is 'anchored' under a church as an anchor is under the side of a ship and dwells under the church to buttress it—though it may be noted that this is a generalized passage, applicable (the author assumes) to any anchoress.[3]

All this, though not very explicit, is clear enough and is the basis of the description of the anchoresses' dwelling regularly given by commentators on *Ancrene Wisse*. But it is not usually observed that these references mostly come in the

[1] Corpus MS., f. 11b/2–5 (Morton, p. 44). That there was only a single priest is implied by the phrase *te preostes tiden* and the singular pronouns *him* and *he*.

[2] Corpus MS., ff. 38b/24–39a/12 (Morton, p. 142).

[3] I do not think that any particular conclusion is to be drawn from the passage in Part VI (Corpus MS., f. 102a/24–102b/5; Morton, p. 378) in which Christ is said to have been a 'recluse' in Mary's womb, and that the anchoresses who suffer bitterness *in nearow stude* are his companions (*feolahes*). It goes on to contrast their *fowr large wahes* with his *nearow cader* and his *stanene þruh*, but any human dwelling-place, in this sort of context, would be described as *large* by comparison; it does not mean that the anchoresses' walls were really spacious.

earlier part of the book. The last but one, the most detailed of all, is the passage concerning the three sisters early in Part IV at a point where, if the two paragraphs had been kept in the Corpus MS., they would have followed the first line of its f. 51b, which is well under half-way through the whole book; and the last is the allusion to the mere wall which separates them from the Host, a remark which might apply to any small religious house in which the chapel was part of the same structure as the living quarters and which still comes in Part IV, less than two-thirds of the way through the work. But in Part IV, after the section on external temptations ending, originally, with the passage about the three sisters, there is a marked change, both in the ampler proportions of the discussion and in its more general quality, and this continues in the following Parts. Sitwell has commented that it is surprising

to find three sections [Parts IV–VI], equal to nearly half the whole work, devoted respectively to temptation, confession, and penance. It is true that the section on Penance . . . might be said to be complementary to the section on Love. But this still leaves two sections, amounting to nearly a third of the whole book, on temptations and confession . . . I think they legitimately raise the question whether they apply to the anchoresses at all . . . it might fairly be argued that they are unsuitable.[1]

But indeed even Part VII, on Love, though the climax of the book and certainly, in its author's view, the most essential part of his teaching for the anchoresses, is not solely directed to them; it sets out, as Sitwell says, 'general principles of the Christian life' and can be read with pleasure and profit by anyone.

Yet it is in Part VIII, as I think, that the change is most remarkable, though not so immediately obvious. Here, among

[1] Introduction to Salu's translation of *The Ancrene Riwle*, pp. xviii–xix.

the detailed instructions for the conduct of the anchoresses' daily lives and the management of their servants, one might have expected to find specific references to the three sisters, to their three-windowed house built on to a church, and to their personal circumstances; but there are none. Though the author, at the beginning of Part VIII, goes out of his way to say that he does not presume to make rules for any anchoresses 'except for you alone', and though most of his precepts are written in the second person plural, the superficial impression that he is writing very particularly is misleading; his instructions are of general application and do not deal with the special circumstances of the three sisters. The section on the servants mostly assumes the hypothetical situation of a single recluse living alone except for her servants, and begins 'For an anchoress who does not have her food near at hand two women are to be employed',[1] though the Nero passage had plainly stated that the three sisters could get all their requirements at a nearby hall; it ends by advising that 'you' should be generous to the servants in respect of food and clothing, 'as far as you can',[2] though again the main point of the Nero passage was that the three sisters and their servants were almost dangerously well-provided for. Similarly the author says, earlier in Part VIII, that 'you' should give a meal to women and children who have done work for you, 'though you have to do without it yourselves'.[3] There are incidental phrases which suggest that he is writing for more women than three only. He lays down in general terms that 'an anchoress shall not degenerate into a schoolmistress'.[4] In the section on the servants, stressing the importance of concord, he urges

[1] Corpus MS., f. 115a/21–2 (Morton, p. 424).

[2] Corpus MS., f. 117a/4–5 (Morton, p. 430).

[3] For the original wording, see Cleopatra MS., f. 192^v/11–13 (before revision) and Nero MS., ed. Day, 190/4–5 (Morton, p. 416).

[4] Corpus MS., f. 114b/20 (Morton, p. 422).

them to hold themselves fast together in love and not to care when the devil may blow, 'especially if many are gathered together and well kindled with love';[1] this allows for a community with many servants. Earlier he says 'You are to provide no feasts nor entice to the gate any strange beggars; though there were no other disadvantage than their unruly noise, it would at times inhibit thoughts of heaven';[2] this sounds much more like the charity that was expected to be doled out at the gate of a monastery or a nunnery than anything that would happen at the door of a hermitage occupied by a single recluse or even by three. Even though he is writing, as he says, only for women in his direct personal charge, he has to allow for other cases than that of the three sisters: for those who do not have their food near at hand as well as for those whose servant had to go no further than the hall of their 'friend', for those whose means were limited as well as those who were comfortably provided for, and for the contrasting cases of a solitary recluse with her recommended two servants and a community where many servants might be gathered together and crowds of beggars might assemble at the gate. And indeed long before Part VIII, in a passage not quite two-thirds of the way through Part IV in the section on remedies for anger[3]—significantly just after one of the passages, discussed below, that uses the word 'lime', and where the Corpus revision introduces one of its major additions—the original text had dealt with the case of women living in different places, between whom some misunderstanding had been caused by the malicious gossip of an ill-disposed person and who were to send trustworthy messengers to each other bearing tactful expressions of

---

[1] Corpus MS., f. 116a/10–22 (Morton, p. 426).

[2] Corpus MS., f. 111b/25–8 (Morton, p. 414).

[3] Cleopatra MS., ff. 113/15–114ᵛ/6; Corpus MS., ff. 69b/14–70a/25 (with an insertion at 69b/19–24); Morton, pp. 256–8.

warning, explanation, and mutual forgiveness. This is in fact clearer, even as first written, than anything in Part VIII, unrevised or revised, in its assumption of women who were each other's 'sisters' but nevertheless lived at some distance from each other, and who can hardly have been the three sisters by birth of the beginning of Part IV, living together (as it seems) in one house built against a church.

Revision of the text of *Ancrene Wisse* began very early. The first thing to be altered was the longer of the two passages referring to the three sisters. The shorter was left unchanged, even in the Corpus revision, probably because it was unobtrusive and was simply overlooked; in any case it gave no details. But the longer passage did give details and was therefore applicable only to the sisters; to any other reader it would be irrelevant, especially to one ill-provided for. It was left unaltered in one line of descent, that which led to the Nero MS. and to the ancestor of the 'generalized' or Titus-type text; though it is rewritten in the Titus MS. (which must merely be following the original generalized manuscript), the rewriting is on the basis of the full version of the two paragraphs. But in the Cleopatra MS.[1] the passage has been so cut down as to remove all the personal details; of the first paragraph only the opening sentence remains, and the first sentence of the second paragraph is also deleted. What is left is entirely general, without reference to the number three, or to the parentage or comfortable circumstances of the sisters. It is also pointless; and it was obviously because the author recognized this that in his final revision (as represented by the Corpus MS.) he deleted the two paragraphs entirely. Now the Cleopatra MS. is certainly earlier than the Corpus revision, as indeed this instance helps to show; but it is most unlikely that this cut was made

[1] f. 81/11–81ᵛ/8. See further the note to the passage in my edition of the manuscript, pp. 144–5, and the references there given.

by the Cleopatra scribe himself.[1] He makes omissions elsewhere, but they are accidental (the result of eye-skip) and
disastrous to the text; I do not recall any other place where
he makes an intelligent cut. Moreover at this point he shows
no sign of hesitation or confusion; he goes straight on from
the first sentence of the first paragraph to the second sentence
of the second, the minimum cut that was necessary to delete
all the personal details and the linked opening of the second
paragraph. One must conclude that the passage had already
been omitted (or, less probably, clearly marked for deletion)
in the exemplar from which the scribe was copying, the lost
manuscript γ, which itself (since it gave an excellent text)
was almost certainly a direct copy of β, the first fair copy of
the original text.[2] The detailed reference to the three sisters
was inappropriate to the readers for whom γ was intended,
even though γ must have been made within a few years
of the publication of the text.

The next revisions (as distinct from minor additions, which
seem to have been made from time to time in various early
copies) were to Part VIII. However carefully it had been
drafted, it did not prove to be finally satisfactory and was
subjected to detailed alteration, first in the margins and
between the lines of the Cleopatra MS. when it was newly
copied and probably before it had been bound, and then
more definitively in the version preserved in the Corpus MS.
The main purpose of the Cleopatra revisions is made clear
by a note at the foot of f. 194, reiterating that none of the
things in the Outer Rule is a command or a prohibition,

---

[1] In the French translation of the Vitellius MS. there is a lacuna in the
text, from Morton's p. 166 (l. 10) to his p. 208 (l. 10), owing to the loss
of leaves in some precursor of the extant manuscript. As this includes the
place where the passage on the three sisters ought to be, one cannot use F
(which like C derives from γ) to confirm that the cut in the passage had
been made already in γ.

[2] See the *stemma codicum* on p. 287, below.

for the Outer Rule is of little importance and may be changed if any necessity or reason requires it; this, with some change in wording, is introduced into the text at a different place in the Corpus MS. (f. 115a/15–21). On f. 191, the first surviving page of the Outer Rule in the Cleopatra MS., there is a note that 'this rule and all others are in your confessor's discretion and your master's breast; he may cut them down or add more to them, as God through his reason counsels him to do according to their need whom he has in his direction'. Most of the detailed changes are mere applications of this general principle; where the original precepts of the Outer Rule had been expressed as absolute commands or prohibitions they are now qualified.[1] But some of the changes are more significant. The phrasing of the concession (f. 195) that 'anyone who wishes' (*hwa se wule*) may have her hair trimmed by the ears (*ieveset*), not clipped or shaven, suggests that he was now writing for a fair number of women, and the long additional attack on anchoresses who 'sin in their wimpling no less than ladies' suggests that amongst them some may have been included who were much vainer of their appearance than he thought fitting. The instruction that women and children who have done work for you are to be

---

[1] The statement that an anchoress who keeps cattle cannot be Mary 'by any means' becomes, by insertion, 'easily or by any means' (f. 193), and in Corpus simply 'easily' (f. 112b/27). They are not to engage in trade—but she may, with her director's leave, sell things that she makes to supply her necessity, though as secretly as possible (f. 193ᵛ). They are to make no purses to win friends with—except for those for whom their director gives his leave (f. 194). They are also to make no silken bandages —nor laces without leave (f. 194). They are not to teach children but ought to attend only to God—though by her director's advice she may direct and help to teach someone (f. 195). Their hair is to be clipped (*idoddet*)—or if 'you' wish shaven, but if 'anyone' wishes it she may have her hair *ieveset*, though in that case she must wash and comb it oftener (f. 195). They are to be bled four times in the year—or if need be more often (f. 195). In each case there is a qualification or relaxation, especially if the director gives permission.

given a meal is altered (f. 192ᵛ) by two additions (both followed, with slight changes, by Corpus, f. 112b/6–10): the insertion of the phrase 'and especially anchoresses' servants', by which must be meant the servants of other anchoresses who have come with messages or done some service, and the addition, after *mak[i]eð ham to eotene*, of the phrase 'with charitable cheer and invite them to shelter (*herbarhe*)', which suggests an establishment with accommodation for guests. The original instruction (f. 192ᵛ) that they were to invite no man to drink 'unless he have need' is modified by the deletion of the qualifying phrase (also omitted by Corpus) and by the addition of 'nor may any eat before you except by your director's advice and by his permission', though they are always and in all circumstances to take care that none shall part from them scandalized or angry or displeased, as far as they can do so with propriety and without sin; this again sounds like the entertainment that might be expected in a nunnery rather than at a hermitage, for though anchorites might offer a man a drink (as forbidden in the original text) it does not seem likely that they would even think of inviting men to eat in their presence. The Corpus version retains this addition in altered form, but modifies it by providing that their director may give general leave for friars, both Dominican and Franciscan, to eat before them,[1] though special leave is required for all others (f. 112b/10–14). There are also important changes to the instruction concerning the acceptance of gifts (ff. 192ᵛ/16–193/5). The original text said that they should accept all that they needed from 'good friends' when the latter offered it, but that they should not accept, in spite of an offer, without

---

[1] Probably not only because the author thought the friars entirely trustworthy, but because they would have had to come a considerable distance to visit the anchoresses and would need food—and were moreover mendicants.

necessity, and they were not to accept less or more from a man they mistrusted, 'not so much as a root of ginger'. 'Great need shall drive you to ask for anything, though humbly show to your dearest friends your distress.' The author alters this by substituting 'true men' for 'good friends'; deleting 'when they offer it' and the following prohibition of acceptance, in spite of an offer, without necessity; deleting 'not so much as a root of ginger'; altering (by deletion) 'great need' to 'need' as the condition for asking for help; and substituting 'good men and women' for 'your dearest friends'. All these changes are followed by the Corpus version except the first.[1] Their general effect is to give much more scope for the receiving of gifts, by allowing them to be accepted from any well-disposed person and even when there is no immediate need;[2] to weaken the absoluteness of the prohibition of accepting gifts from those

[1] On the other hand much of the substance of the original text is repeated in an addition in Corpus to the paragraph 'against gluttony' (originally disproportionately brief) in Part IV (Corpus MS., f. 71a/ 24–71b/18). This addition says that they should not complain of any lack to any man or woman 'except to some true friend who is able to amend it', and that as secretly as if under the seal of confession; and if 'some friend' asks whether they need anything, they may say that it is right for an anchoress to suffer want, for she does not enter her retreat to have ease, but as the friend wishes to know, 'This is a thing of which I have need, and thus our Rule commands, that we show to good friends, as others of God's poor do, their distress with gentle humility, nor are we to refuse the grace of God's sending.' In this passage (which, with its reference to 'God's poor', is perhaps influenced by the mendicant orders) there is no longer an insistence on *great* need as the condition for asking, and it is assumed that there will always be a need which will justify the acceptance of an offer; in these ways it differs from the original passage in Part VIII, though it agrees with it in referring to 'some true friend' and 'some friend', not to 'true men' and 'good men and women', as in the Cleopatra revision.

[2] Cf. also the Cleopatra MS., f. 192/12–13, where the original instruction that an anchoress should not accept what she needs 'except sparingly' (*bute gnedeliche*) is altered to 'except in moderation' (*bute meðfulliche*); so Corpus, f. 112a/18–19 (*bute meaðfulliche*).

they mistrust (though the prohibition remains); and to
allow requests for help to any good men or women, not only
to their dearest friends, in case of necessity (and no longer of
'great necessity'). This seems to me to be a response to the
needs of a larger community which cannot live from hand to
mouth, has to accept offers of help even when there is no
immediate need, cannot rely on the help only of 'good' or
'dearest' friends, and may have to accept help or even seek
actively for it from any 'good men and women'—as Limebrook Priory in 1221 and 1226 accepted donations from the
king's justices and from the king himself.

The further revisions of Part VIII in the Corpus version
do not introduce anything new in principle, but strengthen
the impression that the author is writing for a fair number of
women in more than one place. The prohibition of keeping
other men's possessions 'in your house' becomes 'in your
dwellings (*wanes*)'.[1] There is a more detailed prohibition
(f. 114a/21–114b/8) of the giving and receiving of personal
gifts without the confessor's prior leave given after he has
been told all the circumstances, including the relationship
of the parties;[2] and there is a warning against fine needlework (a common occupation in nunneries): if they make
'amices' and 'apparels'—though this is work more suitable
for worldly ladies—they are not to boast of them, 'none of
you' is to do 'sieve-work' (*criblin*)[3] for love or money, and if

[1] But this may not be significant; cf. *ut of hire wanes* 'out of her dwelling' (Corpus, f. 112a/24; Morton, p. 416), where *wanes* is the word of
the original text.

[2] This obviously would not apply in the case of the three sisters, whose
parentage was known to the author, but in that of women whose kinship
was not well known to their director.

[3] On the meaning of the verb *criblin* see Hall's note (*Early Middle
English*, ii. 397); the most probable explanation, as he says, is 'tambour'
work done on a needlework frame. My mother often did what could be
described as 'sieve-work'—and, I am afraid, was proud of her skill.
But she did it for love, not money.

'someone' sews surplices or albs let her not do other sewing, 'especially over-elaborate', except for great need. There is an added paragraph (f. 117a/11–27) dealing with various matters: how to behave when 'your sisters' maidens' visit you for your relaxation (and a gossip); how long and how often visitors—probably visitors generally, and not the servants—shall be entertained (two nights, and that 'full seldom'); and finally, a prohibition of 'worldly games at the window' and of mutual caresses on the part of both 'the anchoress and her maiden'.

The Corpus MS. has a good many additions to the other Parts of the Rule, most of them brief and of small importance. But there are also a number of long additions of considerable significance, of which the first four (those to Parts I and II) are found also in the French version of the Vitellius MS. (and the fourth at the end of the Vernon MS.).[1] The first is in Part I,[2] and consists of a description of a complicated way of saying a tale of fifty aves used by the author; it increases the preponderance of the cult of the Virgin in Part I. The second is in Part II, in its first subsection devoted to sight.[3] It begins with an instruction that 'all the apertures of all your windows, as those in front in the sight of all men have been closed, so let those at the rear be'; this is certainly not the house of the three sisters or indeed of any small hermitage, but a building with multiple windows, some facing outwards where people pass by.[4] The passage goes

---

[1] See my article on 'The Affiliations of the Manuscripts of *Ancrene Wisse*' in *English and Medieval Studies*, ed. Davis and Wrenn, pp. 152–5.

[2] Corpus MS., ff. 10b/22–11a/18.

[3] Vitellius MS., ed. J. A. Herbert (E.E.T.S. 219, 1944), 46/12–49/24; Corpus MS., f. 15a/1–15b/11. The passage is defective at the beginning in Corpus owing to the loss of two leaves before f. 15; about 18 lines of the addition have been lost and have to be supplied from the French translation, which itself has lacunae because of fire-damage to the manuscript. But the gist is clear.

[4] That would suit very well the situation of Limebrook Priory, the

on to stress the importance of enclosure and the evil consequences that may befall if an anchoress, of all people, should
show herself to the sight of a man. The most important point
of the Outer Rule is that of being well enclosed:

Ouer al þet ȝe habbeð iwriten in ower riwle of þinges wiðuten,
þis point, þis article of wel to beo bitunde, ich wulle beo best
ihalden.[1]

They may show themselves to a woman who desires it, but
are to let well alone if she says nothing about it. They are not
to offer to let any man see their altar, unless he requests it
out of devotion and has permission; if so, they are to be well
veiled and are to draw back the cloth over the altar as quickly
as possible. If he looks towards a bed or asks where they sleep
they are to turn the question aside with a light answer. If a
bishop comes to visit them they are to hasten to meet him, but
if he wishes to see them (i.e. their faces) they are to ask to
be excused and if he insists they are to allow only a short
view and then down with the veil and draw back. These are
instructions for women who are often visited, and there is an
obvious inconsistency with the remark in the original form of
Part VIII, 'Because no man sees you nor you him, it does not
matter about your clothes, whether they are white or black';[2]
the reference to episcopal visitations is especially interesting.

The third addition comes only a little later in Part II,[3]

ruins of which lie between the road down the valley and the brook;
the largest bit of surviving masonry (though it is not very large) is
directly beside the modern road. The front of the building would therefore
have overlooked the road and been clearly visible from it; the back would
have looked towards the brook and the steep wooded rise beyond it.
Anyone in the woods would no doubt have been able to see the rear
windows through the trees.

[1] Corpus MS., f. 15a/8–10.
[2] Cleopatra MS., f. 193ᵛ/9–11; Corpus MS., f. 113a/22–3 (slightly
revised); Morton, p. 418.
[3] Corpus MS., ff. 16b/13–17a/2.

in the subsection dealing with speech, and is the more important of the two references in the Corpus version to the friars of both orders; it says that they are of such a manner of life that they may be trusted and received whenever they come 'to instruct and comfort you in God', and that if the friar is a priest they are to confess to him before he leaves and ask him to take them specially into his good intentions. The fourth addition, much longer, is again in Part II,[1] in the subsection on smell (though it has little to do with this); it follows a passage in the original text which says that an anchoress should not be ease-loving, that it is very unreasonable to enter an 'anchor-house' to seek ease therein and authority (*meistrie*) and 'ladyship' greater than one might readily have had in the world. The addition is essentially to reinforce this and to elaborate it, but the details, and the quotation from Jerome with which it begins, *Quomodo obscuratum est aurum optimum*, suggest that there has been some falling away into worldliness—frivolity or worse in speech, love of ease, bitterness and chiding, and pride of position; and the author calls on his readers to 'row against this world's stream' and to seek the treasure that is in heaven in humility and truth.

Another major addition in the Corpus version is not in the French translation or any other text. It comes about two-thirds of the way through Part IV,[2] and deals with the importance of unity and concord. It is the well-known passage which says that

You are the anchoresses of England so many together—twenty now or more; God increase you in good—that most peace is among, most singleness and unity, and community of a united life according to one rule,

[1] Corpus MS., ff. 28b/21–29b/25.
[2] Corpus MS., f. 69a/12–69b/11 (*Pax uobis . . . cloistre of heouene*). The punctuation of this vital passage in Bennett and Smithers, *Early*

each turned towards the other in one manner of life 'as if you were a community (*cuuent*) of London and of Oxford, of Shrewsbury or of Chester'. This, he says,

that you are all as if one community (*cuuent*) is your high fame. This is pleasing to God. This is now recently[1] widely known, so that your community (*cuuent*) begins to spread toward the extremity of England. You are, as it were, the mother-house from which they are begotten. You are like a spring; if the spring grow muddy, the streams muddy also. Alas, if you grow muddy I shall never endure it.

Middle English Verse and Prose, p. 231, is seriously defective even in the second edition (1968). The citation *Pax uobis* from Luke 24: 36, with which the addition begins, is added to the end of the previous citation (part of the original text) from Acts 4: 32, as if it were part of the same scriptural text; and the important second sentence of the addition is split into two, thus: 'ȝe beoð, þe ancren of England, swa feole togederes—twenti nuðe oðer ma. Godd in god ow mutli þet meast grið is among . . .' This seems designed to force the translation 'You, the anchoresses of England, are so many together—twenty now or more. God increase you in good, you among whom is the greatest peace . . .' But this makes the author opine that the total number of anchoresses in England was 'twenty now or more'. This is a statistic that is most unlikely to have been known even to the clerks of the *curia regis* or the central ecclesiastical authorities; when general surveys were made (which was rarely), they were for taxation purposes and concerned with the annual income of religious establishments, not with the number of their inmates. The author of *Ancrene Wisse* would not have hazarded a guess at the total number of anchoresses in England, and if he had he would have put it far higher than 'twenty or more'; the number is that of the women in the community for which he was writing. Miss Salu's translation (p. 112), though unnecessarily free (as is her custom), is essentially correct.

[1] The word used is *nunan*, which occurs also at Corpus, f. 73b/25, and in *Ste Iuliene*, l. 702. It is a combination of *nu* and *anan* 'anon', and therefore means literally 'now immediately', hence 'in the immediate future, shortly, immediately' or (as Zettersten, p. 162, glosses it) 'presently'; this is the sense it bears in the other two instances. But also it is capable of meaning 'in the immediate past, now recently'; this is the sense it has in the Corpus addition, at f. 69a/26 (rather than 'now, already', as given by Davis in his glossary to Bennett and Smithers, though the difference is slight).

He continues that if any goes her own way and does not follow the community (*cuuent*), but goes out of the flock 'which is as if in a cloister that Jesus is high Prior over', may God turn her back to the flock, to the community (*cuuent*), and grant that

you who are therein may so hold yourselves therein that God the high Prior may at the end take you thence up into the cloister of heaven.

The significance of this is in itself obvious, with the reiterated use of the word *cuuent*, the double use of *cloistre*, and the two references to Jesus or God as a 'high Prior'. The number mentioned, 'twenty now or more', is also relevant, for in monastic tradition thirteen was the number of a 'full convent', the essential minimum for a new religious house, though Augustinian houses in fact were often smaller (Wigmore itself began with two brothers sent over from St. Victor, later replaced by three). A community of over twenty certainly ranked to be described as a *cuuent*. But the placing of the passage is almost as telling: it is inserted into the original text between instances of its apparent play on the word 'lime' (on which see below, pp. 273–9), after the phrase *annesse of an heorte ant of a wil*, which echoes the beginning of the *Regula Tertia* of the Augustinian rule and is its essential principle,[1] and immediately after the quotation of Acts 4: 32, *Multitudinis credentium erat cor unum et anima una*, which is of course the scriptural source of St. Augustine's phrase; and it precedes the passage, discussed above,[2] in which the author had made his most explicit reference in the original text to a number of anchoresses living in separate places who should, if necessary, send trustworthy messengers to each other to explain away any matter that might occasion

[1] See pp. 19–20, above.
[2] pp. 258–9.

discord. The author's placing of his additions is not haphazard; he was very skilful in bringing them in, and it is no accident that this comes where it does. In its context the passage can only mean that the twenty or more anchoresses, though they did not live in one place, nevertheless constituted a single community under a prioress and subject to the Augustinian Rule.

It is particularly because of this addition that some have assumed that the Corpus text is a version of the Rule adapted for a different and larger community. That it was larger is clear; that it was different is not. I myself previously thought that it was the same community which, beginning with the three sisters, had merely grown in numbers,[1] but this is an over-simplification in the opposite direction; the internal evidence of the text shows that even in the original version, in its latter part, the author was writing for an association of anchoresses who did not live in a single place and whose circumstances differed, but that it already included one more numerous household. By the time that the Corpus additions were written this association or community had grown to 'twenty now or more' but was still not concentrated in one place; indeed it was spreading *toward Englondes ende*. It had 'recently' become 'widely known' and included a house of some size (regularly visited by the laity, by friars of both orders, and even by bishops) which was 'as if' the mother-house and which justified allusions to a 'cloister' and to Jesus or God as a 'high Prior'. It is true that the author still writes, without exception, of anchoresses (*ancren*), not of nuns or of canonesses; but the distinction was less absolute than we tend to make it. It was common for hermitages to develop into monasteries or nunneries; but at what stage did someone who had been an anchorite become a monk or canon, a nun or canoness? The Carthusian order

[1] Cf. *Proc. Brit. Acad.*, lii. 205–6.

specifically set out to combine the essential features of a hermit's life with the security and order of a monastic community; and other enclosed houses, especially those which practised a rule of silence, approximated to the same pattern. As late as 1530 a nun of Limebrook was given permission to transfer to a Carthusian house because she desired a stricter discipline; either she did not go or she returned, for she was one of the nuns of Limebrook at its dissolution,[1] but the incident suggests that Limebrook, though less strict than a Carthusian house, appealed to the same sort of woman. Still more significant is the fourteenth-century tradition that the Latin translation of *Ancrene Wisse* was made by Simon of Ghent, bishop of Salisbury from 1297 to 1315, for 'anchorites at Tarrant', for Tarrant in Dorset was a Cistercian house; the writer of the note that records the tradition saw no inconsistency in calling the nuns of a strictly enclosed order 'anchorites'.[2] It is possible, of course, that the author of *Ancrene Wisse* continued to refer to his charges as anchoresses merely for the sake of consistency, especially literary consistency; he had written a book for anchoresses, and anchoresses they must continue to be. But I doubt this; however they had come to be organized, they had begun as anchoresses, some of them still lived in small hermitages, and he still regarded them all, even those in the larger house, as vowed to the anchorite way of life.

That the larger community which is occasionally assumed in the original version and for which the Corpus revisions were particularly made was Limebrook Priory is probable—almost certain—on grounds of topography alone. Apart from Limebrook, the nearest religious house for women to Wig-

[1] See p. 203, n. 3, above.
[2] See G. C. Macaulay, *MLR* ix (1914), 474, and my edition of the Cleopatra MS., p. clxxi and nn. 2, 3.

more Abbey was Aconbury, almost twenty-three miles to the south-south-east; it too was an Augustinian priory, founded after October 1216 by Margaret de Braose.[1] But it was too far away, and probably too recently founded, to be the basis of the allusions in *Ancrene Wisse*; and more conclusively it had not grown from a hermitage, but had been deliberately founded in memory of Margaret's parents and brother. It would not be surprising, perhaps, if a copy of *Ancrene Wisse* had been sent to Aconbury; but it cannot have been the priory alluded to in the Corpus addition or in any sense a member of the spreading community of anchoresses which it describes. There is in any case some evidence, both external and internal, to confirm that Limebrook Priory was the place meant. The addition must have been written about 1230, and says that the anchoresses' unity (that they are all 'as if one community') is their high fame and has 'recently' become 'widely known'; it is a matter of record that the *moniales* of Limebrook had been well enough known in 1221 to receive a donation from the king's justices at the Worcestershire assizes, and in 1226 from the king himself, writing from Shrewsbury to the bailiff of Montgomery, but as these are the earliest known records of the house, though it had been founded by 1190, it must only recently have emerged from obscurity.[2] In 1279 the bishop of Hereford, Thomas de Cantilupe, wrote a long letter[3] to the prioress and nuns of Limebrook in consequence of a recent visitation of their convent; this, he directed, they were to have expounded to them several times a year, in French or English, by their penitentiaries, 'so that you may know it better'.[4] He instructed them

---

[1] See p. 247, above.   [2] See pp. 177–80, above.
[3] *The Register of Thomas de Cantilupe* transcribed by R. G. Griffiths (Canterbury and York Society ii, 1906), pp. 200–2. The date of the letter is lost, but in the register it comes between one dated 21 January and another dated 15 March 1278–9.
[4] Ibid., p. 202.

that they were to choose for themselves confessors from among men living in his diocese,

videlicet de fratribus Minoribus conventus Herefordie, aut aliis religiosis vel secularibus viris competentis litterature boneque conversacionis et vite, in dicta diocesi, ut consuevistis.[1]

It is somewhat surprising that the nuns of an Augustinian house only four miles from Wigmore Abbey should have been accustomed to choose their confessors from the Franciscans of the Hereford convent, seventeen miles away, but it ties up with the advice given in the addition in the Corpus version that the anchoresses were to welcome visits from the friars of both orders and to trust them and, if they were priests, to make confession to them before they left. Early in his letter[2] the bishop writes:

Vos igitur Deo date, que, abnegantes vos ipsas et renunciantes seculo, Christi servicio vos perpetuo mancipastis. Omni custodia vos servare debetis et portas sensuum obserare, ne unquam introitus pateat maligno spiritui ex quo vobis aut aliis, in pravorum desiderium ardore vel saltem levi cogitatione, detur occasio delinquendi.

There is no direct quotation, but it almost looks as though the bishop, on his visit to Limebrook, had been shown a copy of *Ancrene Wisse*, had been glancing through Part II, and had seen in particular the passage[3] which refers to the gates of the senses and repeats in altered form the citation from Proverbs 4 : 23 with which the Part begins, *Omni custodia serua cor tuum.*

The internal evidence in confirmation that Limebrook was the larger house sometimes assumed in the original text and more openly alluded to in the Corpus additions is of

---

[1] Loc. cit.
[2] *The Register of Thomas de Cantilupe*, p. 200.
[3] Corpus MS., f. 27a/25–27b/7 (Morton, p. 104).

secondary importance, for the case stands without it; moreover it is doubtful. But there are a number of passages in Part IV where the author appears to play on the first element of the name *Limebrook*. That there is any play on the second element cannot reasonably be maintained. It is true that in *Ancrene Wisse* there is a passage[1] which refers to the *brokes* that flowed from Christ's wounds on the Cross, and that in the *Ureisun of God Almihti* there is a similar reference to *þe large broc of þine softe side*;[2] but though this metaphorical application of the word *brook* is exceptional from the point of view of general English usage, there is a close parallel in Laȝamon's *Brut*,[3] so that it seems to have been a feature of West Midland literary usage about this time. There are, however, several passages in which the author uses the word *lim* 'lime' in the sense of 'mortar', but applied metaphorically —in a way apparently unknown elsewhere in Middle English[4]—to connote a unifying force, something which binds together, much as we use the noun and verb 'cement'; and from it he coins the verb *limin* (and its negative *unlimin*), again used metaphorically to mean 'to cement together, to unite' (or 'to disunite'), which is also used in *Ste Katerine*[5] in the same sense, though otherwise, according to *OED*, it is not recorded until Shakespeare.[6] The first of the three passages in which the word is used, and the one in which he

---

[1] Corpus MS., f. 70b/8–9 (Morton, p. 258).

[2] Nero MS., ed. W. Meredith Thompson, *þe Wohunge of Ure Lauerd* (E.E.T.S., 241, 1958), p. 7, ll. 98–9; Lambeth MS., op. cit., p. 3, l. 81.

[3] Ed. Madden, l. 30411 (Caligula text): 'Urnen þa brockes of reden blodes'.

[4] *OED*, s.vv. *lime* sb.[1], sense 2; *lime* v.[1], sense 1; and *unlime* v., sense 1. The fascicle of *MED* which should include *lime* is, at the time of writing, the next due to be published.

[5] Ed. Einenkel, l. 1791.

[6] *OED*, s.v. *lime* v.[1], sense 1; but in the sense 'to smear with bird-lime' (sense 2) it is found in the fifteenth century.

most obviously hunts it, is at Corpus f. 61b/12–17 (Morton, pp. 226–8):

ah ne drede ȝe nawt hwil ȝe beoð se treoweliche ant se feste *ilimet* wið *lim* of anred luue euch of ow to oþer, for na deofles puf ne þurue ȝe dreden bute þet *lim* falsi . . . Sone se ei *unlimeð* hire, ha bið sone iswipt forð . . .

As the metaphor is of the stones in a high tower buffeted by the wind, the use of the word is appropriate in the context, but it is certainly emphasized. The second instance is at Corpus f. 68b/9–11 (Morton, pp. 252–4), where *ilimet* is used literally and is not in itself remarkable:

Dust ant greot, as ȝe seoð, for hit is isundret ant nan ne halt to oþer, a lutel windes puf todriueð hit al to nawt; þear hit is in a clot *ilimet* togederes, hit lið al stille.

The third is at Corpus f. 69a/7–12, 69b/11–14 (Cleopatra f. 113/8–21; Morton, pp. 254–6), where the text originally ran:

Al þis is iseid, mine leoue sustren, þet ower leoue nebbes beon eauer iwent somet wið luueful semblant ant wið swote chere, þet ȝe beon aa wið annesse of an heorte ant of a wil *ilimet* togederes, as hit iwriten is bi ure lauerdes deore deciples, *Multitudinis credentium erat cor unum et anima una.* Hwil ȝe haldeð ow in an, offearen ow mei þe feond ȝef he habbeð leaue, ah hearmin nawt mid alle. þet he wat ful wel, ant is for þi umben deies ant nihtes to *unlimin* ow wið wreaððe oðer wið luðer onde.

It is in the middle of this passage that, as we have seen, the Corpus version introduces its long addition (f. 69a/12–69b/11) beginning *Pax uobis* and referring to *cuuents*, to a *cloistre* and a *moder-hus*, and to Jesus or God as *heh priur*. All three passages have the same point, the importance of unity, and this may be sufficient explanation of their recurrent use of *lim*, *limin*, *unlimin*; nevertheless it is exceptional.

Much more remarkable, however, is a still later passage in Part IV, at Corpus f. 77b/14–16 (Morton, p. 284). Here the author refers back to a sentence near the beginning of Part IV (Corpus, f. 49b/2–6; Morton, p. 184) in which he had said that whoever speaks ill of you, or ill-treats you (using the singular pronoun 'thee'), is as it were your file and files your rust away and your roughness caused by sin. The later passage runs:

Of þis is þruppe iwriten muchel, hu he is þi file þe misseið oðer misdeð þe. *Lime* is þe frensch of 'file'. Nis hit or acurset, þe iwurðeð swartre ant ruhre se hit is ifilet mare?

The middle sentence, '*Lime* is the French for "file" ', though true, is one of the most puzzling in the whole work, for it has no apparent relevance. It is not at all in the author's manner to interrupt his argument to give a gratuitous French lesson. Admittedly just after this passage, in Corpus and most manuscripts, there is a short sentence explaining what *or* is,[1] but then he had used the word *or*; he had not used the word *lime*, according to the evidence of all the English manuscripts except one, but the native word *file*. Moreover readers who could understand the sophisticated and technical French-derived vocabulary that he often uses would hardly need to be told what the French word for 'file' was. He has not cited a French source for the metaphor in either passage; it comes in fact from Latin works which speak of the file (*lima*) of adversity, but he does not cite a Latin authority either, and it is the French form that he gives, not the Latin. And if his object were the reverse of what it

[1] See my edition of the Cleopatra MS., p. 209 (note *b* to f. 129). A slightly longer form of the explanation was added by the author in the margin of C, which as originally written was one of the manuscripts that omit it. It was probably in origin a marginal note which was introduced into the text in some manuscripts and omitted in others and was restored by the author, as a marginal note, in C.

seems to be, to explain by a French gloss the meaning of *file*, why should he suppose that people capable of reading so long and difficult an English work, the native vocabulary of which contains so many hard and out-of-the-way words, should need an explanation of so commonplace a term in the later of the two passages in which it is used? The scribes found the sentence as pointless as I do. Its omission by both of the French translations and by the Latin (which naturally use *lime* or *lima* to translate *file*) is for an obvious reason; but it is equally omitted by the Nero and Titus MSS. (and also by Pepys, which is less significant). The scribe of the Cleopatra MS.,[1] after beginning to copy the sentence, jibbed at it and rewrote it in such a way as to show that he did not know the meaning of French *lime* (though the sentence that he should have copied told him); *lime* was, in his altered version, 'that which the file rubs from the iron', which is nonsense in any language. Yet he writes *lime* and *ilimed* for *file* and *ifilet* in the first and third sentences, and we must therefore suppose (since, if he did not understand the French word, he could not have made the substitutions himself) that his exemplar γ had read (in the spellings of the 'AB language'):

Of þis is þruppe iwriten muchel, hu he is þi *lime* þe misseið oðer misdeð þe. *Lime* is þe frensch of 'file'. Nis hit or acurset, þe iwurðeð swartre ant ruhre se hit is *ilimet* mare?

This is a good text in which the middle sentence has real point, but it cannot be the original; Corpus, as remarked above, is supported across the stemma by all other English manuscripts except Cleopatra in reading *file* and *ifilet*, and in the earlier passage to which cross-reference is made the words used are *file* and *fileð* even in Cleopatra. Now the author ('scribe B') corrected the later passage in the Cleopatra

---

[1] ff. 128ᵛ/18–129/4 (p. 209 of my edition, with the notes there).

MS. and in the process took the trouble to restore its puzzling central sentence, which the first scribe had altered, to its original form, but he did not alter the first scribe's *lime* and *ilimed* in the flanking sentences; he left the noun untouched, and above the participle was content to write *ifilet* as a gloss without deleting *ilimed*. He was, it seems, willing to accept the French-derived words, and he certainly wanted '*Lime* is the French for "file" ' as part of his text. But what had been its point in the text as first written, in which the English and not the French words had been used? It is to be remembered that γ, the exemplar of C, was the manuscript in which, it appears, the main reference to the three sisters was first truncated by cutting out all the personal details, just as in this passage it must have been γ that made consistent the use of the French word *lime* (*ilimet*) to the exclusion of the original *file* (*ifilet*). It seems to me that a possible explanation is that γ was a copy intended for Limebrook and that its scribe, with the author's approval and perhaps at his suggestion, had deleted the sentences referring to the three sisters and also, recognizing a play on the first element of *Limebrook*, had made it more obvious and in doing so had much improved the internal run of the passage. But even in the text as originally written the French word had been dragged in; and this, I think, makes it more likely that the metaphorical use in other passages in Part IV of the native word *lim* 'mortar' and the derived verbal forms was also intended to have some special point.

To this explanation there is an obvious objection which must at once be stated: the normal form of the name Limebrook, until 1400 and indeed later, was *Lingebrok* (and variant spellings not significantly different). *Limebrook* is first recorded, as far as is known, in 1348, and its immediate phonetic precursor, *Linbroke*, in 1285 (in a document which makes errors in other place-names); but then **Lindbroc* (spelt *Lyndebrok*), which in etymological and phonetic theory must be an earlier form still, is in fact first recorded in 1383. The chances of record, with place-names, are unpredictable and do not accord with the logical development of forms. If my view of the origin and history of the name is correct,[1] it had always had two alternative forms, one of which gave Middle English *Lingebrok* etc. and early Modern English *Lingbrook*, and the other, Old English **Lindbrōc*, became Middle English *Lyndebrok*, *Linbroke*, and finally *Limebrook* (i.e. the first element *lind-* became *lin-* and then, by assimilation, *lim-*). But the phonetic processes involved in this development, being combinative, are such as could (and did) occur at any date, since of their nature they are always likely in the given phonetic context, the group /ndb/. The analogous Lincolnshire place-name Limber (OE **Lindbeorg*) is already recorded as *Linberge* and *Limberge* before 1100, and the Worcestershire name Limberrow (also from OE **Lindbeorg*) is *Limberga* in 1127. There is no reason why an OE **Lindbrōc* should not have become **Limbrok* well before 1200. Therefore, though there can be no question that the normal thirteenth-century form was *Lingebrok* (however spelt in detail), it is legitimate to assume that **Limbrok* already existed as a variant and might be chosen, for his special purpose, by the author of *Ancrene Wisse* because *lim* was a meaningful word in English (and *lime*, with final *-e*, in French) which might be played on, whereas the normal *linge-* of *Lingebrok*, being meaningless in Middle English and phonetically impossible in Old French, gave no such opportunity.

In the major Corpus addition concerning the increase in size and fame of the anchoresses' community there is one phrase which requires particular notice, that in which the author says that their community *biginneð to spreaden*

---

[1] See Appendix II, pp. 380–92, below.

toward Englondes ende. It has been variously interpreted: Hall took it as a reference to 'the general adoption of the rule by anchoresses all over England',[1] and Shepherd thought that the passage as a whole implied a 'congregation of recluses of which . . . there [were] already communities in London, at Oxford, Shrewsbury, and Chester',[2] as if he too took the phrase (though he does not discuss it) as meaning that their community was spreading throughout England. But *toward Englondes ende* does not mean 'all over England, throughout England'; it means what it still does, 'toward the end (or extremity) of England', towards the border of England.[3] To us it may seem that Wigmore and its district are themselves at *Englondes ende*, and to the clerks of the *curia regis* they were *in Wallia*; Wigmore is but six miles from the modern boundary between England and Wales, and only eight from Offa's Dyke. But plainly it did not seem so to the author himself. He was a man of the Marches, accustomed to living near the border, and we must think as he thought. Wigmore (and Lingen to its south-west) had been English territory at least since the time of Offa and probably much earlier, to judge from the predominantly English place-names. Even during Gruffydd ap Llywelyn's devastation of the borders in 1052 and 1055 they had escaped, unlike the English villages to the west,[4] and since the Norman

[1] *Early Middle English*, ii. 374.

[2] *Ancrene Wisse: Parts VI and VII*, p. xxxv. Compare the note in Bennett and Smithers, p. 409, that the passage apparently means that when it was written 'there really were separate anchor-holds at the places named'. This, as already remarked (p. 133, n. 2, above), misinterprets the sentence, in which the anchoresses' community is merely compared to a *cuuent* in one of these four places; it is not said to include houses in them.

[3] Cf. Davis's gloss 'boundaries', specifically for this instance, in his glossary to Bennett and Smithers; but the singular would be better.

[4] J. E. Lloyd, *A History of Wales*, ii. 366–7, writing of the end of Gruffydd's reign, says that 'a line drawn from Brampton Bryan on the Teme to Willersley on the Wye would roughly indicate the western limit of English occupation at this time; all the English villages between this and

Conquest they had been undisputed English territory, firmly held by Wigmore and its dependent castles. By 'the extremity of England' he would rather have meant lands conquered or reconquered beyond the ancient border and still disputed between the two races. To the south-west of Wigmore was the honour of Radnor, where the English, after Offa's time, had pushed beyond the line of the Dyke. But though it had been devastated by Gruffydd and was still waste in 1086, by about 1096 Philip de Braose was established at Radnor, which had ceased to be debatable border land and was the centre of a Norman lordship;[1] and afterwards it remained one of the chief possessions of his family. It would hardly have seemed a border territory in the early thirteenth century; no one, even a year or so before, could have forseen Llewelyn ab Iorwerth's great outbreak in 1232, when he took Radnor castle and destroyed the town as he swept to the south. Directly west of Wigmore, the province of Maelienydd was claimed by the Mortimers by right of conquest (or reconquest) in 1144, but in 1220 its ownership was in dispute between Hugh de Mortimer and Llywelyn;[2] and whoever its feudal overlord might be, it was undoubtedly Welsh in people, custom, and language, and no part of England. But to a man writing the Corpus addition within a year or two of 1230 the situation would have seemed different to the north-west of Wigmore. The Chirbury district had been one of those worst affected by Gruffydd's warfare, and in 1066 was waste, used only as a hunting-ground.[3] It was recaptured by the Normans

Radnor Forest—Knighton, Radnor, Kington, Huntington and a score of others—had been abandoned to the Welsh, largely, no doubt, as a result of the raid of 1055'. But Lingen was still in English occupation in 1066, as Domesday Book shows; the effective boundary lay to its west.

[1] Lloyd, ii. 402–3.   [2] Lloyd, ii. 479, 501, 657.

[3] Cf. p. 119, n. 1, above. Lloyd (ii. 366) says that 'not only Chirbury, but a score of villages round about, where the English system of hidage

under Roger Montgomery, earl of Shrewsbury, who 'restored the place to something of its old importance' and 'not
far off, in the border forest' built a castle to which he gave his
family name.[1] But Montgomery castle remained a border
fortress, never entirely secure. It was captured in the Welsh
revolt of 1095. In the twelfth century it was not a royal
castle, but a fief of the house of Bollers.[2] Early in 1216 King
John granted it to Gwenwynwyn prince of Powys, and after
the latter's defeat and death later in the year it was in the
effective power of Llywelyn ab Iorwerth of Gwynedd, who
was confirmed in his custody of it in 1218.[3] In 1223, however, the justiciar Hubert de Burgh, alarmed by Llywelyn's
moves, undertook a campaign in the Marches and in October
occupied Montgomery, took the honour into the possession
of the crown, and began building a new castle on a ridge
above the plain. In April 1228 he himself was granted
possession of Montgomery and began a campaign for the
conquest of the Welsh district of Kerry, to the south-west;
but he was strongly resisted by the Welsh under Llywelyn
and by October had been forced back to his base.[4] In June
1231 Montgomery was the first English post to be attacked
by Llywelyn and the new settlement was burnt.[5] It remained
a frontier outpost until the Edwardian conquest of Wales;
it was again attacked, and the town was sacked, by Llywelyn
ap Gruffydd in 1257.[6] To any man of the Central Marches,

had been in full force, had been rendered uninhabitable, and, instead
of fifty hides paying the king's taxes, there was nothing but a great
forest'. At Chirbury a fortress had been built by Æthelflæd Lady of the
Mercians, and there was an ancient church of great importance; before its
devastation it had been the head of an Anglo-Saxon hundred (Lloyd,
i. 331–2 and n. 43).

[1] Lloyd, ii. 389.
[2] Lloyd, ii. 570, or better, Eyton, *Shropshire*, xi. 120–7.
[3] Lloyd, ii. 653–4.
[4] Lloyd, ii. 667–8; Powicke, *The Thirteenth Century*, p. 395.
[5] Lloyd, ii. 673–4; Powicke, pp. 396–7.   [6] Lloyd, ii. 719.

from 1223 onwards, Montgomery would have been pre-eminently the place where the power of the English crown was confronted by that of North Wales. This was the point of conflict, beyond which the king's writ did not run and his army could not advance, where English place-names and the English language gave way to Welsh; this was *Englondes ende*.

If the anchorite community for which *Ancrene Wisse* was written had a recently established cell in the Montgomery area, it would be easy to understand why the author, in an addition written about 1230, should say that *ower cuuent biginneð to spreaden toward Englondes ende* and that *ȝe beoð as þe moderhus þet heo beoð of istreonet*. We have already seen[1] that in a writ of August 1226 dealing with the affairs of the honour of Montgomery and probably issued immediately after a visit there, the king had ordered the bailiff of Montgomery to pay half a mark (6*s*. 8*d*.) to the *monialibus de Lingebroc*. They may have owed their gift to the good offices of the Augustinian canons of Chirbury,[2] but a more direct explanation would be provided if Limebrook had had some connection with Montgomery—if there had been in the area a dependent cell, for which, perhaps, rather than for the mother-house, the gift had really been intended—which might explain both its small amount and the order that it should be paid by the bailiff of Montgomery, not by the official (the sheriff of Herefordshire) within whose jurisdiction Limebrook itself lay. And as the other payments ordered in the writ were in compensation for losses of income occasioned by the taking-over of Montgomery by the crown, it is even possible that Limebrook, or its cell, had also suffered some minor disadvantage for which an *ex gratia* payment was being made. But on the face of the record the payment was a gift (*e dono nostro*).

It is not easy to piece together the history of *Ancrene Wisse*

[1] pp. 178–80, above.   [2] See p. 180, n. 1, above.

and the women for whom it was written from the deliberately oblique, and in some ways contradictory, allusions in the text and from the fragmentary and imperfect record evidence. But it seems to me that the author, shortly after he had begun Part IV—probably about 1218–19—and had made his explicit allusion to the personal circumstances of the three sisters at whose request he had undertaken his work, found that conditions had radically altered. Probably as a consequence of the Lateran Council's insistence on 'a stricter ecclesiastical control of unattached religious',[1] the anchoresses living in the Wigmore district had been reorganized as a unified community, of which Limebrook, founded by 1190 at latest, became the head and 'mother-house' and the other anchorite households were treated as its cells; perhaps as part of this reorganization, Limebrook was placed under a prioress and its members began to be known as *moniales*. It may have been intended that as building progressed at Limebrook the inmates of at least the nearer hermitages should be transferred there, and certainly we know that the chapel of St. Leonard and the lands about it, granted before July 1214 to 'the sisters living in the Deerfold' by the elder Roger de Mortimer, eventually passed into the possession of the priory and were confirmed to it by the charter of his grandson. Either as a direct result of this reorganization or by a coincident appointment the author found his own responsibilities enlarged; he was now in charge not merely of the three sisters, but of a larger association of anchoresses whose circumstances varied and not all of whom he knew so well. He changed the scale of his book and wrote more generally, and made no further direct allusions to the three sisters (though once he may again assume their house built on to the church); and from a point just over ten pages (in terms of the very regular pages of the Corpus MS.) after the

[1] Shepherd, pp. xxiii–iv.

detailed reference to the three sisters he began the first of a series of uses, in Part IV, of the English word *lim* and the French *lime* which may have been plays on the first element of the name *Limebrook*. When he came to Part VIII he was careful to phrase his external rules in such a way that they could apply to a true solitary living separately with her servants, but there are other passages which imply a larger community. But after he had finished his work, during the 1220s, there were further developments: the number of the women in the community increased to 'twenty now or more', new cells had been established (including at least one nearer the English border with Wales, probably in the Montgomery area), the predominance of Limebrook had become more obvious, the community had 'recently' become widely known and frequently visited, and it was subject to episcopal visitation. So he revised Part VIII, first in the Cleopatra MS. and then more fully in his autograph (of which the Corpus MS. was a new copy made after the revision), and also made many changes elsewhere, including the insertion of a number of longer passages (duly reproduced in Corpus) which dealt more fully, among other things, with the need for unity in a larger community and in one of which—if regard be had to its placing—he allowed himself an almost open reference to an Augustinian *cloistre* which had the rank of a priory, might be compared to a religious house in a major centre, and was the mother-house of the whole anchorite community or *cuuent*. This can only be Limebrook. By this time too, about 1230, the friars had arrived and were regularly visiting the anchoresses; and in due course the Franciscans of Hereford became the accepted confessors of Limebrook. Its cells probably ceased to exist as the women living in them died or were removed to the mother-house, for nothing further is known of them;[1] the chapel of St.

[1] In his will of 1320 John of Aquablanca, dean of Hereford, left five

Leonard in the Deerfold remained, but there were probably no longer any members of the anchorite community living at it when the younger Roger de Mortimer issued his charter about 1252, for he was careful to lay on the nuns of Limebrook the duty of providing and maintaining a chaplain to say the divine offices there. In the latter part of the century there was no longer a dispersed community of anchorites living in several places, but a single nunnery, still poor despite the endowments which it received from time to time, in a lonely situation in a quiet valley of the Western March.

The recognition that *Ancrene Wisse* was written not merely for the three sisters, but for a community of anchoresses living in various places including Limebrook Priory, enables us to explain certain features of the transmission of the text and of its further development which otherwise would be difficult to account for. The first is the extraordinarily early multiplication of copies, which becomes more remarkable as evidence accumulates that only a few years—hardly more than ten, and at most fifteen—intervened between the completion of the original version and the making of the definitive Corpus revision. But if the anchoresses lived in a number of separate households, each would need its own copy, especially in view of the duty laid on the anchoresses by the author of reading less or more 'from this book, when you are free to do so, every day';[1] and if the community were growing in numbers and spreading in extent *toward*

shillings to the nuns of Limebrook to have the Office of the Dead said for his soul *in ecclesiis suis*. The plural must refer to the church of St. Thomas at Limebrook and the chapel of St. Leonard in the Deerfold; there is no reason to assume that they had other churches, apart from those appropriated to the nunnery at Clifton-on-Teme and at Stoke Bliss. (For the text, see *Charters and Records of Hereford Cathedral*, ed. Capes, p. 188.)

[1] Corpus MS., f. 117a/27–8 (Morton, p. 430).

Englondes ende the need for extra copies would increase. There was evidently some urgent need for additional copies just before the Corpus revision was undertaken, in view of the way in which two copies, the extant Cleopatra MS. and its congener 'proto-F' (i.e. the English copy on which the Vitellius French translation was based), were made simultaneously, by a form of *pecia* system, from the same exemplar.[1]

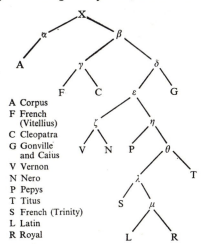

A Corpus
F French (Vitellius)
C Cleopatra
G Gonville and Caius
V Vernon
N Nero
P Pepys
T Titus
S French (Trinity)
L Latin
R Royal

STEMMA CODICUM

of the manuscripts and versions of *Ancrene Wisse*

Originally the work had been 'published' by making a single fair copy, β, from the autograph; this is shown by the fact that all the extant manuscripts and versions except the Corpus MS. share a number of errors and must therefore have a common ultimate ancestor other than the autograph.[2]

---

[1] See my edition of the Cleopatra MS., pp. xxix–xxxvi.

[2] In the account which follows I rely on the findings of my article in *English and Medieval Studies*, ed. Davis and Wrenn, pp. 128–63, and the facts established in the introduction to my edition of the Cleopatra MS.

This ancestor was β, but its errors were so few, considering the length and difficulty of the text, that it must have been made directly from the autograph; and in the circumstances it must have been the copy intended for presentation to the three sisters. But two further very early copies were made, probably directly from β since they still gave relatively good texts (though each introduced a good many additional errors).[1] We have already seen that it is likely that γ was a copy intended for Limebrook, since it truncated the main reference to the three sisters and extended the use, in one passage, of the French word *lime* 'file'; and C and 'proto-F', which were made from it, may also have been intended for Limebrook, to provide for an increase in its numbers, though they too may have been meant for separate anchorite households. The earliest copies were, almost certainly, in the 'AB language' and therefore made in Wigmore Abbey, but for C a scribe living at some little distance and writing a different though related dialect was employed. As C was a little earlier than the Corpus revision of about 1230—its revisions are often earlier drafts of those of Corpus, and the author's work of correcting and revising it was probably the occasion of his undertaking the more extensive revision of his autograph—it is certain that γ, 'proto-F', and C had all been written before the Corpus MS. was made. But δ and its immediate descendants were probably equally early; the Nero and Titus MSS., which descend from them, are

---

[1] They may have been made from β, not from the autograph, simply because scribes found it easier to work from a fair copy, despite the obvious risk that it would contain errors. But it is possible that γ and δ may have been made almost simultaneously with β, by a method analogous to that later used for the making of C and 'proto-F'; as the scribe of β finished a quire he may have handed it over to colleagues who used it to make γ and δ while he himself was still using the autograph. In this way it would have been possible to have three copies ready for presentation to their intended recipients almost at the same time, to the avoidance of jealousy and recrimination.

both dated to the second quarter of the thirteenth century, though they must belong to its latter part (roughly between 1240 and 1250), with T apparently somewhat later than N, so that it is likely that ζ and η are as early as 1230, and ϵ and δ necessarily earlier still. All of them kept, in full, the main reference to the three sisters. Moreover it does not seem likely that the author, while he still kept control of the text (as he evidently did while these manuscripts were newly made), would permit the making of new copies of the un-revised text after he had completed the Corpus revision. The probability is that by about 1230, just before the final revision was undertaken, there were in existence eight copies of the work—possibly even more, for some may have disappeared without trace and without giving rise to any surviving descendants. This is, as I say, a remarkable multiplication of copies of a newly written vernacular work, but explicable in terms of the sort of community for which it was intended, anchorites living in separate households and increasing in numbers.

Another striking feature of the textual tradition of *Ancrene Wisse* will be obvious from a glance at the *stemma codicum*: so far as is known, the revised text had no descendants. Only one copy, the Corpus MS., is extant, and it is so good that there can be no doubt that it was a direct fair copy made from the autograph as revised by the author.[1] But the revised text was not without influence:[2] it affected the detailed readings of several of the later texts of the Nero-Titus group (the descendants of ϵ); and in particular the fragments of

[1] This means that the manuscript denoted a, included in the *stemma codicum* on grounds of general theory, was in fact physically identical with the archetype X but was X as revised; and that X itself, to which there can be attributed no errors except a few that are explicable as an author's slips of the pen, was the autograph as originally written. See *Proc. Brit. Acad.*, lii. 193–9.

[2] See *English and Medieval Studies*, pp. 150–2.

Part VIII preserved in Cotton MS. Vitellius E. vii of the Latin translation and in the Vernon MS. of the English text show that in the vernacular manuscript from which the Latin version was made and in the line of descent which directly led to the Vernon MS. the text of Part VIII had been taken from a fully revised 'Corpus-type' text, not from either the original version or the altered text of the Cleopatra MS. In the subsection of Part IV dealing with the progeny of the Seven Deadly Sins, a series of additions, five in all, within a few consecutive pages is reproduced in full in the Latin version and in the Vernon MS., and four of them also, in rewritten form, in the Pepys MS.[1] The Vernon MS. also adds, as an appendix to its text, a copy of the fourth of the major additions of the Corpus version (that to Part II beginning *Quomodo obscuratum*).[2] From the detailed readings in these additions it is possible to prove that the copy of the revised text which influenced V and L was neither the extant Corpus MS. nor any copy derived from it, but another, evidently at least as good, independently derived from the autograph as revised.[3] Now the revision deals, as we have seen, specifically with the circumstances of a priory, the chief house of the anchorite community, which must in fact have been Limebrook; obviously it was intended that a copy of the revised text should be given to Limebrook. But

[1] See *English and Medieval Studies*, pp. 156–7.

[2] Ibid., pp. 153–5.

[3] A and V, in the *Quomodo obscuratum* addition, share the omission of a phrase correctly preserved in F's text of the addition, and at another point F's phrase is evidently an earlier version than the one used in AV, though both versions are acceptable (ibid., p. 155). As the evidence is that A was based on the revised autograph, not on a faulty copy of it, I would assume that the author sent his original draft of the *Quomodo obscuratum* addition to be interleaved in 'proto-F', and retained, for interleaving in his autograph manuscript, a slightly revised copy of it in which, by homeoteleuton, he himself had carelessly omitted one of his own phrases which was essential for the meaning. But the omission might be independent in A and V, since the cause is obvious.

this cannot have been the Corpus MS., which was un-doubtedly made in the first place for a single person; for at its end, immediately after the author's request for the prayers of his readers (which uses the plural pronoun *ȝe* and plural verbal forms), the scribe adds his own similar request (for which there is no parallel in the other early manuscripts), but by contrast with the author consistently uses the singular:

Iþench o þi writere i *þine* beoden sumchearre, ne beo hit se lutel. Hit turneð *þe* to gode þet *tu bidest* for oþre.[1]

He must have known, by the time he finished his work if not before, that it was to be sent to a single person, perhaps some newly-recruited anchoress whose friends could afford to pay for the making of a very good copy. The copy that went to Limebrook must have been the lost Corpus-type text.

But if these two were the only fair copies made from the revised autograph, it is easy enough to understand why the revised text remained unproductive. One had gone to a single anchoress who, if she were at all young when the Corpus MS. was written about 1230, might easily have lived for another forty years or so, until say 1270; the manuscript was in the possession of a single person and unavailable for copying. She may have lived to the north of Wigmore, for when, about 1300, the manuscript was given back to Wigmore Abbey, it was at the instance of brother Walter of Ludlow and the donor was John Purcell, probably identifiable with a member of a South Shropshire family who held lands at Diddlebury near Ludlow and at Norbury near Bishop's Castle;[2] Nor-bury is only three miles from Snead, eight from Chirbury,

[1] Corpus MS., f. 117b/15–17.

[2] See N. R. Ker's introduction to Tolkien's edition of the Corpus MS., pp. xvii–xviii. But his statement that Norbury is 'within some ten miles of Wigmore' is a slip; this is true of Diddlebury, but Norbury is eighteen miles from Wigmore.

and eleven from Montgomery, so that there is some possibility that the single anchoress for whom the Corpus MS. was made was in a cell in the Chirbury area, near *Englondes ende*. The copy given to Limebrook, for its part, would have been one of the priory's most precious possessions, a fair copy of a revision of the Rule made specially for it; it would be far too valuable to be given away[1] or even lent to the scriptorium of another religious house for copying. It was available for comparison and for the making of copies of Part VIII, which a cursory inspection would show had been much altered, and of any of the additions which were noticed,[2] but not for loan to a scribe to serve as a continuous exemplar of the whole text. But equally Limebrook, knowing that the text had been revised, would have discouraged the making of further copies from unrevised manuscripts; the copy γ of the original text, which there is reason to suppose was Limebrook's, was used as an exemplar *before* the Corpus revision was made, but had, as far as is known, no further progeny (except that the French translation, made from one of the two early copies of γ, continued to be copied until the beginning of the next century). The original fair copy β, made for the three sisters, may perhaps have passed to Limebrook in the end, as the chapel of St. Leonard and the lands granted to 'the sisters in the Deerfold' did, but if so it too would have been highly valued and carefully guarded.[3]

[1] This is a further reason for not identifying the extant Corpus MS., given to Wigmore Abbey by a layman about 1300, with the copy presumed to have been made for Limebrook.

[2] The additions included at their proper place in LV(P), in a few consecutive pages of Part IV (see p. 290, above), are an obvious example. The addition copied at the end of V must have been on a loose leaf which had been slipped in at the back of V's exemplar, behind the damaged or lost leaves at the end of its main text which must be postulated to account for the way in which the V text of Part VIII breaks off. See *English and Medieval Studies*, pp. 153–4.

[3] The copies which may be supposed to have been Limebrook's

The case, however, was very different with δ and its descendants, as again a glance at the *stemma codicum* will show. These must have been copies made for other anchorite households, and it was by means of them that *Ancrene Wisse* escaped into the outside world. As their owners died or were transferred to Limebrook, their copies of the Rule would become available for sale or gift. But I doubt whether this happened immediately; there was probably a period when a considerable number of copies was concentrated in a single centre. For another of the features of the textual tradition is the great extent of the cross-agreements (or 'horizontal agreements') displayed by the descendants of β, and more particularly by those of ε.[1] There are many unoriginal readings in manuscripts of the ε-group derived not by descent, but evidently from γ and/or its two copies, especially from C; but there are also frequent cross-agreements in error between individual manuscripts descended from ε, especially between Nero (N), Pepys (P), and the 'Trinity version' (S). These, and the correction of inherited errors (which also occurs), can only be the result of repeated collation of one copy with another; and the process is associated, as we have seen, with an influence exerted by the lost Corpus-type text (which I assume belonged to Limebrook) on some of the later descendants of ε. Not all of this collation need have occurred before the text 'escaped into the world'; late in the century, at Canonsleigh Abbey in Devon, a man who was probably its

have all disappeared; if they were kept until the Dissolution, as might be expected, they must then have been dispersed and lost. The only exception is the Cleopatra MS., which may have been Limebrook's originally but had passed into other ownership by 1289.

[1] See *English and Medieval Studies*, pp. 136–52. But (as explained in my edition of the Cleopatra MS., p. cxxii, n. 1) I no longer believe that the contamination of the textual tradition was due to a lost early copy π and a line of descent running from it; I now think that there was a direct influence of the γ-group on the ε-group and of the various manuscripts of the latter on each other.

chaplain busily collated the Cleopatra MS., to the detriment of its text, with some lost manuscript belonging to the Nero–Titus group and most closely related to the English original of the Latin version.[1] But most of the contamination of the textual tradition of the ϵ-group had obviously happened much earlier, in view of the dating of N and T themselves to about 1240–50. What I think may have happened was that δ and its descendants ϵ, ζ, and η had been collected in a centre that was distinct from Limebrook but had access to its manuscripts, and that the latter included the lost fair copy of the revised text, and γ and its two copies 'proto-F' and C (but probably not yet β, if it ever did pass to Limebrook); that this other centre had among its inmates men who were trained in the comparison of texts and in the technique of noting and recording textual variants in the margins or between the lines of the several copies, and who were also interested in *Ancrene Wisse* and in publishing it more widely; and that they were allowed occasionally to consult the fair copy of the revised text and more frequently to collate γ and/or its copies—indeed they may have borrowed, or even come to possess, 'proto-F' and C. This hypothesis would explain the very frequent cross-agreements within the ϵ-group, the marked influence of C and 'proto-F', and the later and more infrequent influence of the revised text. Eventually C was sold or given away, by whoever had more recently possessed it; it passed to the great Marcher lady, Matilda de Clare, who on or before her death in 1289 gave it to Canonsleigh Abbey, which she had refounded as a house for women in 1284.[2] But before this it had strongly influenced the texts descended from δ, doubtless because it was known to have been corrected by the author himself.[3]

But what was this 'other centre' which was able to acquire

---

[1] See my edition of the Cleopatra MS., pp. clxv–clxxi.
[2] Ibid., pp. xxv–vi.   [3] Ibid., p. xi.

copies of the Rule (other than those which belonged to Limebrook, the copy β made for the three sisters, and the Corpus MS.) and which was staffed by men capable of exercising a skill which was a product of scholastic training? It was obviously not Wigmore Abbey. That is sufficiently shown by the linguistic forms of N, T, and G, the earliest surviving manuscripts derived from δ and ε; in particular G was written, as Mr. Ker has shown,[1] 'by a scribe who had been trained abroad' and whose command of English orthography was very imperfect. Moreover, Wigmore Abbey may well have still possessed the author's autograph at the time when N and T were written, within twenty years at most of the making of the Corpus revision and of the two fair copies based on the revised autograph; if so, it would not have needed to collate faulty derivative copies in the attempt to form a good text, and when, about the end of the century, it set out to acquire a copy, it recovered one of the two fair copies of the revised text that it had originally made itself. It is certain that η, the source of the so-called 'Titus-group', was held in a house of male religious, for its text was 'generalized' by the inconsistent substitution of masculine pronouns and other forms and by the occasional re-drafting of passages specifically written for women (e.g. the instructions for hair-cutting); but as the alterations were very unsystematic[2] it is unlikely that they were made by a redactor who was making a completely new copy of the work and introducing his changes as he went. Almost

[1] See his introduction to R. M. Wilson's edition of the Gonville and Caius MS. (E.E.T.S. 229, 1954), pp. xi–xiii; the quotation is from pp. xii–xiii.

[2] See Miss F. M. Mack's introduction to her edition of the Titus MS., pp. xiv–xvii. But she appears to assume that the revision was the work of the scribe of T, which was certainly not the case; T is not the original manuscript of the so-called 'Titus-group' or even a direct copy of it. The proximate ancestor of the whole group was η and it was in η that the changes were made.

certainly η was an old copy (as assumed above) sporadically adapted for male readers by changes made between the lines or in the margins. Similarly G (which, despite its high position on the *stemma* as a derivative of δ, has cross-agreements with C and with individual manuscripts of the ε-group[1] and has therefore been affected by the same processes of contamination as the ε-group itself) has occasional substitutions of masculine words and forms[2] and omits a couple of sentences at the beginning of Part VI referring to the 'penance' that the anchoresses endure in their lives,[3] so that it too is adapted for reading by a man. It is a collection of long extracts from all the Parts of the Inner Rule rearranged in what seems a completely haphazard order,[4] and is followed, in the same section of the present manuscript, by Latin extracts from *Vitas Patrum*; it was perhaps intended merely for the personal use of the man who made it, possibly as an aid to preaching.

There is a more definite clue in the Trinity version, a collection of very extensive translated extracts from the Rule, again in rearranged order, embodied in a vast Anglo-

---

[1] *English and Medieval Studies*, pp. 143–4. G, it should be noted, was probably later than N and T, despite its higher position on the *stemma*. Ker dates the hand 'probably in the second half of the thirteenth century or possibly a little earlier' (introduction to Wilson's edition of G, p. ix). The state of its language suggests to me that if it was later than 1250, it was not much later; but it is difficult to judge a scribe who, when he is not reproducing the forms of his 'AB language' exemplar, varies them in so uncouth and ignorant a fashion. Ker's formulation seems to point to a date after rather than before 1250, but not long after. This would make G later than N and T, but not by more than a decade or so.

[2] In particular, *mine leoue sustren* is changed to *mine leoue frend*.

[3] Gonville and Caius MS., ed. Wilson, 28/28–9; contrast Corpus MS., f. 94a/11–23, Cleopatra MS., ff. 159ᵛ/10–160/5 (Morton, p. 348).

[4] Two extracts from Part III are followed by three, almost continuous, from Parts V and VI and by one from Part VII; but then the scribe goes back to Part III (two discontinuous extracts, neither very long) and Part IV (two long but discontinuous extracts, not distinguished in the table on p. xiv of Wilson's edition).

Norman 'Compilation' (as it has been entitled) of which *Ancrene Wisse* was only one of the sources; it is a sort of *Summa Confessorum*[1] and was probably made between 1257 and 1274, though it may have been a little later.[2] Its compiler, adapting the conclusion of *Ancrene Wisse* to serve as a conclusion to his own work (brought together, in his own words, *de plosours escriz*), says that his labour has been 'for the honour of almighty God and of my sweet lady St. Mary and of St. Francis' (*e de seint franceys*).[3] There can be no reasonable doubt that he was a Franciscan. But the English text of the Rule which he used was a copy of the 'generalized' text, an indirect descendant of η and related (though again not directly) to T. It is probable, therefore, that the male house in which the 'generalized' text was formed, and in which G is also likely to have been made by its foreign-trained scribe, was a Franciscan house; and in view of the many cross-agreements of the manuscripts of the 'generalized' text with the descendants of ζ,[4] and especially with N, this house probably also owned ζ, at least for a time, though its text was left ungeneralized.

The question then becomes a more particular one: which was the Franciscan house that was able to collect, and was

---

[1] See W. H. Trethewey's introduction to his edition (E.E.T.S. 240, 1958), pp. xviii ff.   [2] Trethewey, p. xxiii.

[3] ed. Trethewey, 157/28–9. Trethewey himself, though he points the passage out (p. xxiv), looks the gift somewhat in the mouth, saying that it 'may have been carried over from a source'; but the source, except for the phrases quoted above, is the ending of *Ancrene Wisse*, which has no reference to almighty God, St. Mary, or St. Francis. As the compiler and translator himself obviously added the phrase about his having assembled his work from various writings, I can see no reason to suppose that he did not also add the immediately following phrases saying in whose honour he had done so.

[4] These include the Lanhydrock Fragment (ed. A. Zettersten as part of E.E.T.S. 252 (1963), pp. 161–71); see my review in *Medium Ævum*, xxvi (1967), 190–1. It is more closely related to V than to N, but as it is so very brief and the evidence of its textual affiliations is therefore slight it is not included in the *stemma codicum* on p. 287.

interested in collecting, manuscripts of *Ancrene Wisse* and which also had access to the copies held by Limebrook Priory, especially its copy of the revised text? On grounds of contiguity it is likely to have been the Hereford friary,[1] and when we remember the advice given in the Corpus revision that the anchoresses were especially to trust the friars of both orders and the testimony of bishop Thomas de Cantilupe in 1279 that the nuns of Limebrook had been accustomed to choose their confessors from the Franciscans of the Hereford convent the case, it seems to me, is clear. The confessors of Limebrook would certainly have had to study and expound the Rule written for the anchorite community of which Limebrook had been a part, and would thereby become aware of its merits; and they would have been excellently placed to collect manuscripts which had become surplus to the community's requirements or whose owners had died. And again the dates fit, for the centre that was collecting and collating manuscripts of *Ancrene Wisse*, and excerpting, adapting, copying, and finally translating them, must have been active from 1240 at the latest (in view of the datings of N and T), until 1275 or even later (in view of the datings of G and S, and indeed of other indications);[2] the Hereford friary had been founded by

[1] The nearest Franciscan houses to Limebrook, apart from Hereford, were those at Shrewsbury and Worcester, the former about 6 and the latter about 8 miles further away. The friary in Shrewsbury was not founded until 1245–6 (Knowles and Hadcock, p. 228), which is too late. That in Worcester was established between 1225 and 1230, probably by 1226 (ibid., p. 229), so that it is early enough, but it is markedly further away and in another diocese.

[2] Towards the end of the century 'scribe D' of the Cleopatra MS. collated it with a descendant of η related to the English original of L, and L itself was a translation made by a man who was an M.A. of Oxford by 1280 and died in 1315 (Emden, *BROU*, ii. 759–60). Both used manuscripts lower in the *stemma* than the English original of S and therefore probably, though not certainly, written in the third quarter (or even early in the fourth quarter) of the thirteenth century.

1228, it was about 1230 that the author of *Ancrene Wisse* commended the friars to the women in his charge, and 1279 when the bishop recorded that Limebrook had been accustomed to choose confessors from the Hereford house and in effect recommended them to continue to do so. Moreover the English Franciscans, almost from the time of their arrival in the country, were exceptional in their order for their scholarship and academic connections (especially with Oxford), were devoted to preaching, and were in a much better position, because of their widespread influence, to make a vernacular rule, written for an obscure group of women anchorites in a remote part of England, as widely known as it obviously became in the later thirteenth century than if it had remained the concern only of the Victorines of Wigmore and the Augustinian priory of Limebrook. Somehow, after about 1240, it was published more generally; and the evidence, though as always slight, points rather to the friars than to the Augustinians.[1]

The most interesting of the early offshoots of *Ancrene Wisse* is, however, not the 'generalized' Titus-type version or the 'Trinity' version, still less the curious extracts of the Caius version, but the earlier of the French translations, that preserved in Cotton MS. Vitellius F. vii. The surviving manuscript was written about the beginning of the fourteenth century,[2] but is certainly a later copy; the text has errors that must have occurred during the transmission of the French version itself, and a great lacuna due to the loss of

[1] But the Augustinians remained interested; Canonsleigh Abbey was an Augustinian house, and the man who worked there on the Cleopatra MS. was himself almost certainly an Augustinian and not (as Carleton Brown suggested in discussing another manuscript on which he also worked) a friar, probably a Dominican. See my edition, pp. cxvlii–viii.

[2] See J. A. Herbert's introduction to his edition (E.E.T.S. 219, 1944), p. ix.

leaves (probably a whole quire) from some earlier copy of the translation.[1] But it is generally agreed, in view of the forms and the vocabulary of the Anglo-Norman in which it is written, that the translation must have been made in the earlier thirteenth century. Macaulay even argued that it was the original text of the Rule, of which the English version was a translation;[2] but this hypothesis was soon disproved,[3] though it has continued to attract a few scholars. It is completely untenable now that the textual relationships of the various manuscripts and versions have been established; the Vitellius translation (F) shares numerous distinctive errors with C and must be based, as already stated, on an English manuscript ('proto-F') which shares a common ancestor with C, and the evidence that C was made by a form of *pecia* system from an exemplar simultaneously being used for making another copy can leave no doubt that this other copy was 'proto-F'. The latter, however, was finished first[4] and was much more accurate; indeed it was the excellence of its text (though he overestimated it) which was one of Macaulay's grounds for claiming that F was a copy of the original version of the work. 'Proto-F', like C, must therefore have been made shortly before the 'Corpus revision' was undertaken and before the Corpus MS. itself was written. But before the translator began his work

[1] Herbert, pp. xiii–xiv.

[2] *MLR* ix (1914), 63–78.

[3] Miss D. M. E. Dymes, *Essays and Studies* ix (1924), 31–49; also R. W. Chambers, *RES* i (1925), 4–14, and M. L. Samuels, *Medium Ævum*, xxii (1953), 3–6.

[4] This follows from the state of the extant manuscript C. Its scribe was obliged to copy the sections into which the exemplar had been broken up in the wrong order (2, 1, 4, 3), obviously because the scribe of the other manuscript that was being made at the same time was being given them in the right order. But in C the last two sections (5 and 6) were copied in the right order; the simple explanation is that the other scribe had got ahead and had finished section 5 before the C scribe was ready to start it. See the introduction of my edition of C, pp. xxix–xxxvi.

the copy made from γ had been modified. Like C, it had probably been unsystematically corrected by the author and some of its inherited errors had thereby been removed;[1] and it shares with C (or has taken over from C) three minor additions or corrections made by the author in the early part of the work—the first in the Preface, the second in Part I, and the third comparatively early in Part II.[2] It had also been augmented by the four 'Corpus' additions to Parts I and II, which must have been inserted into 'proto-F' in loose-leaf form, since two of them are misplaced (one seriously);[3] and the text of one of these is more correct or earlier than that of the Corpus MS. itself and the Vernon MS. at three of the points where F differs from AV.[4] Another of the additions is the first of the two references to the friars of both orders, which is probably to be dated after the foundation of the Franciscan house in Hereford (before 1228, and probably in 1227). But 'proto-F', as augmented, did not contain the series of additions to Part IV which is found in Corpus and in the later texts LVP,[5] nor the important '*Pax vobiscum*' addition, later in Part IV, which is peculiar to Corpus; and it took no account at all of the extensive revisions of Part VIII, either as written between the lines and in the margins of C, or in their definitive form in Corpus.[6]

[1] This now seems to me the probable explanation of a number of cases in which the extant text of F shares correct readings only with Corpus, against all the other β-group manuscripts (including C); the latter evidently preserve an error inherited from β itself, which in 'proto-F' was corrected. For instances, see *English and Medieval Studies*, p. 139, n. 2.

[2] My edition of the Cleopatra MS., p. cxx. To these should perhaps be added the instance at C f. 16ᵛ/16 (in Part I), where the correction of 'scribe B' (i.e. the author), *þe opere*, agrees with F against Corpus (for details, see ibid., p. cviii).   [3] *English and Medieval Studies*, pp. 152–3.

[4] Ibid., pp. 154–5.   [5] See p. 290, above.

[6] The account given above is not intended to deal with the minor complications of the extant text of F. It has many erroneous readings

Now this is a very strange situation. The translator must have been working while the revision was in progress, since he had been given accurate and independent loose-leaf copies of the additions to Parts I and II, but before it was complete, since he lacked the others. He was apparently working faster than the author, since he translated the later Parts without their additions—which included one of special importance—and used the text of Part VIII in its unrevised form. He must have been in touch with the author, as his receipt of the additions to Parts I and II shows, but it is hard to believe that they were both in residence at the same place; if they were both members of the community of Wigmore Abbey, as is likely, one of them (probably the author) must have been elsewhere at the time. For the translator cannot have been working under the supervision of the author or in close consultation with him; he misplaced two of the four additions that he had been given and he frequently translated literally passages that had been made difficult or unsatisfactory by corruption when, if he had been able to ask the author, he would have been told what the text should be. Why, if he knew that a revision was in progress, did he not wait for it to be completed? He must have known, or been able to guess, that the intention of the revi-

which are not in C and are therefore not derived from their common ancestor γ, but which are often shared by individual manuscripts of the ϵ-group. This is part of the complex problem of the cross-agreements of the descendants of β (see pp. 293–4, above). As far as F is concerned, I now think that the cross-agreements, when not fortuitous (and I doubt if many of them are), are due to influence exercised by 'proto-F' itself on later manuscripts. My previous discussion of the matter, in *English and Medieval Studies*, pp. 142–3, is unsatisfactory and cannot stand; but the instances cited in n. 2 to p. 142 are valid evidence of the cross-agreements of F and the ϵ-group manuscripts. Those in n. 1 to p. 143, except the first two (which are corrections to C's text made by the author, 'scribe B'), show how the unauthorized readings written into C by its 'scribe D' from his lost η-group manuscript sometimes occur also in F.

sion was that a new fair copy should be made at its conclusion; why then did he not wait until he could work from the fair copy of the revised text, or even from the autograph when the author had finished revising it, instead of using a newly made English manuscript which, though good, was imperfect, the copy of a copy of the first fair copy of the unrevised autograph? The whole procedure suggests some haste, in response to a special and urgent need for a French translation of the Rule; and as to make a translation of a long and difficult work, and to make it in a hurry, was no small undertaking, there is also a suggestion that it was thought very important.[1] There is a sharp contrast with the 'Trinity' version, an expansive translation (though usually faithful) made by a scholar assembling his 'Compilation' in a leisurely way from several sources and addressing it to Christian men and women generally. The Vitellius version is a straight word-for-word rendering intended for a woman or a group of women. She (or they) must have been a person (or persons) of some consequence in the Central Marches. And the making of the French translation is but one part of a general flurry of activity: two new copies of the original text made by a *pecia* system from a single exemplar—one (C) by an outside scribe; partial correction certainly of C and probably also of 'proto-F' by the author himself; and finally the revision of the text of the autograph and the making of two fair copies of the revised text. It is the more

[1] The long-term purpose of the translation may of course have been to make available a French version of the Rule to members of the an-chorite community who could not speak English. The bishop of Here-ford's letter of 1279 testifies that some of the members of Limebrook Priory were then French-speaking, and fifty years earlier it would be even more likely that any large community would include some whose first language was French. But this long-term purpose would not account for the haste; it would have been better served by a translation of the revised text when that was ready.

surprising because there is no evidence that either the author[1] or Wigmore Abbey had anything further to do with the text of *Ancrene Wisse*. This, as far as we can tell, was their final effort; thereafter, as I have suggested, the Franciscans of Hereford took over.

Loretta de Braose,[2] some time after 1196, married Robert fitz Parnell, earl of Leicester, who died in 1204. Even in her widowhood she was a wealthy woman, amply provided for by her marriage-portion and her dower lands. She may have been in exile during her family's troubles; in December 1214 she made a deed declaring that she had not remarried and would not do so without the king's consent, and in consequence recovered her lands. But probably in February 1221 she withdrew from the world, and had apparently been making preparations to do so since the summer of 1219. She became a recluse at Hackington, one mile north of Canterbury. In her retirement she continued to be influential; as late as April 1265, when she must have been well over 80, she was consulted by King Henry. She died at Hackington on 4 March, 'in 1266 or one of the next few years'.[3] She was

[1] The visible state of C, and comparison and analysis of the other texts, shows that the author had had an inveterate habit of tinkering with his work, adding in the margins of early copies minor explanations or additions, or citations of authorities (*English and Medieval Studies*, pp. 157–8). But there are only two additions (ibid., p. 158) which are not either incorporated in the definitive revision of the Corpus MS., or included in the text of C (as originally written or as revised) or of F; and of these the more important, that describing how 'our lay brothers' say their hours (pp. 6–9, above), though it survives only in the Nero MS., was certainly copied from some earlier manuscript and may well go back to a date before the Corpus revision. Thus, though there are these two additions which might be later than the revision, there is no proof that they are later. For all practical purposes the author's work ended with the revision.

[2] The facts of the account which follows are taken from F. M. Powicke's article 'Loretta, Countess of Leicester' in *Historical Essays in honour of James Tait* (Manchester, 1933), pp. 247–72; but the application to *Ancrene Wisse* is mine, not his.

[3] Powicke, p. 263.

one of those who had helped the Franciscans on their arrival in England in 1224; according to their historian Thomas of Eccleston,[1]

Lord Simon Langton, archdeacon of Canterbury, lord Henry of Sandwich, and the noble countess, the lady recluse of Hackington, were specially active on their behalf. The lady nourished them in all things . . . by winning for them in her wise way the goodwill of magnates and prelates, by whom she was held in the highest regard.

One of the magnates whom she could very easily have influenced was Hugh de Mortimer, lord of Wigmore, who was married to her sister Annora, and the Franciscans were certainly favoured by the Mortimers; Hugh's nephew, a younger son of his brother and successor Ralph and his Welsh wife Gwladys Ddu (the daughter of Llywelyn ab Iorwerth), became a Franciscan in the Shrewsbury friary, presumably about 1250.[2] The warmth of the regard for the friars expressed by the author of *Ancrene Wisse* in his revised text may well be an indirect result of Loretta's influence. Hugh de Mortimer died in November 1227, and his widow Annora (Eleanor), being childless, retained the right to her marriage-portion during her widowhood; it consisted of the manors of Tetbury and Hampnett (near Northleach) in Gloucestershire, of which her husband had recovered possession in May 1215, after her release from imprisonment in October 1214.[3] She too was well provided for. But by September 1232 she had followed her sister's example[4] and

---

[1] *De adventu fratrum minorum in Angliam*, ed. A. G. Little (1909), pp. 25–6 (Manchester, 1951); cited and translated by Powicke, p. 268.

[2] So the Latin *Fundationis et Fundatorum Historia* (sc. of Wigmore Abbey), in Dugdale's *Monasticon*, vi. 350.

[3] Powicke, pp. 260, n. 2, and 264–5.

[4] Powicke thinks that the two sisters may have withdrawn from the world because of the effect on them of the events that occurred during

had either become, or was about to become, a recluse, for on 28 September the king issued a writ allowing her to retain from her *maritagium* (which, if she withdrew from the world, reverted to her kin, and did in fact revert to the heir of John de Braose) an annual income of 100*s*. in Charlton and Cherington, which were parts of the manor of Tetbury,

ad se sustendendam quamdiu vixerit in reclusagio, ita quod terra illa revertatur ad rectos heredes post decessum ipsius annore.[1]

This must be official consent to a family arrangement, which must have taken time to negotiate and would have been concluded at some interval before the issue of the writ; as Loretta seems to have begun to make her arrangements eighteen months or more before she finally withdrew to her hermitage, Annora had probably taken her decision well before September 1232, possibly in the previous year. She can be identified with Annora, the recluse of Iffley, near Oxford; Powicke accounts for her choice of the Oxford district by the fact that Osney had been the former home of her mother, Maud or Matilda de St. Valéry, and points out that Annora herself had given lands belonging to the manor of Tetbury to Godstow priory, originally founded by the de St. Valéry family.[2] She frequently appears, in the next few years after 1232, 'as the recipient of the royal bounty',[3]

King John's persecution of their family, particularly the deaths of their mother and brother in prison and of their father in exile.

[1] *Pat. R.*, *1225–32*, p. 501, cited by Powicke, p. 265. On the legal position regarding the *maritagium* see Powicke, pp. 252, 265.

[2] Powicke, p. 265.

[3] Powicke, p. 265, who cites evidence in his n. 3 to that page. In September and November 1234 the king repeated the order that 'the recluse of Iffley' was to be allowed 100*s*. a year from the manor of Tetbury, and he also granted oaks for building, wood for the hearth, wheat, and a suitable robe. The gifts cover the period from 1232 to 1201. Powicke's list of the references to Annora in the public records is not quite complete, but nothing of substance is to be added.

and was still living on 26 January 1240–1.[1] She was a *riche ancre* with *rentes isette*.[2]

Annora de Braose was the lady of Wigmore castle from 1214 until her husband's death late in 1227, the period during which *Ancrene Wisse* was written. She would certainly have known of any recluses living nearby in her husband's domains; above all she would know 'the sisters living in the Deerfold', only a mile away, to whom her father-in-law had granted the chapel of St. Leonard and the lands about it and who, if they are identical with the 'three sisters' of *Ancrene Wisse* (as in my view they must be), were accustomed, according to the passage in the Nero MS., to send their servants to the hall of 'their friend' when they had need of food and clothing—which, I have already suggested, means the hall of Annora's husband Hugh. Wigmore Abbey, where *Ancrene Wisse* was written and its early copies made, was under the patronage of her husband's family; she must have known of any book or Rule that had been written at the request of the three sisters by a canon of Wigmore, and no doubt knew what we want to know, who he was—and indeed he may well have been one of her own spiritual directors, since in her widowhood she adopted the way of life which he advocated, especially as it is known that Wigmore Abbey provided a chaplain for the lord of Wigmore.[3] If such a lady—not any great and well-to-do

[1] *Close R.*, *1237–42*, p. 269: two orders dated 26 Jan. 1241, at Marlborough, granting timber and six quarters of wheat. As the grants to Annora had hitherto been fairly frequent, their cessation after this date presumably means that she did not live much longer.

[2] Her annuity of 100s. plus royal grants in kind and (I assume) other help from her kindred, contrasts with the pension of 30s. 5d. a year paid by King John to 'Margaret the recluse' (p. 235, above) and, more sharply, with the annual value in 1291 of Limebrook's 'home estate', assessed at 16s. 4d.—especially as this seems to lump together the original endowment of the community at Limebrook with that in the Deerfold granted to the sisters living there (pp. 232–4, above).   [3] See p. 50, above.

lady, but the one who until 1227 had been mistress of Wigmore castle—had asked for a copy of the book written for anchoresses living near Wigmore to take with her when she retired from the world or to help her to make up her mind whether to do so, or had even let it be known that she herself was considering whether to become an anchoress, and if this request or intimation had closely coincided with a need for additional copies of the Rule and for a revision of its text to take account of the new circumstances of Limebrook, there would be a very adequate explanation of the 'flurry of activity' that the textual facts demonstrate, and of the urgency with which the translation itself was prepared.

To connect the making of the French translation with Annora de Braose's decision to become an anchorite cannot be merely fanciful, for everything fits so well. Obviously, if she had expressed a wish for a copy, or if it had been decided, without a request, that it was desirable to make one for her, it would have to be in French, for she was a member of a great Anglo-Norman noble family and her language must have been French; and even if she could not read herself, she would want the book to be read to her in French. No one else, except possibly her new sister-in-law Gwladys Ddu (who did not become an anchorite, and whose languages were presumably Welsh first and French second), would have had such a claim for special consideration at this time. Wigmore Abbey's interest in vernacular composition was not confined to English; probably a few years before, in the 1220s, it had produced an Anglo-Norman *History of the Foundation of Wigmore Abbey* which was plainly intended, at least in part if not chiefly, for the edification of its patrons the Mortimers. The translator of *Ancrene Wisse* must have known the English dialect of the Wigmore district well; though he was not its author, he had an excellent understanding of what is often a difficult text written in an out-of-the-way form of English, for mistranslations are rare, though they occur, and are not serious.[1] All the circumstances, including his use of a newly-made copy probably corrected, like its congener, by the author, and his receipt of the additions to Parts I and II, make it virtually certain that he was a canon of Wigmore Abbey. The hypothesis that the translation was made in the first instance for such a lady as Annora de Braose would also account for a detail in it which, as our author would say, we considered 'far above' (*feor þruppe*):[2] the modification of the original absolute prohibition on the eating of meat and fat except in great sickness or excessive weakness. She would be pre-eminently a woman who had come to the life of a recluse, as the Augustinian Rule says, from more luxurious circumstances (*ex moribus delicatioribus*) and for whom a complete abstention from meat might well be a hardship that she could not accept. This is the only relaxation of the original text of Part VIII in the French version and occurs only there; it may be chance, but I doubt it. But above all there is the almost exact coincidence of date. As far as I know no one else has ever connected Annora de Braose with *Ancrene Wisse*, though Shepherd in passing, in his discussion of 'the eremitical life', mentions her sister Loretta;[3] yet for at least sixty years it has been generally accepted by scholars that the date of the Corpus MS. is within a few years (five at most) either side of 1230.[4]

---

[1] In this judgement, I allow for copying errors both in the English text from which the translator worked and in the extant Vitellius MS. of the French text. [2] See pp. 41–4.

[3] *Ancrene Wisse: Parts Six and Seven*, p. xxxiii.

[4] M. R. James, *Descriptive Catalogue of the Manuscripts in the Library of Corpus Christi College, Cambridge* (1912), ii. 267–8, merely dates the hand 'early thirteenth century'. But Macaulay in *MLR* ix (1914) says that the hand is 'of the first half of the thirteenth century' (p. 145) and that the manuscript 'can hardly be earlier than 1230' because of the references to the friars (pp. 149–50). Hall in *Early Middle English* (1920), ii. 355, says that it 'cannot be earlier than 1225' because of the mention

The revision of the autograph must of course have been earlier than the date of the extant copy, if only by a little while, but it cannot usefully be distinguished, especially as the earlier limit for the date of the Corpus MS. is set by the two references to the Franciscans, which concern the date of the revision rather than that of the copy; for this reason the revision cannot well be put before 1228 and is probably a year or two later (in view of the date given for the establishment of the Franciscan friary in Hereford),[1] and the same applies to the French translation, which has the first of the references. It too belongs 'about 1230' and the chance of a slightly later date is a little greater than that of an earlier. On the other side of the equation the Crown, on 28 September 1232, formally confirmed the financial arrangement made for Annora's entry into a hermitage; she must have made her decision months before, possibly by the end of the previous year, and have begun to think about it earlier still, at any time after the death of her husband in November 1227. Nothing could fit more closely: the right sort of woman in the right place at the right time.

It makes me wonder whether she did something more than ask for a translation of the Rule, whether she did not also ask its author, who had a good claim to be considered an expert and experienced adviser on the anchorite life, to accompany her to her retreat at Iffley. He certainly knew Oxford, and referred to it in his most important addition to the 'Corpus revision'. If he knew that he was to go with her, it would explain why he undertook, when the French translation was being made, a definitive revision of his work intended, not

of the friars, 'and it is probably later than 1230'. Shepherd, *Ancrene Wisse* (1959), p. xxi, quotes Tolkien's view that the stage of development represented in the dialect cannot 'be put back much before 1225, if as far' (*Essays and Studies*, xiv (1929), 120) and dates the manuscript 'after 1225 and probably before 1235'.

[1] See p. 14, n. 3, above.

for a solitary, but for a community; why, after it was finished, he made no further additions or revisions; and why he advised the anchoresses henceforth to put their trust in the friars. But it would not explain—and this seems a conclusive objection—why he should leave someone else to make the translation from a faulty copy of the unrevised text or why indeed a translation should be at all necessary, since he could himself have expounded his teachings to his patroness. It is more likely that her decision stirred the whole community of Wigmore Abbey into activity, himself included; that he was ageing, and worked more slowly though still with skill; and that, having done this last service to the community of anchoresses and more particularly to Limebrook Priory, he gave up his charge of them—or died.

VI

BRIAN OF LINGEN

It has been well said that 'if we must have an image of the author of the Rule we must seek it in his book',[1] and this will remain true whatever we may be able to discover about his order and his community, about the women for whom he wrote, about dates and places and the transmission of his text; we shall learn nothing significant about the man and his qualities except what he has put in the book, though it may help us a little if we can see him against the background of his time and the particular society in which he lived. One of the things that is clearest is that he was a man of wide reading and indeed erudition; perhaps the most important advance in our understanding of his work has been the stress that has, in recent years, been placed on his indebtedness to the newly developed universities of the twelfth century and to scholastic training.[2] This has now become even more obvious with the recognition of the extent of his dependence on Alexander of Bath's *Moralia super Evangelia*, a work of purely scholastic type written, probably, only some ten or twelve years earlier; and there is also another indication, which I do not think has been pointed out, of the nature of his training. One of the characteristics of the academically trained is their willingness and ability to use

[1] Shepherd, *Ancrene Wisse: Parts Six and Seven*, p. xxix.
[2] C. H. Talbot, 'Some Notes on the Dating of the *Ancrene Riwle*', *Neophilologus*, xl (1956), 38–50, especially p. 50; Shepherd, pp. xxv ff.; G. V. Smithers in Bennett and Smithers, p. 224.

reference-books—dictionaries, concordances, encyclopaedias, bibliographies, and so on—on which indeed scholars rely so much that they encourage their proliferation and give high credit to their compilers; and it was so already in the Middle Ages. Among the most remarkable, though little studied, of these medieval works of reference are the alphabetical lists of *Interpretationes nominum hebraicorum*, which in their aim of including all names found in the Bible (whether or not in fact Hebrew), and in their attempt to give for each name all the variant 'interpretations' that it was supposed to have, approach much more nearly to a modern dictionary than medieval vocabularies themselves do, since the latter deal with a selection only of the Latin vocabulary, mostly the 'hard words'. *Ancrene Wisse* gives 'interpretations' for thirty biblical names,[1] and though some of these come, or may come, from other sources—the text of the Bible itself, the *Glossa Ordinaria*, and in one case from Alexander of Bath—most are undoubtedly taken from one of the fuller and more developed forms of the lists of *Interpretationes*. Two instances may be given, of which the first is the curious error by which the name of Judith's father is given in *Ancrene Wisse* as Merarith[2] instead of Merari. In several of the fuller lists the entry for *Merari* is immediately followed by one for *Merarite* (in classical spelling *Meraritae* 'the Merarites'), with 'interpretations' which are merely

[1] This is far fewer than those 'interpreted' in the *Moralia super Evangelia*, but is still a relatively high number considering the different purpose of the vernacular book, and is a sign of a special interest.

[2] Corpus MS., ff. 84a/5–8, 101a/4–5 (Morton, pp. 308, 372). But in Corpus the name is spelt *Merariht*, with some support from other manuscripts. It can, however, be shown by recension that this is a scribal miscopying of *Merarith*; the common native word-ending -*iht* (as in the word *riht* itself) has been substituted for the rare -*ith*, which occurred only in biblical names such as *Judith*; and though the author is writing of biblical characters he has in fact given Judith's father a non-biblical name. In the first passage S and L correct his error, writing *Merari*.

pluralized forms of those for *Merari*; a variant spelling was *Merarithe*, and in one Bodleian manuscript, a copy of what seems to be the latest developed of all the lists, this is actually abbreviated as *Merarith'*, the mark of suspension being a tiny dot over the bow of the *h* which it is very easy to miss.[1] The second instance is the 'interpretation' of *Melchia(s)* as 'corus domino'.[2] There is no 'interpretation' of the name that I can find in the *Glossa Ordinaria*, and in the lists of *Interpretationes* the name *Melchia(s)* itself has 'interpretations', varying in detail, which derive ultimately from Jerome's 'rex meus'. But the lists also introduce a name *Melechias* which, except in the earliest, is interpreted as 'corus domino', and as it is not properly a biblical name but only an occasional variant of *Melchia(s)* itself, it was sometimes miscopied as (or perhaps consciously corrected to) *Melchias*.[3] In such manuscripts there were as a result two entries for *Melchias* at slightly different points in the alphabetical order, one giving the traditional interpretation derived ultimately from Jerome and the other that invented for the supposed name

[1] MS. Auct. D. 5. 18, f. 323ᵛ. This is a copy (the only one I know) of a rare list beginning 'Aad testificans', a revision of the standard list beginning 'Aaz apprehendens'. But it does not follow that the author of *Ancrene Wisse* used 'Aad testificans'; its compiler certainly worked from a copy of the standard list, and the abbreviation *Merarith'* probably came from it. The same abbreviation may be discoverable in one or more of the almost numberless surviving copies of the standard list; but it is not in any of those in the Bodleian.

[2] Corpus MS., f. 21b/24 (not in Morton). This is an addition to the basic text, though found in most manuscripts; it is lacking from CFN. Only Titus and Corpus give the 'interpretation' without corruption.

[3] So in Paris MS. Bib. Nat. f. lat. 37⁴, f. 347, a copy of one of the versions beginning 'Aaron mons fortitudinis'; Bodleian MS. Auct. D. 5. 8, f. 16ᵛ, the Bodleian copy of the rare list beginning 'Aaz apprehensus' which appears immediately to precede the standard list; and Bodleian MS. Auct. D. 4. 10, f. 571, one of the many copies of the standard 'Aaz apprehendens' list. The 'Aaron' lists appear to be the oldest, but the version given in the Paris MS. is certainly not of the most primitive type.

Melechias; presumably the manuscript used by the author of *Ancrene Wisse* was of this type, unless he himself misread *Melechias* as *Melchias*. Certainly he had been using an academic reference-book, probably in an up-to-date form similar to that used by Alexander of Bath.

It is natural to associate any man of academic training and interests in the late twelfth and early thirteenth centuries directly or indirectly with the university of Paris, as Shepherd has done;[1] indeed he goes somewhat further, saying that the author of *Ancrene Wisse* 'was probably a travelled man, to Paris at least, perhaps to Rome'.[2] I doubt whether the author had been to Rome; at the end of the book he calls God to witness that he would rather betake himself to Rome than begin to write it again. But if he had been to Rome already he would surely have written 'do me *eft* toward Rome', especially as it would have made a neater verbal parallel to 'biginnen hit eft forte donne'.[3] I doubt even whether he had been to Paris, at least to study there. From private discussion with Professor Shepherd I know that one of his reasons for the conclusion expressed in his book that *Ancrene Wisse* could not have been written much after 1200 was that it shows so little acquaintance with the most recent Parisian theological teaching, and especially with that of Stephen Langton. The judgement requires some qualification, for the author of *Ancrene Wisse* knew at least one Langton's Paris sermons[4] (but these circulated early in England); and the study of works extant only in manuscript and not yet available in print may make still further modification necessary.[5] But in general it is true that he lacks

---

[1] *Ancrene Wisse: Parts Six and Seven*, pp. xxviii–ix. Cf. also Talbot, p. 50.   [2] Op. cit., p. xxx.

[3] Corpus MS., f. 117b/3–4 (Morton, p. 430).

[4] See E. J. Dobson, *Moralities on the Gospels* (Oxford, 1975), p. 4 and n. 3.

[5] Cf. Talbot, art. cit., pp. 48–50, who suggests that *Ancrene Wisse*

up-to-date knowledge of the Parisian masters. Moreover, at the very end of the twelfth and the beginning of the thirteenth century the wars between England and France made it more difficult for English scholars to go to Paris. In 1192 Gerald of Wales was prevented 'on account of the wars' from going to Paris to pursue his theological studies, and instead went to Lincoln, where the school was under the famous teacher William de Montibus.[1] One of King John's objections to Stephen Langton as archbishop of Canterbury was that he had lived so long in Paris, the capital of the king's enemy.[2] The Victorines of Paris, of the abbeys of St. Victor itself and of Ste Geneviève, had become estranged from the schools of the Island and the Petit Pont.[3] The English Victorine houses, as we have already seen,[4] in the early thirteenth century were for a time out of touch with their mother-house, and even after they had been received back into relations with St. Victor they had to tell its abbot that, though they would try to get permission from the king and the legate to attend the next chapter, the king was at present unwilling to allow them the full privileges of belonging to the order.

In view of the date of *Ancrene Wisse*, between 1215 and 1222, and probably more narrowly between 1217 and 1220, the most likely time for its author to have been a student of the higher discipline of theology would have been towards the end of the twelfth century, just when Gerald of Wales found himself prevented from going to Paris; and the most

may be influenced by a handbook of Church Offices compiled 'about 1208, perhaps later' by Peter de Roissy, chancellor of Chartres, of which only extracts have been published.

[1] J. de Ghellinck, *L'Essor de la littérature latine au XIIᵉ siècle* (2nd edn., 1955), p. 141; Poole, *From Domesday Book to Magna Carta*, p. 236.　　　[2] F. M. Powicke, *Stephen Langton* (Oxford, 1928), p. 96.
[3] Ibid., p. 27.　　　　　　　　　　[4] See pp. 131–2, above.

recent theological work by which *Ancrene Wisse* is influenced, and that very strongly, is an English one, Alexander of Bath's *Moralia super Evangelia*. It is also probably influenced by Alexander Nequam, who studied and preached in Oxford in the 1190s before he became an Augustinian and withdrew from the world between 1197 and 1201,[1] and there are possible connections with other English scholastic writers. It seems to me much more likely that the author was trained in England than in Paris. There were several flourishing English schools at the end of the twelfth century. That of Hereford itself was very active; there was another at Wells, whose dean Alexander is probably to be identified with the Alexander of Bath who wrote the *Moralia*; and at Lincoln there was the school chosen by Gerald of Wales. But the chief was already Oxford, and I guess that the author of *Ancrene Wisse* may have received some at least of his training there, for it is one of the four major religious centres that he mentions in the most important addition of the Corpus text. Unfortunately the records of the university at the end of the twelfth and the beginning of the thirteenth century are very scanty; there is no hope of tracing him.

It is sometimes held that the author was an old or at least an ageing man; so by Hall, who wrote that 'there is a note of weariness at the end of the book, as of one already advanced in years, and indeed the accumulated experience of a long life must have gone to its making'.[2] But the weariness at the end is rather weariness with a protracted effort of literary composition; it is dangerous to assume from it that he was 'already advanced in years'. A young man can say that he would not willingly start something again. I have myself suggested that the forms of his language, as displayed in his additions to the Cleopatra MS., are, when they differ from

---

[1] Emden, *BROU*, ii. 1342.
[2] *Early Middle English*, ii. 375.

those of the two 'AB' scribes, probably those 'of an older man, possibly less highly trained, and certainly less concerned to adhere strictly to the rule-book of the scribes'.[1] But the two scribes may have been young men, still (say) in their twenties; if the author had been a man approaching fifty when he finished the work about 1220, and approaching sixty when he revised it some ten years later, it would sufficiently account for the linguistic differences. Obviously he was not himself a young man; he warns the anchoresses to be careful about how they confess to young priests,[2] he was clearly experienced, and he would not have been made director of a group of women unless he was mature and trustworthy. But we need not think of him, as Hall did (wishing to identify him with St. Gilbert of Sempringham, who was a hundred years old when he died in 1189), as very old.

At the end of the previous chapter we saw that there is no evidence that either its author or Wigmore Abbey had anything further to do with *Ancrene Wisse*, after he had completed the 'Corpus revision' and the Wigmore scribes had made the two fair copies that we must assume (the Corpus MS. and a similar lost manuscript). I doubt whether this was unforeseen or accidental; it is more likely to have been deliberately planned. If one reads through the author's additions to Parts II and IV, one becomes aware of some ambivalence in his attitude to his charges. On the one hand he is pleased with their success, with the increase in their numbers, their spreading reputation, and the unity which, he asserts, they display more than any other anchoresses in England, so that they are comparable to a community in better-known places. On the other hand he is full of warnings and forebodings of the sort of fault or vice to be expected

---

[1] In my edition of the Cleopatra MS., p. cxl.
[2] Corpus MS., f. 91a/19–21 (Morton, p. 336). He adds 'I mean young in understanding' and equally warns them against 'foolish old' priests.

in a larger and more organized community where not all have a clear religious vocation but some may be worldly or vain or discontented, where friction and quarrelling may arise between one woman and another and there may be ill-natured gossip, where questions of rank and precedence and authority necessarily arise and there may be scope for the ambitious exercise of a little power within a narrow range. I suspect that he was not really happy with the way things had developed, that he had preferred it when there were fewer women of undoubted vocation living a more truly anchorite life in a less organized, more informal association, and that he was conscious of being no longer in full sympathy with this new situation in which some at least of the *inclusae* had become *moniales*. He was doing them a final service by revising his book, embodying in it the minor corrections and additions he had made in various copies during the past few years and making new and important additions intended especially for Limebrook Priory, but he was getting ready to hand over his charge—perhaps had been warned by the bishop or archdeacon that in view of his age he would soon have to do so; and therefore, reiterating and emphasizing, in Part VIII, the power of their *schrift* or *meistre*, whoever he might be, to vary the provisions of the Outer Rule as in his judgement circumstances might require, and in particular commending to them the friars, he took his leave as their preceptor.

Recent scholars, working very properly from the evidence of the book's contents, have emphasized its author's interest in pastoral theology. This was the conclusion that Sitwell drew from the disproportionate length of the Parts on the Sins, Confession, and Penance, and he went on to say that 'it certainly points to the fact that he was a secular priest, rather than a monk, or even a regular canon'.[1] Talbot

[1] See his introduction to Miss Salu's translation, p. xviii ff.

similarly, after arguing that 'he had not a monastic but a scholastic background', continued:[1]

If, further, we consider the eclectic nature of the hymns, prayers, Hours, and other details, the preoccupation with vocal rather than with mental prayer, the insistence on the ascetic rather than the contemplative side of the Recluse's life and the practical knowledge he displays of women's capacities and limitations, it would seem to point to the author being a secular priest rather than a monk, or at least to a member of a religious order with pastoral experience.

Shepherd, summarizing the discussion, says, 'Plainly he had much pastoral experience.'[2] This indeed is obvious from the position he held in relation to the anchoresses: he was not, like Ailred of Rievaulx, a monk writing from the cloister to his sister; he was not even writing only for the three sisters who had asked him for a Rule; he was the spiritual director of a number of anchoresses living at various places, and he cannot therefore have been an enclosed religious himself. The same, I think, is implied by his story of the *loricatus* who 'asks me to teach him . . . and weeps to me . . . and says that God forgets him'.[3] Yet, as we have seen, there cannot be the slightest doubt that he was a member of an order, the Augustinian, and more particularly of the Victorine community of Wigmore. It is as well to recall the classification of canons quoted in chapter I, above,[4] that 'some as far as possible are completely cut off in life, dress, and habitation from the multitude, some are placed near men, others dwell among men, whence they are called seculars'. A Victorine house, whether remote in situation or 'near men'

[1] p. 50. [2] p. xxix.
[3] Corpus MS., f. 103b/8–16 (Morton, p. 382). Cf. also the following reference (ll. 21–2) to the fact that the author knows such a woman as suffers little less. Both allusions imply his pastoral care of the persons concerned. [4] pp. 46–7.

(and Wigmore, surely, would go into the first category), was one of regulars living a life strongly influenced by that of the Cistercians, who deliberately sought lonely sites for their abbeys. But any house of the Augustinian congregations might have parish churches appropriated to it, which might be served not by paid vicars but by canons detached for the purpose; they, dwelling among men, would be 'seculars'. We have also seen that Wigmore Abbey provided a chaplain for the lord of Wigmore, and plainly the domestic chaplain of a baronial household was living 'among men'; indeed the story from which we know of this chaplain shows him accompanying Roger de Mortimer as Roger rode through his domain with his retinue, complaining of his father's generosity to the canons.[1] There is, then, no inconsistency between the author's evident pastoral experience and responsibilities, and his association with Wigmore Abbey; but the conditions to be satisfied are nevertheless very exactly defined. He must have been a member of the Victorine community of Wigmore and yet 'dwelling among men' and therefore 'called a secular'.

There have been several attempts to name the author of *Ancrene Wisse*, all remarkably unsuccessful: attributions to men born, or living, in the wrong places at the wrong dates and belonging to the wrong orders or to none.[2] Shepherd in 1959 wrote that 'it is possible that the author of the Rule will be identified in the future', given 'much more information about the religious life and literature of the late twelfth and early thirteenth centuries in England' and 'a considerable measure of luck'.[3] He also remarked that 'absence of knowledge often serves as a stimulus to speculation'.[4] I take the warning—indeed I agree—but I also take

[1] See p. 228, above.
[2] See Shepherd's summary account, *Ancrene Wisse: Parts Six and Seven*, pp. xxiv–v.   [3] Ibid., p. xxv.   [4] Ibid., p. xxiv.

the risk, observing however that what has seemed to me
to be requisite was not knowledge about religious life and
literature generally but a close analysis of the text and the
relationships between the manuscripts, a careful scrutiny of
the internal evidence, precision of location and dating, and a
deliberate search for record evidence at the right time and
place. It was, in fact, an intelligence officer's job. Nor do I
call it luck if, observing from the map the situation of Limebrook, one conducts a protracted and laborious search for
records of the priory and is rewarded by finding some; the
medieval index in the Black Book of Wigmore leads directly
to the Mortimer charter concerning the chapel of St. Leonard
and the sisters living in the Deerfold, and the Lingen 'genealogy' of MS. Harley 1087 is printed in the section on Limebrook Priory in Dugdale's *Monasticon*.

It is this 'genealogy'[1]—which I have argued is in reality
a list of founder's kin compiled in Limebrook Priory and
last revised between 1522 and 1530—that provides the vital
clue; for almost at its head, in the second generation, is the
name 'Brianus de Lingan Canonicus secularis monesterii
de wigmore'. It is a striking entry: he is the only younger
son recorded in the list, though he lived three hundred
years before it was last revised; and despite the lapse of time
he is precisely described. The description must originally
have been written by someone who had known him during
his lifetime; no one who had received merely a vague
tradition that he had been a canon of Wigmore would, to
give it greater particularity, have added that he was a
secular canon, for this was exceptional and not to be expected
—normally a canon of Wigmore was a regular. Only someone who had certain knowledge that he had been a secular
would have written it. It is this detail that I find conclusive
evidence of the ultimate antiquity of the Harleian list, proof

[1] Printed on p. 199, above.

that it was not a late record of an oral tradition but was based on written documents going back to the first half of the thirteenth century. We must accept that Brian of Lingen was indeed a secular canon of Wigmore Abbey. But why should he be included in the list, and described so precisely, when no other of the younger sons of the family, throughout three centuries, was admitted to it? He must have been a man whose importance to Limebrook Priory was comparable to that of his father Ralph, also carefully described (as 'dominus de Lingan' and 'primus fundator prioratus de Lingbroke'), whose name heads the list; and his status as a secular canon of Wigmore Abbey was evidently relevant. I guess that the Priory, in its early days, had owed him a great debt: that he wrote *Ancrene Wisse*.

There is one sense in which it adds nothing to our knowledge whether he did or not, for he is only a name; I have been able to find no further record of him, though others may be more successful. We have no information about him except what we can deduce from the Harleian list itself. But he is exactly the right sort of man, a canon of Wigmore Abbey yet a secular. He was the son of the 'first founder' of Limebrook Priory. He was born in the district, presumably at Lingen, less than four miles from Wigmore Abbey—certainly he was a member of the family that held Lingen manor and castle for hundreds of years; he must therefore have been a native speaker of the local dialect. Indeed, Lingen almost epitomizes in its history the social conditions that must be assumed to account for the salient features of the vocabulary of the dialect; for in 1066 it had been held as two manors, one by a man with an English and the other by a man with a Danish name, and it is within a few miles of what was, after Gruffydd ap Llywelyn's raids, the effective boundary between England and Wales, so that it must have been commonplace to have Welsh-speaking servants—including nursemaids who would call a cradle *cader*, and perhaps retainers who would be *keis*.[1] It is all but certain that after the Conquest Lingen passed to a family of Norman origin—though it is not a necessary assumption in this district, where some English landholding families continued in possession;[2] but the Normans often intermarried with the dispossessed native families, both because they needed wives and because it was politic to do so, and in any case Norman knights were quickly influenced by the society into which they were introduced and, much sooner than their overlords, had to learn its language to manage their estates. But Brian of Lingen was a man of the knightly class and at this date must have been bilingual, which would explain the high proportion of French-derived vocabulary in *Ancrene Wisse*, and the use, at least in one or two places, of idioms that seem more natural in Old French than in Middle English. His rank would also explain the social assumptions that become explicit in the reference to the sisters being sometimes obliged to endure the arrogance of one who, in other circumstances, 'might have been your thrall'—using the native English word for 'slave'.[3]

[1] There is also a possibility that the Norman Conquest introduced a Flemish element into the local population (cf. next note). The vocabulary of the 'AB language' includes several words apparently of MLG or MDu origin; to *packes*, *spearren*, and *spi* (cf. Zettersten, p. 282) is probably to be added *uleð* 'flatters' (*Ste Katerine*, ed. Einenkel, l. 1486; *Hali Meiðhad*, ed. Colborn, l. 20), which seems more likely to be from MLG or MDu *vleen* than from OE **flæn*, since the latter would be expected to give **fleað* 3 sg. pres. indic. in the 'AB' orthography.

[2] Domesday Book records that at the time of the survey (1086) 'Ralf de Mortimer holds Lingham and Turstin holds it of him'. Turstin was a Norman name (ON *þorstein*), and Round (*VCH Herefordshire*, i. 304) proved that this Turstin was not the 'Turstin the Fleming' who had held Wigmore for a time before the Mortimers gained possession of it. The names of the Lingen family from the mid twelfth century onwards (Ralph and John in the direct male line) are not English, but this is hardly significant; few native personal names continued in use after this time.

[3] See p. 3, above.

He was the son, brother, and uncle of successive lords of Lingen, who were among the chief retainers of the Mortimers of Wigmore; he would have been a very suitable person to be appointed, by the abbot of Wigmore, chaplain to the lord of Wigmore—though I must own that the suggestion that the author of *Ancrene Wisse* may have been a domestic chaplain[1] seems to me to be based either on second sight or on knowledge of some document hitherto unpublished, for I cannot see how it is to be deduced from anything that he wrote in his work.[2] The chaplain of Wigmore castle would certainly have known of anchoresses living only a mile away in the Deerfold, and whether they could rely on his lord for their necessities. And finally the dates—on which I insist (I think rightly)—will fit. Brian of Lingen was the younger brother of a man who succeeded to his inheritance in 1190 and who himself had been succeeded by 1236.[3] I have argued that his elder brother John may not have been of full age in 1190, and in any case was probably a young man still unmarried;[4] if we were to assume that he was born about 1170 (or a year or two later), he would have been 65 or a little less in 1235, the probable date of his death. His younger brother could then have been 45 or more in 1220, the

[1] Shepherd, p. xxix. As none of the three writers to whom he refers in his footnote (Sitwell, Talbot, and Brewer) in fact made this suggestion, it appears to be his own addition; Brewer indeed seems to be improperly cited here, since his argument was that the author was an Augustinian (cf. Shepherd's preceding sentence).

[2] Unless it is assumed that the man mentioned at Corpus f. 103b/ 8–16 was not a religious who wore mail over his hairshirt the better to mortify the flesh (i.e. a *loricatus*, such as St. Edmund of Abingdon is said to have been in a late version of his life), but a lay warrior obliged to wear mail who nevertheless wore also a hairshirt beneath it. This would be a possible interpretation of the words. In the latter case the author, since he knew of the practice of so ascetic a warrior, might have been his chaplain. Cf. p. 320, n. 3, above.

[3] See pp. 207–9, above, and Appendix III, pp. 393–4, below.

[4] See p. 209, above.

approximate date for the finishing of the original version of
Ancrene Wisse, and 55 or more in 1230, the approximate date
of the 'Corpus revision'; and as the elder brother died about
1235, so may the younger have done, soon after this revision
of the Rule, which, as it seems, its author never touched
again. The right sort of man at the right place at the right
time, and the brother of a man who died about the right time.

Unless more documentary evidence can be discovered, it
is pointless to spend much time wondering whether the
three sisters at whose request he began his work were his
sisters in a sense other than spiritual. But it is possible:
they were of his social class, and he not only says that they
were 'the women dearest to me', but also implies that he
was a man very dear to them.[1] When he cites Ailred's *De
vita eremitica*, his words are *as seint Ailred þe abbat wrat to
his suster* (the force of which could be modified by a stress
on *his*), and a few lines later he uses his habitual formula of
address, *mine leoue sustren*.[2] Of course he may be using the
word in a different sense; when he impersonally addresses
any woman reader as *mi leoue suster* he is certainly doing so.
Nevertheless he, like Ailred, may have been writing at the
request of women who were his sisters in more senses than
one; the ambiguity was inherent in contemporary usage.
When Orm dedicated the *Ormulum* to 'brother Walter' he
was at pains to make clear, with the prolixity and repetition
that his metronome metre had forced on him and made a
habit of his mind, that Walter was his 'brother' in three
several ways: *affter þe flæshess kinde*, *i Crisstenndom þurrh
fulluhht and þurrh trowwþe*, and finally *o þe þride wise* because they had both undertaken to follow the same Rule,
in the canonical order and life, as St. Augustine had established it.[3] If Orm had a brother who, like himself, was

[1] See pp. 4–5, above.   [2] Corpus MS., f. 99b/16, 22 (Morton, p. 368).
[3] *Ormulum*, ed. Holt and White (Oxford, 1878), Dedication, ll. 1–10.

subject to the Augustinian Rule, it is conceivable that the three 'dear sisters' who were so very dear to the author of *Ancrene Wisse* were in literal fact his sisters; at the very least they are likely to have been his kinswomen, in so closed a society.

The anonymity of so much medieval literature was largely due to a Christian tradition that it was vainglorious for a writer or an artist to seek fame for himself and perpetuity for his name; talents were given by God and should be used to the glory of God.[1] But the doctrine was sometimes explicitly challenged,[2] and much more often disregarded in practice. Commonly the motive was simply to claim credit or accept responsibility for the work, or to solicit patronage or reward (as in *The Owl and the Nightingale*, if, as is probable, the Master Nicholas of Guildford mentioned both near the beginning and near the end is the author). Even those to whom this might have seemed vainglorious or self-seeking had another powerful motive to give their names: to ensure that prayers might be said for their souls and for the remission of their sins, either by the persons for whom a book had been specifically written or by readers (or hearers) generally.[3] But to give the name in a rubric, whether at the beginning or the end of a work, was risky; scribes often omitted rubrics or even deliberately altered them, transferring the ascription to some other writer. It was

[1] Cf. Julius Schwietering, *Die Demutsformel mittelhochdeutscher Dichter* (Abhandlungen der Königlichen Gesellschaft der Wissenschaften zu Göttingen, Berlin, 1921), c. I, 'Die verhüllende Einkleidung des Autornamens' (pp. 1–36).

[2] E. R. Curtius, *Europäische Literatur und lateinisches Mittelalter* (Bern, 1948), Exkurse xvii, 'Nennung des Autornamens in Mittelalter' (pp. 505–7).

[3] Schwietering, pp. 3–11; K. Sisam, *Studies in the History of Old English Literature* (Oxford, 1953), pp. 23–7 (in the reprint of 'Cynewulf and his Poetry', originally delivered in 1933).

better to work the author's name into the text. Sometimes it was given quite openly. Few authors went so far as Orm, who named his book after himself:

þiss boc iss nemmnedd *Orrmulum*, forrþi þatt Orrm itt wrohhte,[1]

though a little earlier, in the late twelfth century, Gottfried of Viterbo, playing on the etymological meaning of his name (literally 'God-peace'), wrote:

Nomen autem libri est *Panteon* Gotifredi, sicut a *Lucano* Lucanus et ab *oratio* [H]oratius.[2]

In dream-visions the author himself may be named as the dreamer and/or play a part in the action, as Chaucer does in *The Hous of Fame* and is addressed (l. 729) as 'Geffrey', or as Gower does in the *Confessio Amantis*.[3] But commonly the author's name is not openly stated, partly perhaps to avoid scribal meddling or corruption, but mainly, it would seem, to pay lip-service to the doctrine that literary works should be anonymous, while evading it in practice; also men throughout the Middle Ages took delight in literary puzzles, and to set the reader a puzzle was to excite his interest. In verse copied in verse-lines the means most often used for the 'concealed' introduction of the author's name was the acrostic; it was not easy to corrupt, and not too hard a puzzle to set or to solve. In prose, or in Anglo-Saxon verse (habitually not copied in the manuscripts in verse-lines and intended for listeners rather than readers), the acrostic was unsuitable; hence Cynewulf's use of an analogous device, the introduction into the text of the runes that spell his name.[4] The anagram was also used, especially in the later

---

[1] *Ormulum*, ed. Holt–White, Preface, ll. 1–2.   [2] Curtius, p. 507.
[3] See further G. Kane, *Piers Plowman: The Evidence for Authorship* (London, 1965), section iv, 'Signatures' (pp. 52–70), an authoritative and meticulously documented account of this whole matter.
[4] Sisam, p. 25.

Middle Ages (though for reasons discussed below there were limitations on its suitability), and there were various other cryptic devices; Gower in the prologue to Book I of *Vox Clamantis* uses a sort of syllabic cryptogram of his name,[1] and William Langland in *Piers Plowman*, B-text, XV. 148, plays on the elements that make up his name:

'I haue lyued in londe,' quod I, 'my name is longe wille.'

Normally, though not invariably, the name is given near the beginning or end of a work; and most commonly, in religious works and sometimes also in secular, it is embodied in or comes in the immediate neighbourhood of a request for the readers' prayers, or else is mentioned in a direct prayer by the author himself to God for his mercy.[2]

As the purpose was to communicate the author's name and to solicit prayers on his behalf, a writer who used a cryptogram was careful, as a general rule, not to make it too hard, and might even specially draw attention to it. Though the introduction of rune-names (and in particular meaningless rune-names) into verse would itself put an Anglo-saxon audience on the alert, and in the written texts the runes themselves are used by the scribes and stand out from the surrounding roman letters, Cynewulf in the epilogue to *Elene* adds rhyme to alliteration as a means of heightening attention. In *The Fates of the Apostles*, where he exceptionally disarranges slightly the order of the letters of his name in a rudimentary approach to the anagrammatic technique, he goes out of his way to warn the hearer or reader:

Here a man of good wit who takes pleasure in verse may discover who made this poem: *Feoh* stands last . . .[3]

---

[1] *The Works of John Gower*, ed. G. C. Macaulay, iv. 20–1 (ll. 19–24); see also Macaulay's note, p. 370.   [2] Cf. Schwietering, pp. 7–9.
[3] Sisam's translation (p. 22).

and he then introduces, in order, the runes for WUL and CYN. The two obvious solutions are *Wulcynf*, which is impossible, or *Cynwulf*, which of course is right. In a German work (*The Life of St. Ulrich*, by Albert) the author at the end asks the reader to pray for the man whose name is spelt out by an acrostic at the beginning; in case it had been missed, he is explaining where and how to find it.[1] Gower, in *Vox Clamantis*, introduces his cryptogram by the lines:

> Scribentis nomen si queras, ecce loquela
> Sub tribus implicita versibus inde latet,

and lest the puzzle should still have proved too hard several scribes have added, against the lines that follow, the rubric 'Nota de nomine Iohannis Gower' or similar words. But the case would be different with an author who was writing only for a restricted group, whether a secular author writing for an intimate circle of friends or patrons who did not wish his works, or at least his name, to be more widely published, or the author of a religious work intended only for a single community who wished for its prayers but was content (or thought it more virtuous) to remain unknown to the world at large. Then indeed the cryptogram might be intended to be insoluble by outsiders; initiates who already knew the name might be told where it was hidden and given the chance to solve the puzzle, and if they failed would be taught the trick of doing so; and henceforth the knowledge of the secret—that there was a hidden 'signature' and how it was to be decoded—would be a further bond between the author and his chosen audience, an esoteric mystery distinguishing them from all others into whose hands the book might pass. The tradition of slightly cryptic signature—for undoubtedly it became a tradition—would be being put to a more subtle purpose, to reveal and not to reveal or perhaps

---

[1] Schwietering, p. 8.

rather to record and not to reveal: to record the name for those who would take pleasure in the shared secret and in imparting it to any whom they chose to admit to the fellowship, but to conceal it from the uninstructed, who would see only the 'open' meaning of the word or phrase or sentence and would miss, in whole or in part, the 'closed' or secret meaning.

For a writer who did not wish his (or someone else's) name to be easily discoverable two obviously suitable methods were to play on its meaning, if it had one, or to use the anagram. A play on the meaning of a name would be recognizable by those who already knew it but not by outsiders. A very simple example, only in superficial form a secret,[1] is Chaucer's

> And goode faire White she het;
> That was my lady name ryght.

Anyone who moved in courtly circles could have identified the lady called 'White' who had recently died, but it would not be so obvious to others; and this is an exceptionally transparent instance. As for the anagram, modern readers who meet it chiefly in the context of crossword puzzles may tend to underestimate its inherent difficulty. Three different letters can be arranged in 6 different permutations; six different letters in 720; eight different letters in 40,320; ten different letters in 3,628,800. Of course most of these permutations will be unacceptable as solutions to an anagram because they will be unpronounceable and/or contrary to the orthographic conventions of the language being used and/or meaningless in that language. How many of them will make meaningful words (or possible names) will depend partly on the 'mix' of vowels and consonants, partly on chance. The three letters AEV give, in classical Latin spelling,

---

[1] Since the poem is referred to as *The Deeth of Blaunche the Duchesse* in the prologue to *The Legend of Good Women*, text F, l. 418.

three acceptable permutations out of the six that are possible (*ave*, *Eva*, and *vae*) and a fourth (*vea*) that is conceivable as a Latin word but does not in fact exist; on the other hand there can be few languages in which XYZ will yield anything meaningful.[1] If ten different letters are used, with a reasonable admixture of vowels, obviously it will often happen, in any language, that more than one of the 3,628,800 permutations that are possible will prove to be meaningful. But how is the solver of the puzzle to know which, of equally valid answers, is the one intended? And how, without a computer 'print out', or by going through the same process 'by hand', can he be sure that he has thought of all the possible solutions? When anagrams are used in crossword puzzles the number of letters is usually smaller (perhaps half a dozen), the setter of the puzzle generally gives some hint (if only in a riddling way) of the meaning of the solution, and above all the position of some of the letters in the solution is fixed by the answers to clues running at right angles, so that only one of the possible solutions will fit. But unless there is some limiting factor, the anagram of its nature is essentially ambiguous, and the more letters there are the more astronomically the number of theoretical permutations rises,[2] and the more ambiguous, and difficult to solve, the puzzle becomes. For this reason the anagram is of very little use for the conveyance of an encoded message. A relatively simple anagram, set in a context which limits the possibilities of meaning, may be used as one among other devices in an

[1] But the extraordinary English of *The Ayenbite of Inwit* once has *zyx* for 'six'.

[2] For eleven different letters, 39,916,800; for twelve different letters, 479,001,600; for thirteen different letters, 6,227,020,800. The numbers are of course reduced if the clue includes repeated letters; thus if, in a twelve-letter clue, one letter was repeated thrice and two others twice each, the number of permutations would fall to 19,958,400. But this is still large enough.

amateurish code, but there is a grave risk that any censor or interceptor who reads the encoded message will solve the anagram as readily as the intended recipient. A more complex anagram, however, may be used to convey information to a person with whom there is some previous agreement and who knows what sort of information to expect and who will therefore know which of the possible solutions is the one intended.[1]

The anagram was certainly known in the Middle Ages. Cynewulf's disarrangement of the order of the letters of his name in *The Fates of the Apostles*, giving the last letter first, is, as was remarked above, a rudimentary approach to the anagram; it is to be dated, probably, to the ninth century.[2] Also probably of the ninth century is the poem 'Ave, maris stella' which assumes rather than exactly uses the simple *Ave/Eva* anagram which became conventional:

> Sumens illud 'Ave'
> Gabrielis ore,
> funda nos in pace,
> mutans nomen Evae.[3]

A famous thirteenth-century example is in Roger Bacon's *Epistola de secretis operibus naturae et de nullitate magiae*

---

[1] e.g., a man who expects to receive a message saying in which of a limited number of towns an enemy agency has its headquarters.

[2] Sisam, pp. 2–7.

[3] Dreves *et al.*, *Analecta Hymnica*, li. 140 (no. 123), followed by Raby, *Oxford Book of Medieval Latin Verse* (1959), pp. 94–5 (no. 71). Dreves's text appears to be firmly based on the many manuscripts, some of which are very early. Nevertheless it would be easy to emend the text so as to give an exact anagram in place of the inexact one (presumably still more inexact in the manuscripts, which must have *Eue* for Dreves's *Evae*), thus:

> nos in pace funda,
> mutans nomen 'Eva'.

The rhyme-pattern of the stanza as emended would be that of stanzas 3–5.

(*c.* 1248).[1] Bacon certainly discovered how to make gunpowder; in the *Opus Majus* and *Opus Tertium* (1265–8) he refers to explosive toys, and in the *Opus Tertium* openly describes the ingredients. By then the secret had been revealed, but some twenty years before he was intent on concealing from the public so dangerous a piece of information, and very clearly says so:

Insanus est qui aliquid secretum scribit nisi a vulgo celetur, et ut vix a studiosissimis et sapientibus possit intelligi.[2]

So in chapters ix and x of the *De secretis*, mixed up with a pretended discussion of how the alchemists transmuted base metals into gold, he described how to purify the newly-discovered saltpetre and how to make the requisite quality of charcoal (sulphur being already sufficiently well known), and in chapter xi he gave the formula:

Sed tamen salis petrae *luru vopo vir can utri* et[3] sulphuris, et sic facies tonitrum et corruscationem, si scias artificium; videas tamen utrum loquar in enigmate vel secundum veritatem.

Bacon's correspondent seems to have had some understanding with him and perhaps was able to solve the puzzle (which involves abbreviations as well as anagram), but no one else did, as far as is known, until 1904, when an erudite former lieutenant-colonel of the Royal Artillery, who knew all about gunpowder, a handful of languages (including of course Latin), and a lot about ciphers, succeeded in doing so.[4] Yet Bacon had played fair; the nonsense

[1] *Epistola Fratris Rogeri Baconis De Secretis . . . operâ Iohannis Dee Londinensis . . . restituta* (Hamburg, 1618).

[2] *De secretis*, ch. viii.

[3] In the printed texts the *et* is joined to *utri* (thus *utriet*) but it is not in fact part of the anagram; it is 'in clear' and part of the surrounding text.

[4] Henry W. L. Hime, *Gunpowder and Ammunition: Their Origin and Progress* (London, 1904), pp. 141–62, and (more succinctly and improved

syllables in themselves attract attention, there is his hint
that he may be speaking 'in enigmate', and he even obliquely
indicates, just before, that in the solution, after the abbreviations have been expanded, there are thirty letters. Another
famous scientific instance, much later, was Galileo's message
to Kepler recording his observation in 1610 that Venus
imitates the phases of the moon:

Haec immatura a me jam frustra leguntur, O.Y.

which, rearranged, gives

Cynthiae figuras aemulatur mater amorum.

He doubtless felt very sure that no unauthorized person
would work that one out. The elaborate anagram is in fact
a wonderful device for recording information (so that, for
example, its author may later be able to claim priority of
discovery) without divulging it to anyone except like-
minded intimates who can, if necessary, be sent a key by a
later letter.[1]

Several medieval French poets used the anagram as a
means of 'signing' their works. It was 'if not introduced
at any rate put in vogue'[2] by Nicole de Margival, who uses
it in the conclusion (ll. 2630 ff.) of his *Dit de la Panthère*,[3]

in detail) his article 'Roger Bacon and Gunpowder', in *Roger Bacon:
Essays . . . by various writers on the 7th Centenary of his Birth*, ed. A. G.
Little (Oxford, 1914), pp. 321–35 (esp. pp. 329–31). The solution (which
assumes, legitimately, the equivalence of *u* and *v*) is:

Sed tamen salis petrae r[ecipe] vii part[es], v nov[elle] corul[i], v et sulphuris, et sic facies tonitrum et corruscationem, si scias artificium.

In this, *novelle coruli* means 'of young hazelwood', i.e. charcoal made from
it; Bacon had already named hazelwood as one of two woods specially
suitable for making the proper quality of charcoal. Hime comments that
a mixture of saltpetre 41·2 per cent, charcoal and sulphur each 29·4 per
cent, is indeed explosive 'if you know the trick'—if the saltpetre is pure,
the ingredients thoroughly incorporated, and the powder kept dry and
not subjected to undue pressure.

[1] e.g. a list of numbers indicating the true order of the letters.
[2] Kane, p. 54.   [3] ed. H. A. Todd (S.A.T.F., Paris, 1883).

written between 1290 and 1328. He seems to have had a
lively awareness of the inherent difficulty of the anagram,
for, desiring his puzzle to be solved, he went to great pains
to draw his readers' attention to it. He reiterates, almost to
the point of tediousness, that his 'name and surname' are
discoverable from the passage, repeats the clue *digne amour
li cela*[1] three times and explicitly says that he has done so,
and even gives instructions on how to solve an anagram:
the reader must 'disassemble the letters' and 'afterwards
assemble them correctly', and anyone who does the job
properly 'will not find a letter too many or too few' ('plus
ne mains ne trouvera lettre'). But despite his care, the
instance exemplifies a risk that had to be run by the inventor
of an anagram in a vernacular language without a fixed
orthography; for in the earlier and better manuscript[2] the
scribe wrote *amor* for *amour* in the first two places where the
clue is given, omitting a letter necessary to the solution.[3]
More elaborate anagrams are used by Guillaume de Machaut,[4] who has cryptic signatures in nine of his eleven *dits*
(and an open signature in another) and in some of his other
works. He occasionally used a simple numerical code (in
which *1* stood for *a*, *2* for *b*, and so on), but in the *dits*
normally an anagram giving sometimes only his own name,
sometimes both his and that of a patron or lady. It says much

[1] 'Worthy love concealed him.'

[2] Paris Bibliothèque Nationale f. fr. 24432 (late fourteenth century).

[3] This caused some trouble to the first modern solver of the puzzle,
Paulin Paris (*Histoire littéraire de la France*, xxiii (1856), 732–3), who
supposed that *digne* was written for intended *dingne* and that the solution
was 'Nicole de Marginal ou Margival'. It is odd that he did not think of
working from *amour*, actually given at the third place in the manuscript,
since it directly yields *Margival* instead of *Marginal*; but there seems to
have been some doubt about the form of the surname (see p. 342, n. 2,
below). The correction was made by Todd in his edition.

[4] See E. Hoepffner, 'Anagramme und Rätzelgedichte bei Guillaume
de Machaut', *ZfRP* xxx (1906), 401–13. My account is based on his.

for his ingenuity that the clues are always different. He is obviously influenced by de Margival and gives similar instructions: he states that a name (or names) is hidden, repeats the basic direction to *desassembler* and then *(r)assembler* the letters, and sometimes also repeats the statement that no letters except those in the clue are to be used in the solution. But his methods and his instructions are sometimes more complex: he defines by one means or another which line (or lines) contains the clue and whether words or letters (at the beginning or end of the clue-lines) are to be omitted; in one numerical code he says that certain letters (indicated by numbers) are to be used twice in the solution, and there are anagrams in which it is possible that letters are to be similarly repeated even though he does not say so. Nevertheless, despite his instructions, two of the anagrams are insoluble, probably because of faulty transmission of the text,[1] and a third, in the *Voir Dit*, is 'ambiguous and disputed' because it is not agreed what answer should be looked for.[2] It is significant that Machaut takes advantage of variant forms of his Christian name—*Guillaume*, *Guillemin* or *Guillemins*—as suits his convenience in setting the anagram.[3] We may also glance at another French instance described (but very loosely) as an anagram, in Froissart's *l'Espinette Amoureuse*. In lines 4173–82 he says, openly enough, that there are names concealed elsewhere in the poem in 'quatre lignes moult petites', and scholarly scrutiny has chosen, obviously correctly, the four lines (3380–3) which read:

> *Je han*toie a tempre et tart,
> Dont *frois*, dont chaud, navrés d'un d*art*

[1] These are in the *Dit dou Lion* and the *Dit de la Harpe* (Hoepffner, pp. 406, 407–8). In the former Machaut says that the clue is in the penultimate line of the poem, but it yields no solution; perhaps there has been a loss of lines at the end. In the second the clue-lines are probably corrupt.   [2] Hoepffner, pp. 408–9.   [3] Ibid., pp. 404–6.

> D'amours; et lors de flours petites,
> Violetes et margherites . . .

Jehan Froisart is clear enough, and we are told that his mistress's name is there too, *Margherite . . . de Valenchienes*, but there is no agreement on what her family name (represented by the dots) was. If he gave it, he prudently concealed it better than he did his own surname. But when it is argued that in other poems, in which he does not say that he has concealed his and his mistress's names, he nevertheless did so, still in 'four little lines', I must say that I am very sceptical, especially as not even his own stands out clearly.[1]

For there is, of course, another well established but far from reputable use of the anagram—to enable those who are so minded to discover in a text, sacred or profane, a meaning which suits their purposes but is not there on the surface: cabbalists searching for hidden meanings in the Hebrew scriptures, Baconians intent on claiming Shakespeare's works for, as they think, a greater man, and a long succession of cranks, mostly but not entirely religious and literary, of assorted shapes and sizes. Observing them, the cautious scholar may well decide that the only way to avoid imputations of softheadedness is to have nothing to do with cryptograms and especially with cryptic signatures. Yet they

---

[1] See Normand R. Cartier, 'Anagrams in Froissart's Poetry', *Medieval Studies*, xxv (1963), 100–8. The names are in every case made up by Cartier by assembling letters (with two instances of allowing a single letter, *h*, to be counted twice) from a group of four lines, chosen because it provides the requisite letters. Cartier himself grants (p. 106) that he is picking out 40 letters from sections of text consisting of 100 letters 'more or less', and that there are other quatrains in Froissart's works *and in those of other poets* in which the same thing could be done. The chances are obviously high that somewhere in a poem of reasonable length there will occur four consecutive lines containing, among about 100 letters, the 40 that are needed, especially if the letters can be chosen from the larger stock and arranged in order as the solver pleases, without any sort of control.

undoubtedly exist, and in the past have been solved to the increase of our knowledge. How then should a scholar proceed? If, as in the case cited from Froissart, there is a direct statement or a very plain hint that somewhere in a literary work a name (or names) has been hidden 'in four little lines', one is obviously entitled to hunt through the work until four lines are found that will yield names; and if it becomes apparent that the author has hidden the names not in accordance with the conventions of some established puzzle-form but in an arbitrary way of his own (as Froissart did), the investigator is no doubt entitled to adopt arbitrary means of solution—though he must then expect to find it hard to convince other people that his solutions are the only possible ones. But I am concerned with the case where there is no statement that a name has been hidden, and yet the scholar suspects that it may have been. He must then be content to be bound by very strict rules, not arbitrarily formulated but based on common sense and experience.

(1) He must look for the signature only in the places where it is most likely to have been hidden, at the beginning or end of the work; and if there is a request for the reader's prayers, then within that request or immediately next to it. He must not pick some completely unremarkable line out of the middle of the work, just because it suits his purpose, and allege that it contains a hidden signature. This does not mean, of course, that when, in Passus XV of the B-text of *Piers Plowman*, we find the words *londe*, *longe*, and *wille* staring up at us from the page, we are obliged to avert our eyes just because the line is neither at the beginning nor at the end of the work; but I do not regard this as being really a hidden signature— it is almost an open one, at least for anyone who has heard of the ascription of the poem, on other grounds, to William Langland.[1]

[1] But of course it would not be obvious to someone who did not know

(2) If it is alleged that the signature is hidden by means of a recognized type of cryptogram or word-puzzle, the solution proposed must be in strict accord with the principles of that type of puzzle, and the slightest deviation will call for reasoned and convincing justification. An acrostic must be formed by the *initial* letters[1] of lines (or perhaps, exceptionally, of the second halves of lines in which there is a regular and well-marked caesura), and the lines must form a successive group, uninterrupted by others beginning with letters not used in the solution, i.e. the solver must not pick letters to suit himself from a larger stock; for it is of the nature of an acrostic that it should be directly legible by any reader who casts his eye vertically down the row of initial letters.[2] If it is suspected that the name has been anagrammatized, all the letters of the alleged clue must be used in the name. Cf. Kane, pp. 69–70, who describes the signature as 'not wholly open'.

[1] An arguable exception would be when the initial word of a line began with *h*; in this case the second letter might be the one that was intended to be read, for in the Middle Ages there was uncertainty whether *h* was to be counted as a letter (thus in alphabetical lists names beginning with *H* are often entered under the following vowel, e.g. *Hester* and *Holofernes* under *E* and *O* respectively). Moreover scribes often added (or omitted) *h* contrary to the intention of the author.

[2] For this reason the acrostic is a very simple word-puzzle, of no use (as I have already implied) to a man who really wants to hide a name. I should be prepared, at least in theory, to allow the possibility that a truly secret signature might combine the method of the acrostic with that of the anagram, i.e. the letters of the name might be given in a disarranged order at the beginning of verse-lines. But in this case it would be more than ever necessary to insist that the letters should be taken from the *initial* letters of *consecutive* lines, not chosen arbitrarily from a larger stock. The acrostic is not hard to write, and a poet who can please himself in what order he takes the letters of a name has a much easier task than if he is making up a normal acrostic and has to take the letters in a predetermined order. If one believes that the solver is allowed to include non-initial letters or to pick the letters needed for his solution from a larger stock (by arguing that the poet has spread them over a larger group of lines), then one can find almost anything that one wants to, anywhere—as Ethel Seaton did.

the solution—and I would add 'and no others', unless it can be plausibly argued, as in the case of Roger Bacon's anagram, that abbreviation has also been used to make the solution still more difficult, or that it was common practice, at the date in question, to use twice in a solution a letter given only once in the clue. The occasional use by poets of looser and more irregular types of anagram cannot be cited by a scholar who is arguing that there is a hidden signature of which no hint has been given by the original author and therefore no instructions on where to find it or how to solve it; only the demonstration that there is a strict anagram can begin to be convincing in such a case.

(3) There should be something about the line or sentence in which it is alleged that the clue comes to justify this assumption: some special feature of its textual history or its structure or its meaning. It should not be a sentence that arises quite naturally out of the context, was obviously there from the beginning, and has nothing remarkable about it except that it happens to suit the purpose of the would-be puzzle-solver. A good example of the application of this principle is Kane's careful demonstration[1] that the signature-line in *Piers Plowman* 'fails to mesh neatly, dramatically, and inevitably into the structure of meaning', is 'either deeply obscure or not particularly meaningful', and 'taken at its least debatable, literal sense . . . conveys no information which the reader and the personage addressed do not already have, except the Dreamer's nickname and a vague reference to his age'; and his conclusion that 'its form was dictated by another consideration than the advancement of the sense'. These are arguments directed to the particular instance; but the principle is of general validity.

(4) In the case of a truly hidden signature, the name must be known from an outside source and there must be some

[1] pp. 65–9.

reason at least to suspect that it is that of the author.[1] The scholar does not say 'Here is a cryptogram and see how clever I am—I have got from it a name nobody knew before.' He says rather 'I think this is a cryptogram and that it can be so solved as to confirm the suspicion, or the tradition, that the author was so-and-so'—just as Lieutenant-Colonel Hime, knowing already the ingredients of gunpowder, that it was necessary to state their proportions, and what these proportions should be, was able to propose a solution of Roger Bacon's anagram which fitted the grammatical context and gave a credible formula, and by so doing confirmed that Bacon knew, by the date of the *De secretis*, how to make gunpowder. It is of course true that Cynewulf the poet is known only from his runic signatures (though we know from other sources that this was an Anglo-saxon name), and the same applies in some cases of authors whose names are known only from acrostic signatures; but these are not really *hidden* signatures—they are signatures left for the observant to notice, with little or nothing cryptic about them. Paulin Paris, the first modern scholar to solve the well-advertised anagram in *Le Dit de la Panthère*, already knew the name Nicole de Margival as that of the author of another poem.[2] Hoepffner points out that in Machaut's more complex anagrams involving the name of a dedicatee as well as his own, the difficulty of solution (because of the

---

[1] The same, *mutatis mutandis*, applies in the case of the name of a patron or mistress which it is thought may be hidden in a literary work.

[2] See *Histoire littéraire de la France*, xxiii (1856), 723, and the cross-reference there given to p. 279, with its mention of 'une autre pièce *des Trois mors et des trois vis* . . . d'un certain Nicolas de Margival, poëte picard, dont nous ne connaissons point d'autre composition'. Evidently Paris had not yet solved the anagram when he wrote the earlier passage, though it is odd that he did not revise it in proof. The unique copy of this poem on *Les trois Mors et les trois Vis* (now Paris MS. Bib. Nat. f. fr. 25566) has a rubric ascribing it to 'maistres Nicholes de Margiual' (misread *Marginal* in an early edition); see Todd, pp. xxix, xxxi.

number of permutations that are possible) is such that certainty can be attained only if the second name is known from some other evidence, either historical indications (*Andeutungen*) or an open reference in the poems them-selves.[1] We do not know Langland's name from the 'not wholly open' signature in the B-text at XV. 148; we know it from external evidence,[2] and use the internal evidence as proof of the accuracy of the external.

It is my argument that there is a hidden signature in *Ancrene Wisse* and that the author intended that no outsider should ever be able to decipher it. But by a series of strange chances that he could not have foreseen a name has been recorded with a brief but telling description of the status of its bearer. The nuns of Limebrook made, and kept up-to-date until the early sixteenth century, a list of founder's kin on which they inscribed the entry 'Brianus de Lingan Canonicus secularis monesterii de wigmore'; and by a happy chance the list was not lost when the priory was dissolved but fell into the hands of a late sixteenth-century antiquary interested in genealogy, who copied it into his commonplace book, and this in its turn was not lost, as it easily might have been, but passed into the Harleian collection and thence to the British Museum. By another chance that no man in the Middle Ages is likely to have foreseen, enough of the public records of the time have survived for us to be able to date, with considerable accuracy, the deaths of Brian of Lingen's father and elder brother and so to determine the period when he himself lived. By yet another chance—and he would perhaps regard this as the strangest of all—a vernacular book written for a small group of women in a remote part of England has survived in multiple copies and has become the object of long-continued and expert scholarly scrutiny, so that by techniques which he

---

[1] Hoepffner, pp. 406–7.   [2] Kane, pp. 26–51.

could not have foreseen but which, as a man of scholastic training, he would doubtless be able to understand if they were explained to him, it has been possible to define with increasing accuracy in what dialect and therefore where it was written, at what date, in which religious house, and by what sort of man. And in the end all the unforeseen chances were bound to come together: somebody, inspecting the list in the Harleian MS. and recognizing its nature, would see in it the name of Brian of Lingen and wonder why it should be recorded with so particular a description appended, and would realize that this was the right sort of man, at the right time and place, to have written *Ancrene Wisse*—especially if he also had reason to believe that there was a close connection between the work (and therefore its author) and Limebrook Priory. Then the knowledge which was intended to be possessed only by insiders will become a strong suspicion in the mind of an outsider, and the hidden signature which can be deciphered only by someone who already has this knowledge becomes no longer safe; if the hypothesis is correct—but only if it is correct—the code can be broken.

Ancrene Wisse, as originally written, ended with a prayer to God to guard, gladden, and comfort the author's 'dear sisters', and with a doxology, followed by a brief request to them for prayer on his behalf:

Ase ofte as ȝe habbeð ired eawiht heron, greteð þe leafdi wið an Aue for him þet swonc herabuten.[1]

But to this he later appended an additional and final sentence, which in the spelling of the Corpus MS. is

Inoh meaðful ich am, þe bidde se lutel.

That this was an afterthought has not generally been recog-

[1] Cleopatra MS., f. 198ᵛ/18–20; Corpus MS., f. 117b/12–14 (Morton, p. 430). My text follows Corpus.

nized, for it is present in the Nero MS. and therefore in Morton's text, which has been taken as the standard. Nevertheless it is certainly an addition, first made in the Cleopatra MS., as anyone can see who inspects the manuscript or looks at a facsimile of its final page;[1] it is written in the hand of 'scribe B' (i.e. the author), crowded in at the end of the last line of the text (which was the last ruled line on the last page of a quire) and in the right-hand margin, and to make room for it he had to erase pen-work by the original scribe.[2] It was obviously an addition on which he was intent; and I think one may also conclude that he wanted to make it appear, as far as possible, an integral part of the text, since much more easily, and in accordance with his normal practice, he could have written it in the left-hand (outer) margin, where there was plenty of space, and marked it for insertion after *abuten* by oblique strokes either above or below the line.[3] The addition was adopted in the definitive revised text of the Corpus MS.,[4] and was also taken up, ultimately from the Cleopatra MS., by the Nero MS.[5] But it is not in any other text which gives the ending of the Rule:[6] it is lacking in the Vitellius French version (F) as

[1] See, in my edition, the illustration facing p. 316.

[2] Probably decorative scroll-work filling the end of the line, and the word *Explicit* in the margin.

[3] Cf. the two additions made on f. 195; see the illustration facing p. 309 of my edition.

[4] In Corpus the sentence is followed by the scribe's request for the prayers of an individual (see p. 291, above), but this is preceded by the word *Explicit* marking the end of the author's text.

[5] Though Nero gives essentially the basic text of the Rule, it has some additions, and its readings show frequent contamination, direct or indirect, by those of Cleopatra. At four points (apart from the ending) Nero adopts minor additions made by the author ('scribe B') in correcting the text of Cleopatra; see my edition, pp. cxx–cxxi.

[6] In the Vernon MS. (V) and the Latin translation (L) the text of Part VIII is, for different reasons, fragmentary and the ending is missing. The extracts of the Caius version (G) do not include any passages from Part VIII, and the Royal version (R) is based only on Parts II and III.

well as in C as originally written, whence it follows that it was not in their common ancestor, the very good and early manuscript γ, almost certainly a direct copy of β; and it is also lacking in the Titus MS. (T), the Trinity French version (S), and the Pepys version (P),[1] so that it is a reasonable deduction that it was not present in η. The concurrence of γ and η, and the simple physical fact that in C the sentence is added over erasure by the revising author, can leave no doubt that it was not present in β, the fair copy of the text as originally written. If there is a hidden signature anywhere in *Ancrene Wisse* it must be in this sentence deliberately added at the very end, in expansion of the request for the readers' prayers or more precisely for an Ave each time the book was read. It is a sentence with a special textual history at the very point where a signature, if there is one, is most to be expected.

It must at once be granted that there is nothing to attract attention in the sense of the addition, for it fits perfectly into the context; and as far as I know it never has attracted attention. It was not meant to. But if, knowing that it was an afterthought, one looks critically at its shape, then it is more suggestive than it seems at first sight. 'Moderate enough I am, who ask for so little.' Yes, moderate indeed; but are you also being very clever, and perhaps rather pleased with your cleverness, in a way not perfectly humble? 'John Smith I am, who ask for so little.' The words that matter must be those two at the beginning; the sentence is formed for them, and if there is a secret they hide it. But plainly, in that case, we must base our examination on the spelling neither of the Corpus MS. (*inoh meaðful*) nor of the Nero MS. (*inouh*

---

[1] The text of the passage in P is, as usual, freely rewritten, which reduces the value of its evidence; nevertheless it includes an expanded version (ed. Påhlsson, 200/30–201/3) of the sentence asking for an Ave each time the book is read, and nothing at all to correspond to the comment on the moderation of the request.

meðful), but on that used by the author himself in revising the Cleopatra MS., *inoh meðful*;[1] for if the form of the words is significant for the solution, only the author's form can be considered.

I believe that *inoh meðful* is indeed a signature, and that it works on two levels, both semantic and formal. Any scholastically trained man of the author's time would have accepted that a name had, if not a meaning, at least an 'interpretation'. Sometimes, in the course of biblical exegesis, a writer may say that a name *significat* ('means') such-and-such, but the more usual expression is *interpretatur* ('is interpreted'); the schoolmen were aware of the grammatical commonplace that though an ordinary word has a meaning, or connotation, known to all intelligent users of a language, a name has strictly only a denotation, identifying the person(s) who bear it. But they also accepted that a name had a more esoteric meaning or 'interpretation' (or commonly a set of alternative 'interpretations') known to specialists in that branch of knowledge, which they could look up in the appropriate works of reference, particularly the alphabetical lists of *Interpretationes nominum hebraicorum*—just as the ordinary educated modern accepts that all words have etymologies worked out by specialists and discoverable by reference to a dictionary. The parallel is closer than it may seem, for study of the lists of 'interpretations' shows clearly that they were based on a sort of etymological principle. The main lines of an 'interpretation' were determined by the root syllable, or

[1] OE (WS) *mæð*, Anglian **með*, should be spelt *með* in the 'AB language', as in any Anglian dialect. The spelling *meað*, though regular in the Corpus MS. and in MS. Bodley 34, both in the simplex and in its derivatives, is contrary to expectation, one of only three words (the others being *breað* and *deadbote*) in which the spelling *ea* is used instead of *e* without any possible phonetic reason. The author ('scribe B') not only used *meðful* in the added sentence on f. 198ᵛ of the Cleopatra MS., but also *meðfulliche* in two minor revisions on f. 192; it was apparently his normal spelling.

at least the initial syllable; names with the same beginning normally have similar 'interpretations', based on the meaning, real or supposed, of the root.[1] But the ending also played a part, modifying the basic meaning; the forms *Paulus* and *Saulus* differ in their 'interpretations', and differ in the same way, from those of *Paul* and *Saul*; and the 'interpretations' of feminine forms of names differ in consistent ways from those of the corresponding masculine forms. Non-biblical names were also assumed to have etymologies and therefore a basic significance—a reasonable enough assumption indeed, even if the etymology actually proposed (*[H]oratius* from *oratio*) was often absurd. Now the author of *Ancrene Wisse*, as we have seen, was familiar with this doctrine and was indeed a rather sophisticated exponent of it; the name *Oloferne* 'Holofernes', he tells us,[2] is not only, 'according to the interpretation' (*secundum interpretationem*), 'infirmans uitulum saginatum', which he would have found in most of the medieval lists of *interpretationes*,[3] but also, 'according to the etymology' (*secundum nominis ethimologiam*), 'olens in inferno', for which I have not yet found a source, though obviously there must be one, probably in some text-book. He would undoubtedly have thought that any name had an etymology, if only it could be discovered.

[1] Ultimately the medieval lists of interpretations derive from sources compiled by men who knew Hebrew; but this is not to say, of course, that the etymologies of the names, and their basic meanings, were necessarily correctly identified, and in the medieval lists there is obviously a great superstructure of pseudo-science.

[2] Corpus MS., f. 37b/7–12 (Morton, p. 136).

[3] It is not in what seem to be the earliest forms of the medieval lists: Bodleian MS. Auct. D. inf. 2. 1, f. 461 (a list beginning 'Aaron mons fortitudinis'); Bodleian MS. Auct. D. inf. 2. 3, f. 363ᵛ (a second, different, list beginning 'Aaron mons fortitudinis'); Paris MS. Bib. Nat. f. lat. 393, f. 3ᵛ (a third list beginning 'Aaron mons fortitudinis'). It is however in Paris MS. Bib. Nat. f. lat. 37⁴, ff. 332ᵛ and 354 (a fourth list beginning 'Aaron mons fortitudinis'); Bodleian MSS. Auct. D. 5. 6, f. 319, and Auct. D. 4. 8, f. 693ᵛ (related versions of a list beginning 'Aaron mons

The name *Brian*, which was common in England in the Middle Ages—and which was so regularly borne by the eldest son of the family (later known as the Harleys) which held Brampton, just over three miles north-west of Wigmore, that the place became known as Brampton Bryan—is of Celtic origin and ultimately derived from British and Irish *bre* 'hill' (< *brigā*).[1] But the author of *Ancrene Wisse* could not possibly have known this; even if he spoke Welsh (which is unlikely), he would not have associated *bre* 'hill' with *Brian* or the Latinized form *Brianus*. He would expect an etymon to have a more obvious superficial resemblance to its derivative, and as *Brianus* seems a genuine enough Latin form (i.e. is not an obvious Latinization of a vernacular name) he would look for an etymon in Latin itself, the learned and ancient language of the Western world. His whole training would make him think first of Latin for any name that was not obviously English or French.

There was in late Latin a noun *bria*, first recorded in the Christian writer Arnobius Afer (*c.* 300), which means, according to the *Glossarium Philoxeni* (*c.* 500), a sort of wine-vessel (εἶδος ἀγγείου). In the Middle Ages it is fairly commonly recorded, and the *Revised Medieval Latin Word-List* gives it as occurring in British Latin from *c.* 1194 to *c.* 1470 (*Catholicon Anglicanum*).[2] Its primary sense was

fortis'); Paris MS. Bib. Nat. f. lat. 227, f. 688ᵛ (a list beginning 'Aaron mons fortis', but blended with a list of the type of Bodleian MS. Auct. D. inf. 2. 1); Bodleian MS. Auct. D. 5. 8, f. 18 (a list beginning 'Aaz apprehensus'); the standard 'Aaz apprehendens' list, e.g. Bodleian MSS. Auct. D. 5. 21, f. 384, and Auct. D. 4. 10, f. 18; Bodleian MS. Auct. D. 5. 18, f. 325 (a list beginning 'Aad testificans').

[1] E. G. Withycombe, *Oxford Dictionary of English Christian Names* (2nd edn., 1950), pp. 50–1; J. Morris Jones, *A Welsh Grammar* (Oxford, 1913), § 65. ii (3).

[2] Mr. R. E. Latham, the editor of the *Word-List*, has kindly sent me the references to Gerald of Wales, cited below. He adds that among later instances are two which are 'apparently quoting earlier sources': Fordun,

still 'a measure (especially for wine)', but it had also developed a secondary abstract sense, 'measure, moderation', as in the (now obsolete) Italian word *bria* in the phrase *fuor di bria* 'beyond bounds, beyond measure'.[1] Évrard (Eberhard) of Béthune (*d.* 1212), in the versified rules of usage of his misnamed *Grecismus*, defines the word thus:

> Hæc *bria* si dicas, modus est; vas Romipetarum
> Hic *bria*, quo vinum sibi distribuunt, quasi *libra*.[2]

Bria, if you use it as a feminine, means 'moderation'; if as a masculine, the bowl of pilgrims to Rome, in which they serve wine to each other, like [the word] *libra* [in its sense 'a measure for liquids'].

This makes the distinction of sense, somewhat surprisingly, correspond to a distinction of gender, but there is other evidence to the same effect. The abstract sense is used several times by Gerald of Wales, but it is significant of the rarity of the word that he is always careful to define it by some addition: 'extra briam . . . sobrietatis poni';[3] 'debriatus et extra modestiæ briam longe positus';[4] 'vino . . . trans modestiam omnem et sobrietatis metam, ultraque justæ mensuræ briam . . . dato';[5] 'cum potibus quoque, tam vino videlicet quam cervisia, forte trans briam omnem et modestiam sumptis'.[6] It is also significant that in each case he uses

Scotichronicon, vi. 43, referring to bishop Abel of St. Andrews (1253), and Abbot Whethamstede's *Register* (Rolls Series), i. 157.

[1] Alfred Hoare, *An Italian Dictionary* (Cambridge, 1925), who gives *fuor di misura* as an equivalent, and glosses 'beyond bounds'; Barbara Reynolds, *Cambridge Italian Dictionary* (1962), who glosses 'beyond measure'.

[2] Eberhardi Bethuniensis *Græcismus*, ed. J. Wrobel (Bratislava, 1881), xii. 345–6.

[3] *Gemma Ecclesiastica* (*c.* 1198), ed. J. S. Brewer (Rolls Series, 1862), p. 260.

[4] Ibid., p. 303.

[5] *Speculum Ecclesiæ* (1215–18), ed. J. S. Brewer (Rolls Series, 1873), p. 203.   [6] Ibid., p. 209.

it in the context of sobriety (or the opposite, inebriation), for
it is clear that it was very largely a 'dictionary' word,
especially cited as the supposed etymon of *ebrius* and *sobrius*.
The tradition was ultimately derived from the mid fourth-
century Latin grammarian Charisius,[1] and was well established by the later twelfth century. Peter Lombard (d.
1160), in his *Commentary on the Epistle to the Romans*,
says (apparently implying the same distinction of gender as
Évrard of Béthune):

Briam enim genere masculino dicimus calicem aptum potationi,
a quo dicitur *ebrietas*, quæ est nimia potatio vini.[2]

Ugutio of Pisa in his *Derivationes*, completed 'about the end
of the twelfth century',[3] has an entry

Item a *brachos* hec *bria* est; ubi enim nimietas est, mensura non
est. Et componitur *ebrius*, *-a*, *-um*, [ex] *extra briam*, id est extra
mensuram positus uel bibens; unde *ebriosus* . . . et *ebrietas* et hec
ebriositas.[4]

This again makes the abstract *bria* feminine and in its use of
'extra briam . . . positus' parallels Gerald's use of *poni* and
positus in the first two examples cited from him above.
Guilielmus Brito, in his *Summa* or *Expositiones difficiliorum
verborum* of about the mid thirteenth century,[5] derives
sobrius from *se* and *bria*, 'que dicit "mensura", unde *sobrius*

[1] i.e. Flavius Sosipater Charisius. See *Charisii Artis Grammaticae
Libri V*, ed. C. Barwick (2nd corr. imp., Leipzig, 1964), p. 105: '*Eber*
et *ebriacus* ne dixeris. *Bria* enim est vas vinarium, unde *ebrius* et *ebria*
dicitur, *ebriosus*que et *ebriosa*, sicut a *negotio negotiosus* et *negotiosa*. Cui
contrarium est *sobrius* . . .'
[2] Migne, *Pat. Lat.*, cxci, col. 1510, where *brian* is printed for *briam*.
[3] Lloyd W. Daly and B. A. Daly, 'Some Techniques in Medieval
Latin Lexicography', *Speculum*, xxxix (1964), 235.
[4] Text conflated from Bodleian MSS. e Museo 96, f. 48[vb], and Bodley
376, f. 19[va].
[5] It was 'already being cited by Jean Gilles about 1270 and by Roger
Bacon in 1272' (Daly, p. 237).

quasi *se brius*, id est secum habens *briam*, id est mensuram'.[1]
Janua (Giovanni di Genova, also known as Balbus), in his
Catholicon completed on 7 March 1286,[2] follows Ugutio
almost word for word in deriving *bria* from *bracos*,[3] and says
that *ebrius* is compounded of *e* and *bria*, 'id est extra mensuram bibens'.[4] In Germany Caesarius of Heisterbach (*c.*
1180–1240) derives *ebrietas* from '*extra briam*, id est super
mensuram', and Albertus Magnus O.P., bishop of Ratisbon
(*c.* 1200–80), similarly explains *sobrietas* as being 'quasi
sub bria, quod est mensura'; *ebrius*, he says, is applicable
'non quod multum potet, sed quando est extra hanc *briam*
sive mensuram', and, again, in Latin a man is described
as *ebrius* 'qui extra mensuram bibit, quia βρία Græce Latine
dicitur mensura'.[5] The English Dominican Ralph Bocking
(d. 1270), in his *Life* of St. Richard of Chichester, also has
the derivation of *sobrius* 'quasi *sub bria* constitutus, id est, sub
mensura'.[6]

It is evident that by the thirteenth century the 'etymology' of *ebrius* and *sobrius* was a scholastic commonplace,
and it necessarily brought with it the knowledge of the
'hard word' *bria* meaning *mensura*, *modus*, or *modestia*, the
currency of which in early thirteenth-century British Latin
is attested by Gerald of Wales. But *bria* would provide an
even more obvious etymology for *Brianus*: as *Romanus*
from *Roma*, *capellanus* from *capella*, the name *Silvanus* (and
later the adjective *silvanus*) from *silva*, so *Brianus* from *bria*.
A man who accepted that the etymology of *Olofernes* was
olens in inferno would have no reason to jib at so sensible a

---

[1] Bodleian MS. Douce 239, f. 75rb.   [2] Daly, p. 237.
[3] Bodleian MS. D'Orville 44, f. 201vb.   [4] Ibid., f. 308rb.
[5] *Mittellateinisches Wörterbuch*, Band I A–B (Munich, 1967), s.v. *bria*
f. 'mensura (vini), (Wein-) Mass'. There is no warrant for Albertus's
guess, in the last of these citations, that *bria* was a Greek word; but
evidently he did not regard it as an ordinary Latin word.
[6] *Acta Sanctorum*, ix. 291 (under *Tertia Aprilis*).

derivation as *Brianus* from *bria*, which is formally unexceptionable—there is indeed nothing at all wrong with it except that it does not happen to be right, and it can be disproved only by knowledge of the history of languages and of names that the Middle Ages did not possess. But if *Brianus* was taken as a derivative of *bria* it would, in form, be adjectival, and inevitably its 'interpretation' would have to be *mensurabilis, modestus*, 'moderate'.[1] My name is Brian, *Brianus sum*; *Brianus interpretatur 'modestus'*; therefore *meðful ich am*.

This is the main reason for suggesting that the sentence added at the end of *Ancrene Wisse* contains a hidden signature —that the word *meðful* coincides in sense with the only reasonable 'interpretation' of the name *Brianus* that could occur to a medieval scholar. But merely to hint at the author's Christian name would not be enough for full identification; some indication of his surname, or territorial designation, might also be thought necessary—just as Langland, in addition to giving the dreamer's name as Will (two or three times in each of the three versions of *Piers Plowman*), also plays once (in the B-version) on the elements of his surname. Moreover the phrase used in *Ancrene Wisse* is not simply *meðful ich am*, but *inoh meðful ich am*. If there is a hidden signature, *inoh* may be part of it. Its purpose, in the supposed puzzle, could only be to supply additional letters, for it does not aid—indeed it slightly hinders—the apparent play on meaning; and this suggests the possibility, which I must at once own cannot be fully demonstrated, that there may also be an anagram to make more precise the designation of the author. One way of rearranging the letters of *inoh meðful* is *of linðehum*, which is in form a territorial designation but will not do as it stands, for it is impossible to conceive of a Middle English or Old French place-name *Linðehum*. But

[1] The alternative possible meaning, 'appertaining to a drinking-vessel', would hardly be considered.

it is different if one replaces *ð* by *th*; for *Linthehum* would be, in the 'AB language', a characteristic development of an Old English place-name **Lindhegum*. In this dialect, as in the West Midlands more generally, final consonants were often unvoiced, and in particular /nd/ and /ld/ frequently became /nt/ and /lt/ at the end not only of words (as in *hunt* 'hound') but also of the first element of compounds and derivatives: so, among other examples, *schentfule* (Corpus MS., ff. 42b/24, 53a/7, etc.) beside *schendfule* (f. 33a/24, etc.); *golthord(es)* (ff. 29a/25–6, 29b/4, 41a/16, 17, 23, 25, 26) beside *goldhord* (f. 41a/14, two lines before one of the instances of -*lt*-); and, in successive lines, *iblintfeallet* p.p. 'blindfolded' beside *blindfeallede* pa. t. (f. 28a/16–17).[1] But it is also a regular and distinctive feature of the orthography of the 'AB language' that it uses *h* (not *ȝ*) for OE *g* in all words in which it had not been vocalized, and particularly in those in which, in OE, it had represented the voiced back palatal spirant [ɣ], as in *wahes* 'walls' (OE *wagas*), *drehen* 'endure' (OE **dregan*), *halhen* 'saints' (OE *halgan*);[2] and this was certainly characteristic of the spelling not only of the scribe of the Corpus MS., but of the author himself, who uses it regularly in his corrections and additions to the Cleopatra MS.[3] If, therefore, the dative plural ending -*um* was preserved unaltered, as it often was in place-names,[4]

---

[1] Cf. d'Ardenne, *Ste Iuliene*, pp. 196–7 (§§ 33–4). For such forms in the Cleopatra MS. see my edition, pp. lxxiv (the original scribe) and cxxxi ('scribe B', i.e. the author). The form *hunt* 'hound' occurs in *Ste Katerine* (ed. Einenkel, l. 1859; MS. Bodley 34, f. 12ᵛ).

[2] Cf. d'Ardenne, p. 173 (§ 2). This use of *h* for intervocalic *g* began in OE; Campbell, § 447, says that it occurs especially in the OE *Boethius*. The closest parallel to **hegum* (with *ĕ* before *g* but a back vowel after) would be the comparative *fehere* 'fairer', which develops as if from an OE (Mercian) **fegura* < Gmc. **fagrōzon* with abnormal loss of *r* (probably after the *z* had become *r*; cf. loss of /r/ in /febjuəri/ for *February*), where the normal form would be **fegerra* (WS *fægerra*).

[3] See my edition, pp. cxxvi–vii.

[4] See A. H. Smith, *English Place-Name Elements*, Part II, pp. 224–6,

OE *Lindhegum* would give, in the 'AB language', *Lindhe-hum* as its direct descendant and *Linthehum* as a common variant.[1] But it is argued in Appendix II, below (pp. 380–90) that the etymologies of the place-names Limebrook and Lingen are such that we must assume, in Old English, the variants *Lindbrōc* and *Lindhegum* beside *Lindga brōc* and *Lindgum hegum* (later remodelled as *Lin(d)ge hein*), whence Middle English *Lingebrok* and *Lingein*; if this is valid, then *of Linthehum* would be a variant, in the spelling of the 'AB language', of the normal Middle English *of Lingein*, and *inoh meðful* would be an anagram (with substitution of *ð* for *th*) of a phrase meaning 'of Lingen'.

I said above (pp. 340–1) that any deviation from the strict rules of the type of cryptogram alleged to have been used calls for 'reasoned and convincing justification'. Obviously a solution which assumes that *ð* may be replaced by *th* is such a deviation. Nevertheless it is not arbitrary to take *th* and *ð* as equivalents. The spelling *th* was used for [þ] and [ð] in the earliest Anglo-saxon documents, but it had

---

s.v. *-um*. Examples are Dilwyn, Herefordshire (*Dilun* 1138, *Dilum* 1193 < OE *dīlgum, dīglum*); Stockham, Cheshire (*Stoccum c.* 1173 and 1288, *Stockum* 1288); Halam, Notts. (*Halum* 1198, 1331 < OE *healum* 958); Downham, Lancs. (*Dounum* 1251 < OE *Dūnum*). But the ending *-um* also survived in certain old dative plurals used as adverbs and therefore isolated from the ME inflexional system; the obvious example is *whilum*, *whilom* < OE *hwīlum*, but there are others, e.g. Langland's *litlum and lytlum*, B-text (ed. Skeat), XV. 599.

[1] From the case of *golthord*, which has *-ld-* only once, beside *-lt-* seven times and once also in MS. Bodley 34 (the only occurrence there, in *Ste Margarete*), it seems indeed that it was more common for unvoicing to take place than to fail before /h/; cf. d'Ardenne, p. 197 (§ 34). There is a similar preponderance of *-lt-* in *goltsmið* (Corpus, f. 49a/1, 15, 64a/3) beside *goldsmið* (f. 49a/14); Tolkien's text is in error in printing *goldsmið* at f. 49a/15. Corpus has only *hondhwile* (thrice), but Cleopatra has *honthwile* (ff. 38ᵛ/3, 60ᵛ/7) beside *hondhwile* (f. 61ᵛ/3), and MS. Bodley 34 has *honthwile* at *Ste Katerine* (ed. Einenkel), ll. 1617 and 1942 (ff. 10ᵛ and 13); this however is not the same case as before the simple aspirate.

almost entirely disappeared from later Old English usage,[1] and its reintroduction was probably due to Anglo-Norman scribes,[2] though where they got it from is unclear.[3] It occurs occasionally in Domesday Book both for initial [þ] and for medial [ð].[4] In Anglo-Norman it is used to express the sounds [ð] and more rarely [þ] in the twelfth-century Hildesheim MS. (from St. Albans) of the *Vie de St. Alexis* and in British Museum MS. Cotton Vespasian B. x[1] (*c.* 1200) of the *Voyage of St. Brendan*.[5] In official records of the twelfth century (written by Anglo-Norman scribes) *th* occurs in spellings of place-names chiefly in documents originating from, or dealing with places in, the east of the country: Zachrisson says that there is 'a strong and, no doubt, intentional tendency' to denote initial [þ] by *th* in the Leicestershire survey (1124–9) and the Northampton-

---

[1] It occurs, however, in the interlinear gloss *thollan* (marginal gloss *þollan*) on f. 39ᵛ of Brussels MS. Bibliothèque Royale 1650 of Aldhelm's prose *De Laude Virginitatis*; see K. Schiebel, *Die Sprache der altenglischen Glossen zu Aldhelms Schrift 'De Laude Virginitatis'* (dissertation; Halle, 1907), p. 40. N. R. Ker, *Catalogue of Manuscripts containing Anglo-Saxon* (Oxford, 1957), pp. 6–7, dates the glossing hands to the first half of the eleventh century. The manuscript is almost certainly from Abingdon (Ker, p. 3). Conceivably the interlinear gloss was copied from some much earlier manuscript.

[2] Cf. Sweet, *History of English Sounds*, § 600. Zachrisson's view (*Anglo-Norman Influence on English Place-Names* (Lund, 1909), p. 116) that the use of *th* for [þ] and [ð] in Anglo-Norman manuscripts may 'very well have been borrowed from English' is most unlikely, since it was virtually unknown in later OE.

[3] It might be worth considering whether it was due to Welsh (or possibly Breton) influence, since Old and Medieval Welsh used *th* (and also *t* after *r*) to represent [þ], and *d* to represent [ð] (J. Morris Jones, *A Welsh Grammar*, §§ 19. iii and 20. ii); there are obvious analogues with Anglo-Norman practice, though they may be the coincidental results of restricting oneself to the letters of the roman alphabet.

[4] O. von Feilitzen, *The Pre-Conquest Personal Names of Domesday Book* (Uppsala, 1937), p. 100 (§ 105, on initial *þ*) and pp. 101–2 (§ 108, on medial *ð*).

[5] Pope, *From Latin to Modern French*, § 1215.

shire survey (Henry I–Henry II),[1] and spellings which he cites[2] show that OE medial [ð] was also sometimes written *th* in the Northamptonshire survey, in the *Inquisitio Eliensis*, and in charters preserved in the British Museum dealing with Rothwell (Lincs.) and Stepney (Middlesex), as well as in others listed in the *Calendar of Documents preserved in France* dealing with Siddington (Gloucs.) and Hendred (Berks.). In the thirteenth century, *th* for both initial [þ] and medial [ð] becomes much more common in the records. In vernacular English texts it is used six times in the mid twelfth-century gloss to Eadwine's Psalter (MS. Trinity College Cambridge R. 17. 1), from Christ Church, Canterbury.[3] It occurs thrice (beside *þ* often, *ð* once, and several instances of *d* for *ð*) in the charter of Henry II issued from York in February 1155 in favour of Christ Church, Canterbury,[4] and over forty times in the last continuation of the Peterborough Chronicle, written at Peterborough in or shortly after 1155. There is a single instance (*burth*) in the brief text of St. Godric's so-called 'hymns' on an inserted leaf (of the beginning of the thirteenth century) in British Museum MS. Royal 5 F. vii, a life of St. Godric by Geoffrey, a monk of Durham,[5] and there are twenty-six in the text of the song 'Ar ne kuthe ich sorghe non' in the *Liber de Antiquis Legibus* (London, Guildhall; before 1250), beside *d* seven times and *t* once;[6] the scribe was probably Anglo-Norman, since the English text is accompanied by, and seems to be a translation of, one in Anglo-Norman. In MS. Maidstone A.

---

[1] Zachrisson, pp. 41–2. [2] Ibid., pp. 83–9, 99, 111–12.

[3] W. Schlemilch, *Beiträge zur Sprache und Orthographie spätaltenglischer Sprachdenkmäler der Übergangszeit* (Studien zur englischen Philologie xxxiv, Halle, 1914), p. 58; Ker, *Catalogue*, pp. 135–6 (no. 91).

[4] Hall, *Early Middle English*, no. IV (pp. 11–12).

[5] Hall, no. II (p. 5).

[6] Carleton Brown, *English Lyrics of the Thirteenth Century* (Oxford, 1932), no. 5 (pp. 9–13).

13 (written in Northampton about 1250) there are nine instances of *th* (beside -*t*) in the text of the song 'Man mei longe liues wene',[1] and the East Anglian MS. Arundel 248 (late thirteenth century) has over twenty in the four English songs which it includes.[2] In the 'Kentish Sermons'[3] of Bodleian MS. Laud Misc. 471 (late thirteenth century) *th* is very common in final position (beside *þ*, *t*, *d*, and even *dh*), though *þ* is used initially; the scribe was again perhaps Anglo-Norman, and the same part of the manuscript contains items in Anglo-Norman.

The use of *th*, however, was contrary to normal West Midland scribal practice. It is not found in the so-called 'Worcester Fragments'[4] of MS. Worcester Cathedral F. 174, written in the 'tremulous hand' which Ker dates to the beginning of the thirteenth century,[5] nor in the early manuscripts of *Ancrene Wisse* and the *Katherine*-group. But it occurs once (*north* corrected from *nort*) in the charm against a wen[6] in MS. Royal 4 A. xiv, which Ker dates to the middle of the twelfth century;[7] the manuscript may have been written at Winchester, but was later at Worcester, 'perhaps already in the twelfth century', and since the linguistic forms of the charm are undoubtedly West Midland,[8] it was probably added to the manuscript in Worcester. MS. Lam-

[1] Carleton Brown, *English Lyrics of the Thirteenth Century*, no. 10A (pp. 15–16). [2] Ibid., nos. 44–5, 46A, 47 (pp. 75–80, 83–5).

[3] Hall, no. XXIII (pp. 214–22).

[4] Ibid., no. I (pp. 1–4).

[5] *Catalogue*, p. lvii. The older dating to the later twelfth century (Hall, ii. 223) is less probable.

[6] E. V. K. Dobbie, *The Anglo-saxon Minor Poems* (The Anglo-saxon Poetic Records, VI; New York, 1942), p. 128.

[7] *Catalogue*, p. 320 (no. 250). Dobbie's dating (p. cxxxii) to the late eleventh century cannot be right, in view of the linguistic forms, and is contrary to the judgement not only of Ker, but of earlier scholars; cf. F. Holthausen in *Beiblatt zur Anglia*, xix (1908), pp. 213–15.

[8] Note in particular *et* 'at', *weter* 'water', *scring* 'shrink', and *linsetcorn* for OE *linsǣdcorn* 'linseed corn'.

beth 487 (s. xii–xiii, possibly from Llanthony Priory, Gloucester) of the *Poema Morale* once has *with* (l. 216), perhaps a relic of the spelling of the eastern original of the poem. In the Caius version of *Ancrene Wisse*, written by a foreign-trained scribe 'probably in the second half of the thirteenth century or possibly a little earlier',[1] *th* occurs occasionally and *t* often in final position, though the usual spelling is ð or *d*.[2] Bodleian MS. Rawlinson G. 18 (second half of the thirteenth century) has three instances of *th* (two final and one medial), beside frequent *t* and one instance of *d*, in its text of the song 'Worldes bliss';[3] its erratic spelling again suggests an Anglo-Norman scribe. The Caligula MS. of Laȝamon's *Brut*, it is reported, has isolated instances of the use of *th*.[4] A thorough search would undoubtedly add further instances,[5] but it is sufficiently clear that even in the later thirteenth century the use of *th* was much less frequent in western than in eastern manuscripts. Nevertheless throughout the thirteenth century any educated westerner, especially one who was bilingual in French and English, must have been aware of the possibility of using *th* in place of þ and ð and that Anglo-Norman scribes, especially in the east of the country, often did so use it.[6]

---

[1] N. R. Ker, in his introduction to the edition of the Caius version (E.E.T.S. 229), p. ix.　　　　　　　　　　　[2] Ibid., p. xi.

[3] Brown, no. 46B (pp. 80–2).

[4] Jordan, *ME Grammatik*, § 16, Anm. 2.

[5] Some spellings with *th* in printed editions, however, are editorial errors. MS. Jesus College Oxford 29 does not have *thikke* at l. 29 of *The Owl and the Nightingale*, as printed by Hall, p. 150, and in the last line of Thomas of Hales's *Luue Ron* it reads *haueþ*, not *haueth* as printed by Brown, p. 74, followed by Dickins and Wilson, *Early Middle English Texts*, p. 109 (with a special comment on the alleged spelling on p. 217).

[6] A man of the Welsh Marches, even if he did not speak Welsh, might also have known of the use of *th* in Welsh in spelling such a name as *Iorwerth*, where English would have used ð. Ralph de Mortimer, lord of Wigmore from 1227 to 1246, was married to the daughter of Llywelyn ab Iorwerth.

In considering the legitimacy of the replacement of ð by *th* one must in any case look at the matter from the point of view not of the solver, but of the setter of the puzzle. The substitution is then in the opposite direction: *th* is replaced by ð. He would probably first think of a play on the 'interpretation' of the name *Brianus* and decide to use an English word meaning 'moderate'. Then he would consider the possibility of a cryptogram to convey the sense 'of Lingen', his territorial designation. He would soon realize that the normal thirteenth-century form *of Lingein* would get him nowhere. But if he knew (as I assume) that there were variants, he would try them too, as Machaut used variants of his Christian name; and he would find that *of Linthehum*, permuted, would give *inoh methful*, which would be just what he wanted—except that it involved the new-fangled spelling *th*. If he used this, it would be entirely unparalleled in his book[1] and would attract undesirable attention; moreover the first scribe that copied the sentence would almost certainly normalize the spelling.[2] It would be better for the author himself to adopt *meðful*, since this spelling would be unobtrusive. He could explain to those who were to share the secret that the solution of the anagram required, after the letters had been rearranged in order, the replacement of ð by *th*;[3] and the need to do this would not only

---

[1] The use of *th* in biblical names such as *Iudith* is of course not parallel; in these *th* was almost certainly pronounced /t/, as in *Thomas* (though in some of them Orm uses þ or þþ in writing English, against *th* in his Latin texts). The main scribe of the Cleopatra MS. once has *Marðe* (f. 191ᵛ/14–15) for normal *Marthe*, a clear case of unthinking substitution of ð for *th*; MS. Bodley 34 has *beðleem* (*Ste Iuliene*, l. 600) for the Royal MS.'s *bethlehem*, but this is a less certain instance, since it is one of the names for which Orm has þ(þ).

[2] As the Corpus scribe, applying his unvaried rule, in fact altered the spelling from *meðful* to *meaðful*.

[3] This would be comparable to Machaut's instructions that certain words or letters in clue-lines were to be omitted from the solution—with the difference that Machaut was giving open instructions for the solution

avoid attracting the attention of outsiders, but also make it harder for them to solve the puzzle—just as Roger Bacon some twenty years later, though he left it obvious that there was a puzzle, made its solution very difficult by abbreviating some of the words before he disarranged the order of the letters.[1]

My argument supposes that the author used the form *Linthehum* instead of the normal thirteenth-century *Lingein* primarily because it enabled him to construct a meaningful and apt anagram, just as I have earlier argued (pp. 273-9, above) that he played on the form *Limebrook*, not found in the records until the fourteenth century, in preference to the normal thirteenth-century *Lingebrok* because the latter was unsuitable for word-play. The two hypotheses run parallel; in each case he uses a form derived from an Old English compound with the noun *lind* as its first element, and in each he plays on what was then a rarer form because it was the suitable one. But he may not have thought this a disadvantage if he wanted his puzzles to be intelligible only to initiates; for an outsider would find the common forms the

of anagrams to which he had openly called attention, whereas the author of *Ancrene Wisse* would be giving a secret instruction for the solution of a hidden signature.

[1] An alternative explanation might be to suppose that the author started from a form of the place-name *Lindehum*, developed from OE *Lindhegum* by loss of the /h/ at the beginning of the second element (a common process, especially in place-names) and with the usual orthographic substitution of *h* for OE *g*. Then *of Lindehum* would, rearranged, give *inoh medful*, which could be turned into *inoh meðful* by substitution of ð for *d*. This would be an extremely simple substitution, for ð is both historically and calligraphically only a modification of *d*, and even well-trained Western scribes (including the 'AB' scribes themselves) often write *d* where ð is required (and less often ð for *d*). The author himself, in his additions to the Cleopatra MS., writes *d* by error for ð four times; see my edition, p. cxxv, n. 2. But though it would be even easier to assume the substitution (in the clue) of ð for *d* than of ð for *th*, it seems to me that in the 'AB language' *Linthehum* is more likely than *Lindehum* as a development of OE *Lindhegum*.

easiest to recognize. And it would also be in keeping with the pervasive traditionalism of the 'AB language', the consciously literary form of West Midland English developed in Wigmore Abbey, to retain and still to use in the early thirteenth century an old-fashioned variant of the name Lingen otherwise unrecorded, just as it uses words of undoubted Anglo-saxon origin which would be unknown but for their occurrence in this remarkable group of texts.

Colonel and Mrs. Friedman, writing from professional experience of the solving of cryptograms, say that

the point must be reached where he [the cryptanalyst] begins to feel that the whole thing did not and could not happen by accident. But it is not simply a matter of his *feeling* this; the assessment can be far more rigorous. The mathematical theory of probability can be applied, and the chances calculated exactly. . .[1]

The trouble is that few literary scholars are competent in the mathematical theory of probability. I do not see how one can begin to calculate the chances that a sentence added at the end of a work will include, as its most prominent word, a Middle English synonym of the only interpretation that could be given to the name *Brianus* by a man whose training and knowledge would lead him to suppose, however wrongly, that it was of Latin derivation; I can only assert a belief that they must be extremely slight. But one can perhaps, in an amateurish fashion, do something to estimate the chances that this word and the one that precedes it, making up together ten different letters (including four vowels), will be capable of being anagrammatized in a particular way. The 'AB language' had an effective alphabet of twenty-five letters.[2] Of these, twenty were consonant-letters, three

[1] William F. Friedman and Elizabeth S. Friedman, *The Shakespeare Ciphers Examined* (Cambridge, 1957), p. 21.

[2] Of the letters of the modern alphabet, *j* and *v* were not yet distinguished from *i* and *u*, and *w*, *y*, and *z* were so seldom used, especially in

(*a*, *e*, *o*) were vowel-letters only, and two (*i* and *u*) could represent either vowels or a consonant, but in the following calculations are counted as vowel-letters.[1] If one assumes a combination of ten letters, all different,[2] of which at least two are to be vowels so as to give a possibility of meaningful permutations,[3] then from twenty consonant-letters and five vowel-letters the number of combinations that can be formed is 1,259,700 with two vowels, 775,200 with three, 193,800 with four, and 15,504 with five. Every one of these ten-letter combinations is capable of 3,628,800 permutations, but even so many of them will presumably not yield a single permutation which can be split up into a sequence of two or more real words (or names) in the orthography of the 'AB language'. If one assumes, quite arbitrarily, that only one in a hundred of the combinations with two vowels, one in ten of those with three, but all of those with four or five will, when permuted, yield at least one sequence of real words (or names), then one still has a total of at least 299,421; and this, it seems to me, is after making an extremely generous provision for 'unproductive' combinations. In most cases, of course, though the permutation of ten letters may be divisible into two or more recognizable words or names, the collocation of these words (or names) will be such as to make

native words, that they can be disregarded in practice. This leaves twenty-one letters, to which are to be added the four special English letters *p* (for *w*), *þ*, *ð*, and *ȝ*.

[1] The chief effect of the ambivalence of *i* and *u* is to increase the chances that a combination into which they enter will yield permutations that can be read as real words, since *i* and *u* can be taken as either vowel or consonant as may be convenient.

[2] I assume ten letters, all different, because this is the combination that occurs in the phrase actually used, *inoh meðful*. But of course the author was under no obligation to use a phrase of ten letters, or one in which no letter was repeated; the number of combinations in fact open to him was much larger than the calculations allow.

[3] In ME as in MnE, two vowels can 'carry' eight or nine consonants, as in ME *hwit flesch, strong child*.

it impossible or very difficult to fit the sequence into a meaningful and grammatical sentence. But even if we were again to assume, improbably, that only one in a hundred of the 'productive' combinations will give, when permuted, a *usable* sequence of two or more words (or word(s) plus a name), we should still be left with just under 3,000, and of these only one will be the combination which, permuted one way, gives *of Linðehum*. The chances of finding two or three successive words[1] to make up this combination of letters *somewhere* in a book of about 70,000 words, as *Ancrene Wisse* is, must be within the range of the odds that a bookmaker would lay on a difficult steeplechase in which there were many starters but a rank outsider might be the only horse to stay on its legs with its rider on its back; that is to say, it might occur fortuitously. But the odds against finding it at one particular point—at the head of a sentence of suggestive form, a deliberate later addition immediately after the original request for the readers' prayers and at the very end of the book—are so very high as virtually to rule out the hypothesis that it is the result of chance. If a bookmaker offered odds of 3,000 to one against, one would know that in his estimation the risk of the event occurring by chance was so very slight that he could ignore it; and if he thought that it could be deliberately contrived he would not bet. Of course extraordinary chances do come off; every few weeks someone who knows nothing about football and who picks with a pin wins a football pool, though the mathematical odds against his doing so are enormous. But in such cases someone must win, whereas there does not have to be a pair of words at the head of an added sentence capable of

---

[1] Beside *inoh meðful* one could have, for example, '*nu foð Mihel* ant Gabriel . . .' or (on the sort of principle sometimes followed by Machaut) '. . . *fuleð min hon*d'. Neither sequence in fact occurs, and the recorded form of 'Michael' in the Corpus and Cleopatra MSS. is *Mihal*; but Nero and Titus have *Mihel*.

being anagrammatized. The probability that there will be such a pair, that it will yield (with the substitution only of *th* for *ð*) a possible variant form of the territorial designation 'of Lingen', and that at the same time the key word will bear the meaning of the only etymological interpretation of the Christian name *Brianus* reasonably open to a medieval scholar, is so infinitesimal that in my considered judgement one can rule out chance; the possibilities are present in the sentence because its author meant them to be.

We have always to remember that the sentence is a later addition and is therefore self-evidently not essential, though I think it a marked stylistic improvement which gives a better ending. Even granted its general sense and form, its precise wording is not inevitable. The adjective *me(a)ðful* occurs only here in *Ancrene Wisse*, though the adverb *me(a)ðfulliche* occurs twice;[1] *OED* records the adjective from Ælfric until the early fifteenth century, but it was never common. The author could equally well have used the adjective *(i)mete* 'moderate', since he thrice has its negative *unimete* 'immense, immeasurable',[2] or have formed an adjective **metelich* (cf. OE *gemetlic*) on the noun *mete* 'moderation', which he uses twice,[3] especially as he once has

[1] Cleopatra MS., f. 192/13, 15 (*meðfulliche* in alterations by 'scribe B', i.e. the author); Corpus MS., f. 112a/19, 21 (*meaðfulliche*). But the words originally used were *gnedeliche* at the first point, **nearowliche* at the second; see Cleopatra as written by the original scribe and Nero, 189/22, 24 (Morton, p. 414). *Me(a)ðful* and *me(a)ðfulliche* are used only in the alterations and the addition in Cleopatra and at the corresponding points in the revised text of Corpus, as though the author had only recently become aware of the word and had it on his mind as he was revising Part VIII.

[2] Corpus MS., ff. 10a/10, 39b/16, 54b/15 (Morton, pp. 40, 144, 202). Cf. also the adverb *unimete* 'immeasurably', Corpus f. 27a/17 (Morton, p. 102).

[3] Corpus MS., ff. 78a/23 and 80b/24 (Morton, pp. 286, 296); cf. also *Sawles Warde*, ed. Bennett and Smithers, l. 50, where the word is glossed 'meosure'. Zettersten, pp. 186–7, whose discussion of this group

the adverb *unmeteliche* 'excessively';[1] and as he uses the French noun *meosure* in the sense 'moderation',[2] he might conceivably have used **meosurable*. And though *inoh meðful* fits the context well and is idiomatic (*inoh* is similarly used elsewhere in *Ancrene Wisse*),[3] it is not the only possible thing that he could have written even if he had decided on *meðful* rather than a synonym; he could have used, with equal suitability in the context, *swiðe meðful* or *swa meðful* or *meðful i* (or *for*) *soðe* or simply *meðful* alone. *Meðful ich am, þe bidde se lutel* 'I am moderate, who ask for so little', though less wry than 'I am moderate enough', is indeed really more suitable; to ask for so little in return for so great a labour is not 'moderate enough', but absolutely moderate. Yet the phrase he chose was *inoh meðful*, and it is this alone which gives the anagram.

The weakness of the argument, in fact, is not the assumption of an anagram (a proper anagram, not a juggling with letters arbitrarily selected from a larger stock), nor the secondary assumption that the author substituted *ð* for *th* in the clue to avoid attracting attention to an orthographic irregularity, but my failure, despite long search, to find any documentary evidence of variant forms of the place-name Lingen descended from an OE **Lindhegum*. I believe, as a

of words fails properly to distinguish the various parts of speech, takes *ouer mete* at f. 80b/24 as a compound adjective *ouermete* 'excessive' (perhaps because in manuscripts GNT it is written as one word), but this is certainly mistaken; cf. the translation of F (ed. Herbert, 208/34–209/1), *vltre mesure*. The noun *mete* is from OE **mǣte* (Anglian **mēte*), cognate with OHG *māza*, MHG *māte* (cf. Stratmann–Bradley, s.v. *mǣte*, sb.).

[1] Corpus MS., f. 108a/4 (Morton, p. 398).

[2] Corpus MS., ff. 19a/11, 100b/10 (Morton, pp. 74, 372). Cf. *Sawles Warde*, ed. Bennett and Smithers, ll. 51, 197, and *Hali Meiðhad*, ed. Colborn, l. 598.

[3] Cf. *inoh sari* (Corpus MS., f. 26b/24; Morton, p. 102), *inoh is etscene* (Corpus, f. 55b/24; Morton, p. 206), *inoh ich wes abuten* (Corpus, f. 22b/24; Morton, p. 88), and the common adverb *inohreaðe* 'quickly enough, etc.'.

professional English philologist, that the philological argument for this Old English form is valid, but I cannot support it by direct evidence—only by inferential evidence from the variants of the associated name Limebrook/Lingbrook. If anyone ever finds Old or Middle English evidence—just one single occurrence—of a village-name in north-west Herefordshire plainly derived from OE *Lind-hegum*, then the proof that Brian of Lingen wrote *Ancrene Wisse* will be complete.

Nevertheless my hypothesis that he was the author does not rest on an alleged anagram of an unrecorded place-name form, nor even on what I consider the high probability that there is, in the deliberately added final sentence, a play on the 'interpretation' of the name *Brianus*. It depends rather on the two seemingly inconsistent propositions that the author must have been a member of the community of Wigmore Abbey, and yet a secular cleric or at least a man with pastoral interests, experience, and duties. These two requirements can both be met if we suppose that he was a secular canon of Wigmore; but as the abbey was a house of regular canons, it is unlikely to have had among its members, at any one time, more than two or three (if as many) who were seculars. The name of one such, who lived at the very time when *Ancrene Wisse* was written, is recorded in a document which shows clear signs of being a copy of a list of founder's kin compiled at Limebrook Priory. Brian of Lingen must in all the circumstances have been one of a mere handful of men who could have been the author, and it is legitimate to ask why his name and status should have been remembered so long in a nunnery which there is reason to connect with the work, especially in its revised form. 'Prei for me, mi leue suster', wrote the author of *þe Wohunge of ure Lauerd*,[1] just as the author of *Ancrene Wisse* (who may

[1] ed. Meredith Thompson, p. 37, ll. 645–6.

well have been the same man) asked that the women on whose behalf he had spent a great while writing 'this book' should, whenever they had read anything in it, 'greet the Lady with an Ave for him who laboured on it'. The evidence of the list of names in MS. Harley 1087 is that they did pray for him, they and their successors for three hundred years, until Henry VIII swept away for ever their little poor nunnery, but not his book.

APPENDIX I

DANISH LANDHOLDERS IN HEREFORDSHIRE AND SHROPSHIRE

DOMESDAY BOOK records a good number of men with Scandinavian names as having held lands in Herefordshire and Shropshire *tempore Regis Edwardi*, i.e. in 1066. The following account excludes (i) men with Scandinavian-derived names recorded as holding lands at the time of the survey in 1086, unless it is explicitly stated that they had also held them in 1066 (since many Normans bore names that were ultimately Scandinavian); (ii) the names mentioned on p. 118, n. 3, above.

The Domesday records for the two counties are translated, with identifications of the place-names and with notes, in the Victoria County History, *Herefordshire*, i. 309–45, and *Shropshire*, i. 309–49; there are introductions by J. H. Round (*Herefordshire*, i. 263–307) and James Tait (*Shropshire*, i. 279–308). I follow the identifications of the place-names given in these two editions; those in Shropshire are based on Eyton's in his *Antiquities of Shropshire*. Both volumes include sketch-maps showing the locations of the Domesday place-names, but they are not easy to use; though based on careful research, they are badly drawn and on too small a scale.[1] For Shropshire, the maps in Eyton are much better drawn and on a larger scale (half-inch to the mile). Unless otherwise stated, I accept the etymologies of the personal names given by O. von Feilitzen, *The Pre-Conquest Personal Names of Domesday Book* (Uppsala, 1937), the standard investigation. I give first a list of the Scandinavian personal names, with details of the places in the two counties where the men who bore

[1] The map in the Herefordshire volume (between pages 308 and 309) appears to be at the scale of one inch to six miles; that in the Shropshire volume (also between pages 308 and 309) is at one inch to five miles.

these names held lands, and then a summary of the places where the lands were held. The identifiable places are plotted on the sketch-map on p. 120, above.

(A) *Scandinavian names of landholders in* 1066

(1) Alchen (ODan *Alfkill*) held at Felton Butler, Salop.

(2) Anschill (ON *Áskell*), 'a man of the bishop of Hereford', held at Pixley, Herefords.; Oschetell, Oschill (also ON *Áskell*) held at Wollerton, Besford, and Ruthall, Salop.

(3) Ansgot (ON *Ásgautr*) held at *Lecce* (perhaps Lea) in *Bremesse* Hundred, the SE. extremity of Herefords.

(4) Archill 'a thane of Earl Harold', Archetel (ODan *Arnketil*, ON *Arnkell*) held at Yarkhill, Upton, and Laysters in Herefords. and at Womerton and Faintree, Salop.

(5) Aregrim, Ærgrim, Ergrim (ON *Argrimr*) held at Upton and Laysters in Herefords.; at Pedwardine, now Herefords. (then Salop); and at Womerton, Salop.

(6) Asci (ON *Aski*) held at *Sudtelch* (unidentified; probably in Baschurch Hundred) in Salop.

(7) Austin (ON *Auðsteinn*?) held at Cardington, Meadowley, and Broome in Salop; the first was held with another Austin, the last with Turstin. This name is taken by von Feilitzen as from OF *Austin* < Latin *Augustinus*, but in view of the company it keeps in the Shropshire Domesday it is much more likely to be a Scandinavian name, and *Auð-* and *-stein* are common elements.

(8) Auti, Outi (ODan *Auti*) held at Womerton, Lydley Heys, and Leebotwood in Salop, and at Quatt, then in War. in Stoneleigh Hundred, but now in Salop.

(9) Azor (ODan *Azur*) held at Leinthall in Herefords., at Sheinton, Upper Ashford, Neenton, Burwarton, Norton in Hales, and Beckbury in Salop, and also held (with two other men, Sewar and Oslac) hunting rights over extensive lands in the vicinity of the site of Montgomery Castle (partly in modern Montgomeryshire and partly in SW. Salop), which were then waste.

(10) Batsuen (ON *Batsveinn*) held at Howle, Salop.

(11) Carle, Carlo (ON *Karl(i)*) held at Great Wytheford, Salop.

(12) Chetel (ON *Ketill*) held at Lower Poston, Stanton (now Castle Holdgate), Wilderley, Woolstaston, and Wrentnall, Salop.

(13) Colegrim (ON *Kólgrimr*) held at *Lacre* (unidentified; in *Plegeliet* Hundred) in Herefords.

(14) Collinc (ON *Kollungr*) held at Steele, Salop.

(15) Dot (ON *Dottr*?) held at Rowton, Salop.

(16) Einulf (ON *Einulfr*) held at Womerton, Salop.

(17) Ertein (ON *Hersteinn* or *Hiǫrsteinn*?) held at Middleton, Salop. According to von Feilitzen, the name is 'perhaps OG *Herithegen*', but a Scandinavian etymon seems more likely; cf. DB's *Turtin* for *Turstin* < *þorsteinn*.

(18) Gamel (ON *Gamall*) held at Waters Upton, Marston near Diddlebury, and Millichope, Salop.

(19) Gheri (ODan *Geri*, ON *Geiri*) held at Acton Pigot and Monks Albrighton, Salop.

(20) Grim (ON *Grímr*) held at Rowden in Edwin Ralph and at Marston, Herefords., and at Dawley Magna (formerly Dawley Pantulf, in the manor of Wellington), Salop. In 1086 Rowden was held by Grimchetel, presumably Grim's heir.

(21) Grimchetel, Grinchetel (ON *Grímkell*) held at Birley, Herefords., and at Coton near Wem, Salop.

(22) Gunner (ON *Gunnarr*) held at Pontshill in Weston, at Weston under Penyard, and at *Calcheberge* (unidentified; like the other two places, in *Bremesse* Hundred) in Herefords.

(23) (*a*) Gunward, Gunwar (ON *Gunnvarðr*) held at Brampton Bryan, now Herefords. (then Salop), and at Clungunford, Salop.

(*b*) Gunuert, Gunuer held at Weston Beggard and at *Merestun* (stated to be the site of Wigmore Castle) in Herefords., at Lingen, now Herefords. (then Salop), and at Choulton, Salop. The forms *Gunuer(t)* are derived by von Feilitzen from ON *Gunnfróðr*; he rejects Björkmann's derivation from *Gunnvarðr* on the ground that OE, ON unstressed -*ard*, -*arð* does not normally give -*er(d)* in DB (see his § 24). But his own examples show that -*erd* does occur in both the suffixes -*weard* and -*heard*; and the location of the holdings makes it virtually certain that Gunuer(t) was the same man as Gunwar(d).

(24) Hagene (ODan *Haghni*) held at Sollers Hope, Herefords.

(25) Morcar (OSw *Morkar*) held at Rowton, Salop.

(26) Orgrim (either ON **Úlfgrímr* or OG *Ordgrim*, according to von Feilitzen) held at Peplow, Salop.

(27) Otro (ON *Óttarr*) held at Gretton, Salop.

(28) Rauechetel (ON *Hrafnkell*) held at Dilwyn Sollers and at *Lutelei* (Luntley in Dilwyn?), Herefords.

(29) Rauensward, Rauesuard, Reuensuard (ON *Hrafnsvartr*) held at Adley in Brampton Bryan, now Herefords. (then Salop), at Steventon, Salop, and at Tyrley (now Staffs., then Salop).

(30) Saxi, Saisi, Saissil, Sessi (ON *Saxi*) held at Staunton on Wye and Lyde, Herefords., at Buckton, now Herefords. (then Salop), and at *Lude*, probably Ludlow (cf. Ekwall, *ODEPN*, s.n. *Ludford*, though this has been doubted), and Aston Eyre, Salop. According to von Feilitzen, *Saisi* and *Saisil* may either represent Old Welsh *Seisill* (which he appears to think more likely) or be Normanized forms of *Saxi*. But as a man called *Saxi* is recorded at Buckton, it seems to me that *Saisi* and *Saissil* are more likely to be forms of that name; and von Feilitzen himself takes *Sessi* to be a form of *Saxi*. The form *Saissil* is given for the man who held at Staunton on Wye, and *Saisi* for the one who held at Lyde; the locations suggest that these may be the same man, perhaps distinct from the one who held further north, and to that extent are consistent with von Feilitzen's suggested distinction of the etymologies. On the other hand there was at Lyde another landholder with the undoubtedly Danish name of Turchill. On balance it seems much more likely that *Saisi* is a form of *Saxi* and it probably takes *Saissil* with it. I have therefore marked Staunton on Wye on the map on p. 120.

(31) Sistain (ON *Sigsteinn*) held at Dawley Parva, Salop.

(32) Steinulf, Stenulf (ON *Steinólfr*) held at Venn, Herefords., and at *Bolebec* (perhaps The More in Eardington), Salop.

(33) Sten (ON *Steinn*) held at Great Wytheford, Salop.

(34) Suain, Suen (ON *Sveinn*) held at Golding, Langley, Clunbury, Kempton, Sibdon Carwood, Coston near Clunbury, and Edgton, Salop.

(35) Thoret, Toret (ON *Þorðr*) held at Berrington, Eaton Mascott, Wroxeter, Lee Gomery, Rodington, and Norton, Salop.

(36) Tosti, Thostin (ON *Tosti*) held at *Nerefrum* (Castle Frome?), of Queen Edith, and at Putley, Herefords. If this was Earl Tosti Godwinson, DB does not say so.

(37) Turgar (ON *þorgeirr*) held at Pixley, Herefords., and at Steele, Salop.

(38) Turgod, Turgot (ON *þorgautr*) held at Hatton, Cosford, Bishton, and *Newetone* (unidentified; in *Mersete* Hundred, the NW. extremity of the county), Salop.

(39) (*a*) Turchil(l) (ON *þorkell*) held at Old Radnor (now Radnorshire, then Herefords.), at Lyde, Little Marcle, Stretton Grandison, and Whitwick (holding all four of Earl Harold), and at *Frome* (Bishop's Frome?), Evesbatch, Leadon, Credenhill, Lyonshall, and *Bernoldune* (in *Hezetre* Hundred; see below), all in Herefords.; also at *Buterel* (said to be modern Buttery, i.e. Buttery Farm near Kynnersley, in Wrockwardine Hundred), in Salop.

(*b*) Turchill Wit (ON *þorkell vítr*) held at Fownhope and Wellington, Herefords., and one Elric held of him at Eaton in Foy, also Herefords. Turchill Wit was probably the same man as the preceding Turchil(l), for all these estates in Herefords. went after the Conquest to the same Norman, Hugh Lasne.

(40) Turmod (ON *þormóðr*) held of Earl Harold at Colwall, Herefords.

(41) Turstin, Turtin (ON *þorsteinn*) held at Broome and Harcourt, Salop.

(42) Ulchet(e), Ulchetel (ON *Úlfkell*) held at Downton, Monkland, and Mansell Gamage, Herefords., at Whitton, Faintree, and Betton in Hales, Salop., and at *Hibrihteselle* (unidentified) in Leintwardine Hundred (which was then in Salop. but most of which was later transferred to Herefords.).

(43) Ulf (ON *Úlfr*) held at Isombridge, Salop.

(44) Wil(l)egrip (ODan *Vilgrip*) held at Great Wytheford and Kynnersley in Salop.

(45) Wiuar (ON *Viðfari*) held at Ryton in Salop.

(B) *Location of Scandinavian landholdings*

The men listed above held lands at 43 places in modern

Herefordshire, in addition to Old Radnor (now in Radnorshire) and *Bernoldune* (probably in Radnorshire), and at 70 places in modern Shropshire,[1] in addition to Tyrley (now in Staffordshire). At many of the places there were more landholders than one, and a landholder with a Scandinavian name may be found in association with one bearing an English name; so at Lingen, held as two manors by Gunwar, a Dane, and Edric, an Englishman. In some instances there was more than one Scandinavian landholder at the same place: so in Herefordshire at Laysters (Ergrim and Archetel, stated to be holding it as two manors), Lyde (Saisi and Turchil), Pixley (Anchil and Turgar), and Upton (again Ergrim and Archetel holding it as two manors); and in Shropshire at Faintree (Archetel and Ulchetel), Rowton (Dot and Morcar), Steele (Collinc and Turgar), Womerton (Archetel, Aregrim, Auti, and Einulf), and Great Wytheford (Carle or Carlo, Sten, and Willegrip). On the other hand a single man often held at more places than one. For this reason the number of names is doubtless more significant than the number of locations, though there were probably (or even certainly) instances of more men than one bearing the same name; but at each of his manors a landholder must have had his dependants and servants, and though these may often have been English, many of them must have been Danish. When lands are distributed to the officers of a disbanded army, they do not go off to them unaccompanied; they take with them their subordinates to help secure and protect their new properties, to work their estates, and to share in the profits. Each landholding, even when it was only one of a number belonging to a single owner, must have been at least a potential centre of Scandinavian linguistic influence.

In the lists of locations that follow, the numbers in brackets are four-figure National Grid references[2] (i.e. references to the nearest square kilometre). The grid letters are not prefixed; for

---

[1] Assuming that the unidentified *Hibrihteselle* in Leintwardine Hundred was in the smaller northern part that remains in modern Shropshire.

[2] But in the original of the sketch-map on p. 120 (which was drawn at the scale of 1:25,000), the positions of the places where the lands were held (or rather, of the modern towns and villages) were plotted from six-figure grid-references.

Herefordshire and southern Shropshire up to a line drawn east and west through Much Wenlock (6200) they are SO, for northern Shropshire they are SJ. Without the prefixed letters, it is possible for a place in southern Herefordshire to have the same grid-reference as one in northern Shropshire, but within each county it is impossible for two places to have the same reference. On the sketch-map on p. 120, above, grid-lines are marked at ten-kilometre intervals, i.e. the place with the reference 3667 (Lingen) is to the right of the line numbered 3 and above the line numbered 6. The grid-references are given to facilitate reference to modern Ordnance Survey maps. Almost all the places are marked on the 1-inch maps; in the few cases in which they are not, I give a grid-reference based on calculations from the maps in the *VCH* and Eyton.

In modern Herefordshire, men with Scandinavian names held lands at the following places identified by *VCH*: Adley (3874) in Brampton Bryan; Birley (4553); Brampton Bryan (3772); Buckton (3873); Colwall (7542); Credenhill (4543); Dilwyn Sollers (4255); Downton (4273); Eaton (6027) in Foy; Evesbatch (6848); Fownhope (5834); Bishop's Frome (6648) if this is DB's *Frome*, as assumed by *VCH*; Castle Frome (6646) if this is DB's *Nerefrum*, as conjectured by *VCH*; Sollers Hope (6133); Laysters (5563); Lea (6621) if this is DB's *Lecce*; Leadon (6846); Leinthall Earls (4467); Lingen (3667); Luntley (3956) in Dilwyn; Lyde (5044); Lyonshall (3355); Mansell Gamage (3944); Little Marcle (6736); Marston (3657); *Merestun*, said by DB to be the site of Wigmore Castle (4069); Monkland (4657); Pedwardine (3670); Pixley (6638); Pontshill (6321) in Weston; Putley (6437); Rowden (6356) in Edwyn Ralph; Staunton on Wye (3645); Stretton Grandison (6344); Upton (5466); Venn (5348); Wellington (4948); Weston Beggard (5841); Weston under Penyard (6323); Whitwick (6145); Yarkhill (6042). Now outside Herefordshire and in Radnorshire is Old Radnor (2559).

Places in Herefordshire unidentified by *VCH* are *Bernoldune* in *Hezetre* (Haseltree) Hundred, *Calcheberge* in *Bremesse* (Bromsash) Hundred (the SE. extremity of the county), and *Lacre* in *Plegeliet* Hundred (the ENE. part of the county, around and south of Bromyard). Of these the most interesting is *Bernoldune*, which, as it was in *Hezetre* Hundred and was described in 1428 as *Bernaldeston in Marchia Wallie*,[1] must have been somewhere on or near the border north-west or north of Kington (since if it had been on the border between Presteigne and Knighton it would have been in Leintwardine Hundred, in 1086 part of Shropshire). The schedules of the Feudal Aids in 1303, 1346, and 1428 put *Bernaldeston* under Stretford Hundred, immediately to the south of the old *Hezetre* Hundred, and list it (in 1346 and 1428) between Staunton (on Arrow) and Radnor; this must mean that it was towards the south of the old *Hezetre* Hundred in the vicinity of Old Radnor. Another pointer in the same direction is that Turchil, who held *Bernoldune* in 1066, had another holding at Old Radnor. A very suitable site which has been suggested[2] is Barland (2862), $2\frac{1}{2}$ miles NE. of Old Radnor, now just over the border in Radnorshire but east of Offa's Dike, where there is a village beneath a hill and the ruins of a motte and bailey castle. The connection between the ancient and the modern forms of the name is not very direct, but the reported forms[3] show a development from DB *Bernoldune* to *Barnaldon* 1422; metathesis of the consonants in the second syllable and substitution of the suffix *-ton*[4] produce the forms *Barlonton* 1449, *Barlenton* 1452. If then the suffix *-ton* were dropped, as it undoubtedly was in the case of Adley, some twelve miles to the NNE.,[5] we should be left with *Barlen, a form comparable to three neighbouring place-names in *-len* which were altered to

[1] As was Wigmore; but Radnor was described as *in Wallia* (*Feudal Aids*, ii. 412). Earlier references to *Bernaldeston* in the *Feudal Aids* occur at ii. 377 (dated 1303) and ii. 392 (dated 1346).

[2] Cf. B. G. Charles, *Non-Celtic Place-names in Wales* (London Medieval Studies, Monograph No. 1, 1938), p. 172, though he does not say by whom the suggestion had been made. He himself thinks that 'the identification is not certain', but he seems, rather surprisingly, not to have known the evidence of DB and the *Feudal Aids*, which is strongly in favour of it.

[3] See Charles, loc. cit. (except for the forms of DB and the *Feudal Aids*).

[4] Evidenced, as early as 1303, by the form *Bernaldeston*.

[5] In 1524 Adley is still recorded as *Adlaghton* (Bannister, *The Place-names of Herefordshire*, p. 3).

-land (*Eardisland*, *Kingsland*, and *Monkland*);[1] the same change would alter **Barlen* to *Barland*, which is already recorded (as *Barlond*) in 1544. I regard the identification as sufficiently certain to warrant the marking of Barland on the map on p. 120; but this is the only instance in which I have adopted an identification not suggested by *VCH*.

In modern Shropshire, men with Scandinavian names held lands at the following places identified by *VCH* (mainly in reliance on Eyton): Acton Pigot (5402); Monks Albrighton (4918); Upper Ashford, also known as Ashford Jones (not marked on the O.S. one-inch map, but shown by Eyton's map (vol. iv, facing p. 138), and by that in *VCH*, at 5271, about ¾ mile north of Ashford Carbonel);[2] Aston Eyre (6594); Beckbury (7601); Berrington (5307); Besford (5525); Betton (6936) in Hales; Bishton (8001); *Bolebec*, identified by Eyton[3] as the Moor (More) in Eardington and marked on his map by Westwood, just over 1¼ miles WNW. of Eardington, i.e. at 7091; Broome (5298); Burwarton (6185); Buttery (6817); Cardington (5095); Choulton (3788); Clunbury (3780); Clungunford (3978); Cosford (7804); Coston (3880); Coton (5334) near Wem; Dawley Magna (6807); Dawley Parva (6806); Eaton Mascott (5305); Edgton (3885); Faintree (6689); Felton Butler (3917); Golding (5403); Gretton (5195); Harcourt (5725); Hatton (7604); Howle (6923); Isombridge (6113); Kempton (3683); Kynnersley (6716); Langley (5400); Leebotwood (4798); Lee Gomery (6712); Ludlow (5174) if this is DB's *Lude*, as is generally assumed; Lydley Heys near Leebotwood (not on the O.S. one-inch map, but marked on the *VCH* map about two-thirds of a mile SSE. of Leebotwood, i.e. at 4897);[4] Marston near Diddlebury (5085);[5] Meadowley (6692);

---

[1] The early forms of these three names, which are frequently recorded, normally have *-len* (varying, e.g., with *-lan*), representing the old district-name *Leon* found also in *Lyonshall* and *Leominster*; cf. Ekwall, *ODEPN*, and Bannister, op. cit., s.nn.

[2] The identification of this manor, unnamed in DB, is due to Eyton, v. 79.   [3] i. 128–30.

[4] Eyton's map, in his vol. vi, places Lydley Heys slightly differently, about one mile ESE. of Leebotwood.

[5] Eyton, v. 110, says that *Merestun* (Marston) 'seems to have been in

Middleton (2999); Millichope (5289); Neenton (6387); Norton (6382); Norton (7038) in Hales; Peplow (6224); Lower (Lesser) Poston (5382); Quatt (7588), which was in Stoneleigh Hundred, Warwickshire, at the time of the Domesday survey; Rodington (5814); Rowton (6120); Ruthall (5990); Ryton (7602); Sheinton (6104); Sibdon Carwood (4183); Stanton, now Castle Holdgate (5689); Steele (5436); Steventon (5273); Waters Upton (6319); Whitton (3409); Wilderley (4301); Wollerton (6230); Womerton (4697); Woolstaston (4598); Wrentnall (4203); Wroxeter (5608); Great Wytheford (5719). Now just outside Shropshire and in Staffordshire is Tyrley (6933 approx.; there is now no village of Tyrley, but a parish, and Tyrley Castle 6833, Tyrley Locks 6932).

Places in Shropshire unidentified by Eyton and *VCH* are *Newetone* in *Mersete* Hundred (the NW. extremity of the county, bordering on Wales, north of the Severn), *Sudtelch*, probably in Baschurch Hundred (the west-central part, E. of *Mersete* Hundred), and *Hibrihteselle* in Leintwardine Hundred in the extreme SW. of the county, most of which was later to become the NW. extremity of Herefordshire. The third of these is listed by DB as the last of the holdings, in 1086, of Picot de Say in Leintwardine Hundred, immediately after Clungunford (3978), Bedstone (3675), and *Edelactune*, which Eyton[1] identified, doubtless correctly, as Adley (3874), now just inside Herefordshire. It seems almost certain that *Hibrihteselle* was in the same area, near the modern border between Herefordshire and Shropshire, NW. of Wigmore and possibly in Herefordshire (since the list, in the three preceding names, is moving south). Presumably the name meant 'Hygberht's hill',[2] and there are plenty of hills in the

the parish of Diddlebury, but its exact situation I am unable to trace'; obviously for this reason, it is unmarked on his map and on that in *VCH*. If the first element is *mersc* 'marsh', one might expect that Marston would have been E. or SE. of Diddlebury near the river Corve; but as the exact site is unknown, I have marked the location on my map on p. 120 at Diddlebury itself, which must be right within a mile or two.

[1] xi. 312.

[2] For the OE name *Hygebeorht* (Anglian *Hyg(e)berht*) cf. Withycombe, *ODECN*, s.n. *Hubert*.

vicinity. *Hibrihteselle* is therefore one more location to be added to the cluster of Scandinavian landholdings in the Wigmore area, but as it is unidentifiable it is of course not marked on the map on p. 120.

APPENDIX II

THE PLACE-NAMES *LINGEN* AND *LIMEBROOK*

THE early forms recorded for the two names are:

Lingen

1. *Lingham* 1086 DB, *Lyngham* 1425 Cal. I.p.m.
2. *Lingein* (*Lyn-*, *-guein*, *-geyn(e)*, *-gaine*, *-gayne*, etc.) 1177 onwards, Pipe R. 23 Hen. II, p. 21, and similar entries in succeeding years; for other references see Ekwall, *ERN* and *EPN*, and Bannister, *PN Herefordshire*, though their lists are selective. This is overwhelmingly the normal medieval form.
3. *Lingen* c. 1150 (*Charters Hereford Cathedral*, ed. Capes, p. 15; so printed,[1] but suspicious at this date); *Lingen* B.M. MS. Add. 34633 (s. xiii);[2] *Lyngen* 1452–3 Cal. I.p.m., and similarly with normal *-en* in modern times.
4. *Lyngem* 1398 Cal. I.p.m. (scribal misreading of *Lyngein*).
5. *Lingan* in MS. Harley 1087 (late s. xvi).

Limebrook

1. *Lingebrok(e)* (*Lynge-*, *Lyngge-*, *-broc*, *-bork*): ten times by 1300, beginning with *Lingebrok* 1221 Ass. R., *Lingebroc* 1226 Close R.
2. *Lingbroke* 1303 Ep. Reg., *Lingbroc* 1320 *Charters Hereford Cathedral*.
3. *Linbroke* 1285 Inq. ad q. d.[3]

---

[1] Capes has expanded a contraction; compare *Calendar of the Earlier Hereford Cathedral Muniments* (Hist. MSS. Com.: National Register of Archives), i (1955), 16, where the form is given (in typescript) as (Ralph de) *Ling'e*. Probably a medieval scribe, copying the document, misread *Lingein* as *Lingem* and abbreviated it *Lingē*; cf. the form *Lingem* in 1398.

[2] On this record see pp. 390–2, below.

[3] P.R.O. Chancery Inquisitions A.Q.D., File 8, no. 1 (calendared in

4. *Limebrook* 1348 Ep. Reg., *Limebrok* 1384 Ep. Reg.
5. *Lyndebrok* 1383 Ep. Reg.

Ekwall, *ERN* and *EPN*, suggests that the name *Lingein* (later *Lingen*) was originally that of the stream and only secondarily that of the village; he sets up, tentatively, a Welsh etymon, **llyn cain* with the proposed meaning '(brook with) clear or beautiful water', which he assumes would become **llyngain* by the Welsh phonetic process of lenition. But the hypothesis is full of difficulties.

(*a*) The Welsh collocation postulated, though not impossible, is doubtful. Professor I. Ll. Foster informs me that if an Old Welsh **Lincein* or Middle Welsh **Llyngein* had existed, one would expect (i) that the first element would be the MW *llyn* (m. and f.) 'pool in a river, lake, pond' rather than the related *llyn* 'liquid, drink', and (ii) that the second element would be, not an adjective qualifying the first element, but the actual name (OW *Cein*) of the stream.[1] If so, to MW **Llyngein* there should correspond a ME **Keinbrok* not *Lingebrok*, unless one were to assume

Calendarium Genealogicum, p. 360). The writ uses the spelling *Linbroke* (first syllable in full), but also has *Radenonere* for Radnor and *Watmor* [*sic*] for Wigmore (Abbey). It is dated 28 May 13 Edw. 1. The return to the writ, reporting the inquest held on the Thursday after the Nativity of St. John the Baptist (24 June), uses the forms *Radenor*, *Wygemore*, and *Lyngebroke*. The clerk who copied the writ was obviously careless, and it is possible that his *Linbroke* was simply an error (by omission of letters) for *Lingebroke*. But if so he produced a form which one would in any case hypothesize, and it seems hard on him to suppose that he got three of the four place-names in the writ wrong (the fourth being *Erleslane*, which the return spells *Erleslen*, the modern Eardisland).

[1] In Welsh names in which *Cain* (*Cein*) appears, such as *Nant Cein*, *Inis Cein*, *Afon Cain*, *Cilcain* (*Cilcen*), Professor Foster takes it to be the name of the stream. He compares also *Gelli Gain* and *Llyn Gelligain* 'the lake near the wood or grove on the Cain' (Merioneth). The river-name *Llyndeg* (a tributary of the Wye in Radnorshire), from *llyn+teg* 'fair, bright', is derived from the name of the source of the stream.

Old Welsh *cein* 'fair, beautiful, bright' occurs as a descriptive personal name. *Kein* (*Cain*), daughter of Brychan, is listed among Welsh saints, and her name occurs in place-names, e.g. Llan-gain in Carmarthenshire and OW *Lan Cein* for Kentchurch in Herefordshire. Tacit, son of Cein son of Guorcein, occurs in early Welsh genealogies.

(improbably, so near the border) that the English had adopted
Llyngein without knowing its meaning.

(*b*) Ekwall must have regarded the medieval form *Lingebrok*
as a tautology in which the English *brok* 'brook' had been added
to *Lingein*, itself (according to his theory) the original name of the
stream and containing, disguised, a Welsh word meaning 'water'.
But it is odd that we never find, even in the earliest (thirteenth-
century) records, the forms **Lingein-brok* or **Lingen-brok*, but
only *Lingebrok* with *e* (not *ein* or *en*) in the second syllable.
There is no special phonetic reason why the medial syllable of
Lingebrok should have been invariably reduced to *e* when the
second syllable of *Lingein* (*Lingen*) invariably kept its *n*. Certainly
no one in the thirteenth century or later can have thought that
Lingebrok was a compound of *Lingein* and *brok*.

(*c*) On Ekwall's hypothesis the variant forms *Linbroke*,
Limebrook, and *Lyndebrok* are very difficult to explain. We might
suppose that, after *Lingebrok* had, by syncope of the medial *e*,
become *Lingbroke* (which is recorded), the latter then became
Linbroke, and that at this stage the first element began to be
associated with the word for 'lime-tree', giving rise to *Lyndebrok*
and *Limebrook*; but this seems very unlikely, especially as a
phonetic change of *ng* [ŋg] through [ŋ] to [n] would be abnormal.

(*d*) His hypothesis disregards the evidence of DB, which not
only gives the form *Lingham* (the second element of which Ekwall
must have regarded as entirely corrupt) but also says that among
the appurtenances of the manor are 'three *haiæ* for catching
roe-deer' (*iii. haiæ capreolis capiendis*, vol. i, f. 260). The Latinized word *haia* was used in medieval times to denote 'a part of
a forest fenced off for hunting' and is derived from OE (*ge*)*hæg*
(Mercian (*ge*)*heg*) 'fence, enclosure' in the sense 'a fenced-in
piece of ground' exemplified in OE in the phrases *horsa gehæg* and
oxena gehæg;[1] here in DB its meaning would be 'three fenced
enclosures for catching roe-deer'. This evidence from DB indicates that the second element of the name *Lingein* is the plural
of Mercian *heg*, and if so the form must represent the OE dative

[1] A. H. Smith, *English Place-Name Elements*, Part I, pp. 214–15,
s.v. (*ge*)*hæg*.

plural, since the nominative of this masculine noun would give a ME form in -(*e*)*s*.[1]

Place-names which originally occurred in the dative plural were sometimes subjected to early re-formation; a 'weak plural' in -(*e*)*n*, formed on the nominative singular, was substituted,[2] and such a process would be especially likely in a West Midland dialect, in which the weak plural showed a marked tendency to proliferate. The importance of the point is that in a mono-syllable such as OE *hæg*, Mercian *heg*, in which the palatal *g*, being final, was part of the same syllable as the vowel, it was early vocalized to *i* and became part of a diphthong;[3] *hæg* would

[1] For the dative plural in place-names, see Smith, Part II, pp. 224–6, s.v. *-um*. In place-names the dat. is very common, being used in locative function ('at X'), and the dat. pl. is used when a plural sense is appropriate. The dat. pl. type seems to belong to Anglian territory, especially the North of England E. of the Pennines, but examples 'occur sporadically everywhere in Anglian territory' (p. 225), as in: Lindon, Worcs. (*Lindon* 1225 etc., *Linden* 1275 etc., from OE *lindum* 'at the limes'); Hawne, Worcs. (*Halen* 1294, from OE *healum* dat. pl. of *healh*); Oaken, Staffs. (from OE *ācum*); Stockham, Ches. (*Stoccum c.* 1173 and 1288, *Stockum* 1288, from OE *stoccum*); and in Herefords. itself Dilwyn (*Dilun* 1138, *Dilum* 1193, *Dilewe* 1277, from OE *dīglum* and metathesized *dīlgum*; see Ekwall, *EPN*). The dat. pl. occurs also in compounds, including words 'denoting enclosures, clearings, etc.', as in Acklam, Yorks., E. Riding (*Aclum* 1130, *Acclum* 1154–70) and N. Riding (*Achelum*, *Aclun* DB), both from OE *āc-lēum* dat. pl. of *āc-lēah*, and Cleatlam, Durham (*Cletlum* 1271, from OE *clǣt(e)-lēum*).

Formally it would be possible to derive the second element of *Lingein* from OE **hægen* (Mercian **hegen*) 'enclosure', which occurs as an independent word *hain* 'walled enclosure, park' in Laȝamon (cf. Ekwall, *EPN*, s.n. Hainford, and Smith, s.v. **hægen*, **hagen*, in part diverging from *OED*, s.v. *hain*, which treats the independent word as of purely Scandinavian origin). But the evidence of DB on the three *haiæ* at Lingen requires a word plural in sense.

[2] Cf. Smith, I. 10–11 (s.v. *-an*) and II. 225–6 (s.v. *-um*). Smith says that such re-formations are characteristic of the 'South Country', but they are to be expected also in the West Midlands, where equally the weak plural was extended in range in early ME. The starting point of the re-formation is the change to *-en* of both the OE weak plural ending *-an* and the dative plural *-um*. But despite Smith I do not think that ME *heghen* is such a re-formation; if it is, the stem chosen as the basis is not that of the nom. sg., which would be *hei* not **hegh*.

[3] Luick, *Hist. Gram.*, § 257 (2); Campbell, *OE Gram.*, § 430.

thus become *hæi* > *hai* and Mercian *heg* would become *hei*, and the new weak plurals formed on these singular forms would be *hain* and *hein*. DB's *Lingham* (MS. *Linghā*) is almost certainly due to scribal misreading of **Linghain*; the normal ME *Lingein* is a development of **Linghein*.[1] But in forms such as the dative plurals **hægum*, **hegum*,[2] in which the *g* was separated from the stressed vowel by the syllable-division, it did not vocalize early and in OE no diphthong was formed, especially in cases in which it was followed by a back vowel;[3] thus the dative singular **hege* normally gives early ME *heȝe* (*heghe*, etc., according to the orthographic system of the dialect), and the dative plural **hegum* would likewise give **heȝum* (**heghum*, etc.) or **heȝe(n)* (*heghe(n)*, etc.), depending on whether the inflexion was preserved in full or reduced.[4]

---

[1] Loss of *h* at the beginning of the second element of a compound no longer clearly apprehended as such has been a continuing feature of English since pre-literary times: cf. Bülbring, *Alteng. Elementarbuch*, § 526; Luick, *Hist. Gram.*, §§ 646, 656, 716, 778 (1); Campbell, *OE Gram.*, § 468; Jordan, *ME Gram.*, § 195. It is especially common in OE personal names and in place-names. Examples of the latter (in addition to those given by Luick and Jordan) are Hookey, Worcs., from OE (Mercian) *hōc-heg*, which is *Hokeye* and *Okeye* in 1275 (Mawer and Stenton, *PN Worcs.*, pp. 327–8); Ankerdine, Worcs. (*Oncredam* 1240, 1247 beside *Oncredeham* 1240, 1275), of which the final element is OE *hamm* 'meadow along a stream' (Ankerdine Hill takes its name from the meadow beside the Teme at its foot; op. cit., p. 46); and William of Occam (Ockham in Surrey, from OE *āc-hām*).

[2] The latter would itself be an analogical re-formation on the Mercian singular *heg*, for the Gmc. dat. pl. **hagumiz* would give WS **hagum*, Mercian **hægum* (cf. WS *dagum*, Mercian *dægum* dat. pl. of WS *dæg*, Mercian *deg*). But in words of this sort, with variation between WS *æ*, Mercian *e* in the sg. and WS *a*, Mercian *æ* in the pl., analogical re-formation, in one direction or the other, was very common (Campbell, §§ 160–1): *hwælum* for *hwalum*, and conversely *hwales* for *hwæles*, occur in Alfred's *Orosius*, and VP itself has *degas*, *dega*, *degum* beside the phonologically normal *dægas*, *dæga*, *dægum* (the forms in *e* amounting to about one-third of the instances of the plural). Obviously **hegum* beside **hægum* is exactly parallel to VP *degum* beside *dægum* (*daegum*).

[3] Luick, § 372; Campbell, § 430.

[4] Ekwall, *EPN*, explains the name Hayne (Dorset) as descended from a dat. pl.; early forms are *Heghe(n)* and *Hachen*, of which Ekwall takes the

If this explanation of the second element of *Lingein* is accepted, it follows that Ekwall's whole postulate of a Welsh etymon, in which the name was taken to divide *lin-gein*, must be rejected. It remains, then, to identify the first element. A. T. Bannister in his *Place-Names of Herefordshire* tentatively suggested that it was the word *ling*. This might be topographically suitable, for there are now areas of heath near Lingen (cf. in particular Heathy Park, $2\frac{1}{2}$ miles to the NNW.); late OE **ling-hegum* would then mean '(at) the enclosures in the heath'. But Bannister himself pointed out that *ling* is a Scandinavian word and is not recorded by *OED* until *c.* 1357. These are not necessarily conclusive objections; the dialects of Herefordshire and Worcestershire, as evidenced by *Ancrene Wisse* and Laȝamon, contained many words from Norse, and words often occur earlier—even much earlier—in place-names than as independent words. This is in fact the case with *ling* itself.[1] But from *OED*'s evidence it seems that *ling* was not current in the West Midlands; its examples before 1500 all come from the North and East of England and the word seems to have been confined to the old Danelaw. Even there *ling* rarely occurs in place-names; Smith, *PN Elements*, does not list it, but it is found in a few minor names in Danelaw counties.[2] It would be unlikely to occur with a native second element. All told, it is very improbable that *ling* can be the first element of *Lingen*; Bannister himself put forward the suggestion only to withdraw it. Moreover on this hypothesis we should have to regard the name *Limebrook* as having been derived from the village-name *Lingen*; the early form *Lingebrok* would mean 'the Lingen brook'. But if so, the question is more than ever posed why the thirteenth-century form is regularly *Lingebrok* and never **Lingein-brok* or even **Lingen-brok* when the village-name is regularly *Lingein*; it would be much better if we could assume

latter to represent OE *gehagum* dat. pl. of *gehæg*, the former OE *hegum* dat. pl. of *hege* 'hedge'.

[1] A. H. Smith, *PN East Riding Yorks.*, p. 117, records the minor name *Lingholme* 1180 (ON *lyng+holmr*); cf. Gover, Mawer, and Stenton, *PN Notts.*, p. 287, for a thirteenth-century example.

[2] See preceding note.

that *Lingein* was from **linge-hein*, so that we could have a formal parallelism between **linge-hein* 'the *linge* enclosures' and *linge-brok* 'the *linge* brook', whatever *linge* might be. And finally, if *Linge-brok* meant 'the Lingen brook', we should still be left to explain the forms *Linbroke*, *Lyndebrok*, and *Limebrook* as abnormal variants on *Lingbroke* < *Lingebrok*.

The variation *lind-*, *lin-*, *lim-* is in fact closely paralleled in place-names in which the first element is the OE word *lind* 'lime-tree', in particular in two names in which the second element begins with the consonant *b*. Limber in Lincolnshire, of which the etymon is OE **lind-beorg* 'lime-tree hill', is already recorded with the three forms *Lindbeorghe*, *Linberge*, and *Limberge* before 1100 (Ekwall, *EPN*, s.n. *Limber*); and Limberrow (Cottages) in the Pershore hundred of Worcestershire, which has the same etymology, occurs as *Limberg(a)* in 1127 and 1321 (Mawer and Stenton, *EPN Worcs.*, pp. 215–16). The phonetic process is loss of /d/ in the group /ndb/, followed by assimilation of /n/ to /m/ before /b/ (as in *Bambury* for *Banbury* and many other instances).[1] If we were to take the first element of the modern name Limebrook as being for once what it seems to be, we should immediately have explained the recorded thirteenth-century *Linbroke* and the fourteenth-century *Limebrook* and *Lyndebrok*; the normal OE form would have been **Lindbrōc*, with **Linbroc* and **Limbroc* as phonetic variants that could occur by 1100, on the model of the closely analogous Limber and Limberrow.[2] The difficulty, with this etymology, is to explain the village-name *Lingein* and the common—in the thirteenth century the dominant—variant *Lingebrok* (later also *Lingbrok*) of the name of the stream.

---

[1] The variant *lime* (tree) for older *lind*, first recorded by *OED* as a form of the independent word in 1623 (s.v. *lime* sb.[3]), must have been deduced from special combinations, e.g. from **lind-bough* or **lind-wood* with the change of /nd/ through /n/ to /m/, or else from **line-bough*, **line-wood* after the word *lind*, even when used independently, had become *line* in the early sixteenth century by the common eMnE loss of final /d/ after /n/.

[2] In the compound **lind-brōc* the vowel of the first element would be expected to retain its original short quantity, as in Limber and Limberrow.

One of the characteristic features of the West Midland dialect, in particular of the 'AB language', is that in it the OE voiced back palatal spirant [ɣ] often becomes a stop [g] in initial position in unstressed syllables.[1] The phenomenon is discussed by Miss d'Ardenne in § 32 of the Phonology of her edition of *Ste Iuliene*. She rejects Jordan's explanation (*ME Gram.*, § 186 Anm. 2), that the development occurs only before secondarily-stressed vowels, for the conclusive reason that it will not account for the common *witege* 'prophet' < OE *witega*, *witga*, and herself explains it as a natural change of [ɣ] to [g] after *d*, *t*, and certain spirants, 'combinations that only arose naturally in the contracted forms related to adjectival *-ig*'. But she goes on to point out that 'both *awildgin* and *wurdgin* have a *g* not present in OE', i.e. the recorded OE *awildian* and *wurþian* have been remodelled as if from **awild(i)gian* and **wurþ(i)gian*,[2] which in turn are as if formed on an unrecorded **wildig* and the recorded adjective *wurþig* (the former related to *wilde* as *wurþig*, *weorþig* is to *weorþe*).[3] In the same way OE **lind-hegum* '(at) the lime-tree enclosures' (or 'enclosures among the lime-trees') and **lind-brōc* 'lime-tree

---

But in the simplex *lind* it would become long and the long vowel could be imported into the compound if the sense of the latter continued to be understood, as it evidently did.

[1] That OE *g* in such words as *syngian* 'sin', *wērgian* 'grow weary' was not fronted, but remained [ɣ], before a front vowel derived by *i*-mutation from a back vowel is an assumption made, obviously correctly, by Luick, § 637 (2), and Campbell, § 420; it is supported by the analogy of back palatal [ɣ], later [g], before mutated vowels in such words as *gylden* 'golden', *gēs* 'geese'. All the words in which OE spirantal *g* becomes a stop [g] in ME are such as must or can have the back palatal spirant in OE; none has a *g* which must have been fronted.   [2] Cf. German *würdigen*.

[3] Miss d'Ardenne herself says (Glossary, s.v. *wurdgin*) that the alteration to *wurþ(i)gan* was 'probably but not necessarily by association with *wyrþig*, *wurþig*; the verbal ending *-gian* was extended to words without any parallel adjective in *-ig*: so A *awildgin*, *awilgin*, go mad (OE *a-wildian*)'. One might similarly hypothesize the extension of an adjectival ending *-(e)ge* (as in *witege*) to words used in adjectival function, such as the first elements of compounds, whose stem ended in *t* or *d*; after a short stem the ending would be *-ege*, after a long stem *-ge*. But it seems simpler to assume **wildig* and **lindig*.

brook' might be remodelled as if from OE *lindgum hegum and *lindga broc,[1] in turn presupposing an adjective *lindig 'pertaining to lime-trees'.[2] Then by West Midland phonetic development the spirantal g [ɣ] will become [g], and *lindgum hegum (hægum), remodelled as a weak plural (see pp. 383–4 above), will be altered to *lindge hein (hain); this in turn, with loss of d (cf. OE myndgian > myngian, ME awildgin > awilgin), will give *linge hein (hain), whence, with elision of e before weak-stressed h,[3] *linghein (*linghain; cf. DB Lingham). Loss of h at the beginning of the second element will finally produce Lingein. Likewise *lindga broc will become *linge broc, with no possibility of elision of the -e, to give the recorded thirteenth-century Lingebrok; the variant Lingbroke is by later syncope (not elision) of the medial e of a trisyllabic word.[4]

I assume this explanation, according to which Lingein is 'the lime-tree enclosures' and Lingebrok 'the lime-tree brook'. It might be no less accurate, and would certainly be more elegant, to gloss the names 'the forest enclosures' and 'the forest brook';[5]

---

[1] On the use of the weak adjective in place-names see Ekwall, EPN, p. xv.

[2] Adjectival formations in -ig are not uncommon in place-names. Smith, Eng. PN Elements, s.v. -ig, cites among others OE *brērig 'briery', *colig 'coaly', *gorstig 'gorsy', *scearnig 'sharny', and *stubbig 'stubby', none of which is recorded in OE as an independent word or by OED until after 1500, and brōmig 'broomy', recorded once for OE by the Supplement of Bosworth–Toller and from 1649 by OED. *Lindig would be closely comparable to wudig 'full of woods and trees', recorded once as an independent word by Bosworth–Toller ('Waldend scop wudige moras', Az. 120), especially if lind were used in a generalized sense to mean 'tree'; *lindig might then mean 'woody' or 'forest' (adj.). See n. 5, below.   [3] Luick, § 452.   [4] Luick, § 456(2).

[5] Place-name scholars (Ekwall, Smith, and others) regularly gloss names with lind- as a first element (e.g. *Lindbeorg) as 'lime-tree (hill)', etc. This is of course literal and safe. But in ME poetry lind is used to refer to trees generally and the phrase under linde is used to mean 'under the greenwood tree', 'in the forest', and OED cites from a text dated ante 1400 the phrase in feld or lynde, evidently meaning 'in field or wood'; OED takes this to be an erroneous use, but it is not evidently so—it is rather a development of the sense implicit in the phrase under linde. It seems to me that such compounds as *lind-heg, *lind-brōc etc. may often

the whole of the area was originally well forested (Lingen is still surrounded by woods) and it was of course in the forest that the roe-deer lived and were hunted. But the literal sense may be appropriate; the large-leaved lime, we are told, 'seems to be native near Aymestrey',[1] and certainly now grows in the valley of the Lime Brook. If the etymology and phonetic explanation given are true, the form *Limebrook* is not an abnormal development of earlier *Lingebrok* but a parallel formation with the noun *lind* (and its special combinative by-forms *lin-* and *lim-*) as the first element; the continuing use of *Limebrook* and *Lingbrook* as alternative forms even in the sixteenth century strongly suggests that they are parallel and not successive developments. And in that case the form **Limbroc*, later spelt *Limebrook*, though not in fact recorded until 1348, might well be expected from the late eleventh century, when the analogous *Limberge* 'Limber' is already recorded. In the whole course of the thirteenth century, forms of the name Limebrook, by my count, have been found only eleven times; the number is not large enough to be statistically significant, and it may be chance that in ten of these occurrences the form is *Lingebrok* (and variant spellings), only in one *Linbroke* (1285), and in none *Limbroke*. Indeed, if the etymology proposed is correct, it must be chance, for the basic OE form would be **Lindbrōc*, and yet *Lyndebrok* is the last of the ME forms to appear, in 1384. In all such work one must reckon with the vagaries of record and survival.

It follows from my argument that just as **Lindbrōc* and its developments existed as an alternative formation beside *Lingebroke*, so OE **Lindhegum* > ME **Lindheʒum* must have existed beside late eleventh-century **Linghein* > *Lingein*; yet in this case only *Lingein* and related forms are recorded. But it is to be observed that after DB almost all the records of the name are references not to the village itself, but to members of the family

have been intended to mean simply 'forest enclosure', 'forest brook', and that **lind-beorg* may not have meant specifically 'hill with lime-trees on it', but more generally 'wooded hill'. This would of course involve assuming that the generalized sense of *lind* already existed in OE.

[1] *VCH Herefordshire*, i (1908), 49.

which took its name from the village.[1] This was, almost certainly, a Norman family in origin,[2] and the early records must have been written, at least predominantly, by Anglo-Norman scribes. It is easy to see that the form *Linghein > Lingein would be readily acceptable to a speaker of French, for it presents no phonetic difficulties and is directly comparable in structure to French names and words ending in -ein (-ain); but OE *Lindhegum > ME *Lindheʒum would be a very different matter, for its structure is characteristically Anglo-Saxon, and alien to French, in stress-pattern (/ \ ×), the sounds involved (especially [ɣ]), and the fossilized dative plural inflexion. It might well have been deliberately avoided by an Anglo-Norman family and by Anglo-Norman scribes until their usage had made Lingein the dominant and in the end the only form; but the variant *Lindheʒum could well have survived for a time in colloquial use among native speakers of English. It would be very surprising if there had been no variation of form in the case of Lingen to parallel that so clearly established, after 1300, for Limebrook/Lingbrook. The early records for Lingen must be even more defective than those for Limebrook.

It is necessary to add a note on the record of the name Lingen in the thirteenth-century B.M. MS. Additional 34633, which is discussed by Professor H. P. R. Finberg in *The Early Charters of the West Midlands* (Leicester, 1961), pp. 197 ff.[3] The second item (ff. 206–16ᵛ) in this composite manuscript is a life of St. Mildburg attributed to Goscelin, a monastic hagiographer, and written about 1100. The author embodies in it, professedly in the original words (as seems very probable), a 'testament' written by Mildburg, who was abbess of a religious house at Much Wenlock

---

[1] Just as, indeed, the records of Limebrook are all references to the nunnery, not to the stream.   [2] See p. 324, n. 2, above.

[3] Cf. also his handlist of charters, p. 139, no. 405. Finberg is followed by P. H. Sawyer, *Anglo-Saxon Charters: an Annotated List and Bibliography* (London, 1968), p. 473, no. 1801 (under 'Lost and Incomplete Texts'), where the charter is calendared as 'Cenred, king of Mercia, to the nun Feleburg: grant of land at Lingen (or Lye), Herefords.' In view of what is said below, this requires qualification, especially as the text is described as 'authentic'. The place-names are not.

and died about 722. In this document[1] she gives an account of the lands of the minster and how they came into her possession, with summaries of the relevant charters. Towards the end she relates how a nun called 'Felaburga' gave to her eight hides of land together with the letters by which they had originally been granted to Felaburg, 'hunc tenorem habentes':

Keonred rex pro redemcione anime sue terram octo manencium in Lingen ⟨*with* Liya *interlined above*⟩ famule Dei Feleburge in propriam perdonavit potestatem, hiis testibus presentibus atque consencientibus: Turchtello episcopo, Wihctsi, et Eadberto.[2]

Coenred reigned from 704 to 709, and Tyrhtel was bishop of Hereford from 688 to between 705 and 710. There seems no reason to doubt the authenticity of the record, but there can be no question that the forms of some of the names have been modified; in particular somebody—probably the scribe of the extant thirteenth-century manuscript—has modernized the form of the place-name, certainly in post-Conquest times.[3] The important question is, what earlier form gave rise to the variant interpretations *Lingen* and *Liya*, and I think the answer can only be **Lige*, which might first be taken as an error for *Linge*n (with the mark of abbreviation for *n* omitted from both vowels) and then more knowledgeably as a form of the name 'Leigh' < OE (Anglian) *lēh*, *lēge* (WS *lēah*, *lēage*). But even **Lige* was probably an alteration of original **Lege*, for Anglian *ē* < *ēa* before *g* is not known to have become *ī* before the earlier thirteenth

[1] Finberg, pp. 201–4 (text), 204–6 (translation).

[2] MS., f. 211; Finberg, pp. 201 (text), 204 (translation). The scribe first wrote *Wihctsi*, as printed by Finberg, but subpuncted the second *i*. The interlined *Liya* is in the hand of the text-scribe himself.

[3] The form *Lingen* instead of *Lingein* is very rare until after 1450; note also that no inflexion has been added. *Liya* is obviously a medieval Latinized form; moreover it uses *y* for the consonant /j/, a specifically English usage first found about the middle of the thirteenth century, and has *i* for Anglian *ē* < *ēa* before *g*, a development of the second half of the thirteenth century (cf. next note). Ekwall, *EPN*, s.n. *Leigh*, records *Lia* in 1242 (*Book of Fees*) for Leigh in Wiltshire, but in view of the location this might go back to the WS fem. dat. sg. *līeg*. *Ancrene Wisse*, which represents the local dialect of the Wigmore area, has (*wude-*)*lehe*.

century,[1] though Anglian *ē* < *ēo* before *g* occasionally becomes *ī* in Old Mercian.[2] Finberg, in his index, takes *Liya* to be Upper Lye, near Lingen, but the only warrant for this is that *Liya* in the late manuscript is given as an alternative to *Lingen*; it might be any place with a form of the name 'Leigh'. There is no record that St. Milburga's Priory at Much Wenlock ever held lands at Lingen or at Upper Lye (or for that matter Lower Lye), nor is it easy to believe that there could have been room for eight hides around Upper Lye, which in the early eighth century was probably a small clearing in the forest. But the Priory did have important holdings at Hughley (earlier *Lega, Leghe, Leye, Lee*)[3] in Shropshire, four miles WSW. of Much Wenlock, where there was plenty of space; these are much more likely to represent the lands granted by Coenred to Felaburg and transferred by her to Mildburg. The thirteenth-century copy, therefore, tells us only that the form *Lingen* was already in use by that time; it gives no information at all on the OE form of the name, and has been introduced into the late copy only by a scribal error.

[1] Cf. Luick, *Hist. Gram.*, § 407. 1, who dates the change of *ẹi* to *ī* to the second half of the century. But Wyld, *Short History of English* (London, 3rd edn., 1927), § 172 (2), cites Miss Serjeantson's view, based on place-name forms, that the change had occurred in certain Midland dialects in the first half of the century.

[2] Bülbring, *Ae. Elementarbuch*, § 323.

[3] See p. 191, above.

APPENDIX III

THE LINGEN FAMILY

In what follows, my primary concern is to trace the main line of descent from Ralph of Lingen in the late twelfth century to his descendant Jane Lingen in the later sixteenth, so as to permit comparison with the 'genealogy' of MS. Harley 1087.[1] But I add, at the end, notes on other men of the family, from the thirteenth to the early sixteenth century, who do not appear in the Harleian list and seem to have no place in the direct line of descent. I normally substitute the modern form Lingen for the forms of the records; these are (especially before 1400) usually spelling-variants on the form *Lingein*, thus *Lingein(e)*, *Lyngein(e)*, *Lyngeyne*, *Lingayne*, but other forms also occur, thus *Lyngoyn*, *Lyngham*, *Lyngam*, *Lynghen*, *Lyngeigne*, as well as errors and corruptions such as *Lygarn*, *Lyngton*.

(1) Ralph of Lingen I (omitted from the Harleian list) who witnessed a charter of Hereford Cathedral dated *c.* 1150 (see p. 205, above); this man I take to be distinct from the next Ralph (and, in that case, probably his father), since the Ralph who died in 1190 left a young heir and was therefore probably not old himself.[2]

(2) Ralph of Lingen II (included at the head of the Harleian list), who died in 1190; for further details see pp. 205–7, above.

(3) John of Lingen I (included in the Harleian list) was probably a young man of about 20 at the time of his father's death in

---

[1] Accounts of the Lingen family are given in Burke, *The Commoners of Great Britain and Ireland*, iv (1838), 266–7 (very confused), and in R. W. Eyton, *The Antiquities of Shropshire* (1854–60), v. 75–9 and vii. 333–4, who gives a helpful if incomplete account of the earlier history of the family, based on original sources.

[2] See pp. 208–9, above.

1190.[1] In 1193–4 he resumed the litigation about extensive lands in Gloucestershire and Wiltshire that his father had begun in 1177, with the same lack of result.[2] In 1221, at the Shropshire assizes, he was defendant (successfully) in a suit concerning a tenement at Lingen.[3] Also in 1221, in Easter Term, he was sued by William de Stuteville and his wife Margery (i.e. Margery de Say) in a custody action.[4] In 1221–2 he was involved, as tenant (under the Mortimers) of Huntington south of Ludlow, in a complex action concerning a subtenant of his named Ralph de Cambray at Ashford (probably Ashford Jones).[5] In 1226 he again was a successful defendant in another suit, brought by a different plaintiff, concerning a tenement at Lingen.[6] In Easter Term 1231 he was appointed a member of a jury of Grand Assizes in Shropshire[7] (which implies that he was a knight). In 1235 a John of Lingen was again engaged in litigation;[8] this was probably the same man, though it may have been his son.

(4) John of Lingen II (described as *miles* in the Harleian list) is unlikely to have been born before 1200.[9] In 1236 he brought a suit, under the assize of *mort d'ancestor*, against his overlord Ralph de Mortimer for possession of 40 acres at Lingen; and on 16 November of that year Mortimer acknowledged his right and restored the land, on payment of 25 marks by the plaintiff.[10] As the process of *mort d'ancestor* was designed to protect 'an heir from being wrongly kept out of his inheritance' and 'was directly pointed at the practice of the lord of seizing on one pretext or another the land of his dead tenant',[11] there can be no reasonable doubt that this action means that Lingen had recently

[1] See pp. 208–9, above.   [2] See pp. 207–8, above.
[3] *Rolls of the Justices in Eyre . . . for Gloucestershire* [etc.] *1221, 1222*, ed. D. M. Stenton (Selden Soc., 1940), p. 509 (no. 1154); Eyton, vii. 333.   [4] *Curia Regis Rolls*, x. 96.
[5] Eyton, v. 76–7; D. M. Stenton, pp. 457 (no. 1033) and 589 (no. 1401).
[6] Eyton, vii. 333 (citing the Assize Roll, 10 Hen. III, m. 4ᵈ).
[7] *Curia Regis Rolls*, xii. 261.   [8] *Close R. 1234–9*, p. 181.
[9] See p. 209, above.
[10] Eyton, vii. 333 (who assumes that this was a second John of Lingen, as I do; cf. also Eyton, v. 77).
[11] Poole, *From Domesday Book to Magna Carta*, p. 408.

passed from one John to another. In 1237 John of Lingen acted as surety for his subtenant William de Cambrai.[1] In 1242 he is recorded as holding Lingen and Covenhope of Ralph de Mortimer,[2] and as also having a holding in Kenchester;[3] in 1249 he is recorded as holding Covenhope of Roger de Mortimer,[4] and in 1255 as holding Huntingdon, also of Roger de Mortimer.[5] On 6 July 1247 he delivered £200 to the keeper of the Wardrobe at Winchester on behalf of Roger de Mortimer and of the executors of Ralph de Mortimer.[6] On 31 July 1253 a covenant was drawn up to arrange the terms on which Constance, the daughter of 'Sir John de Lingayn', was to marry Grimbald, son and heir of Sir Richard Pancefot.[7] On 12 November 1253 he was held guilty of contempt of court in an affair in which weapons were drawn in the presence of the king's justice and in which he caused the men of Roger de Mortimer to leave without fulfilling any of their pledges.[8] In 1255 there is a record that two subtenants held Catsley of John of Lingen.[9] Also in 1255 he was exempted for life from service on assizes and juries or as coroner, escheator, verderer, forester, or other royal bailiff;[10] in 1256 he was granted rights of free warren.[11] From 1259 to 1262 he was one—apparently the first in precedence—of the plenipotentiaries or 'dictators', on the king's side, of the truce with Llywelyn, prince of Wales,[12] and on 9 February 1263 he (among others) was granted protection until Midsummer or during the Welsh war,[13] which implies

---

[1] Eyton, v. 78 (citing the Pipe Roll for the year, in which the name is given as *Lingede*; Eyton rightly assumes that this is an error for *Lingein*).

[2] *Book of Fees*, ii. 804, 963. [3] Ibid., p. 814.

[4] Ibid., p. 1481. [5] Eyton, v. 77–8 (citing *Rot. Hundred.*, ii. 70).

[6] *Cal. Liberate R.*, iii. 130.

[7] Duncumb, *History and Antiquities of the County of Hereford*, ii. 97–9; Eyton, v. 77. The Latin text, given by Duncumb, styles both John de Lingayn and Richard Pancefot *dominus*, which Eyton renders as 'Sir'. [8] *Abbreviatio placitorum*, p. 137.

[9] Eyton, iv. 260 (citing *Rot. Hundred.*, ii. 81).

[10] *Cal Pat. R. 1247–58*, p. 455. [11] Duncumb, i. 183.

[12] *Cal. Pat. R. 1258–66*, pp. 45, 57, 65, 69–70; *Close R. 1256–9*, p. 423; *Close R. 1259–61*, pp. 4–5, 89, 163, 309–10; *Close R. 1261–4*, p. 136; *Cal. Liberate R.*, v. 11.

[13] *Cal. Pat. R. 1258–66*, p. 248.

that he was expected to go on the campaign. In Easter Term 1260 he was among various defendants sued by Felicia, widow of Nicholas of Hints (Shropshire), in actions concerning lands.[1] At various dates from about 1240 onwards he was a witness of surviving deeds, in several of which he is described as a knight.[2] He was still alive on 24 February 1270, when he witnessed a charter,[3] and probably survived until about 1275.

(5) Ralph of Lingen III (omitted from the Harleian list). On 8 August 1276 his appointment as coroner of Herefordshire was countermanded on the ground that he was not resident in the county but in the Marches, 'where he has much land, for the defence of his lands and the adjoining lands'.[4] In Easter Term 1283 he was sued (with others) for trespass at *Bereford* (Burford, Shropshire?).[5] In 1287 he held *Kyngeshemed* (Kinsham, south of Lingen), one of the family properties, of Robert de Mortimer.[6] He was still alive in June 1292, when, answering a writ of *quo warranto*, he produced a charter granted by Henry III to his father John (explicitly so described) to justify his right of free warren in his manors of Aymestrey and Covenhope.[7]

(6) John of Lingen III (omitted from the Harleian list) in 1297 witnessed grants made by Edmund de Mortimer,[8] and in the same year, as a man holding lands or rents worth £20 and more, was summoned from Shropshire for foreign service, the muster being fixed for 7 July in London.[9] In 1301 he was similarly summoned from Herefordshire for service against the Scots, the

---

[1] Eyton, iv. 367 (citing *Placita*, Pasch. Term, 44 Hen. III, m. 32ᵈ).

[2] Cf. Eyton, iii. 27 (n. 22), 52 (nn. 11 and 12), 54 (n. 21). Thus in MS. Harley 1240 (*Liber Niger de Wigmore*), f. 40ᵛ, John of Lingen is one of a number of witnesses who are described as *milites* in document no. xxxii, a grant by Ralph de Mortimer (lord of Wigmore 1227–46), and is given the appellation *dominus* in document no. xxx, a grant to the same Ralph de Mortimer.

[3] Eyton, vii. 30 (citing *Salop Chartulary*, no. 289).

[4] *Cal. Close R. 1272–9*, p. 307.

[5] Eyton, v. 78 (citing *Placita coram Rege*, no. 75, m. 15).

[6] *Cal. I.p.m.*, ii. 395 (no. 640).

[7] *Placita de Quo Warranto*, p. 272.

[8] *Cal. Pat. R. 1292–1301*, pp. 290–1.

[9] Eyton, v. 78 (citing *Parliamentary Writs*, i. 291).

muster being fixed for 24 June at Berwick on Tweed.[1] He died
before 30 July 1304, when the king, at Stirling, granted to his
yeoman Walter of Woodham, at the instance of the queen,
the custody of John of Lingen's land during the minority of
his heir, and the marriages of his widow Matilda and of his
heir.[2]

(7) John of Lingein IV (included in the Harleian list), though
a minor in July 1304, is recorded as holding family lands as a
tenant of Edmund de Mortimer at the inquisition on the latter's
death held in Hereford on 5 February 1305.[3] He was knighted,
with many others, on the occasion of the knighting of Edward,
Prince of Wales, at Whitsuntide 1306.[4] In 1307, specifically
described as *miles*, he served on a jury at Bromyard.[5] In 1308,
at the death of Matilda (Maud), the widow of Hugh de Mortimer
of Richard's Castle, John of Lingen held lands at Knull and
at *Kyngeshemed*;[6] and in March 1316 he is recorded as holding
land at Credenhill, Covenhope, and Lye in Herefordshire.[7] In
March 1317 he witnessed a deed at Wigmore.[8] In 1324 he was one
of those summoned from Herefordshire to attend parliament at

[1] Eyton, v. 78 (citing *Parliamentary Writs*, i. 349.)

[2] *Cal. Pat. R. 1301–7*, p. 245.

[3] *Cal. I.p.m.*, iv. 165 (no. 235). The lands listed were Aymestrey,
Covenhope, and *Schurlet*; the latter is perhaps an error for Shirley, but
in later inquisitions we find Richard of *Lington* (for Lingen) holding at
Aymestrey, Covenhope, and *Shirlythe* in 1398, and John Russell and
Isabel his wife holding at Aymestrey, Covenhope, and *Shirhethe* or
Shirhech in 1425 (see p. 410, below). There seems some continuing confusion about the name. The form of 1305 suggests Shirlet Forest in
Shropshire, those of 1398 and 1425 suggest Shirl Heath (between Kingsland and Eardisland). But Shirley near Lingen was the traditional
property of the Lingens, and the grouping with Aymestrey and Covenhope suggests that this is what is meant.

[4] Elias Ashmole, *Institutions . . . of the Most Noble Order of the Garter*
(1672), pp. 38–9; William A. Shaw, *The Knights of England* (1906),
i. 118.

[5] *Registrum Ricardi de Swinfield*, ed. Capes, p. 413.

[6] *Cal. I.p.m.*, v. 25 (no. 57); cf. p. 26 (no. 58), and *Cal. Close R.
1307–13*, p. 178.

[7] Eyton, v. 78 (citing *Parliamentary Writs*, iv. 365).

[8] MS. Harley 1240 (*Liber Niger*), f. 40 (no. xxviii).

Westminster on 30 May.[1] For his marriage, see pp. 201-2, above. I have found no evidence of the date of his death.

(8) Ralph of Lingen IV (included in the Harleian list) must have been born after 1304, but probably before 1310. He is said to have married Margery, daughter of Fulk of Pembridge (*Pembruge*, etc.), of Tong in Shropshire.[2] In July 1332 Ralph of Lingen was one of the jurors at the inquest at Wigmore on Edmund de Mortimer.[3] His arrest and imprisonment in Hereford Castle (with that of many other gentlemen of the county) was ordered in April 1337,[4] and his release in May.[5] In July 1340 there is a record that Ralph of Lingen, knight, was owed a debt of £220 to be levied in Herefordshire.[6] I have found no record of his death, but after 1340 there is a long interval before the name Ralph of Lingen reappears in the public records, and when it does we must have moved on to his son of the same name.[7]

(9) Ralph of Lingen V (included in the Harleian list) was probably born about 1340. He was, as the list shows, the brother-in-law of Brian Harley, a neighbour who held lands of Roger de Mortimer in 1396[8] and defended Dolverin and Montgomery Castles for Henry IV during Glendower's rebellion.[9] His elder

---

[1] Eyton, v. 78 (citing *Parliamentary Writs*, iv. 639).

[2] Burke, *Commoners*, iv. 266. Burke does not cite his evidence, but his statement is very probable. Fulk of Pembridge was born on 25 August 1291 (*Cal. I.p.m.*, iii. 208-9 (no. 340)), and was therefore probably about seven years younger than the John of Lingen who was knighted in 1306; his daughter may well have been of an age to marry John's son Ralph. Fulk died apparently after 6 March 1326 (*Cal. Pat. R. 1324-7*, p. 248) but before 17 March 1326, leaving a widow Matilda holding his manor of Tong (*Cal. Close R. 1323-7*, p. 456). His daughter must have been born by 1326, and probably before 1320; her marriage to Ralph of Lingen could well have taken place before 1340, which would fit the chronology.

[3] Eyton, vii. 334.   [4] *Cal. Pat. R. 1334-8*, pp. 446, 451-2.

[5] *Cal. Close R. 1337-9*, p. 132.

[6] *Cal. Close R. 1339-41*, p. 490.

[7] Burke, *Commoners*, iv. 266, makes the father the man who was 'M.P. for Herefordshire' in the time of Edward III, but his chronology is confused.   [8] *Calendarium I.p.m.*, iii (1821), 234 (22 Ric. II, no. 34).

[9] Burke, *Commoners*, iv. 266. A Brian Harley is again recorded as a tenant of Edmund de Mortimer, the last Mortimer earl of March, at

sister Isabel (to be identified with the Elizabeth of the Harleian list, for the two are forms of the same name) is said to have married, as his second wife, her cousin Fulk of Pembridge (who died without issue in 1408–9),[1] and founded a college at Tong in 1410–11;[2] she must by then have been a woman of 60 or more. On 3 July 1370 a commission was issed to Ralph Lingen and others to inquire into allegations of the abduction of Elizabeth de Mortimer from a house in which William Devereux had lodged her after they had exchanged vows of marriage before witnesses and until the religious ceremony could be performed.[3] On 5 November 1373 a commission was issued to Ralph Lingen, knight (among others), to raise men for the Irish campaign,[4] and on 10 December an order was issued for the payment to him of £11. 12s. 0d. for his expenses for 29 days as knight of the shire for Herefordshire.[5] On 2 May 1379 a pardon was granted, at the supplication of Ralph Lingen, knight, to a tailor of Leominster.[6] On 7 May and 23 May 1379 he gave recognizances for the payment of sums of £80 and of 500 marks, to be levied in Herefordshire and Shropshire respectively.[7] On 6 December 1379 protection for one year was granted to Ralph of Lingen and Brian of Harley, going with others in the company of Edmund de Mortimer on the expedition to Ireland,[8] and the grant was repeated, to Ralph Lingen knight and Brian of Harley, going to Ireland on the king's service with Edmund earl of March, on 10 November

the latter's death in 1425 (*Calendarium I.p.m.*, iv (1828), 93 (3 Hen. VI, no. 32)), but as the name Brian was in constant use in this family this may not be the same man.

[1] Eyton, ii. 240, who calls her 'Isabel or Elizabeth' Lingen.

[2] *Monasticon*, vi. 1401–11; Burke, *Commoners*, iv. 266; Eyton, ii. 240. Burke's chronology is again confused, for at this point he identifies the Ralph Lingen who died before March 1390, the brother-in-law of Brian Harley, with the Ralph Lingen who died in 1452. He has failed to recognize the omissions of the Harleian list.

[3] *Cal. Pat. R. 1367–70*, pp. 471–2.

[4] *Cal. Pat. R. 1370–4*, p. 353.

[5] *Cal. Close R. 1369–74*, p. 611.

[6] *Cal. Pat. R. 1377–81*, p. 345.

[7] *Cal. Close R. 1377–81*, pp. 242, 251.

[8] *Cal. Pat. R. 1377–81*, p. 409.

1380.[1] He died before 4 March 1390, when the king, having custody of the lands and heir of Ralph of Lingen, knight, granted to David Vaghan ap David the free chapel of St. Michael, Lingen;[2] in December 1391 the king is again found disposing of the chapel.[3]

(10) John of Lingen V (omitted from the Harleian list) must have been still a minor in 1390–1, but in 1398 he is recorded as holding Lingen at the death of Roger de Mortimer, fourth earl of March,[4] and again in a document of 16 March 1399.[5] He still held Lingen at the death of Edmund de Mortimer in 1425.[6] He is a shadowy figure and would seem to have played little part in affairs. Probably because of his minority, in 1394 a Richard Lingen, presumably his father's younger brother, was carrying out the military duties which would ordinarily be those of the head of the family (and which Ralph V had performed), and was also holding several of the chief family manors, probably by virtue of a marriage settlement.[7]

(11) Ralph Lingen VI (omitted from the Harleian list) is presumably the man mentioned in a record of 1425 which says that 'Elizabeth wife of Ralph Lingham' then held Upper Lye.[8] As this was one of the properties of Isabel, the widow of Richard Lingen, it would seem that Elizabeth was her daughter by her third marriage (after 1406) to John Russell and that she had settled Upper Lye on her daughter as her marriage-portion.[9] Elizabeth obviously predeceased her husband, for he had married

[1] *Cal. Pat. R. 1377–81*, p. 556.

[2] *Cal. Pat. R. 1388–92*, p. 229. As the Lingens were not tenants-in-chief, but subtenants of the Mortimers, their lands would not ordinarily have fallen into the king's hand; but at this time Roger de Mortimer (1374–98) was himself a minor and the king's ward.

[3] *Cal. Pat. R. 1391–6*, pp. 9, 10.

[4] *Calendarium I.p.m.*, iii (1821), 234 (22 Ric. II, no. 34).

[5] *Cal. Close R. 1396–9*, p. 457.

[6] *Calendarium I.p.m.*, iv (1828), 93 (3 Hen. VI, no. 32).

[7] See p. 410, below.   [8] *Calendarium I.p.m.*, iv (1828), 94.

[9] See p. 410, below. It is not inconsistent with this view that in 1428 Upper Lye is recorded as being held by John Russell and 'Isabel his wife'; if Elizabeth was their daughter she would hold Upper Lye by right of her mother.

again before his death. He was appointed escheator of Hereford-shire on 26 November 1431,[1] but had ceased to hold the office by 1 December 1432;[2] he was again escheator in July 1433,[3] and was reappointed on 4 November 1433.[4] He was appointed sheriff of Herefordshire on 6 November 1444,[5] and with others was commissioned to hold an inquisition in January 1446.[6] He died on 2 January 1453, leaving as his next heir his son John, aged 21 on the previous 3 November.[7] He had appointed feoffees in trust to take control of his lands; and at uncertain dates before (probably) the end of 35 Henry VI (i.e. at the outside, before 31 August 1457) his widow Joan and her new husband Thomas Fitz-Harry engaged in litigation with these feoffees concerning the manor of Sutton Overcourt and other lands in Herefordshire.[8]

(12) John Lingen VI (the *Johannes de Lingan miles* at the foot of the Harleian list) was born on 3 November 1431, and must have been the son of his father's first wife, Elizabeth Russell.[9] On 13 May 1457 he and other gentlemen of Hereford-shire were required jointly to enter into a recognisance of 5,000 marks and, having been committed to the custody of the marshal of the king's marshalsea, to be true prisoners according to law.[10] He was appointed sheriff of Herefordshire for the first time on 5 November 1465,[11] and was knighted by Edward IV on the field of the battle of Tewkesbury on 4 May 1471.[12] He was

---

[1] *Cal. Fine R.*, xvi. 79.   [2] *Cal. Pat. R. 1429–36*, p. 253.
[3] *Cal. Close R. 1429–35*, p. 218.
[4] *Cal. Fine R.*, xvii. 285.   [5] *Cal. Fine R.*, xvii. 303.
[6] *Cal. Pat. R. 1441–6*, p. 466; *Cal. Close R. 1441–7*, p. 400.
[7] Chancery Inquisitions *post mortem*, Henry VI, File 149, no. 21; writ of *diem clausit extremum* (dated 22 January 1453) also in *Cal. Fine R.*, xix. 2. The return to the writ says that the inquisition was held at Hereford on 12 April, and names Ralph Lingen's wife as Joan, daughter of Laurence Merbury, knight. The inquisition is briefly listed in *Calendarium I.p.m.*, iv (1828), 254 (31 Hen. VI, no. 21), but the details here given are from the original in the P.R.O.
[8] *Early Chancery Proceedings*, vol. i (P.R.O. Lists and Indexes xii, 1901), pp. 134 (no. 304), 218 (no. 107), 259 (nos. 526, 529).
[9] See p. 410, below.
[10] *Cal. Close R. 1454–61*, pp. 222–3.   [11] *Cal. Fine R.*, xx. 168.
[12] Shaw, *The Knights of England*, ii. 14.

appointed sheriff for a second term on 9 November 1471,[1] for a third on 5 November 1486,[2] and finally on 5 November 1495.[3] At numerous dates between July 1471 and December 1484 he received commissions of various sorts, including commissions of the peace,[4] and similarly during the reign of Henry VII, on 11 May 1486, 24 October 1490, and 24 February 1498.[5] On some of these occasions he was appointed jointly with Sir John Devoreux and/or Sir William Devoreux; according to the Harleian list, his sister Matilda was married to Robert Devoreux. He died on 2 March 1507, aged 75, leaving as his heir his son, Sir John Lingen 'the younger', then aged '40 years and more'.[6] He married, presumably about 1460, Isabel, third daughter and co-heiress of Sir John Burgh.[7] In July 1482 she and her husband are recorded as joint patrons of the living of Wentnor, which was part of her heritage.[8] She died early in 1522, probably on Thursday 30 Janu-

---

[1] *Cal. Fine R.*, xxi. 30 (no. 79).

[2] *Cal. Fine R.*, xxii. 54 (no. 128). But the clerk wrote simply 'John Lyngeyn', without appellation (whether 'knight' or 'esquire'); such omissions occur elsewhere and have no necessary significance. In this case, however, the *List of Sheriffs for England and Wales* (P.R.O. Lists and Indexes ix, 1898) enters the appointment as 'John Lyngeyn (afterwards knighted)', from which Shaw, *Knights*, ii. 23, concludes that in addition to the 'John Lyngeyne' who was knighted by Edward IV in 1471, there was another 'John Lyngeyn sheriff of Hereford' knighted by Henry VII 'after 5 November 1486'. This is merely a misconception based on the clerk's omission of the appellation, coupled with later records of John Lingen's period of office which correctly described him as 'knight'. The sheriff of 1486 could not have been John Lingen VII, who was not knighted until 1504, and there is no evidence at all that there was at that time a third John Lingen, also a sheriff of Herefordshire and also a knight.   [3] *Cal. Fine R.*, xxii. 225 (no. 535).

[4] *Cal. Pat. R. 1467–77*, pp. 288, 350, 407, 616; *1476–85*, pp. 110, 111, 226, 242, 392, 394, 401, 491, 561.

[5] *Cal. Pat. R. 1485–94*, pp. 106, 134; *1494–1509*, p. 148.

[6] *Cal. Fine R.*, xxii. 383 (no. 855, writ of *diem clausit extremum* dated 13 April 1507); *Cal. I.p.m. Hen. VII*, iii. 239 (no. 377).

[7] *Cal. Fine R.*, xxi. 35 (no. 95, dated 14 November 1471); the document rehearses *inter alia* that 'John Lingen knight' has had issue of his wife Isabel.

[8] *Registrum T. Myllyng*, ed. A. T. Bannister (Canterbury and York Soc. xxvi, 1920), p. 173.

ary.[1] Her heir was her son Sir John Lingen, who according to the most probable account, that of the return from Gloucestershire, was then aged '60 years and more'.[2]

(13) John Lingen VII (not included in the Harleian list) on the evidence just cited was born before 1462. He was appointed escheator of Shropshire on 6 November 1489[3] and sheriff of Herefordshire for the first time on 5 November 1497 (being then 'John Lyngeyn esquire'),[4] was knighted on 18 February 1504 on the occasion of prince Henry's being created Prince of Wales,[5] and was appointed sheriff for the second time on 1 December 1505.[6] On 29 January 1507 a commission of the peace again describes him (his father still being alive) as 'John Lyngen the younger, knight'.[7] Later periods of office as sheriff of Herefordshire were in 1516, 1520, and 1528.[8] He died on 29 April 1530.[9]

---

[1] So the return from Gloucestershire, which says she died on Thursday before the feast of the Purification (2 February, which fell on Sunday). The return from Shropshire says she died on Thursday before the feast of the Annunciation (25 March), evidently an error. The return from Warwickshire says she died on 4 February. The writ of *d.c.e.* was dated 12 May.

[2] The return from Warwickshire says '50 years and more', that from Shropshire gives no age. The returns of the inquisitions *post mortem* in the P.R.O. are: (i) from Shropshire, Chancery Series II, vol. 38, no. 31 (= Exchequer Series II, File 843, no. 2); (ii) from Gloucestershire, Chancery Series II, vol. 39, no. 80; (iii) from Warwickshire, Chancery Series II, vol. 39, no. 103.   [3] *Cal. Fine R.*, xxii. 133 (no. 325).

[4] *Cal. Fine R.*, xxii. 263 (no. 602).

[5] Shaw, *Knights*, ii. 34.

[6] *Cal. Fine R.*, xxii. 377 (no. 843). But his name is given as 'William Lingern the younger, knight', an error corrected in the *List of Sheriffs*, p. 61.   [7] *Cal. Pat. R. 1494–1509*, p. 642.

[8] *List of Sheriffs*, p. 61.

[9] Inquisition *post mortem* in the P.R.O.: return from Herefordshire, Chancery Series II, vol. 51, no. 19 (= Exchequer Series II, File 429, no. 1); from Shropshire, Chancery Series II, vol. 51, no. 65 (= Exchequer Series II, File 851, no. 1). The returns, especially that from Herefordshire, set out in detail the elaborate legal dispositions Sir John had made for his property.

A complication is introduced by a record that among the men who were summoned to attend the king's person, accompanied by specified numbers of troops, during the Lincolnshire rebellion of 1536, and to whom

He was twice married. His first wife was Eleanor, only daughter and heiress of Thomas Mylwater (Mylewater). Mylwater died on 1 February 1473,[1] having appointed feoffees in trust to hold his manor of Stoke Edith for his daughter, who was under age; on 9 July 1490 an order was issued to these feoffees for the delivery of her lands, as she had become of full age on the preceding 2 February.[2] From the wording of the order one would assume that she was still unmarried, but this is probably misleading; her son John Lingen was reported to be aged 40 years 'and more' at the time of his father's death in 1530, and must therefore have been born in 1490 at latest.[3] She died, at latest, in 1522, for at the end of that year her husband married Elinora, widow of Sir Thomas Cresset, of Upton within the manor of Sutton.[4]

(14) Sir John 'the younger' was succeeded by his son John Lingen VIII (not included in the Harleian list); he was aged '40 years and more' at Sir John's death. Within his father's lifetime he was living at Stoke Edith, his mother's manor, of which he was the heir. He married, probably in 1507–8,[5] Mar-

countermanding orders were sent when it collapsed, was 'Sir John Lyngham' of Herefordshire (*Letters and Papers of Henry VIII*, vol. xi, no. 580 (p. 233, twice) and no. 670). Apparently, in the flurry of sending out the orders, old lists were used, and it was not realized that Sir John Lingen had been dead for six years, or alternatively that his son had not been knighted.

[1] *Cal. Close R. 1485–1500*, p. 123 (no. 431), as calendared, says that he died on '1 February last', but the 'last' (which would mean February 1490) is some error; the writ of *d.c.e.* was issued on 8 February 1473 (*Cal. Fine R.*, xxi. 38 (no. 100)), and the inquisition was held at Ledbury on 11 March 1473 (*Cal. Close R.*, loc. cit.).

[2] *Cal. Close R.*, loc. cit.

[3] Duncumb, *Herefordshire*, ii. 184, dates Eleanor Mylwater's marriage '4 Hen. VIII' (1512–13), and Burke, *Commoners*, iv. 267, dates it 1514, but this makes nonsense of the chronology. Probably Duncumb's '4 Hen. VIII' is an error for 4 Hen. VII (1488–9), which would be about right.

[4] A dispensation for the marriage was granted by the bishop of Hereford on 26 November 1522 (*Registrum Caroli Bothe* [etc.], ed. Bannister, p. 349).

[5] In 23 Henry VII (1507–8) Sir John Lingen 'the younger' made legal agreements whereby the manor of Weston was placed in the hands of

garet, the daughter of a Sir Thomas Englefield and the sister of another man of the same name, a justice of the Court of Common Pleas who died in 1537.[1] Margaret Englefield can have had little joy of her marriage; for a petition dated 6 June 1524 from Charles Bothe, bishop of Hereford, to the king asks for the arrest of John Lingen of Stoke Edith and Anne Giles of Withington as adulterous persons who remained recalcitrant after excommunication.[2] John Lingen of Stoke Edith was cited under the Privy Seal to appear before Mr. Secretary Cromwell on 15 June 1533;[3] and on 8 June his brother-in-law, Sir Thomas Englefield, wrote to Cromwell to say:

You were good enough to send to John Lyngen the elder, to appear before you . . . As he thinks the privy seal refers only to his fine for not being knighted, he will appear . . . I shall not be able to be in London the first day of term to declare to you his abominable and beastly living, for the continuance whereof he and his naughty queans are accursed; also his unreasonable demeanor towards my sister, his wife, and children, who, but for their friends, would have been famished . . .'.[4]

Lingen appeared, but 'obstinately departed without leave', and was summoned again to appear before Cromwell on 3 November 1534.[5] In 1539 and 1542 the reprobate was still living at Stoke

trustees for the use and benefit of John Lingen knight and 'Alionora then his wife' during their lives, and after their deaths for John Lingen esquire and Margaret the daughter of Thomas Englefield knight, his wife. This was obviously a marriage settlement. See the return of the inquisition *post mortem* on Sir John Lingen held at Hereford on 22 October 1530 (Chancery Series II, vol. 51, no. 19 = Exchequer Series II, File 429, no. 1). Duncumb, ii. 184, dates the marriage 22 Henry VIII (1530–1), but this is the date of Sir John's death and of the inquisition, not of his son's marriage.

[1] *DNB*, s.n. Englefield, Sir Francis.

[2] *Registrum Caroli Bothe*, p. 160.

[3] *Letters and Papers of Henry VIII*, Addenda vol. i, part I, p. 297 (no. 855).

[4] *Letters and Papers of Henry VIII*, vi. 280–1 (no. 607).

[5] *Letters and Papers of Henry VIII*, Addenda vol. i, part I, p. 333 (no. 947).

Edith, apparently undisturbed.[1] He died on 22 February 1545, having survived excommunication for 21 years.[2]

It is not clear whether he was the same man as the John Lingen of Whitton (Witton), Shropshire (one mile WSW. of Westbury), who on 23 January 1526 at Westbury attacked Lodovic ap Hoel by force and arms and wounded him so severely that he died on the following 13 April. Lingen repeatedly failed to appear to answer the charge against him and orders for his arrest were ineffective, and he was finally outlawed by the king's coroners in Shropshire; an inquisition held by the escheator of Shropshire at Wellington on 3 November 1530, after rehearsing these facts, declared his lands at Westbury and Whitton forfeit to the Crown,[3] and they were subsequently leased to other men.[4] Three facts argue in favour of the identification of this John Lingen of Whitton with John Lingen of Stoke Edith. (i) The inquisition into the case of John Lingen of Whitton was held by the escheator of Shropshire on 3 November 1530, nine days after his inquisition *post mortem* on Sir John Lingen (held on 25 October 1530), at which John Lingen of Stoke Edith was declared the heir; it looks as though the escheator was dealing with related cases. (ii) In 1541 Whitton was held by William 'Lyngam',[5] and it is known that John Lingen of Stoke Edith had a younger son named William. (iii) The elaborate legal arrangements made by Sir John Lingen in 1529 or earlier for the family properties seemed designed to guard against forfeiture. These arrangements are carefully rehearsed in the returns of the inquisitions *post mortem* on Sir John, and there is clear evidence in that from Herefordshire that Sir Thomas Englefield, the justice of the Court of Common Pleas, had a hand in them. In general Sir John placed the family properties in the care of trustees,

---

[1] *Letters and Papers of Henry VIII*, vol. xiv, part I, p. 273; vol. xvii, pp. 501–2.

[2] Return of inquisition *post mortem* held at Hereford on 21 October 1545 (P.R.O., Exchequer Series II, File 440, no. 1).

[3] P.R.O., Exchequer Series II, File 851, no. 3.

[4] *Letters and Papers of Henry VIII*, v. 287 (no. 627 (27), of December 1531); vi. 191 (no. 418 (15), of April 1533).

[5] *Letters and Papers of Henry VIII*, xvi. 293.

either by deeds drawn up at earlier dates or by his will in 1529, to be held for the use and benefit of himself and 'Alienora his wife' during their lives, and after their deaths for the use and benefit of his son and heir John Lingen esquire 'for his life only',[1] and thereafter for the latter's son and heir-apparent John Lingen (Sir John's grandson) and his heirs. That is, the son, John Lingen VIII, was given only a life interest in properties held by trustees, with eventual remainder to the grandson, John Lingen IX. But these arrangements might have been made only to avoid the possibility that John Lingen VIII, the adulterer, might dissipate the family wealth in favour of his 'naughty queans'.

(15) John Lingen IX (not included in the Harleian list) was aged '30 years and more' at his father's death in 1545, and was therefore born at latest in 1515, and probably about 1510. He was listed as 'John Lyngen junior' in the musters of the army prepared against France in 1544, his father still being alive.[2] He was appointed sheriff of Herefordshire on 16 November 1544, still listed as 'John Lingen the younger, esq.'[3] In May 1547 and December 1550 he received, with others, the commission of the peace.[4] In 1550 he and his wife Isabel disposed temporarily of the manor of Stoke Edith.[5] In October 1553 he was granted certain offices for life 'in consideration of his services'.[6] He received the commission of the peace again on 18 February 1554,[7] but died soon after; on 6 May of that year the offices that he had been granted the previous October, and 'which John Lyngham lately held', were filled.[8] The writ of *diem clausit extremum*, though badly rubbed, seems to be dated 8 May; the inquest was

---

[1] An exception is that a deed of 4 March 1522 placed the manor of Kenchester in the hands of trustees for the use and benefit, after the death of John Lingen knight, of his son Thomas Lingen (evidently a younger son) for the duration of his life only, and after his death to the direct heirs of John Lingen knight.

[2] *Letters and Papers of Henry VIII*, vol. xix, part I, p. 153.

[3] *List of Sheriffs*, p. 61.

[4] *Cal. Pat. R. 1547–8*, p. 84; *Cal. Pat. R. 1553*, p. 354.

[5] *Cal. Pat. R. 1549–51*, p. 230 (of date 18 October 1550).

[6] *Cal. Pat. R. 1553–4*, p. 394.

[7] *Cal. Pat. R. 1553–4*, p. 20.   [8] *Cal. Pat. R. 1553–4*, p. 161.

held at Hereford on 19 July. The return of the inquisition is very badly rubbed at the foot and is in part illegible. It does not seem to give the date of John Lingen's death, but appears to say that his wife 'Isabell' died on 20 May last.[1] Their daughter was therefore left an orphan.

(16) Jane Lingen (not included in the Harleian list) was the only child and sole heiress of her father John and his wife Isabel. She was 10 years old at his death in 1554, and the custody of her lands and person was given, during her minority, to the marquis of Winchester, treasurer of England.[2] On 28 May 1560 a licence was granted for her to enter upon her lands, to issue from the time when she attained the age of 16.[3] She died in 1610, and was succeeded by her first cousin Edward Lingen,[4] the son of her father's younger brother William, who had died in 1569.[5] This Edward Lingen had a most unhappy career;[6] he was probably a Catholic recusant. But with the break in the direct line of descent we may end our account of it, for we have already passed the date at which the Lingen 'genealogy' was copied into MS. Harley 1087.

The records have, however, many references to other members of what is evidently the same family, though these members do not figure in the direct line. On 29 February 1268 a pardon was granted, at the instance of Roger de Mortimer, to John son of Walter of Lingen for the death of John of Showdon (Shobdon?).[7]

---

[1] Inquisitions *post mortem*, Chancery Series II, vol. 102, no. 79.

[2] *Cal. Pat. R. 1554–5*, p. 88.

[3] *Cal. Pat. R. 1558–60*, p. 448.

[4] Burke, *Commoners*, iv. 267.

[5] Uncalendared I.p.m. in P.R.O.; see *Index of Inquisitions*, vol. ii: Elizabeth (P.R.O. Lists and Indexes xxvi, 1908), p. 221.

[6] On 16 May 1603 Edward Lyngen was attainted of treason (Historical MSS. Commission, *Hatfield House XV*, p. 92). On 7 November 1623 an order was issued that Edward Lyngen of Stoke Edith was to be sent to Stoke Edith or to his other house of Sutton, he being and long having been a prisoner for contempt in the Porter's Lodge prison, but having been found a lunatic and committed to the care of Sir John Scudamore, bart. (Historical MSS. Commission, vol. xiii, part IV, p. 271).

[7] *Cal. Pat. R. 1266–72*, p. 198.

A little later there are Richard of Lingen and Thomas of Lingen, ordained priests in 1277 and 1278 respectively, and probably younger brothers of the contemporary Ralph.[1] In 1309 it is recorded that Thomas of Lingen was a tenant of Matilda, widow of Hugh de Mortimer of Richard's Castle, at her death.[2] In 1327 a pardon was granted to John son of John son of Nicholas of Lingen for the deaths of William Wilmot and Thomas David.[3] On 7 September 1352 a pardon of special grace was granted to Thomas of Lingen, chaplain, for the death of Henry, late porter of *Lyngebrok*[4]—evidently not a happy incident in the association of the Lingens with Limebrook Priory. From 1361 until 1400 there are records of what is evidently a continuing family of Lingens in the service of the royal household—Henry Lingen who received a grant for long service in 1361 and 1363,[5] Hugh Lingen (his son?) and Agatha, Hugh's wife, who served Queen Philippa, Edward III, and Richard II from at latest 1363 until 1400,[6] and what is perhaps a second Henry, who was Richard II's esquire.[7] The Thomas Lingen who was keeper of a park in Essex in 1400[8] perhaps belonged to the same branch of the family. To go back a little, in 1372 Robert Lingen held the manor of Oxenden,[9]

[1] *Register of Thomas de Cantilupe*, ed. Griffiths, pp. 301, 303.

[2] *Cal. I.p.m.*, v. 25 (no. 57) and 26 (no. 58), which give the name of the place as *Herton; Cal. Close R. 1307–13*, p. 178, which gives *Heriton*.

[3] *Cal. Pat. R. 1327–30*, p. 45.

[4] *Cal. Pat. R. 1350–4*, p. 319.

[5] *Cal. Pat. R. 1361–4*, pp. 4, 279; *1377–81*, p. 176; *1385–9*, p. 452.

[6] *Cal. Pat. R. 1361–4*, p. 306; *1367–70*, pp. 342, 374, 386; *1374–7*, p. 384; *1377–81*, pp. 178, 389; *1381–5*, p. 435; *1385–9*, pp. 5, 452, 491; *1389–92*, pp. 77, 312, 455; *1391–6*, p. 251; *1396–9*, p. 569; *1399–1401*, pp. 176, 185; *Cal. Close R. 1377–81*, p. 371; *1381–5*, pp. 50, 124; *1385–9*, pp. 111, 442. Agatha drops out fairly soon, but Hugh continues; he was buyer for the royal household and is described as 'esquire' and as 'serjaunt', and finally got, on 27 January 1400, a tun of Gascon wine yearly for life from Henry IV for his good service to the king's predecessors. But he did not enjoy it long, for he was dead by 16 September 1400 (*Cal. Close R. 1399–1402*, pp. 210, 388).

[7] *Cal. Pat. R. 1385–9*, p. 34; *Cal. Close R. 1385–9*, p. 483; *1389–92*, p. 313.

[8] *Cal. Close R. 1399–1402*, p. 140.

[9] *Cal. Close R. 1367–74*, pp. 396, 469.

and in 1388 Philip Lingen of Ludlow received a pardon of out-lawry for failure to pay a debt of 40s.[1]

In the Wigmore area itself, in 1394 Richard Lingen esquire, who on 10 August 1394 had been granted protection for half a year as one of those going on the king's service to Ireland with Roger de Mortimer, earl of March and Ulster,[2] held important family lands at Aymestrey, Covenhope, and *Shirlythe* in 1398.[3] He must have been a younger brother of Ralph V, and the uncle of John V, who in 1394 may still have been a minor. The family lands had clearly been divided for the time being. Richard's wife Isabel, formerly the wife of John Sentowen, held lands of her own, including Upper Lye SE. of Lingen.[4] He died in 1406,[5] and it is recorded that in 1426 Aymestrey, Covenhope, and *Shir-hethe* (or *Shirhech*), and in 1428 Upper Lye, were held by John Russell and 'Isabel his wife'.[6] The probable explanation is that by a marriage settlement life tenancies of Aymestrey, Covenhope, and Shirley, which would make a compact property with Upper Lye, had been granted to Richard Lingen and Isabel his wife; that Isabel and her tenancy had survived Richard by 22 years at least; and that John Russell was a third husband, holding by right of his wife. In due course the Lingen lands returned to the possession of the head of the family. The shield of arms in Aymestrey parish church above the tomb of Sir John Lingen (John VI) quarters the arms of Russell with those of Lingen,[7] which must mean that he had inherited the lands of both families; this justifies the assumption made above that he was the son of Elizabeth, his father's first wife and the daughter (evidently also the heiress) of Isabel and her third husband John Russell.

Other Lingens are met with in the fifteenth century. In

[1] *Cal. Pat. R. 1385–9*, p. 487.   [2] *Cal. Pat. R. 1391–6*, p. 481.

[3] *Calendarium I.p.m.*, iii (1821), 239. Richard's surname in some of the records is incorrectly given as *Lington* or *Lingem*.

[4] *Calendarium I.p.m.*, iii (1821), 239; *Cal. Close R. 1396–9*, p. 459; *1402–5*, p. 328; *1405–9*, p. 310; *Cal. Fine R.*, xiii. 170, 173–4.

[5] *Cal. Fine R.*, xiii. 78.

[6] *Calendarium I.p.m.*, iv (1828), 94; *Cal. Close R. 1422–9*, p. 252; *Feudal Aids*, ii. 413.

[7] R.C.H.M., *Herefordshire*, iii. 10.

1403 and 1407 a 'William Lyngeyn clerk' is recorded as holding land at Eastham.[1] In 1411 there is a record of a Walter Lingen, deceased, who had been keeper of the forest of Highwood of Leominster,[2] and in 1427 John Lingen 'late of Worcester, yeoman' (perhaps not a member of this family) was a member of an armed poaching party.[3] In 1428 and 1431 Philip Lingen was assessed for various landholdings in Leominster Hundred,[4] and in 1434 was among many in Hereford who took an oath to maintain the peace.[5] In 1441 and 1444 William Lingen was appointed escheator of Shropshire;[6] he may be the same man as received the commission of the peace at Westminster in July 1449[7] and was one of the feoffees in trust of the manor of Middleton Stony, Oxfordshire, in 1450.[8] It is not so clear whether he was the same as the William Lingen, esquire, 'late of London', who was granted a pardon for non-appearance concerning a debt of £23. 6s. 8d. in Middlesex in June 1469, or the William Lingen 'late of Caurs alias Caus co. Salop' who likewise was pardoned for non-appearance concerning a debt of the same amount (though to answer a different plaintiff) in London in June 1474.[9] But he was certainly not the same as the William Lingen who as Sewer of the Chamber took part in the funeral of Henry VII in 1509;[10] this was probably a younger son of Sir John Lingen 'the elder'. He received a grant for life in June 1510,[11] which he surrendered in May 1511 for another grant.[12] In 1527 a pardon was granted to Roger Lingen, 'late of Hereford, chaplain', for robbing Edward Frowceter, deacon of Hereford, of golden jewellery valued at £10.[13]

[1] *Cal. Close R. 1402–5*, p. 75; *1405–9*, p. 183.
[2] *Cal. Pat. R. 1408–13*, p. 290.   [3] *Cal. Pat. R. 1422–9*, p. 423.
[4] *Feudal Aids*, ii. 413, 421.   [5] *Cal. Pat. R. 1429–36*, p. 377.
[6] *Cal. Fine R.*, xvii. 206, 304.   [7] *Cal. Pat. R. 1446–52*, p. 594.
[8] *Cal. Pat. R. 1446–52*, pp. 311–12.
[9] *Cal. Pat. R. 1467–77*, pp. 143, 432.
[10] *Letters and Papers of Henry VIII*, vol. i, part i, p. 20.
[11] *Letters and Papers of Henry VIII*, vol. i, part i, p. 305.
[12] *Letters and Papers of Henry VIII*, vol. i, part i, p. 424.
[13] *Letters and Papers of Henry VIII*, vol. iii, part 2, p. 1595 (no. 3540 (15)).

This last glimpse of the occasional lawlessness of the Lingens brings us to the period (1522–30) at which the list of MS. Harley 1087 was finally revised. The relationship of all these Lingens to each other is not apparent, but it is at least evident that there was no lack of younger sons who could have been included in the Harleian list if its compilers had so desired. But it omits even the Richard Lingen who seems to have been so prominent a member of the family from 1394 to 1406, and the William who held the responsible post of escheator of Shropshire in 1441 and 1444. It is true that it has a blank, even in the direct male line, from 1390 to 1452; but its concentration on the lords of the manor of Lingen, and their sisters and wives, is clear.

APPENDIX IV

THE CROFT FAMILY

THE following account of the lords of Croft from the later twelfth to the early fourteenth century has as its object the identification of the Hugh of Croft who witnessed Roger de Mortimer's charter to Limebrook Priory, which must fall between 1246 (when Roger succeeded to the barony) and the end of 1269 (when Robert Corbet died). In view of its limited purpose, it makes no pretence of completeness. The account given by O. G. S. Croft, *The House of Croft of Croft Castle* (Hereford, 1949), is distinguished by family piety rather than by scholarly accuracy (whether in statement of fact, or in citation—if there is citation—of authority, or in printing the texts of documents); and Croft seems undoubtedly to confuse and even to omit generations, probably because of lack of information and uncritical reliance on the family trees of earlier antiquaries and genealogists. But I follow him where I can.

In 1086, at the time of the Domesday Survey, Croft, Wharton, Newton (in Hope under Dinmore), and other lands in Herefordshire were held by (1) Bernard of Croft, who later (in 1103, according to O. G. S. Croft) became a monk at Thetford Priory after having granted it the tithes of Wharton.[1] He was succeeded as lord of Croft by (2) his son Gilbert, who confirmed the grant of the tithes of Wharton 'by his father Bernard before he was made a monk'.[2] His tenure probably lasted from 1103 to about 1130. He was succeeded by (3) Hugh of Croft I, who with his brothers confirmed the grant of the tithes made by his grandfather Bernard and his father Gilbert.[3] By a deed which Croft

[1] Croft, pp. 10, 11.
[2] B.M. MS. Cotton Vitellius E. xv, f. 163ᵛ.   [3] Ibid., f. 163.

dates between 1130 and 1135 he was granted a mill between Yarpole and Croft by the abbot of Reading.[1] His tenure must have lasted from *c.* 1130 to 1160 or a little later. Thereafter the line of succession seems to have been as follows.

(4) Hugh of Croft II had probably come newly into his inheritance at Michaelmas 1163, when the Pipe Roll for 9 Henry II records him, under *Nova Placita*, as owing 30 marks *pro terra sua*, of which he had already paid 5 marks; he paid off the rest by instalments between 1163 and 1167.[2] In the 'Herefordshire Domesday' (*c.* 1160–70) he is recorded as holding one hide in Croft, one in Wharton (*Wauerton*'), and a half-hide in Hope-under-Dinmore.[3] In the Pipe Roll of 1176 he is recorded, with three others, as a knight of the shire in Herefordshire.[4] In 1191 he confirmed, by a charter, the transference in 1189 of the tithes of Wharton from Thetford Priory to Osney Abbey; the deed was witnessed by (among others) *Roberto avungulo meo* and *Milone filio meo*.[5] There is no later record of him.

(5) Milo of Croft is apparently known only from his witnessing of his father's charter of 1191. The natural inference is that he was Hugh II's eldest son and heir, consenting to his father's grant.

[1] Croft, pp. 10, 12.

[2] *Pipe R. 9 Hen. II*, p. 7; *10 Hen. II*, p. 6; *11 Hen. II*, p. 101; *12 Hen. II*, p. 84; *13 Hen. II*, p. 70. Croft, p. 12, takes the Pipe Roll references (inaccurately dated 1163–5) as referring to Hugh I, though on p. 13 he says that Hugh II held lands in Herefordshire between 1165 and 1168. He has carelessly not distinguished the generations. The sum assessed on Hugh of Croft in 1163 *pro terra sua*, and paid off by 1167, must have been a relief, and therefore an indication that he had recently been given seisin of his lands.

[3] *The Herefordshire Domesday*, ed. V. H. Galbraith and James Tait (Pipe Roll Soc., N.S. xxv), pp. 13, 54, 78; cf. also the notes on pp. 105–6, 127. [4] *Pipe R. 22 Hen. II*, p. 45.

[5] For the transference of the tithes from Thetford to Osney see Croft, p. 14, where it is dated 1189, evidently correctly (though on p. 13 the date is given as 1180, probably a misprint). The terms of Hugh II's deed of confirmation and its list of witnesses were recited in a later confirmation by his descendant John II in 1289; this is Bodleian Charters: Oxon., Oseney Abbey, no. 214b (MS. Charters Oxon. a. 3). Its text is given by Croft, pp. 21–2, but with errors and omissions (probably again due to the printer).

As he was a competent witness, he must have been of full age, and therefore born by 1170 at latest. Though E. O. G. Croft does not recognize him as belonging in the direct line of descent, and though I have found no other record of him, he fits well into the twenty-year gap between Hugh II (last heard of in 1191) and Hugh III (first heard of in 1211–12).

(6) Hugh of Croft III was, according to E. O. G. Croft, the son of Hugh II and the elder brother of Milo,[1] but this, since it would imply that he was born before 1170 (see above), makes nonsense of the chronology.[2] He must rather have been the son of Milo and the grandson of Hugh II, and have been born by 1190 (since he held a knight's fee in 1211–12), probably between 1180 and 1190. He is recorded as holding one knight's fee of the honour of Brecon in 1211–12.[3] In 1220 he is said to have acted as surety for Brian of Brampton.[4] In 1229 he witnessed, with Ralph de Mortimer and others, an important charter granted by Hubert de Burgh to the town of Montgomery.[5] In March 1230 he was one of those against whom attorneys were appointed by Gladusa, widow of Reginald de Braose[6] (i.e. Gwladys Ddu, daughter of Llywelyn ab Iorwerth, who married Ralph de Mortimer in that year and became the mother of Roger de Mortimer). In 1233 the Close Roll describes him as a knight and records the grant to him of lands in order that he may continue to serve the king.[7] In May 1234 Henry III, on the nomination of Llywelyn ab Iorwerth, prince of Aberffraw,

---

[1] p. 14.

[2] Croft, p. 15, treats only the records of 1211–12 and 1220 as referring to this Hugh of Croft, and plainly believes that he died between 1220 and 1240. But he is unaware of the evidence of the public records, which show a continuous career in the royal service from 1233 onwards, ended in 1255 by dismissal on account of old age. The records of 1211–12 to 1230 must be linked with those of 1233 to 1255. The man who was appointed escheator in 1246 (and dismissed in 1255) cannot have been born before 1170.

[3] *Red Book of the Exchequer*, ed. H. Hall (Rolls Series, 1896), ii. 601.

[4] Croft, p. 15.

[5] *Inspeximus* dated 6 October 1229, *Cal. Charter R.*, i. 101.

[6] *Close R. 1227–31*, pp. 389–90.

[7] Ibid., pp. 282, 335.

appointed him (with Brian of Brampton and John fitz Geoffrey) to supervise in Herefordshire the carrying out of the terms of truce between the king and the prince.[1] In 1235 and 1237 he was one of the receivers in Herefordshire of the royal taxation imposed in those years.[2] In 1242 he is recorded as holding Croft, Wharton, and Newton of the honour of Dilwyn,[3] and in 1249 he is similarly recorded as holding land at Marston, of the honour of Weobley.[4] On 23 June 1246 he was appointed escheator of Herefordshire,[5] and in November 1252 a record shows him exercising his functions as such;[6] but on 1 May 1254 the king ordered him to be replaced in the office,[7] and when for some reason this proved ineffective a further order on 1 July 1255 dismissed him 'on account of his old age and feebleness'.[8] This is the last record that certainly refers to him, though it is probably he (and not Hugh IV) who is recorded in the Pipe Rolls for 1258–9 and 1260–1 as owing one mark as an amercement for failure to produce a man for whom he had stood surety.[9] The date of the Herefordshire account in which this debt is first recorded is 27 January 1260,[10] but it is possible, to judge from its position in the Pipe Roll, that the amercement was originally imposed at assizes held by Master Simon de Wauton (Walton). The latter was appointed, in April 1255, to conduct assizes

[1] *Close R. 1227–31*, p. 562.

[2] *Close R. 1234–7*, pp. 191, 551.

[3] *Book of Fees*, ii. 798–9, 810, 813.

[4] Ibid., ii. 1482.

[5] *Cal. Pat. R. 1232–47*, p. 483.

[6] *Cal. Inq. Misc.*, i. 58 (no. 174).

[7] *Close R. 1253–4*, p. 52.

[8] *Close R. 1254–6*, p. 92 ('propter senectutem et debilitatem suam').

[9] P.R.O. E372/103 (Pipe R. 43 Hen. III), rot. 13d, m. 1; E372/105 (Pipe R. 45 Hen. III), rot. 15d, m. 1. The following six Pipe Rolls contain no Herefordshire account, but the record is repeated in that for 52 Hen. III (P.R.O. E372/112, rot. 10d, m. 1); here, however, there is a note giving a cross-reference to the roll for 3 Edw. I, and comparison with the latter (P.R.O. E372/119, rot. 11d, m. 1) shows that the debt was one of many then removed from the rolls unpaid.

[10] Lord Treasurer's Remembrancer's Memoranda Roll, 44 Hen. III, m. 23.

in Herefordshire, Shropshire, and Worcestershire.[1] He was in Worcestershire in late October[2] and in Herefordshire by mid November,[3] and had reached Shropshire by January 1256.[4] He was elected bishop of Norwich in May to June 1257,[5] and thereafter would not have been referred to merely as 'Master'; the roll of amercements must therefore have been written before that date, though not copied into the Pipe Roll until later. If then it was Hugh III who was amerced, and if the amercement was imposed by Simon de Wauton at his Herefordshire assizes, Hugh III was still alive in November 1255, but need not have been in January 1260, the date when the amercement was entered in the Pipe Roll.[6]

Assuming that all these records refer to the same man, he must have been born by 1290 at latest, and probably earlier, in which case he would have been at least 65, and probably more, when dismissed for 'old age and feebleness' in 1255.

(7) John of Croft I, whose existence is not recognized by O. G. S. Croft,[7] is known from a record in the Close Rolls. On 8 February 1263, when protection during the Welsh war was given to Roger de Mortimer and a number of his leading retainers,

---

[1] *Close R. 1254–6*, pp. 183–4; the document is enrolled between one dated 26 April and another dated 29 April. Cf. *Cal. Pat. R. 1247–58*, p. 438, which records the appointment, on 22 June 1255, of Simon de Wauton and William le Bretun to enquire into the king's rights in Gloucestershire, Worcestershire, and Herefordshire. But in fact Wauton seems to have held the assizes in Worcestershire, Herefordshire, and Shropshire; later (28 May 1256) he and Henry de Bathonia were sent to Bristol to conduct an inquiry into an alleged error at the recent assizes there held by William Trussell and John de Cave (*Cal. Pat. R. 1247–58*, p. 519).

[2] *Close R. 1254–6*, p. 229.

[3] Ibid., p. 238.

[4] Eyton, *Shropshire*, i. 145, 187; iii. 53, 75, 210; vii. 80–2, 307.

[5] Cf. *Cal. Pat. R. 1247–58*, recording the royal assent on 10 June 1257 to the election.

[6] The preceding account of the amercement imposed on Hugh of Croft is largely based on information supplied by Dr. David Crook, who kindly searched the Pipe Rolls for me. He also searched the Fine Rolls from 1 July 1255 to October 1265, without finding any references to the Crofts.   [7] pp. 15 ff.

it was John of Croft (and not Hugh) who was included among them.[1] In view of the nature of the list and the names which it comprises, there can be no doubt that John of Croft was at that time head of the family and the lord of Croft Castle, but he can have held the inheritance only for a comparatively short while, presumably because of the longevity of Hugh III. It is possible that John was a casualty of the heavy fighting with the Welsh under Llywelyn ap Gruffydd in 1263–4. He had been succeeded by Hugh IV by 1265.[2]

(8) Hugh of Croft IV is said to have been the son and heir of one Christina, who, if the statement is correct, was presumably the wife of the preceding John of Croft.[3] Hugh IV, though taken by O. G. S. Croft to be the son of Hugh III, is much more likely to have been his grandson. On 1 July 1265 his name is listed among those ordered to assemble at Hereford in preparation for the Evesham campaign.[4] If the story is true that a lord of Croft assisted in Prince Edward's escape from custody on 28 May 1265,[5] this was the man; but contrary to O. G. S. Croft's assumption, he was newly come into his inheritance and probably young (like Edward himself and his other companions), not the

[1] *Cal. Pat. R. 1258–66*, p. 248. On 23 November 1263, when the protection was renewed without detailed listing of the names, it was described as covering Roger de Mortimer 'and his knights and free tenants' (ibid., p. 299).

[2] In the *Curia Regis Rolls* there are records of a John of *Crofte* in Hilary Term 1225 (vol. xii, no. 59 (p. 10)) and of a John of *Craft* in Trinity Term 1231 (vol. xiv, no. 1701 (p. 363)). It is unlikely that these records relate to the John of 1263. The *Liber Niger de Wigmore* (MS. Harley 1240) contains on f. 62^r-v two deeds witnessed by 'magister' John of Croft (Eyton, *Shropshire*, iii. 54 (n. 21) and iv. 276), but this must be a cleric, probably a younger brother of Hugh III and an uncle of the John of 1263. But the name John was evidently one that ran in the family in the thirteenth century.

[3] Croft, p. 15, who treats Christina as the wife of Hugh III. But this appears to be a mere assumption, based on Croft's omission of John of Croft and his consequent belief that Hugh IV was the son of Hugh III.

[4] *Close R. 1264–8*, p. 127.

[5] See Croft, pp. 16–17. The source is the Latin chronicle of Wigmore Abbey entitled *Fundationis et Fundatorum Historia* (printed in Dugdale, *Monasticon*, vi. 348–55), which adds to the account of Prince Edward's

man who had held Croft in 1240.[1] The story itself, that he rode with Edward, outstripping the pursuers, to the safety of Wigmore Castle, implies an active man, not one enfeebled by old age. A record dated 52 Henry III (i.e. 1268–9) says that Hugh of Croft had married Isabel, daughter and co-heiress of Roger Longberch *alias* Longborne.[2] At some date 'between 1268 and 1287' he witnessed a grant to the abbot of Reading.[3] It is not known when he died; perhaps about 1280–5.

(9) Robert of Croft was the eldest son of Hugh IV. He died without issue by 1289; in January 1289–90 his wife Eva claimed dower in Croft and Wharton from John of Croft,[4] from which it is to be presumed that Robert had held the inheritance, however briefly, after his father's death. In an undated charter he granted lands to Wormesley Priory.[5]

(10) John of Croft II was the younger brother and heir of Robert. It was presumably this man who in May 1282 gave an acre of meadow in *Ayston* to Limebrook Priory.[6] The compiler of the genealogy in Bodleian MS. Rawlinson B.66, f. 8[v], had evidently seen a document referring to him dated 15 Edw. I (1286–7), for the genealogy has the note *vixit 15 Edw. I* against his name. In October 1289 he confirmed the charter of 1191 in which his ancestor Hugh of Croft II had approved the transfer

escape, found in various sources, the detail that the man mounted on a white horse 'sitting on the top of a hill toward *Tullinton*' (i.e. Tillington, Herefordshire) was 'dominu[s] de Crofte ad tunc ut dicitur' (p. 350). As the source is a local one, it deserves credence; it is certainly evidence of a local tradition.

[1] Croft, it will be remembered, makes the line of division between Hugh III and Hugh IV fall between 1220 and 1240; see p. 415, n. 2, above.

[2] Bodleian MS. Rawlinson B. 66, f. 8[v]. This is an early seventeenth-century antiquary's compilation, and gives on f. 8[v] a very incomplete and inaccurate genealogy of the Croft family. But the genealogist had obviously consulted early documents, probably legal records, and in this instance quotes the text of the document recording the marriage, without stating its source. The date given is obviously that of the record, not of the marriage, but it serves to show which Hugh of Croft is involved.

[3] Croft, p. 15.   [4] Croft, p. 21.   [5] Croft, p. 18.
[6] See p. 184, n. 4, above.

of the tithes of Wharton from Thetford Priory to Osney Abbey;[1] in the document he is explicitly described as the son of Sir Hugh of Croft. In January 1289–90, as son and heir of Hugh, he was defendant in a suit about land in Nupton, and on 7 July 1297 he was summoned to serve beyond the seas.[2] He died before 1303.

(11) Hugh of Croft V held Croft, Wharton, and Newton in 1303,[3] and may therefore be presumed to have been born before 1282. He was created a knight of the Bath in 1305 and was present at a tournament at Dunstable in 1308.[4] On 22 April 1309 he was appointed sheriff of Shropshire and Staffordshire,[5] and on 23 February 1310 he and others stood surety for a large debt owed by Roger de Mortimer of Chirk.[6] He was replaced as sheriff on 28 January 1312,[7] but was summoned in 1313 and 1315 to fight against the Scots[8] and was present on 9 September 1314 in the parliament at York.[9] According to Holinshed,[10] in 1317 he was murdered in Ireland by the de Lacys, to whom he had been sent as a messenger by Roger de Mortimer, first earl of March, who was then campaigning against them. The writ of *diem clausit extremum* was issued on 15 June 1317; at the inquest at Hereford on 8 February 1318 it was stated that his next heir was his son Hugh, aged 11 'at the feast of St. Michael last'.[11]

(12) Hugh of Croft VI, according to this evidence, was born at Michaelmas 1306. He was still alive in 1348,[12] but had died before Michaelmas 1356.[13]

---

[1] See p. 414, n. 5, above.

[2] Croft, p. 21.

[3] Croft, p. 22 (without citing source).

[4] loc. cit.

[5] *List of Sheriffs*, p. 117; cf. *Cal. Close R. 1307–13*, pp. 263, 381.

[6] *Cal. Close R. 1307–13*, p. 246.

[7] *List of Sheriffs*, p. 117.

[8] Croft, p. 23.   [9] Croft, p. 22.

[10] Cf. Croft, p. 24. But on p. 23 Croft says that he was murdered at a tournament in Stepney.

[11] *Cal. I.p.m.*, vi. 58 (no. 77).

[12] Croft, p. 25.   [13] Croft, p. 27.

APPENDIX V

THE TEXTUAL TRADITION OF *STE KATERINE* AND *SAWLES WARDE*

BOTH works exist in three manuscripts, Bodley 34 (B), B.M. Royal 17 A. xxvii (R), and B.M. Cotton Titus D. xviii (for which I use the siglum T, though C is often used by editors of works belonging to the *Katherine-group*). None of these is the source, direct or indirect, of either of the others, for each contains frequent errors which the other two avoid. But in both works B and R often share errors, or have related erroneous readings, which are not in T; B and R therefore must have a common proximate ancestor α of which T is independent. Again in both works, all three extant manuscripts at a number of points have identical (or only slightly varied) erroneous readings which must descend from their archetype X; and as the errors are not such as might be explained as an author's slips of the pen, it follows that in neither work is X to be identified with the author's holograph O. In each case the stemma is

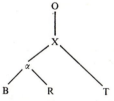

Such a stemma does not of course imply that any manuscript shown on it is a direct copy of its proximate ancestor. But B and R, which are nearly contemporary, do not diverge more widely than could be explained by the assumption that one or other (or both) of the scribes of the extant manuscripts has varied from his exemplar. It is not necessary to assume, from the state of the texts, that either

B or R was separated from α by an intermediate copy, and it is probable that B was in fact a direct copy of α; but R, which gives a less good text and is not in the 'AB language', may be a copy of a lost intermediate manuscript in which the works contained in R were first collected together.[1] In its turn α (as reconstituted from the readings of B and R) does not diverge from the readings to be attributed to X more than can be explained by the assumption that the scribe of α, whether by carelessness or deliberately, has himself modified X; that is, α may well have been, and probably was, a direct copy of X. But T, though independently descended from X, is unlikely to have been a direct copy of it, in view of T's later date. Moreover T's text, in both works, shows a good deal of deliberate innovation, 'emending' errors or supposed errors and otherwise modifying the expression; and though its scribe was doubtless himself responsible for the altered linguistic forms, the analogy of his copy of *Ancrene Wisse* suggests that the textual innovations were the work of a predecessor. It also seems unlikely that the T scribe was solely responsible for collecting the various works found in the manuscript; he probably combined only two sources, (*a*) the 'generalized' text of *Ancrene Wisse*, and (*b*) a manuscript in which there had already been collected *Sawles Warde*, *Hali Meiðhad*, *þe Wohunge of ure Lauerd*, and *Ste Katerine* (in that order).[2] As for X, the errors to be attributed to it in the two works

---

[1] The manuscript α shown in the stemma as the proximate common ancestor of B and R in these two works is unlikely to have been one in which a collection of works belonging to the *Katherine*-group had already been formed; for though both B and R are collections, their contents are not identical nor are they in the same order. I mean no more by the stemma than that the same pattern of manuscript-relationships applies to both *Ste Katerine* and *Sawles Warde*. The manuscript α assumed for the one was probably not physically identical with the α assumed for the other, i.e. the two works were probably not bound in a single volume (see next note). But as, in each case, the copy denoted α was available both to the compiler of the Bodleian collection and to the compiler of the Royal collection, it may be that a single owner (or group of owners) possessed the α copy of *Ste Katerine* and the α copy of *Sawles Warde*.

[2] The order in T suggests that though *Ste Katerine* and *Sawles Warde* had the same sort of textual history, they did not originally circu-

are not very numerous, considering the length of the texts, and are never complex; in each case it was probably a direct copy of the holograph.

Detailed evidence of the errors linking B and R, and of the errors attributed to the archetype X, is set out below. It is assumed, in view of the stemma, that normally the agreement of T with either B or R is conclusive of the archetypal reading. Line-references, in the case of *Sawles Warde*, are to the edition in Bennett and Smithers, *Early Middle English Verse and Prose*; in that of *Ste Katerine*, to Einenkel's edition, for want of a better (though it is planned to replace it). Normally I expand abbreviations without notice, and the forms are those of the manuscript first cited.

Errors linking B and R

Einenkel (p. xv) accepted that in *Ste Katerine* B and R were related, against T, but his view was based partly on their resemblances in linguistic forms, which are not valid evidence of textual affiliation. Nevertheless B and R certainly do share false readings which T avoids; some of these Einenkel pointed out in his notes. Instances are: (1) 278 *schulen* BR, *sehen* T; (2) 393 *wastu* BR, *wastu nu* T; (3) 472 *to* B, *for* R, *and to* T

late together in a single volume, for T separates them. So does B, in which *Ste Katerine* is first and *Sawles Warde* last (the reverse of the situation in T); they come together only in R, in which *Sawles Warde* is first (as in T) and is immediately followed by *Ste Katerine*. There is a contrast with *Ste Margarete* and *Ste Iuliene*, which come together in both B and R (in B as second and third, in R as third and fourth); they may well have been combined in one volume at an early stage of their history. Only B has achieved a rational arrangement of the works: the three lives of the virgin saints first, then a tract in praise of virginity (*Hali Meiðhad*), and finally *Sawles Warde*, which is not specifically about virginity (though it significantly expands its source when dealing with the high place allotted to virgins in heaven).

The position in R is complicated by the fact that at the foot of f. 10ᵛ, after the end of *Sawles Warde*, there is a request for prayers 'for iohan þet þeos boc wrat'. As R itself was written by three scribes (of whom the one who copied the request for prayers wrote only the last two leaves of *Sawles Warde*), John was presumably the scribe of an antecedent manuscript, either of a copy of *Sawles Warde* alone or of a collection in which *Sawles Warde* was the final item, as in B.

correctly; (4) 1522 *bune* B, *bunen* R, *buue* T; (5) 1635 *his icorene* BR, *his leue icorene* T with required alliteration on *l*; (6) 1642 *bur* BR, *burh* T (*civitas* Latin); (7) 1762 *þes lease maumez* BR, *þes mix and lease maumez* T (cf. ll. 202 and 2069 and *Ste Iuliene* (B), l. 164); (8) 1887 *þu bipench(e) me* BR, *þu bipenche þe* T (*tu . . . excogitare ne differas* Latin); (9) 1933–8 *þet Katerine schal . . . swiken . . . ant . . . wurchen* BR, *þat Katerine . . . swike . . . and . . . wurche* T (*ut* with subjunctives in Latin); (10) 1971 *Her amidde(n)* BR, *her amidheapes* T (see d'Ardenne, *Ste Iuliene*, p. 145); (11) 2048 *al wraðe* B, *ant wreððe* R (each attempting to emend a false reading *al wreaððe*), *al o wraððe* T; (12) 2055 *weren isehen(e)* BR, *weren isihen* 'had journeyed' T (*convenerant* Latin); (13) 2136 *earni* BR, *slakie* T for original *earhi* < OE *eargian* (*deficere* Latin); (14) 2210 *sathanesse* B, *sathanesses* R, *Sathanase* gen. sg. T correctly (cf. *Judase* 'Judas's'; see d'Ardenne, op. cit., p. 208 (§ 63 n. 1); the precursor of BR seems to have thought that it meant 'of a female Satan'); (15) 2276 *cuð icudd* BR, *cuð and icud* T; (16) 2377 *bileaue* BR, *bileafde* T (*credentium* Latin); (17) possibly 2385 *i tale* BR, *i þe tale* T. BR also have in common Latin citations which T either lacks (ll. 482–3; differently placed in B and R) or has in different form (l. 634). At l. 245, where BR read *unwit(e)lese* (for which cf. *unwitlese* BR at *Ste Margarete* 20/13 and Miss Mack's note), T's *witlese* is the scribe's 'emendation' (initial *wynn* altered from *u*). There is a long gap in B, owing to the loss of three leaves, from l. 878 to l. 1255.

On *Sawles Warde* see R. M. Wilson's edition (Leeds, 1938), pp. xxxii–xxxiii, though he understates the extent of the evidence for a BR grouping. The two manuscripts share errors, exactly or with further modifications, at eleven points: (1) 73–4 *hweonene he* BR, *hwenne ha* T (*ubi et . . . quando* Latin); read *hweonene ant hwenne ha*, conflating BR and T; BR themselves switch to *ha* 'she' in the next clause, and the answer is *Ich nat nawt þe time*; (2) 94 *wiðute met* BR, *wid wiðute met* T (*latus . . . sine mensura* Latin); (3) 156 *iwis . . . a þusent* BR, *þis . . . and þusand* T (*haec . . . et millies* Latin); (4) 173 *ant for his wrenches* BR, *for hise wrenches ich con* T (not in Latin, but T plainly right, despite

Bennett and Smithers); (5) 188 *wone* BR, *nesche* T (again T plainly right, despite Bennett and Smithers); (6) 244 omission in BR, *þat helden us swa stille hwil fearlac us agrette* T (*si . . . nos, dum timor et memoria mortis loqueretur, tacuimus* Latin); (7) 257 *ȝe iseoð* 'you see' BR for *ȝe i soð, ȝoi isoð* T (half-corrected in Bennett and Smithers); (8) 273 BR omit *wordes* 'hosts, orders', *weoredes* T (*ordines* Latin); (9) 291 *poure ant lah on eorðe* B, ⟨*þet*⟩ *poure* ⟨*weren*⟩ *ant lahe* R (obviously 'emending' B's text), *of poure and lahe on eorðe* 'from being poor and lowly on earth' T (Bennett and Smithers accept the easy reading of B, but T agrees with the Latin, *de pauperibus et de infirmis*); (10) 358 *þis loft songes* B, *þis loft song* R (emending), *his loft songes* T, obviously rightly (accepted by Bennett and Smithers); (11) 370-1 *ah nower neh ne neh ich al* B, *ah nower neh ne neh al* R (making the best of it that the scribe could), *ah nower neh ne seh ich al* 'but I did not see anywhere near everything' T (free translation of *neque ut sunt vidi* Latin; adopted by Bennett and Smithers).

Errors of the archetype

In *Ste Katerine* there are some twenty archetypal errors, for even if a few of those listed below are doubtful (or in two cases probably independent in BR and T) a closer scrutiny of the text than it has yet been given might reveal others that I have not noticed; Einenkel, though he did not follow any manuscript uncritically and was all too willing to pick and choose between (or even alter) the linguistic forms, rarely considered the possibility that all three manuscripts might be erroneous in substance, and when he did, showed no skill in emendation. My provisional list is as follows. (1) 176 *geinen* RT, *geinen* corrected to *geinin* B; archetype *geinen* for regular AB form *geinin* < ON *gegna*, but alliteration seems to require *ȝeinin* < OE *gegnian* (for which see *OED* s.v. *yain* v.). (2) 320 *hefde lahe sprung* BRT, for *hefde lahe[t] sprung* 'had an origin lawfully ordained' (*rationalibus manasse primordiis* Latin). (3) 407-8 *iselede writes wið his ahne kinering* BRT, for *writes isealede . . .* (*litteras regio anulo signatas* Latin). (4) 742 *stot hercnede* B, *stod her⟨c⟩nede* R, *stod hercnende* T. Though T's reading makes good sense it is probably a scribal emendation of the BR reading; the pres. p. should be *hercninde* in the AB language, which is unlikely to have been corrupted to *hercnede*. Emend rather to *stod* (or *stot*) *hercneð* or less probably to *stod hercnet*, both meaning 'stood listening'; cf. in *Ancrene Wisse* the idioms *lið bipencheð him* 'lies considering' (Corpus f. 88a/24, Cleopatra f. 148ᵛ/14) and *cumeð iswenchet* 'come working' (Corpus f. 112b/7). (5) 817 *ant þet* BRT, for *þet* (*quod* Latin). (6) 900 *þah he luðere ahte* R, *þah þe luðere* T (lacuna in B); archetype undoubtedly corrupt; read probably *þah we luðere [wr]ahte*. (7) 1057 *ah wes* RT (lacuna in B), for *ah þes*. (8) 1249 *ageide* R, *agide* T (lacuna in B), with alliteration on /g/. Corruption of some word meaning 'terrified', perhaps *agride; cf. *gryed* in *GGK* 2370, *agruwie* in *Ancrene Wisse* (Nero) 40/22, and *OED* s.v. *grue* v.[1] (9) 1311 *þet he* BRT, for *þet* rel. pron. (10) 1313–14 *lihtlich(e) of* BRT, for *lihtliche [te leoten] of* 'to be lightly esteemed'; clear case of omission in archetype. (11) 1319 *haueð us acomen* B, *haueð* R, *haueð mot* T. All corrupt, but probably independently. At 1311 B reads *acomen* for *al tom* 'completely tame, subdued' RT, which suggests that in 1319 its *acomen* is again a substitution for essentially the same word, but here the p.p. of a verb 'to tame'—either *atemet* < OE *atemian* (cf. *OED*, s.v. *teme* v.) or more probably *atomet* from a new formation *atomien (cf. *OED*, s.v. *tame* v., not recorded until the fourteenth century). B's *acomen* would then depend essentially on misreading *t* as *c*, with 'correction' of the inflexion -*et* to -*en*. R's omission of *us atomet* (or of *us acomen*, as in B) may have been because the scribe could not understand it; T has misread the last three letters as *mot* (which occurs repeatedly in the context) and has left out the rest.[1] The corresponding Latin is *nos in stuporem et admirationem adeo convertit*. Other possible emendations would be *amead* 'maddened' or *mat* adj. 'overcome,

---

[1] As B also has *acomen* in 1311, it is probable that there too we should read *atomet*. It would be possible to explain the agreement of RT in reading *al tom* in 1311 by supposing that this was a gloss to *atomet*, introduced first in the archetype and preserved in α, which had been independently substituted for *atomet* in the lines of descent which led to R and T but not in B, which dropped the gloss and corrupted *atomet* to *acomen*.

confounded' (cf. 1989), but it is less likely that the scribes would corrupt these words. (12) 1552 *Bicom to þet* BR, [*B*]*icom þat* T, for *Bicom þo þet* (*Accidit autem ut* Latin). (13) 1635–6 *lure*(*n*) *ant tis worldliche* (ð for *d* B) *lif* BRT, for *luren i þis worldliche lif* (*dampnis temporalibus* Latin); *Ʒ* for *i*. (14) 1751 *þear as me þe*⟨*a*⟩*r as me rihte bileaue* B, *þer as mi rihte bileaue schawde me* R, *þer is al mi rihte bileaue* T; R and T attempting to emend corrupt text. Einenkel, p. 143, correctly deduced that the archetype must have been corrupt at this point, but his emendation will not do; read *þear as me rihte bileaue* [*learde*], supplying omitted alliterating verb. (15) 1790 *þet he ham wule leasten* BT, *þet wule ham ilesten* R, for *þet lif ham wule leasten*. (16) 1928–9 *þurhspitet mid kenre þen ei* (*eni* R) *cnif* BR, *þurhspited mid kenre þikes þen eni cnif* T. Word omitted after *mid* by archetype; *þikes* conjecturally supplied by T after *kenre*. But read *þurhspitet mid* [*spakes*] *kenre þen eni cnif*; cf. *Ste Iuliene* (B), l. 546. (17) 1931 *hit* BRT where plural referring to *hweoles* 'wheels' (1919, 1928, 1941) is required; *rotas* Latin. Read probably *ham*, though *hit* 'the thing' may be defensible. (18) 1988 *ƷMaxence* BRT, for *Ʒ þ Maxence* (*ant tet Maxence*) 'and so that Maxentius'. (19) 2065 *to him* BR, *to him* with *to* subpuncted T, for *him* accusative; correct emendation in T by scribe himself. (20) 2278 *lead* BRT, for *let* 'hinder, delay' (*protrahas* Latin). (21) 2348 *me iweddet* BRT, for *min iweddet* (*sponsus meus* Latin); cf. 2419. (22) 2391 *þe to luue lauerd* BR, *to þe leue lauerd* T, for *þe to loue, lauerd* 'in thy praise, o Lord' (*in laudem et gloriam tuam* Latin); probably independent error in BR and T, and perhaps an instance in which T's error is best explained as building on one in an intermediate copy (*leue* replacing *loue* because previously the order of *þe to* had been inverted).

In *Sawles Warde* I would list eight or nine points where the archetype must have been in error, as follows. (1) 34 *castel* BT, reflecting archetype (note agreement across stemma), for original *catel*; *chatel* R by emendation, but this form will not account for the BT error. (2) 85 *hire* BRT, probably for *hine* (see d'Ardenne, p. 222 (§ 87)). (3) 149 *rueð* B, *ruueð* R (clearly not *runeð* as reported by Wilson, followed by Bennett and Smithers), *runeð*

T, for *rungeð*; see p. 105, n. 2, above. (4) 167 *false* B, *fahe* RT for *flahe* 'deceitful' < OE *flāh* (J. R. R. Tolkien's emendation, made in lectures; cf. *RES*, i (1925), 214); B's reading, though good sense, is shown to be an emendation by the agreement of RT across the stemma on a meaningless (because corrupt) form. (5) 202 *ha* BRT, for *hwa* 'one who'. (6) 204–5, archetype *ant ure alre ehnen ant demeð* (preserved in T, with ampersand for *ant*); B 'emends' by omitting second *ant*, R much more neatly by substituting *to* for first *ant*, but correct emendation *at* (in same sense as R's *to*) for first *ant*. (7) Possibly 247, *þet* BRT, perhaps for *þer* (*et ibi* Latin); it is argued that *þet* can bear the sense 'where', but confusion of the abbreviations for *þer* and *þet* (or of the full forms) seems more likely. (8) 354 *þet ha nimeð* BRT, for *hu nimeð ha* (*quomodo capit* Latin); Hall suggested the replacement of *þet* by *hu* but failed to note that *ha* must then follow the verb; the emendation is spoiled in Bennett and Smithers, 2nd edn., which omits *ha* altogether though professing to follow Hall.[1] (9) 370 *nower* BRT, for normal spelling *nohwer*.

---

[1] It is possible that the author of *Sawles Warde* misread the abbreviation for *quomodo*, in his Latin source, as that for *quod* (or alternatively that in his manuscript of the Latin the wrong abbreviation had been used). If so, the meaningless text given by the three manuscripts at 354 would go back to the autograph; but it would be an isolated instance of the failure of the English author to write sense.

APPENDIX VI

A SOURCE OF *HALI MEIÐHAD*

In Chapter III above (pp. 164–5) reference was made to a passage in the *Moralia super Evangelia* by Alexander of Bath, Book III, chapter 92, which the author of *Hali Meiðhad* must have read, since in the English work there is a series of passages (in Colborn's edition, Bodley text, ll. 40–64, 150–63, 240–60, 300–19, 324–45) which expand and develop the ideas of the Latin. The passage, edited from MSS. Lincoln College Oxford Lat. 79, f. 180^(r–v), and Trinity College Oxford 50, f. 300^(r–v) (with editorial emendations in square brackets), is as follows.

Ad commendationem cuiusuis uirginis facit quod eadem uirginali flore ditata est, eo quod fructui tricesimo coniugium, sexagesimo uidualis, centesimo uero status uirginalis donandus est. Hinc est quod iuxta Ambrosium primus argento, secundus auro, tercius lapidi precioso assimulatur. Primus stellis, secundus lune, tercius sole comparabilis est. Commendant etiam uitam uirginalem corporis et anime libertas, celibatus, status, fructus, canticum, et corona. In uirgine igitur corporis et anime libertas[1] perspicua est: non enim in reddendo debito coniugali seruituti subicitur, nec habet alius potestatem corporis eius. De coniugatis dicit apostolus, 'Tribulationem carnis habebunt', huius sollicitudinem scilicet quam plurimam de domo regenda, de rebus necessariis prouidendis sibi et coniugibus suis, filiis, filiabus, et famulis. Hanc curam mordacem ceteraque matrimoniorum onera[2] uitat uirginitas. Patet etiam celibatus uirginis, cum angelicam uitam ducat in terris et sequatur agnum quocumque ierit, hoc est [in][3] integritate anime et corporis. Status etiam uirginalis statui [matrimoniali][4] precellit. Iuxta illud Exodi, 'Facies tabernaculi operimentum de pellibus rubricatis, et super hoc de iacinctinis pellibus', celestis scilicet

---

[1] libertas] ubertas T   [2] onera] honera L   [3] in] *om.* LT   [4] matrimoniali] m̄rm *for* matrimonium LT

coloris—hinc patet quod uirginitas etiam martyrio precellit. Item in¹ Ysaia dicit dominus eunuchis, 'Dabo nomen melius a filiis et filiabus', id est excellentius quam si filios et filias generassent. Uirginum etiam est canticum spirituale: id est, gaudium et gratiarum actio, de natiua² sue³ carnis integritate, perseuerantur⁴ conseruata. Earundem preter [lucem]⁵ auream est corona aureola; nec mirum, quia, ut ait Ambrosius, 'Maior⁶ est uictoria uirginum quam angelorum'. Uirgines itaque⁷ iuuencule sunt tympanistrie uel filie chore,⁸ que carnem suam crucifigunt cum uiciis et concupiscentiis et sic in carne de carne triumphant, et propter amorem sponsi⁹ Iesu Cristi regnum mundi et omnem ornatum seculi contempnunt. Nam mariambule sunt et cornua cerastis, id est, luxuriam et superbiam castitate et humilitate quasi gemino pede conterunt. Ecce duplex uictoria cui duplex debetur corona.

The passage proceeds to compare the flesh of virgins to that of elephants, but the author of *Hali Meiðhad*, who had a sense of humour, drew the line at that. A pity, from my point of view; if he had used it, nobody could possibly doubt that he was following the *Moralia*.

¹ in] *om.* T   ² natiua] natura T   ³ sue] siue T   ⁴ perseuerantur] perseueratur T   ⁵ lucem] *om.* LT   ⁶ maior] melior *with* maior *interlined above* T   ⁷ itaque] namque T   ⁸ chore] thore T   ⁹ amorem sponsi] sponsi amorem T

INDEX

This index omits some names of persons, places, and literary works referred to only incidentally; in particular it does not include references to most of the persons and places mentioned in the Appendixes, or to scholars (and their works) later than 1600. Names of persons are entered under the family name if there was one (including a territorial designation which was clearly used as, or became, a family name), but under the Christian name if any further designation appears to have been merely the name of their place of birth or residence, monastery, etc., or a title or nickname. The manuscripts and versions of *Ancrene Wisse* and the *Katherine-*group are listed under those headings; other manuscripts under their names.